Britain and the Arab Gulf after Empire

Although Britain's formal imperial role in the smaller, oil-rich Sheikhdoms of the Arab Gulf – Kuwait, Bahrain, Qatar, and the United Arab Emirates – ended in 1971, Britain continued to have a strong interest and continuing presence in the region. This book explores the nature of Britain's role after the formal end of empire. It traces the historical events of the post-imperial years, including the 1973 oil shock, the fall of the Shah in Iran, and the beginnings of the Iran–Iraq War; considers the changing positions towards the region of other major world powers, including the United States; and engages with debates on the nature of empire and the end of empire. The book is a sequel to the author's highly acclaimed previous books *Britain's Revival and Fall in the Gulf: Kuwait, Bahrain, Qatar, and the Trucial States, 1950–71* (Routledge 2004) and *Ending Empire in the Middle East: Britain, the United States and Post-war Decolonization, 1945–1973* (Routledge 2012).

Simon C. Smith is Professor of International History at the University of Hull, UK.

Routledge Studies in Middle Eastern History

The region's history from the earliest times to the present is catered for by this series made up of the very latest research. Books include political, social, cultural, religious and economic history.

British Somaliland
An Administrative History, 1920–1960
Brock Millman

War and State Formation in Syria
Cemal Pasha's Governorate during World War I, 1914–1917
M. Talha Çiçek

The Druze Community and the Lebanese State
Between Confrontation and Reconciliation
Yusri Hazran

The Secret Anglo–French War in the Middle East
Intelligence and Decolonization, 1940–1948
Meir Zamir

Histories of the Jews of Egypt
An Imagined Bourgeoisie
Dario Miccoli

The Empress Nurbanu and Ottoman Politics in the Sixteenth Century
Building the Atik Valide
Pinar Kayaalp

Britain and the Arab Gulf after Empire
Kuwait, Bahrain, Qatar, and the United Arab Emirates, 1971–1981
Simon C. Smith

For a full list of titles in the series: www.routledge.com/middleeaststudies/series/SE0811

First published 2019
by Routledge
2 Park Square, Milton Park, Abingdon, Oxon OX14 4RN

and by Routledge
52 Vanderbilt Avenue, New York, NY 10017

Routledge is an imprint of the Taylor & Francis Group, an informa business

© 2019 Simon C. Smith

The right of Simon C. Smith to be identified as author of this work has been asserted by him in accordance with sections 77 and 78 of the Copyright, Designs and Patents Act 1988.

All rights reserved. No part of this book may be reprinted or reproduced or utilised in any form or by any electronic, mechanical, or other means, now known or hereafter invented, including photocopying and recording, or in any information storage or retrieval system, without permission in writing from the publishers.

Trademark notice: Product or corporate names may be trademarks or registered trademarks, and are used only for identification and explanation without intent to infringe.

British Library Cataloguing-in-Publication Data
A catalogue record for this book is available from the British Library

Library of Congress Cataloging-in-Publication Data
A catalog record for this book has been requested

ISBN: 978-1-138-83869-7 (hbk)
ISBN: 978-1-315-73388-3 (ebk)

Typeset in Times New Roman
by Apex CoVantage, LLC

Printed and bound in Great Britain by
TJ International Ltd, Padstow, Cornwall

Britain and the Arab Gulf after Empire

Kuwait, Bahrain, Qatar, and the United Arab Emirates, 1971–1981

Simon C. Smith

LONDON AND NEW YORK

For Reyhan

Contents

List of abbreviations	viii
Acknowledgements	x
Preface	xi
Map: The Modern Gulf	xiii
Introduction	1
1 The trials of independence, 1971–1972	26
2 The oil revolution, 1973	50
3 Challenges and opportunities, 1974–1977	72
4 Revolution and reaction, 1978–1979	102
5 War and peace, 1980	124
6 The empire strikes back? 1981	146
Conclusion: imperialism after empire?	168
Appendix 1 British Ambassadors to the Gulf States	178
Appendix 2 Heads of the FCO's Arabian/Middle East Department	182
Appendix 3 Secretaries of State for Foreign and Commonwealth Affairs	184
Appendix 4 British Prime Ministers	186
Appendix 5 Gulf Rulers	187
Bibliography	189
Index	202

Abbreviations

ADDF	Abu Dhabi Defence Force
BAe	British Aerospace
BD	Bahraini Dinar
BDF	Bahrain Defence Force
BL	British Leyland
BP	British Petroleum
BSC	British Steel Corporation
C-in-C	Commander-in-Chief
DHSS	Department of Health and Social Security
DMAO	Director of Military Assistance Office
DoT	Department of Trade
DTI	Department of Trade and Industry
EAD	Euro–Arab Dialogue
EC	European Community
EEC	European Economic Community
ELT	English Language Training
FCO	Foreign and Commonwealth Office
FO	Foreign Office
GCC	Gulf Co-operation Council
GEC	General Electric Company
GHQ	General Head Quarters
GNP	Gross National Product
GOK	Government of Kuwait
HMG	Her Majesty's Government
ICI	Imperial Chemical Industries
IDTC	Industrial Development Technical Centre
JIC	Joint Intelligence Committee
KCMG	Knight Commander of the Order of St Michael and St George
KLT	Kuwait Liaison Team
LSP	Loan Service Personnel
MAT	(British) Military Advisory Team
MoD	Ministry of Defence

NATO	North Atlantic Treaty Organization
OAPEC	Organization of Arab Petroleum Exporting Countries
OECD	Organization for Economic Co-operation and Development
OPEC	Organization of the Petroleum Exporting Countries
QNPC	Qatar National Petroleum Company
QPC	Qatar Petroleum Company
QSF	Qatar Security Force
PDRY	People's Democratic Republic of Yemen
PFLOAG	Popular Front for the Liberation of the Occupied Arabian Gulf
PLO	Palestine Liberation Organization
PUSS	Parliamentary Under-Secretary of State
RAF	Royal Air Force
RDF	Rapid Deployment Force
SAVAK	Sazman-e Ettela'at va Amniyat-e Keshvar (Organization of Intelligence and National Security)
UAE	United Arab Emirates
UN	United Nations
USG	United States Government

Acknowledgements

I should like to thank staff at the National Archives in the US and the UK, the Lyndon Baines Johnson Library (Austin), and the Hull History Centre for their assistance in researching this book. I should also like to record my gratitude to the University of Hull for granting the study leave which allowed the completion of the project.

Preface

The end of formal empire in 1971, symbolized by Britain's military egress from the Gulf, did not equate with the end of British interests in this oil-rich region. Britain's relative decline in the post-war era, however, made the task of maintaining existing relationships and building new partnerships a challenging undertaking. In some respects, the former British-protected states of the Lower Gulf offered favourable circumstances for successfully achieving this transition. Britain's role had always been less visible than in more strictly colonial settings, whether in Aden, Africa, the Mediterranean, or the Far East. The ruling families of the Gulf States, moreover, were eager, at least in the short term, to maintain links with their erstwhile protector. Nevertheless, early British hopes of preserving influence and interests after empire were challenged by the encroachment of Britain's industrial rivals into the lucrative and expanding Gulf markets. Similarly, the intrusion of the politics of the Arab world into the Gulf, which had the emotive issue of Palestine at its heart, provided a further challenge to Britain. This was highlighted most conspicuously by the Gulf States' participation in the use of the 'oil weapon' at the time of the 1973 Arab–Israeli conflict which Britain proved powerless to prevent. Such palpable limits on Britain's ability to sway the Gulf States just two years after formal withdrawal calls into question the extent to which it was able to maintain informal imperial influence into the period of formal independence.

In response to US Secretary of Defense James R. Schlesinger's blunt observation in the wake of the 1973 Yom Kippur War that the British were 'just incompetent', Deputy Secretary of State Kenneth Rush pointed out that 'They are competent. They have a plan but no power'.[1] Indeed, a lack of power restricted Britain's ability to protect its position in the Gulf and preserve its remaining economic and strategic interests there after withdrawal. This is demonstrated in Chapter 1 which examines the Gulf in the immediate aftermath of the Britain's formal military and political departure in 1971 and underlines its relative impotence in the face of growing regional instability. Chapter 2 investigates the new pressures to which the Gulf States were subjected, especially from the Arab world to use their oil wealth for political reasons. The wielding of the 'oil weapon' at the time of the 1973 Arab–Israeli conflict demonstrated that British efforts to influence the Gulf States and preserve interests were threatened as never before. The hike in oil prices, however, provided an opportunity for British commerce to exploit the Gulf States' swollen revenues. Chapter 3 analyses British attempts to shore up its economic interests in the Gulf States against the background of growing competition from its industrial rivals in the Western world, underlining the common experience of British commerce to struggle to preserve market share in the new competitive environment.

Chapter 4 interrogates the impact of the Iranian Revolution on both the Gulf States themselves and on British interests in the region. The chapter emphasizes that the decline of British influence and the growth of commercial competition from industrial rivals belie the notion that Britain seamlessly made the transition from formal to informal empire in the Gulf, still less that it achieved the status of a neo-colonial power.

Chapter 5 explores the effects of regional developments, especially the Soviet invasion of Afghanistan and the outbreak of the Iran–Iraq War, on the Gulf States. It also studies the ways in which these dramatic events provided Britain with an opportunity to strengthen its ties with these territories, especially in the military field. Indeed, the chapter highlights that times of crisis, especially when the Gulf States were confronted with an external threat, offered Britain the chance to re-assert its role in the region. Equally, the reluctance of the Gulf States to countenance too close an association with the US meant that there was a tendency to look to Britain for assistance.

Chapter 6 considers the ways in which Margaret Thatcher sought to solidify British links with, and interests in, the Gulf through her two historic visits to the region in 1981, the first by a sitting British Prime Minister. While Thatcher's visit coincided with some notable successes for British defence sales to the region, the chapter also stresses that far from the empire striking back in the Gulf in the form of informal imperialism, British decision-makers sought to pursue a more demonstrably modern and recognizably post-imperial relationship with the Gulf States. The conclusion points out that where Britain did attempt to preserve invisible or informal influence in the Gulf, it was, at best, a diluted form of influence which lacked the exclusivity of former imperial ties. By engaging with debates about the applicability of the concept of informal empire to decolonization, the book as a whole seeks to contribute to our understanding of the nature of the end of empire in the Gulf and its consequences for both Britain and the Gulf States.

Note

1 Memorandum of conversation, Washington, 29 November 1973, cited in *Foreign Relations of the United States, 1969–76: Volume XXV: Arab–Israeli Crisis and War, 1973* (Washington, DC: United States Government Printing Office, 2011), p. 1003.

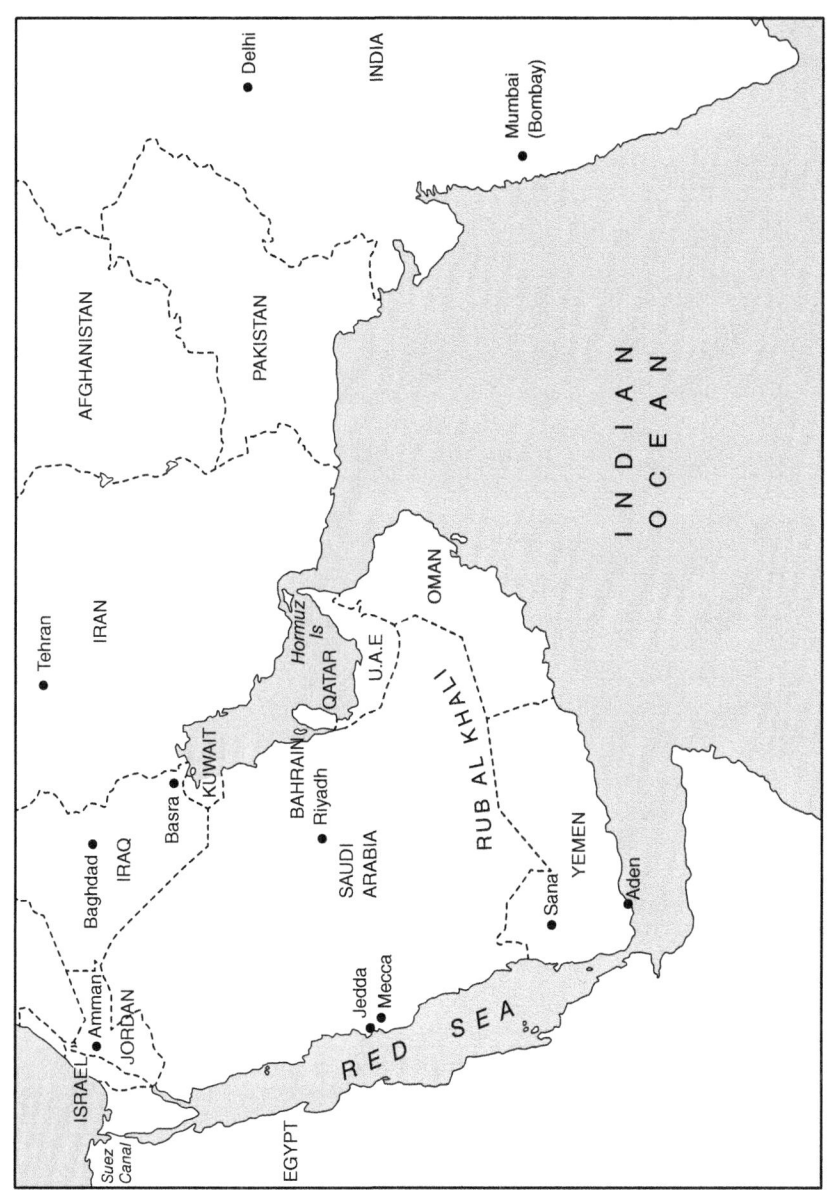

Map 0.1 The modern Gulf in its regional context
Source: Smith 2013.

Introduction

That the definition of empire does not necessarily equate with the territory under the direct sovereignty or control of the imperial power has long been recognized. John Gallagher and Ronald Robinson famously wrote that considering such areas alone as part of the British Empire is 'rather like judging the size and character of icebergs solely from the parts above the water-line'.[1] To characterize those portions of the world which, while not under direct British control, were nevertheless under Britain's imperial sway, Gallagher and Robinson used the term 'informal empire'. Writing on his own, Gallagher asserted:

> 'empire', as a set of colonies and other dependencies, was just the tip of the iceberg that made up the British world system as a whole, a system of influence as well as power which, indeed, preferred to work through informal methods of influence when possible, and through formal methods of rule only when necessary.[2]

While they were principally referring to the nineteenth-century British Empire, Gallagher and Robinson's ideas permeated debates about empire in the following century. In his analysis of decolonization, Robin Winks ruminates that 'the final irony of informal empire was that precisely because it was informal, it was the most tenacious of all'.[3] Examining the period after the First World War, Glen Balfour-Paul refers to Britain's 'informal empire in the Middle East',[4] while John Darwin coins the term 'undeclared empire' to describe Britain's imperial engagement with that region in the inter-war years, pointing out that it was 'ruled (for the most part) by proxy'.[5] Indeed, collaboration with local elites to preserve British imperial interests has proved central to the informal empire paradigm.[6]

Writing in the early 1960s, the leader of the Malta Labour Party, Dom Mintoff, posited: 'Colonialism to survive must find reliable allies rising from the same soil – the maharajahs, the sheiks, etc, to whom a political change often means a social change and the consequent loss of material privileges and benefits'.[7] Drawing on such ideas in his essay on the non-European foundations of European imperialism, Ronald Robinson highlighted the co-option of powerful elements within the local population who acted as advocates, intermediaries, or even instruments of imperial power.[8] 'The theory of collaboration', he asserts, 'suggests that at every stage from external imperialism to decolonisation, the working of imperialism was determined by the indigenous collaborative systems connecting its European and Afro-Asian components'.[9] In a similar vein, Martin Thomas, who has coined the phrase 'intelligence states' to characterize the British and French empires in North Africa and the Middle East in the inter-war years, observes that these states were 'in constant flux, reliant on indigenous intermediaries to sustain imperial control'.[10] For Shohei Sato, 'Local cooperation was the essential device of the informal empire, which enabled Britain to yield maximum benefits to the dying British Empire with minimum economic, military and administrative costs'.[11] Equally, Michael Doyle contends that 'Informal imperialism can ... effect the same results as formal imperialism; the difference lies in the process of control, which informal imperialism achieves through collaboration of a legally independent (but actually subordinate) government in the periphery'.[12]

As regards the era of decolonization, Ronald Robinson insists that 'when the colonial rulers ran out of indigenous collaborators, they either chose to leave or were compelled to go'.[13] Summarizing his argument, Robinson asserts that 'Any new theory must recognise that imperialism was as much a function of its victims' collaboration or non-collaboration ... as it was of European imperialism'.[14] In a further extension of his analysis in conjunction with Wm. Roger Louis, Robinson argues that decolonization by the European imperial powers (principally Britain and France) should be seen as attempts at 'exchanging formal control for informal tutelage'.[15] Referring specifically to British policy in Africa, Robinson and Louis contend that officials nurtured independence in order to 'prolong imperial sway and secure British economic and strategic assets. It was increasingly urgent to exchange colonial control for informal empire'.[16] Equally, they emphasize that British policy-makers considered that 'The good will of amenable national leaders had to be won before independence, if they were to be allied after independence'.[17] Louis and Robinson refer to British statesmen setting their sights on an 'empire in the post-colonial world', in which 'Influence had to be won by converting discontented subjects into loyal allies'.[18]

The notion that the end of empire did not necessarily mark the end of Britain's presence in parts of its former imperial demesne has been explored by other scholars and writers. Juan Romero has argued that 'the post-Second World War decolonization process did not necessarily lead to reduced influence of the metropole over a colony or dependent state'.[19] The first Prime Minister of independent Ghana, Kwame Nkrumah, observed that

> The young countries are still the providers of raw materials, the old of manufactured goods. The change in the economic relationship between the new sovereign states and the erstwhile masters is only one of form. Colonialism has achieved a new guise. It has become neo-colonialism, the last stage of imperialism.[20]

Speaking at the United Nations General Assembly in 1960, Nkrumah declared:

> African countries need to be on their guard against what I call clientele-sovereignty, or fake independence, namely, the practice of granting a sort of independence by the metropolitan power, with the concealed intention of making the liberated country a client-state and controlling it effectively by means other than political ones.[21]

Nkrumah's ideas have influenced academics and political thinkers. Writing in 1978, Rhoda Howard argued that the Ghanaian regimes which followed the ending of formal empire in 1957 inherited a 'colonially-imposed state with little economic independence'.[22] Referring to Africa more generally, G. Ugo Nwokeji has stressed that 'The British case shows that there was indeed a deliberate scheme to establish a neo-colonialist system. The colonial powers looked to reform the colonies into neo-colonies after realizing that classical colonialism had been rejected and could no longer guarantee the benefits for which colonies had been acquired'.[23] From a Marxist standpoint, Jack Woddis opined in 1967 that 'One of the aims of neo-colonialism is to retain essentially the same economic relationship between imperialism and the developing countries as has existed up until now'.[24] In a similar vein, Harry Magdoff remarked in the early 1970s that 'both the economic and political structures of the former colonies are well suited to the perpetuation of economic dependence along with political independence'.[25] Writing in 1977, D. K. Fieldhouse observed that

> The current fashion, particularly though not exclusively, on the political left, is to say that decolonisation made very little difference. Empire had been a tool of monopoly capitalism; but when empire was wound up international capital adjusted its methods and continued to dominate less developed countries through a complex of devices conventionally summed up as 'neo-colonialism'.[26]

For economist Lim Mah Hui, the fact that in the mid-1970s some 67 per cent of directors in Malaysia's top 100 companies were still non-Malaysian indicated that his country had 'attained its political independence without substantive economic independence'.[27]

Fred Halliday argues that in the decades following the Second World War, 'imperialism went through a major transformation, partly forced upon it by the War and partly resulting from increased opportunities for capitalist development both in the industrialized countries and the colonial world. Politically this transformation took the form of decolonization'.[28] 'Just as the members of the indigenous state began to play a larger political role as partners in this expanding system', he explains, 'so local state economic officials and private bourgeois now participated as a subordinate section of the imperialist economy'.[29] He concludes: 'the truth was that imperialism had taken a new form, distinct from the previous colonial model. The global expansion of capitalism was forced, and was able, to incorporate new junior partners into its system'.[30]

While writing from neither a Marxist nor colonial nationalist perspective, S. R. Ashton has noted that 'Historians of the British empire have long debated the question of when empire began. Equally open to interpretation are questions of when it ended or whether it continued in a different form'.[31] In a similar vein, John Darwin muses that 'The "end of empire" is in fact a deceptively enigmatic phrase. In reality, it is not only difficult to say exactly when empire did end, but what precisely that empire was'.[32] This is a particularly prescient observation with regard to debates on the nature of British decolonization, especially the extent to which Britain either attempted, or achieved, a return to 'informal empire'.

The sociologist Julian Go contends that 'Formal and informal empire might be better thought of as two ends of a blurry continuum'.[33] He adds that imperial states 'might shift modes, decolonizing a territory only to replace formal colonialism with informal control'.[34] Drawing the strands of his interpretation together, Wm. Roger Louis emphasizes the idea of the 'imperialism of decolonization' which he defines as the 'reversion to indirect control or influence rather than direct colonial rule'.[35] Giving this notion further definition, Louis remarks that the 'British aim was to harness American capitalism to British purposes and to alter the structure of Empire from formal rule to more indirect control, or at least influence. Such is the imperialism of decolonization'.[36] He also contends that 'In the post-war period the history of the Empire may be read as the attempt to convert formal rule into an informal basis of equal partnership and influence. . . . The purpose of this transformation was the perpetuation of Britain as a "world power"'.[37] In a similar vein, Darwin argues that British policy was 'geared, above all, to the preservation of British world power in increasingly adverse circumstances'.[38] '[E]ven after the timetables for independence had shifted from "a generation hence" to "this time next year"', posits Darwin, 'plans and schemes for the preservation of "influence" were being busily drafted'.[39] He adds that

> speeding up the transfers of power in the colonial Empire was not meant, whatever the actual outcome, to signal the final, lasting and complete retreat from the extra-European world but should be seen as a hasty and sometimes involuntary expedient to stabilize the spheres of British influence amid rapidly changing international and local circumstances.[40]

'The spirit of British policy', concludes Darwin, 'was one of pragmatic readjustment not painful renunciation'.[41]

Frank Heinlein has stressed that in the era of decolonization British policymakers operated on the basis that 'it was the transfer of power, rather than as in the past the acquisition, possession, and defence of empire, which held out the prospect of maximising metropolitan influence and standing in the world'.[42] Similarly, Nicholas J. White asserts that 'for all European, and non-European decolonisers, the end of colonial rule was never predicated on the principle of abandonment of influence'.[43] In the opinion of Bernard Porter, 'When Britain surrendered her colonies, she didn't give up everything. This is what most of the struggles with the nationalists were about: not whether Britain could hold on to their territories ... but whether their "free" successor governments would still do her bidding in certain particular areas'.[44] Francis Owtram, moreover, insists that with the decline of formal imperialism, 'efforts turned to securing post-colonial states on the Arabian peninsula conducive to Western and specifically British interests'.[45] Summarizing British attitudes towards African decolonization, D. K. Fieldhouse observes: 'On the assumption that independence was bound to come sooner or later, policy was to make it sooner, in the hope that a friendly parting would have the fewest possible bad effects on British political and also economic interests in Africa'.[46]

Drawing on earlier ideas of collaboration, Martin Thomas and Andrew Thompson contend that 'The quest for favoured post-colonial relationships – neo-colonialism in the eyes of its critics, essential aid, advice, and investment to its defenders – mirrored the cultivation of preferred elites before independence'.[47] Referring specifically to the Gulf, Shohei Sato argues that the independence of Bahrain, Qatar, and the United Arab Emirates 'enabled both Britain and the US to maintain an international order favourable to the west by means of consensus and collaboration, whilst minimising direct involvement and the use of coercive measures'.[48] He proceeds to note that 'In the end, the whole process did not alter the collaborative relationship that had developed during the period of Britain's informal empire, instead only entailing the rearrangement thereof'.[49]

For Gordon Martell,

> Abandonment of certain territories and commitments is better understood as the political equivalent of 'downsizing' or 'restructuring' in the contemporary corporate world of the globalised marketplace, i.e. a calculated effort to sell off dwindling assets and reinvest in promising ones – not a decision to get out of the business of empire altogether.[50]

In a similar vein, Sarah Stockwell notes that British decolonization was 'directed to an "end" which aimed at salvaging from unhappy circumstances as much prestige and influence for Britain as possible'.[51] In her important work on 'exporting Britishness', Stockwell goes on to argue

> the transfers of power did not necessarily result in the cessation of colonialism in all its other guises, whether economic, cultural, or military. That this was the case was the inevitable consequence of the asymmetric relationship between imperial metropole and colony, with the former not only ambitious to exercise influence, but also in a strong position from which to do so.[52]

Sarah Stockwell's namesake, A. J. Stockwell, insists that in the era of decolonization the British set their sights on the 'maintenance of an imperial role as opposed to imperial rule'.[53] For Martin Thomas, 'by late 1960 the key decision-makers in [Harold] Macmillan's second government had crossed the Rubicon from imperial to post-imperial mind-sets. Conserving international reputation and post-colonial influence meant letting go sooner, not later'.[54] In a similar vein, Timothy Parsons argues that

> In attempting to peacefully transfer power to a sufficiently Anglicized and cooperative generation of nationalist leaders, Macmillan's government sought to preserve the economic and strategic benefits of empire without incurring the costs of direct imperial rule. In effect, this was an attempt to turn back the clock to the informal empire of the mid-nineteenth century.[55]

Dietmar Rothermund, however, argues that 'the influence which the colonial rulers had hoped to gain by handing over power more or less gracefully receded very soon'.[56] John Darwin also casts doubt on the success of British plans for the post-imperial era. On the one hand, he records that British leaders 'insisted that the end of colonial rule symbolized the success of the British method of empire, and was merely the prelude to a new and more equitable partnership'.[57] On the other, he notes that 'They only saw very late that Britain was grossly under-equipped to act the role of the metropole in such an informal empire'.[58] Darwin adds that as the British moved towards informality, 'the more vulnerable their old spheres became to the entry of the new world powers'.[59] If Britain did indeed see decolonization as an attempt to return to empire through informal means, Darwin argues that its hopes were largely dashed. For Darwin, the maintenance of informal empire required influence and strength which Britain no longer possessed. As he puts it: 'Informal imperialism was not an easy option for a declining power. . . . The transition to more informal empire required a stronger not a weaker Imperial centre'.[60] Equally, he points out that 'Self-government and independence turned out in most cases to be far more real than the British expected; the influence which the British hoped to exercise over their former colonies faded away as their economic fortunes declined'.[61] In sum, Darwin indicates that 'the optimistic prospectus on which winding up empire became the political orthodoxy was soon belied in reality. The "empire" of influence that was imagined in Whitehall shrivelled all too quickly'.[62]

Referring specifically to Britain's diplomatic reverse at the hands of President Nasser of Egypt at the time of the 1956 Suez crisis, Darwin remarks 'What Suez had shown was that Britain lacked the resources – of financial muscle, military power and geopolitical leverage – to sustain an empire of influence, and certainly not in a region as rough and dangerous as the postwar Middle East'.[63] In a similar vein, Martin Lynn contends that Suez 'marked a major turning point in British hopes of maintaining an independent role, indeed any significant role, overseas'.[64] In the estimation of Asher Orkaby, Nasser in 1956 'delivered the greatest blow to the British Empire in the Middle East'.[65] Peter Hahn goes even further, arguing that the Suez crisis 'destroyed all vestiges of Britain's influence in the Middle East'.[66] While recognizing that the Suez episode 'did not strategically dissolve British power or economic clout', Gregory Barton stresses that the

> loss of prestige led to a hardening of the resolve of elites in the Middle East, indeed around the British Empire, to resist further British influence. This

denouement demonstrates how relationships with subordinate elites provide the key to informal empire. When relationships between elites dissolve, so, too, does informal empire.[67]

For L. J. Butler, it was the attempt to substitute formal control for informal influence which exposed the degree to which British power had declined following the Second World War. 'To be successful', he argues, 'this strategy would require strong economic underpinnings, enabling Britain to consolidate its commercial ties, provide aid and offer attractive defence packages. In the event, Britain's capacity, especially in the provision of aid, was simply overtaken by the United States and international agencies'.[68] In a similar vein, Nicholas J. White asserts that 'Declining British industrial competitiveness, and the growing financial difficulties of the UK, made it impossible to maintain an "informal empire" by the latter half of the 1960s'.[69] For P. J. Cain and A. G. Hopkins,

> neo-colonialism could not have been planned in 1945 for the simple reason that decolonisation was not then envisaged. It was only later, in the 1950s, that serious thought was given to ways of perpetuating British influence in the post-imperial world, but by then Britain's aims were limited by her changing interests and not simply by the resources at her disposal.[70]

Focussing specifically on East Africa, Ichiro Maekawa contends that 'Britain, the old colonial power, had a relatively limited impact on the outcome of events. British aid was too inconsequential and incoherent to form a consistent neo-colonial policy in the newly independent states. Private investment, the "informal" side of neo-colonialism, was also of declining significance'.[71]

For Bernard Porter, it was the oil crisis of 1973–1974 which revealed the limits on Britain's neo-colonial capabilities. '[T]he West's domination of the [oil] market did not survive decolonisation', he explains, 'and the oil-producing countries banded together to raise prices to the very great detriment of those economies – which meant most industrial economies, including Britain's – which had grown dependent on cheap imported petroleum to a vulnerable degree'.[72] Even Wm. Roger Louis, in his analysis of the immediate post-war years, comments that 'The history of the British Empire in the Middle East during this period may be read as the unsuccessful attempt at conversion from formal rule and alliances to an informal basis of equal partnership and influence'.[73] Highlighting British expectations that 'imperialism would be sustained by means other than domination', Louis accepts that the 'actuality did not conform to the hope'.[74] As he points out: 'The idea of ostensible equal partnership never quite overcame Asian and African scepticism. What emerged was an accommodation based on self-interest'.[75] How far Britain and its erstwhile clients among the Gulf Sheikhdoms achieved such an accommodation will be a central feature of this study.

The extent to which empire, whether formal or informal, is an accurate description of British relations with the Gulf Sheikhdoms is a debatable point. Certainly Britain's locus standi within the Sheikhdoms rested on treaties signed with the individual rulers in the nineteenth and early twentieth centuries.[76] Under these agreements, the Gulf Sheikhdoms' foreign relations were conducted through the British government which, as Peter Lienhardt pointed out, 'came close to excluding all other powers absolutely'.[77] In internal affairs however, the Sheikhdoms enjoyed considerable autonomy.[78] Speaking to Trucial chiefs in 1903, the Viceroy of India, Lord Curzon, even declared: 'We saved you from extinction at the hands of your neighbours. . . . We have not seized or held your territory. We have not destroyed your independence, but have preserved it'.[79]

Christopher Davidson has gone so far as to characterize British relations with the Gulf Sheikhdoms as a '"cut-price" imperial system of indirect control'.[80] 'In contrast to its generalized failure across the wider Middle East', argues Gregory Barton, 'Britain did hang on successfully in the Persian Gulf, drawing on its long history of informal empire over these small Sheikhdoms to achieve the grand aims that failed elsewhere in the region'.[81] Similarly, Shohei Sato insists that 'the essence of the British presence in the Gulf up to the 1960s can be comprehended as an informal empire – the holding of indirect control over the region, achieved by means of cooperation with local elites'.[82] Allen Fromherz, moreover, argues that in the Gulf Britain was 'Less of a colonial power than an advisory service'.[83] In practice, however, the British were prepared to intervene to protect their perceived interests.

'Although the Persian Gulf protectorates of Kuwait, Qatar and the United Arab Emirates (Trucial States) were purportedly autonomous polities', observes Dane Kennedy, 'their affairs were overseen by British imperial agents'.[84] In a similar vein, Tancred Bradshaw has noted that in the Gulf 'it was taken for granted by British officials that the rulers would accept their advice'.[85] James Onley, moreover, emphasizes with respect to the Gulf Sheikhdoms that Britain ensured 'rival imperial influence was excluded'.[86] For Mark Hayman, the Second World War marked something of a watershed whereby the 'policy and practice of leaving internal arrangements to the ruling sheikhs could not be sustained' since the 'self-declared policy of non-involvement in internal affairs was severely compromised by the exigencies of war'.[87] Referring to the immediate post-war period, Rowena Abdul Razak contends that 'in clear contradiction to its stated policy that it would not intervene in Bahrain's internal affairs, Britain asserted control and ensured that the Ruler adhered to British interests, thereby securing its prime position in Bahrain and by extension the Gulf'.[88]

Helene von Bismarck has pointed out that Britain's de facto role in the Gulf Sheikhdoms went 'far beyond Britain's formal treaty-based rights and commitments'.[89] The principal reason for this was that the growing importance of the Gulf after 1945, not least as a vital source of oil and as a market for British manufactures, precluded the laissez-faire approach which had characterized British policy in the pre-war years. Indeed, the post-war expansion of oil revenues coincided with a shift in policy which witnessed a more interventionist stance by the British. In 1950, for instance, Britain's Political Agent in Bahrain, C. J. Pelly, remarked: 'His Majesty's Government's interest in the Persian Gulf Arab States is *NOT* confined merely to conducting their "external relations" even if in the case of these States a sharp dividing line could be drawn between "external relations" and internal affairs'.[90]

The need to pay more attention to the Gulf Sheikhdoms was underlined by the nationalization of the British-owned Anglo–Iranian Oil Company in 1951 by Iranian Prime Minister Muhammad Mussadiq. Indeed, the increased importance of oil from the Arab side of the Gulf following Mussadiq's demarche, coupled with the prospect of immense and growing wealth flowing into the relatively primitive Gulf Sheikhdoms, prompted the Permanent Under-Secretary at the Foreign Office, Sir William Strang, to call for a comprehensive review of the situation in the region.[91] Deputy Under-Secretary of State at the FO, Sir Roger Makins, was selected for the task, visiting the Gulf between 12 February and 12 March 1952. In the resulting report, Makins claimed that 'the efficiency of the administration in an Arab country is proportionate to the amount of British administration and advice which they have received in the past'.[92] In calling for British advice to be made more widely available, Makins did concede that 'Her Majesty's Government are responsible only for the external affairs of the States and have no direct responsibility for their internal administration'.[93] Nonetheless, he insisted that these responsibilities could not 'remain in watertight compartments', and that the 'administrative efficiency and economic stability of the States must be a matter of concern to Her Majesty's Government'.[94] 'The provision of British advisers', asserted Makins, 'is essential in order to preserve the administrations from collapse and to protect the great interest of Her Majesty's Government arising from the prospective accumulation of sterling balances in the hands of Kuwait and Qatar'.[95]

The growth in sterling balances stemmed not only from increases in Gulf oil production following the disruption in supplies from Iran, but also the extension of the type of 50/50 profit-sharing agreements between the oil companies and the host governments which Saudi Arabia had secured from the Arabian American Oil Company in December 1950.[96] By 1953, Kuwait, which had signed a 50/50 profit-sharing agreement with the Kuwait Oil Company in December 1951, saw revenues from oil exports reach the annual figure of £60 million.[97] Although Kuwait moved towards full independence by 19 June 1961, such was its immutable significance that within days Britain despatched a sizable force to deter an Iraqi move on the Amirate.[98] Calling to mind Kuwaiti Ruler Sheikh Abdullah's reaction to news of the imminent arrival of British troops, the Political Resident wrote: 'I have seldom seen a man more relieved or grateful than was the Amir'.[99] Abdullah's successor, Sheikh Sabah, also placed a degree of reliance on the British, informing the British Ambassador to Kuwait in 1966 that 'the important thing was to be frank with the British in private, to take their advice wherever possible and to lean on them as much as he liked, but in public to maintain his independence'.[100] For its part, Britain remained committed to the defence of Kuwait throughout the 1960s, albeit on an ever-decreasing scale.[101] On the eve of the cessation of Britain's formal military protection of Kuwait in 1971, the Joint Intelligence Committee intoned that such was the scale of Britain's continuing economic interests in the Amirate that it remained 'of the first importance' for the national interest.[102]

The post-war shift in British policy is highlighted by the instructions Bernard Burrows received from the Foreign Office upon taking up his position as Britain's Political Resident in the Gulf in 1953:

> The Shaikhdoms of the Gulf have become of first importance to the United Kingdom and to the Sterling Area as a whole. It is essential that Her Majesty's Government should exert sufficient influence in them to ensure that there is no conflict between the policies of the Rulers and those of Her Majesty's Government.[103]

Reflecting the renewed importance of the Gulf to Britain, one of Burrows' successors, Sir William Luce,[104] observed towards the end of 1961:

> it is no exaggeration to say that Britain at this moment stands more deeply committed in the Persian Gulf, both politically and militarily, than at any time since the last war, a situation which stands in marked contrast with the great contraction of our political and military commitments elsewhere in the world over the past fifteen years.[105]

Musing on British relations with the Gulf States three years later, Luce noted:

> After the Second World War and coincidental with, though not altogether consequential upon, the transfer of responsibility for Gulf affairs to the Foreign Office, there was a marked change in interpretation and application of British rights and obligations in respect of the States. Foremost was the recognition that protection of the States and responsibility for their external relations carried with them an indirect but none the less real responsibility for what went on, inside the States.[106]

In July 1959, the Foreign Office Deputy Under-Secretary of State, Sir Roger Stevens, had told a meeting of British diplomats in Middle Eastern countries that 'it had never been contested that we should hold our position in Aden, the Aden Protectorate and the Persian Gulf. In any conflict between those positions and anything else it was paramount that we should hold on'.[107] While Britain's resolve in Aden, and South Arabia more generally, was weakened by terrorism and instability fomented by Egypt's President Nasser, its commitment to the Gulf appeared to be immutable.

Rory Miller contends that 'By the beginning of the 1960s, British governments no longer had the money, the political will or the popular support at home to continue to provide security and play a leading role in the eleven Sheikhdoms of the Arab Gulf'.[108] A contrasting interpretation is produced by Christopher Davidson. Referring specifically to Britain's approach to the Gulf Sheikhdoms in the 1960s, he asserts that 'as events unfolded Britain increasingly began to intervene in the domestic politics and affairs of these proto-states'.[109] Indeed, well into that decade Britain still took it upon itself to interfere in the succession of the ruling families to ensure more amenable regimes among the Sheikhdoms. The most significant example of this was the deposition of the recalcitrant Sheikh Shakhbut of Abu Dhabi, who evinced resistance to development in his increasingly oil-rich state and shunned cooperation with neighbouring Sheikhdoms, and his replacement with his more reform-minded brother, Sheikh Zaid.[110] Responding to claims that the deposition of Shakhbut would be inconsistent with Britain's public assurances that the Gulf States were independent entities, immune from internal interference by the protecting power, Luce remarked: 'Does anyone in the Arab world . . . believe that we do not interfere in the internal affairs of the Gulf States and do we get any credit from our assertion?'[111] Britain not only assured Zaid of its support but also offered him military backing if he required it.[112] 'It can be concluded', notes von Bismarck, 'that Shaikh Shakhbut's eventual deposition in August 1966 was a joint enterprise between the British Government and Shaikh Zayed'.[113]

A year earlier, Britain had also played a significant role in the deposition of Sheikh Saqr of Sharjah whose flirtation with Arab nationalism, and readiness to permit Arab League personnel into his state, appeared to threaten British interests.[114] As Sir William Luce remarked shortly before Saqr's deposition:

> For years our position in the Gulf has been based on prestige and belief in our power and will to maintain our predominance. If this is proved after all to be a mere bubble by unwillingness or inability to restore the present situation we shall have nothing left with which to influence the future course of events.[115]

'It is inconceivable to me', expatiated the Political Resident, 'that Her Majesty's Government could abandon their peace-keeping role in this economically vital area at the first flick of the whip by Nasser and a couple of insignificant, self-serving Sheikhs'.[116] However, the British decision, announced in January 1968, to withdraw its military forces from the Gulf within three years meant that a new, more recognizably post-imperial, relationship had to be forged with the Sheikhdoms.

In some respects, the British announcement provided an unpropitious backdrop for this endeavour. On the one hand, the Sheikhs were taken aback by Britain's impending departure from the Gulf, not least in the context of Foreign Office Minister Goronwy Roberts' assurance during a visit to the region in November 1967 that the British presence would continue as long as it was necessary to maintain peace and stability. To nervous Gulf Rulers, moreover, the British decision seemed ominously reminiscent of British policy towards Aden and the Federation of South Arabia. There, Britain's declaration that the Federation would receive independence no later than 1968, coupled with its decision to close the military base in Aden and not provide any military commitment to the Federation after independence,[117] had led to the toppling of Britain's allies among the ruling families of South Arabia in the course of 1967.

Reflecting the dismay of the Gulf Rulers at Britain's January 1968 withdrawal announcement, the Political Resident, Sir Stewart Crawford, remarked: 'In the light of [the] South Arabian experience they consider that this is bound to encourage subversive elements, frighten away foreign investors and increase difficulties all round'.[118] Expanding on this theme, Crawford emphasized:

> It had been expected that the withdrawal of British forces from South Arabia would cause a severe shock to the Rulers of the Southern Gulf; but when it came, it proved the more severe because of the events leading up to it: the collapse of the South Arabian Federal Government, the flight of the Sultans, the emergence of the National Liberation Front and the discovery that Her Majesty's Government were prepared to treat with its leaders despite their revolutionary political affiliations and the violent methods they had used to seize power.[119]

Sheikh Rashid of Dubai himself told Goronwy Roberts at the beginning of 1968 that once the British departed there would be the 'same outcome as in South Arabia' where they had 'abandoned the Sultans'.[120] Rashid also spoke for many of his fellow Gulf Rulers when he condemned 'the decision, its timing and presentation and impending announcement of a date'.[121] Sheikh Ahmed of Qatar depicted Britain's apparent U-turn as a 'bad mistake' which could only mean that it 'wanted trouble in the Gulf'.[122] In a similar vein, Sheikh Zaid of Abu Dhabi asserted that if Britain 'went just like that' it would not only be 'severely criticised', but also lose all its friends in the Gulf,[123] while Sheikh Saqr bin Mohamed al-Qasimi of Ras al Khaimah lamented that the 'northern five Rulers[124] were too poor to arrange their affairs by themselves'.[125]

From his vantage point in Manama, Britain's Political Agent in Bahrain, Anthony Parsons, reported: 'the Ruler and his brothers consider that they have been betrayed by an unvarnished volte face only two months after the reassurance of November 1967; and that they are being faced with the sudden and unilateral termination of 150 years of mutual relationship with no warning or genuine consultation'.[126] The Chairman of Bahrain's Administrative Council, Sheikh Khalifah bin Salman, went so far as to accuse Britain of abandoning Bahrain to be 'kicked like a football between the players in the Gulf game'.[127] Despite having achieved formal independence from Britain in 1961,[128] Kuwait demonstrated equal consternation at the 1968 withdrawal decision, the Amir of Kuwait in particular conveying uneasiness about the future of the states of the Lower Gulf.[129] Relations between the Gulf Rulers and Britain were strained still further when Secretary of State for Defence Denis Healey contemptuously dismissed their offer to contribute to the costs of maintaining British forces in the region with the remark: 'it would be a great mistake if we allowed ourselves to become mercenaries for people who would like to have a few British troops around'.[130]

Given the strength of the reaction to news of Britain's impeding military departure from the Gulf, in no real sense can this decision be seen as deriving from a desire to sponsor independence in order to win the goodwill of elites and so preserve British interests after independence as may have been the case in other colonial settings. Rather, Britain's task after 1971 was to try and re-build and re-establish co-operative relations with the Sheikhly regimes of the Gulf whose loyalty to the British connection had been sorely tested by the precipitate withdrawal decision. As Lord Carrington, who served as Secretary of State for Defence from 1970 to 1974, recalled, Britain's formal departure from the Gulf meant that 'our interest in those areas would never again be underpinned by military means; or, if it were, it would involve new forces in a new situation'.[131] Some comfort regarding the future of the Gulf could be drawn from the attitude of the Abu Dhabi ruler, however.

Despite prophesying even before the January 1968 announcement that a swift British withdrawal would cause chaos in the Lower Gulf,[132] Sheikh Zaid pledged himself to embark upon persuading the other Trucial Rulers 'to accept cooperation and togetherness'.[133] Zaid emphasized the importance of impressing upon his fellow Rulers of the Lower Gulf that 'whether the British withdrawal took place in three, five or ten years' time it was going to happen and they must begin organising themselves now, not in six months' time'.[134] Indeed, Sheikhs Zaid and Rashid were quick to react to news of Britain's impending departure, proclaiming the unification of Abu Dhabi and Dubai on 18 February 1968.

Reflecting earlier in the decade on the difficulties of effecting closer association among the Sheikhdoms of the Lower Gulf, Sir William Luce observed:

> The Trucial States, with a combined population of about 85,000, are linked with Qatar, with about 45,000 inhabitants, by a long narrow strip of desert; both are more accessible to Saudi Arabia than they are to each other. Bahrain, with a population of about 150,000, is separated from Qatar by 40 miles of sea and is more accessible to Saudi Arabia on whom she is economically dependent.... The most ardent federalist would boggle at the task of making any political or military sense out of such a situation.[135]

In the course of the tortuous discussions which led to the creation of the United Arab Emirates from among the former Trucial States on 18 July 1971, the British were eager to avoid too prominent a role. As the Head of the Foreign Office's Arabian Department, M. S. Weir, noted in the immediate aftermath of the British government's decision to quit the Gulf by 1971, there could be 'no question of trying, or even being thought to be trying, to promote another "Whitehall Federation" on the lines of South Arabia'.[136] Equally, Weir's successor, A. A. Acland, doubted the value of a structure imposed by Britain, declaring: 'A successful Union which will survive our military withdrawal from the Gulf can only be brought about if the Rulers enter into it willingly with a genuine desire to make it work'.[137] The Labour Foreign Secretary, Michael Stewart, had already insisted that 'the will to unite must exist first among those concerned and cannot be imposed'.[138] Indeed, the impetus for unity came from the Trucial States themselves, the emergence United Arab Emirates essentially resting on an accommodation between the Rulers of the two leading states, Abu Dhabi and Dubai.

Ruminating on the ostensible relinquishment of Britain's identity as a world power ushered in by the impending departure from East of Suez, of which the presence in the Gulf was a key component, Labour Cabinet minister and diarist

Richard Crossman observed: 'the status barrier is as difficult to break through as the sound barrier; it splits your ears and is terribly painful when it happens'.[139] Former Labour Foreign Secretary Patrick Gordon Walker, moreover, characterized the decision to withdraw as 'the most momentous shift in our foreign policy for a century and a half'.[140] Writing shortly after the withdrawal announcement, renowned historian of international history D. C. Watt characterized it as 'the reversal of long-standing official Labour government policy and a crowning exhibition of weakness in an area where visible strength counts a good deal'.[141] 'It puts at hazard', he continued, 'very considerable British economic and financial interests'.[142] In 1969, the Labour Secretary of State for Defence, Denis Healey, himself declared that Britain had changed 'from a world power to a European power'.[143] John Darwin has largely followed these contemporary assessments.

In *Unfinished Empire*, Darwin contends that Prime Minister Harold Wilson's announcement on 16 January 1968 of the end of Britain's East of Suez commitment marked the 'terminus of Britain's three-century career as a great Asian power. It signalled the final collapse of the postwar campaign to remain a world power'.[144] In his earlier work, *Britain and Decolonisation*, Darwin similarly argued that the January 1968 announcement 'helped to transform the *partial* withdrawal which the British intended to be the result of the colonial transfers of power into a conscious retreat from the old burdens and privileges of imperial power'.[145] In a similar vein, Ronald Hyam has remarked: 'Here was the moment of the recall of the legions, the end of the Pax Britannica in the Indian Ocean, the removal of the last remnants of a physical British presence in the Middle East, the effective termination of the British imperial-global cosmoplastic system'.[146]

For P. L. Pham, the Wilson government's decision to withdraw from East of Suez 'sealed Britain's descent from its former status as a world power'.[147] Writing somewhat earlier, Colin Cross asserted that 'So far as the end of the British Empire can be set at a definite point in time, it was the afternoon of January 19 [sic], 1968, when the Labour Prime Minister, Harold Wilson, announced the final homecoming of the British legions'.[148] Scathing in his criticism of the withdrawal decision, J. B. Kelly insists that 'By 1970 the permanent officials at the Foreign Office had also come round to the view that Britain's destiny lay in Continental Europe and not, as in the past, in the lands and seas beyond'.[149] More recently, Peter Mangold has maintained that 'The 1970s mark a watershed in British engagement with the Middle East. Informal empire had finally all gone, and with it the framework within which Britain had pursued its interests in the region for well over a century. No longer able to prioritise those interests over the will of local states, or to claim special privileges, Britain now accepted that its relations with Middle Eastern countries were on a new moral and political basis, more appropriate to a post-imperial age'.[150] Other scholars have challenged declinist interpretations.

Taking the events of 1956 as his starting point, G. C. Peden contends that 'it would be wrong to portray the British as being in full retreat from the Middle East after Suez. Officials advised against a policy of scuttle; instead, they believed in gradual disengagement, with every effort made to maintain British prestige with friendly governments'.[151] He adds that while Britain 'no longer had the economic and military power it had enjoyed in its heyday, it could still hope to exercise substantial influence in world affairs, taking advantage of its position as a link between the USA, the commonwealth, and Europe'.[152] For Greg Kennedy and Christopher Tuck, 'influence remains at the heart of British foreign policy. The British government continues to trade on the notion of Britain's position as a global "hub", an idea which reflects the British aspiration to continue to be able to exert global influence in the defence of British interests'.[153] Equally, Spencer Mawby argues that 'For the first post-war generation Britain's identity remained tied up with its global role, and the events of the last two decades from the Falklands war to the invasion of Iraq in 2003 suggest that a part of this globalist instinct has survived into the present'.[154] Mawby also observes that 'even after all were agreed that the formal British Empire was no more, its influence was still strongly felt in the former colonial territories, in Britain itself and in the international system'.[155] Referring specifically to Tony Blair's New Labour government, elected in 1997, Julia Gallagher insists that it 'wanted to make sure that Britain was a major world player'.[156]

Ashley Jackson, moreover, plays down the significance of decolonization and emphasizes the 'hardy survival of Britain as an international player that never ceased to seek a global role and that retained manifold international interests and responsibilities, together with the political and security capabilities to support them'.[157] Jackson asserts that his interpretation aims to qualify the

> common, even hackneyed, picture of a sudden shift from empire to postempire in the 1960s, a shift that in reality never really took place, and thus challenges the 'now you see it, now you don't' view of empire that struggles to capture the more complex reality of Britain's world role in the last half century.[158]

Indeed, Jackson is keen to stress the 'continuation of the world role into the 1970s and beyond'.[159] In a similar vein, Philip Murphy argues that there is a 'danger of exaggerating [the] retreat from a global role and missing the continuities in British policy'.[160] Equally, D. George Boyce stresses that 'England did not relinquish her imperial and great power status easily. If she was obliged to change, then she did so in order to stay the same: she aspired to remain a great power, or at least influence, in, for example, the Middle East, even after the Suez crisis'.[161] David M. McCourt, furthermore, contends that British policy-makers 'did not conceive of the decisions taken in early January 1968 as signifying a retreat from world affairs'.[162] He proceeds to point out that 'whilst Britain now had no specific "capability for use" east of Suez, her economic and political interests in a safe and secure world beyond Europe remained'.[163]

In his study of Britain's international role after 1970, Michael J. Turner insists that the 'political and economic problems of the 1970s and the limits they imposed on Britain's international role and influence were not as debilitating as was claimed'.[164] Reacting to notions that the 1970s represented the 'nadir' of British power,[165] Turner points out that 'Historians who focus on the reasons for

Britain's decline perhaps lose sight of an equally important phenomenon: how and why decline was minimized. Britain did decline, but despite the lack of resources and despite events that did not go its way, Britain remained one of the world's great powers'.[166] So far as the Middle East is concerned, Turner notes that its ongoing economic and strategic importance meant that, the announcement of formal withdrawal from East of Suez notwithstanding, 'Britain's involvement did not end, even if its role was much smaller than in former times'.[167] Equally, Ashley Jackson contends that 'Despite the apparent finality of the decision to withdraw from East of Suez . . . there was no firm handshake and swift departure – more of a long lingering goodbye which is yet to end'.[168] In a similar vein, Tore Petersen insists that 'The British, despite liquidating most of its fixed positions in the Persian Gulf and Arabian Peninsula, successfully made the transition from formal to informal empire in the region'.[169] Petersen even suggests that 'British influence remained large and almost paramount' in the Gulf.[170]

Referring to its role in the Gulf after 1971, Jeffrey Macris has remarked that 'Great Britain – without substantial military forces in the area for the first time in over a century – attempted to prolong whatever influence it still possessed'.[171] Similarly, Shohei Sato comments that 'In essence, Britain's goal was to leave in peace and to retain some informal influence after its retreat'.[172] Ruminating on the announcement to withdraw from East of Suez, Rob Johnson insists that 'the threat posed by the Marxist rebellion in Oman's Dhofar province and then on the Musandam Peninsula, supported by the same revolutionary forces that had been active in neighbouring Aden, posed a particular challenge to the British government and forced a change of policy from disengagement to reinforcement'.[173] He goes on to stress that 'While both Labour and Conservative governments wanted to limit their liabilities, they certainly did not want a repetition of the debacle that had marked Britain's withdrawal from Aden'.[174]

J. E. Peterson argues that a significant legacy of the British presence in the Gulf States has been a 'continuing preference for British standards, practices, products and companies'.[175] In retirement, the former Head of the FCO's Middle East Department, Sir Alan Munro, pointed out the paradox that, despite the withdrawal from East of Suez, Britain's 'inherited role' role in the Middle East 'persisted at a time of generally recessive British diplomacy in the 1970's while we took stock of our status. The Middle East still remained an area of active diplomacy for us'.[176] Referring in his memoirs to British policy towards the Gulf States in aftermath of the Iranian Revolution, moreover, Munro asserts that Britain took steps to 're-engage with their security, no longer with garrisons as in earlier days of empire, but through diplomatic support, bolstered by military training and equipment'.[177]

Focusing on British policy towards Oman in the 1970s, James Worrall has also cast doubt on notions of British decline. In a detailed analysis, Worrall demonstrates Britain's commitment to Oman in terms of military assistance in defeating the rebellion in Dhofar which threatened not only the authority of the pro-British Ruler, Sultan Qaboos, but also the existence of the Sultanate itself. He also draws attention to Britain's role in the construction of the modern state of Oman 'almost from scratch'.[178] This heavy commitment was undertaken, argues Worrall, to ensure that instability in the Sultanate did not threaten Britain's wider interests, particularly economic ones, in the Gulf.[179] Worrall also points out that while the RAF's withdrawal from Salalah and Masirah in Oman in April 1977 marked the end of the last permanent British bases in the Gulf, 'Britain has by no means abandoned its role in the region'.[180] 'What happened in Oman', stresses Worrall, 'does not show that Britain was in inexorable decline'.[181] He goes on the claim that his study of Oman has 'contributed to the literature on Britain's decline in the second half of the twentieth century by demonstrating that any loss of will was by no means complete, especially when vital national interests were at stake'.[182] Worrall concludes that 'even whilst Britain was moving further into the European Circle, responsibilities in the old Commonwealth/World Circle were still being willingly fulfilled, thus challenging the notion of Britain becoming purely a European power'.[183] Indeed, far from marking a 'dramatic farewell to Britain's world role'[184] as John Darwin suggests, the announcement of Britain's formal withdrawal from East of Suez did not end extensive British involvement in the Gulf region. In 1969, FCO Minister of State Goronwy Roberts assured the Ruler of Sharjah, Sheikh Khalid, that 'Britain was not leaving the Gulf entirely. After 1971 Britain's presence would probably be even stronger, but it would be commercial and technical rather than military'.[185] Britain's attempts to preserve as much of its influence, and as many of its interests, as possible into the post-imperial era will be reflected in the first chapter.

Notes

1. John Gallagher and Ronald Robinson, 'The imperialism of free trade', *Economic History Review*, 6, 1 (1953), p. 1.
2. John Gallagher, *The Decline, Revival and Fall of the British Empire* (Cambridge: Cambridge University Press, 1982), p. 75.
3. Robin W. Winks, 'On decolonization and informal empire', *The American Historical Review*, 81, 3 (1976), p. 556.
4. Glen Balfour-Paul, 'Britain's informal empire in the Middle East', in Judith M. Brown and Wm. Roger Louis (eds.), *The Oxford History of the Twentieth Century: Volume IV: The Twentieth Century* (Oxford: Oxford University Press, 1999), pp. 490–514.
5. John Darwin, 'An undeclared empire: The British in the Middle East, 1918–39', *Journal of Imperial and Commonwealth History*, 27, 2 (1999), p. 159.
6. Ronald Robinson, 'The excentric idea of imperialism, with or without empire', in Wolfgang J. Mommesen and Jürgen Osterhammel (eds.), *Imperialism and After: Continuities and Discontinuities* (London: Allen and Unwin, 1986), p. 273; John Darwin, 'Gallagher's empire', in Wm. Roger Louis (ed.), *Yet More Adventures with Britannia: Personalities, Politics and Culture in Britain* (London: I. B. Tauris, 2005), p. 239.
7. Dom Mintoff, *How Britain Rules Malta: A Brief Analysis of the Report of the Malta Constitutional Commission 1960* (Valletta: Union Press, undated), p. 3.
8. Ronald Robinson, 'Non-European foundations of European imperialism: Sketch for a theory of collaboration', in B. Sutcliffe and R. Owen (eds.), *Studies in the Theory of Imperialism* (London: Longmans, 1972), pp. 117–42.
9. Ibid., pp. 138–9.
10. Martin Thomas, *Empires of Intelligence: Security Services and Colonial Disorder After 1914* (Berkeley: University of California Press, 2008), p. 44.

18 *Introduction*

11 Shohei Sato, *Britain and the Formation of the Gulf States: Embers of Empire* (Manchester: Manchester University Press, 2016), p. 23.
12 Michael W. Doyle, *Empires* (Ithaca: Cornell University Press, 1986), p. 38.
13 Robinson, 'Non-European foundations of European imperialism', p. 139. For a similar interpretation, see Doyle, *Empires*, p. 369.
14 Robinson, 'Non-European foundations of European imperialism', p. 118. Robin Winks agrees that the 'role of collaborator . . . was critically important within the informal empire' (Winks, 'On decolonization', p. 552).
15 Wm. Roger Louis and Ronald Robinson, 'The imperialism of decolonization', *Journal of Imperial and Commonwealth History*, 22, 3 (1994), pp. 493–4.
16 Ibid., p. 485.
17 Ibid., p. 487.
18 Wm. Roger Louis and Ronald Robinson, 'Empire preserv'd: How the Americans put anti-communism before anti-imperialism', in Prasenjit Duara (ed.), *Decolonization: Perspectives from Now and Then* (London: Routledge, 2004), p. 157.
19 Juan Romero, 'Decolonization in reverse: The Iranian oil crisis of 1951–53', *Middle Eastern Studies*, 51, 3 (2015), p. 483.
20 Kwame Nkrumah, *Neo-Colonialism: The Last Stage of Imperialism* (London: Nelson, 1965), p. 31.
21 Timothy H. Parsons, *The Second British Empire: In the Crucible of the Twentieth Century* (Lanham: Rowman & Littlefield, 2014), p. 144.
22 Rhoda Howard, *Colonialism and Underdevelopment in Ghana* (London: Croom Helm, 1978), p. 223.
23 G. Ugo Nwokeji, 'African economies in the years of decolonization', in Toyin Falola (ed.), *Africa: Volume 4: The End of Colonial Rule: Nationalism and Decolonization* (Durham, NC: Carolina Academic Press, 2002), pp. 150–1.
24 Jack Woddis, *Introduction to Neo-Colonialism* (New York: International Publishers, 1967), p. 87.
25 Harry Magdoff, 'Imperialism without colonies', in Roger Own and Bob Sutcliffe (eds.), *Studies in the Theory of Imperialism* (London: Longman, 1972), p. 167.
26 D. K. Fieldhouse, *Unilever Overseas: The Anatomy of a Multinational, 1895–1965* (London: Croom Helm, 1978), p. 599.
27 Cited in Nicholas J. White, *British Business in Post-Colonial Malaysia, 1957–70: 'Neo-colonialism' or 'Disengagement'?* (London and New York: RoutledgeCurzon, 2004), p. 2.
28 Fred Halliday, *Arabia Without Sultans* (Harmondsworth: Penguin, 1979), p. 497.
29 Ibid., pp. 497–8.
30 Ibid., p. 499.
31 S. R. Ashton, 'Introduction', in S. R. Ashton and Wm. Roger Louis (eds.), *East of Suez and the Commonwealth 1964–1971*, Part I (London: The Stationery Office, 2004), p. xxix.
32 John Darwin, *The End of the British Empire: The Historical Debate* (Oxford: Blackwell Publishing, 1991), p. 3.
33 Julian Go, *Patterns of Empire: The British and American Empires 1688 to the Present* (New York: Cambridge University Press, 2011), p. 11.
34 Ibid.
35 Wm. Roger Louis, 'Suez and decolonization: Scrambling out of Africa and Asia', in Wm. Roger Louis (ed.), *Ends of British Imperialism: The Scramble for Empire, Suez and Decolonization* (London: I. B. Tauris, 2006), p. 28.
36 Ibid., p. 29.
37 Wm. Roger Louis, 'Introduction', in Brown and Louis (eds.), *The Oxford History of the British Empire: Volume IV* (Oxford: Oxford University Press, 1999), p. 27.
38 John Darwin, 'British decolonization since 1945: A pattern or a puzzle?' *Journal of Imperial and Commonwealth History*, 12, 2 (1984), p. 206.

Introduction   19

39 John Darwin, 'Last days of empire', in Miguel Bandeira Jeronimo and Antonio Costa Pinto (eds.), *The Ends of European Colonial Empires: Cases and Comparisons* (Basingstoke: Palgrave Macmillan, 2015), p. 273.
40 John Darwin, 'Britain's withdrawal from East of Suez', in Carl Bridge (ed.), *Munich to Vietnam: Australia's Relations with Britain and the United States Since the 1930s* (Carlton, VIC: Melbourne University Press, 1991), p. 149.
41 Ibid.
42 Frank Heinlein, *British Government Policy and Decolonisation 1945–1963: Scrutinising the Official Mind* (London: Frank Cass, 2002), p. 297.
43 Nicholas J. White, *Decolonisation: The British Experience Since 1945* (London: Longman, 1999), p. 106.
44 Bernard Porter, *British Imperial: What the Empire Wasn't* (London: I. B. Tauris, 2015), p. 98.
45 Francis Owtram, *A Modern History of Oman: Formation of the State Since 1920* (London: I. B. Tauris, 2004), p. 124.
46 D. K. Fieldhouse, *Black Africa, 1945–1980: Economic Decolonization and Arrested Development* (London: Routledge, 2011), p. 9. Fieldhouse adds that 'it was generally assumed that, if the colonies were liberated quickly and good relations established with the successor regimes, there would be little or no economic loss to the metropolises. African markets would remain open; colonial exports would continue to flow to their traditional European terminals or entrepots' (ibid., p. 232).
47 Martin Thomas and Andrew Thompson, 'Empire and globalisation: From "high imperialism" to decolonisation', *International History Review*, 36, 1 (2014), p. 159.
48 Sato, *Britain and the Formation of the Gulf States*, p. 4.
49 Ibid. See also pp. 134–5.
50 Gordon Martell, 'Decolonisation After Suez: Retreat or rationalisation?' *Australian Journal of Politics and History*, 46, 3 (2000), p. 414.
51 Sarah Stockwell, 'Ends of empire', in Sarah Stockwell (ed.), *The British Empire: Themes and Perspectives* (Oxford: Blackwell Publishing, 2008), p. 281.
52 Sarah Stockwell, 'Exporting Britishness: Decolonization in Africa, the British state and its clients', in Miguel Bandeira Jeronimo and Antonio Costa Pinto (eds.), *The Ends of European Colonial Empires: Cases and Comparisons* (Basingstoke: Palgrave Macmillan, 2015), p. 169.
53 A. J. Stockwell, *Ending the British Empire: What Did They Think They Were Doing?* (Egham: Royal Holloway, University of London, 1999), p. 24.
54 Martin Thomas, *Fight or Flight: Britain, France, and their Roads from Empire* (Oxford: Oxford University Press, 2014), pp. 275–6.
55 Parsons, *The Second British Empire*, p. 146.
56 Dietmar Rothermund, *The Routledge Companion to Decolonization* (London and New York: Routledge, 2006), p. 2.
57 John Darwin, *Unfinished Empire: The Global Expansion of Britain* (London: Allen Lane, 2012), p. 343.
58 Ibid.
59 John Darwin, 'Diplomacy and decolonization', in Kent Fedorowich and Martin Thomas (eds.), *International Diplomacy and Colonial Retreat* (London: Frank Cass, 2001), p. 18.
60 John Darwin, 'Decolonization and the end of the British empire', in Robin W. Winks (ed.), *The Oxford History of the British Empire: Vol. V* (Oxford: Oxford University Press, 1999), p. 551.
61 Darwin, 'British decolonization since 1945', p. 206.
62 John Darwin, 'The geopolitics of decolonization', in Alfred W. McCoy, Josep M. Fradera, and Stephen Jacobson (eds.), *Endless Empire: Spain's Retreat, Europe's Eclipse, America's Decline* (Madison, WI: University of Wisconsin Press, 2012), p. 202.
63 Darwin, *Unfinished Empire*, p. 363.

64 Martin Lynn, 'Introduction', in Martin Lynn (ed.), *The British Empire in the 1950s: Retreat or Revival* (Basingstoke: Palgrave Macmillan, 2006), p. 8.
65 Asher Orkaby, *Beyond the Arab Cold War: The International History of the Yemen Civil War, 1962–68* (New York: Oxford University Press, 2017), p. 152.
66 Peter L. Hahn, *The United States, Great Britain, and Egypt, 1945–1956: Strategy and Diplomacy in the Early Cold War* (Chapel Hill and London: University of North Carolina Press, 1991), p. 240.
67 Gregory A. Barton, *Informal Empire and the Rise of One World Culture* (Basingstoke: Palgrave Macmillan, 2014), p. 163.
68 L. J. Butler, *Britain and Empire: Adjusting to a Post-Imperial World* (London and New York: I. B. Tauris, 2002), p. 195.
69 White, *British Business in Post-Colonial Malaysia*, p. 16.
70 P. J. Cain and A. J. Hopkins, *British Imperialism, 1688–2000* (Harlow: Longman, 2002), p. 640.
71 Ichiro Maekawa, 'Neo-colonialism reconsidered: A case study of East Africa in the 1960s and 1970s', *Journal of Imperial and Commonwealth History*, 43, 2 (2015), p. 333.
72 Bernard Porter, *The Lion's Share: A History of British Imperialism 1850 to the Present*, 5th edition (Harlow: Pearson, 2012), p. 295.
73 Wm. Roger Louis, *The British Empire in the Middle East, 1945–1951: Arab Nationalism, the United States and Postwar Imperialism* (Oxford: Clarendon Press, 1984), p. 15.
74 Wm. Roger Louis, 'The dissolution of the British Empire', in Judith M. Brown and Wm. Roger Louis (eds.), *The Oxford History of the Twentieth Century: Volume IV: The Twentieth Century* (Oxford: Oxford University Press, 1999), p. 329.
75 Ibid.
76 See Rosemarie Said Zahlan, *The Making, of the Gulf States: Kuwait, Bahrain, Qatar, the United Arab Emirates and Oman* (Reading: Ithaca Press, 1998), pp. 14–17, Uzi Rabi, 'Britain's "special position"' in the Gulf: Its origins, dynamics and legacy', *Middle Eastern Studies*, 42, 3 (2006), pp. 353–4; C. U. Aitchison, *Treaties and Engagements Relating to Arabia and the Persian Gulf* (Gerrards Cross: Archive Editions, 1987), pp. 181–266.
77 Peter Lienhardt, *Shaikhdoms of Eastern Arabia* (Basingstoke: Palgrave Macmillan, 2001), p. 3. See also Ivor Lucas, *A Road to Damascus: Mainly Diplomatic Memoirs from the Middle East* (London: The Radcliffe Press, 1997), pp. 32–3.
78 Lienhardt, *Shaikhdoms of Eastern Arabia*, pp. 8–9; Anthony Parsons, *They Say the Lion: Britain's Legacy to the Arabs: A Personal Memoir* (London: Jonathan Cape, 1986), pp. 118–19.
79 Cited in Zoe Holman, 'On the side of decency and democracy: The history of British-Bahraini relations and transnational contestation', in Ala'a Shehabi and Marc Owen Jones (eds.), *Bahrain's Uprising: Resistance and Repression in the Gulf* (London: Zed Books, 2015), p. 175.
80 Christopher M. Davidson, *Dubai: The Vulnerability of Success* (London: Hurst and Company, 2008), p. 17.
81 Gregory A. Barton, 'Informal empire: The case of Siam and the Middle East', in Alfred W. McCoy, Josep M. Fradera, and Stephen Jacobson (eds.), *Endless Empire: Spain's Retreat, Europe's Eclipse, America's Decline* (Madison, WI: University of Wisconsin Press, 2012), p. 261.
82 Sato, *Britain and the Formation of the Gulf States*, p. 23.
83 Allen J. Fromherz, *Qatar: A Modern History* (London and New York: I. B. Tauris, 2012), p. 65.
84 Dane Kennedy, *The Imperial History Wars: Debating the British Empire* (London: Bloomsbury Academic, 2018), p. 111.
85 Tancred Bradshaw, 'The dead hand of the Treasury: The economic and social development of the Trucial States, 1948–60', *Middle Eastern Studies*, 50, 2 (2014), p. 328.

86 James Onley, *The Arabian Frontier of the British Raj: Merchants, Rulers, and the Nineteenth-Century Gulf* (Oxford: Oxford University Press, 2007), p. 32.
87 Mark Hayman, 'Economic protectorate in Britain's informal empire: The Trucial Coast during the Second World War', *Journal of Imperial and Commonwealth History*, 46, 2 (2018), p. 324.
88 Rowena Abdul Razak, 'When guns are not enough: Britain's response to nationalism in Bahrain, 1958–63', *Journal of Arabian Studies*, 7, 1 (2017), p. 65.
89 Helene von Bismarck, *British Policy in the Persian Gulf, 1961–1968: Conceptions of Informal Empire* (Basingstoke: Palgrave Macmillan, 2013), p. 182.
90 Cited in Jill Crystal, *Oil and Politics in the Gulf: Rulers and Merchants in Kuwait and Qatar* (Cambridge: Cambridge University Press, 1990), p. 122.
91 Minute by Sir William Strang, 10 September 1951, FO 371/91341/EA 15316/2.
92 Report on a visit to the States of the Persian Gulf under British protection, with some observations on Iraq and Saudi Arabia and with conclusions and recommendations by Sir Roger Makins, 20 March 1952, FO 371/98343/EA 1051/53.
93 Ibid.
94 Ibid.
95 Ibid.
96 Simon C. Smith, *Kuwait, 1950–1965: Britain, the al-Sabah, and Oil* (Oxford: Oxford University Press, 1999), pp. 32–3.
97 Letter from B. A. B. Burrows to Anthony Eden, 12 March 1954, in *Foreign Office Annual Reports from Arabia, 1930–1960: Iraq, Jordan, Kuwait, Persian Gulf, Saudi Arabia, Yemen* (London: Archive Editions, 1993), p. 713.
98 See Nigel Ashton, 'Britain and the Kuwaiti crisis, 1961', *Diplomacy and Statecraft*, 9, 1 (1998), pp. 163–81.
99 Letter from Luce to Crawford, No. 1040/64, 3 July 1964, FO 371/174489/B 1052/26/G.
100 Robert L. Jarman, *Sabah al-Salim al-Sabah: Amir of Kuwait, 1965–77: A Political Biography* (London: London Centre of Arab Studies, 2002), p. 277.
101 See Ash Rossiter, ' "Screening the food from the flies": Britain, Kuwait, and the dilemma of protection, 1961–1971', *Diplomacy and Statecraft*, 28, 1 (2017), pp. 85–109.
102 Ibid., p. 102.
103 Letter from the Foreign Office to Bernard Burrows, No. 125, 24 July 1953, FO 371/104270/EA 1053/8.
104 Sir William (Henry Tucker) Luce (1907–1977): Sudan Political Service, 1930; Private Secretary to Governor-General, 1941–1947; Deputy Governor, Equatoria Province, 1950; Governor, Blue Nile Province, 1951; Adviser to the Governor-General of the Sudan on Constitutional and External Affairs, 1953–1956; Governor and Commander-in-Chief, Aden, 1956–1960; Political Resident in the Persian Gulf, 1961–1966; Personal Representative of the Foreign and Commonwealth Secretary for Persian Gulf Affairs, 1970–1972.
105 Letter from Luce to Lord Home, No. 98, 22 November 1961, T 317/41.
106 Letter from Luce to Patrick Gordon Walker, 11 November 1964, cited in Ashton and Louis, *East of Suez and the Commonwealth 1964–1971*, Part I, p. 398.
107 Robert McNamara, 'The Nasser factor: Anglo–Egyptian relations and Yemen/Aden crisis 1962–65', *Middle Eastern Studies*, 53, 1 (2017), p. 53.
108 Rory Miller, *Desert Kingdoms to Global Powers: The Rise of the Arab Gulf* (New Haven and London: Yale University Press, 2016), p. 5.
109 Christopher Davidson, *Shadow Wars: The Secret Struggle for the Middle East* (London: Oneworld, 2017), pp. 31–2.
110 Uzi Rabi, 'Oil politics and tribal rulers in Eastern Araba: The reign of Shakhbut (1928–1966)', *British Journal of Middle Eastern Studies*, 33, 1 (2006), pp. 48–50. Peter Lienhardt, who acted briefly as an adviser to Shakhbut in 1961, recalled: 'In Abu Dhabi itself, the fact that people were getting very little out of their oil caused

22 Introduction

increasing dissatisfaction among both the ruling family and the general public. It was clear that the situation could not go on like that indefinitely . . . his own brother [Sheikh Zaid] had told him that unless he spent more money the people would come and burn the palace down' (Lienhardt, *Shaikhdoms of Eastern Arabia*, pp. ix–x). The Political Agent in Abu Dhabi at the time of Shakhbut's ouster, Archie Lamb, recalled that the Ruler's inability to trust others 'made him instantly suspicious, where money was concerned, of everyone's motives and interests and regrettably made him very receptive to hints that he was being "cheated, betrayed and played around with", to use one of his comments soon after my arrival. It also made him a ready prey for any second-rate contractor or entrepreneur who claimed that he could do a job on the cheap; and confirmed the Ruler in his belief, when the second-rate job proved a non-starter or a failure, that every businessman was out to rob him' (Sir Archie Lamb, *A Long Way from Swansea: A Memoir* (Clunderwen: Starborn Books, 2003), pp. 106–7).

111 M. W. Daly, *The Last of the Great Proconsuls: The Biography of Sir William Luce* (San Diego: Nathan Berg, 2014), pp. 223–4.

112 It was the Deputy Political Resident in Bahrain, Glencairn Balfour-Paul, who not only delivered the unwelcome news to Shakhbut that his family wanted him out, but also stationed two companies of the British-officered Trucial Oman Scouts 'sufficiently near the palace to intervene forcibly if needed' (Glencairn Balfour-Paul, *Bagpipes in Babylon: A Lifetime in the Arab World and Beyond* (London and New York: I. B. Tauris, 2006), pp. 203–04). See also Tom Walcott, 'The Trucial Oman Scouts 1955 to 1971: An overview', *Asian Affairs*, 37, 1 (2006), p. 20.

113 Von Bismarck, *British Policy in the Persian Gulf*, p. 184.

114 See Helene von Bismarck, '"A watershed in our relations with the Trucial States": Great Britain's policy to prevent the opening of an Arab League office in the Persian Gulf in 1965', *Middle Eastern Studies*, 47, 1 (2011), pp. 1–24; Glen Balfour Paul, *The End of the Middle East: Britain's Relinquishment of Power in her Last Three Arab Dependencies* (Cambridge: Cambridge University Press, 1994), p. 121.

115 Von Bismarck, *British Policy in the Persian Gulf, 1961–1968*, p. 152.

116 Telegram from Luce to the Foreign Office, No. 528, 21 June 1965, FO 371/179918/ BT 1103/195.

117 *Statement on the Defence Estimates 1966: Part I: The Defence Review* (London: HMSO, 1966), Cmnd. 2901, p. 8. In his annual report for 1966, the Political Resident in the Gulf, Sir Stewart Crawford, recorded that 'The decision to withdraw our forces from South Arabia caused serious shock to the Gulf rulers and the repercussions of this decision are still working themselves out' (Letter from Crawford to George Brown, 27 January 1967, cited in cited in A. L. P. Burdett (ed.), *Records of the Emirates, 1966–1971: Volume 1: 1966* (Slough: Archive Editions, 2002), p. 4).

118 Telegram from Crawford to the Foreign Office, No. 34, 10 January 1968, FCO 8/47.

119 Letter from Crawford to George Brown, 17 January 1968, cited in A. L. P. Burdett (ed.), *Records of the Emirates, 1966–1971: Volume 2: 1967* (Slough: Archive Editions, 2002), p. 4.

120 Record of a meeting between Mr Goronwy Roberts, MP, Minister of State, Foreign Office, and Their Highnesses the Rulers of Qatar and Dubai in Dubai, 8 January 1968, cited in A. L. P. Burdett (ed.), *Records of the Emirates, 1966–1971: Volume 3: 1968* (Slough: Archive Editions, 2002), p. 212.

121 Telegram from D. A. Roberts to the Foreign Office, No. 25, 11 January 1968, FCO 8/47. In mid-1969, Rashid impressed upon Prime Minister Harold Wilson that 'the British decision to withdraw by 1971 left too short a period for adjustment. This period might have been suitable for more advanced and well-established societies but conditions in the Gulf were such that the area needed a longer period. Although the Emirates were rich they were not politically strong enough to face the world without help' (A. L. P. Burdett (ed.), *Records of the Emirates, 1966–1971: Volume 4: 1969* (Slough: Archive Editions, 2002), p. 210).

Introduction 23

122 Record of a meeting between Mr Goronwy Roberts, MP, Minister of State, Foreign Office, and Their Highnesses the Rulers of Qatar and Dubai in Dubai, 8 January 1968, cited in Burdett, *Records of the Emirates, 1966–1971: Volume 3: 1968*, p. 213.
123 Record of meeting between the Minister of State for Foreign Affairs and the Ruler of Abu Dhabi, 9 January 1968, at 12.00, cited in ibid., p. 207. Britain's Political Resident in the Gulf, Sir Stewart Crawford, subsequently told Sheikh Zaid that the 'withdrawal of H.M. forces and the lapsing of the Treaties did not mean H.M.G. would not wish to maintain their traditional friendship with the Gulf States. On the contrary, H.M.G. hoped to strengthen that friendship' (Record of a meeting between the Political Resident and the Ruler of Abu Dhabi in Abu Dhabi, 30 January 1968, cited in ibid., p. 241).
124 Umm al Qaiwain, Ras al Khaimah, Ajman, Sharjah, and Fujairah.
125 Record of a conversation between Mr Goronwy Roberts, MP, Minister of State, Foreign Office, and HH the Rulers of the Northern Trucial States in Dubai, 9 January 1968, cited in Burdett, *Records of the Emirates, 1966–1971: Volume 3: 1968*, p. 215.
126 Letter from Parsons to Weir, No. 2/3, 13 January 1968, FCO 8/48. In retirement, Parsons recalled that the British determination to withdraw from the Gulf came as a 'terrible shock' and that the Ruler of Bahrain was 'absolutely devastated by this decision to go into reverse' (British Diplomatic Oral History Project: Jane Barder interviewing Sir Anthony Parsons, 22 March 1996, p. 12, DOHP 10, Churchill Archives Centre, Cambridge).
127 Letter from Parsons to Weir, No. 2/3, 13 January 1968, FCO 8/48.
128 Miriam Joyce, *Kuwait, 1945–1996: An Anglo–American Perspective* (London: Frank Cass, 1998), p. 87.
129 Telegram from Arthur to the Foreign Office, No. 12, 8 January 1968, FCO 8/145.
130 Telegram from the Foreign and Commonwealth Office to certain missions, No. 23, 23 January 1968, FCO 8/48.
131 Lord Carrington, *Reflect on Things Past: The Memoirs of Lord Carrington* (London: Collins, 1988), p. 218.
132 'Talk with Shaikh Zaid', Note by Crawford, 18 October 1967, FCO 8/848.
133 Letter from Lamb to Crawford, No. 3/1G, 11 January 1968, FCO 8/48.
134 Ibid.
135 Daly, *The Last of the Great Proconsuls*, pp. 223–4.
136 Letter from Weir to Crawford, No. 1/5, 1 February 1968, FCO 8/828.
137 'The Union of Arab Emirates', Minute by A. A. Acland, 18 May 1970, FCO 8/1293.
138 Letter from Stewart to Crawford, 10 December 1969, FCO 8/925.
139 John Darwin, *Britain and Decolonisation: The Retreat from Empire in the Post War World* (Basingstoke: Palgrave Macmillan, 1988), p. 297.
140 Chris Wrigley, 'Now you see it, now you don't: Harold Wilson and Labour's foreign policy', in R. Coopey, S. Fielding, and N. Tiratsoo (eds.), *The Wilson Governments, 1964–1970* (London: Pinter, 1993), p. 133.
141 D. C. Watt, 'The decision to withdraw from the Gulf', *Political Quarterly*, 39, 3 (1968), p. 310.
142 Ibid.
143 James Worrall, *Statebuilding and Counterinsurgency in Oman: Political, Military, and Diplomatic Relations at the End of Empire* (London: I. B. Tauris, 2014), p. 23.
144 Darwin, *Unfinished Empire*, p. 380. See also John Darwin, *The Empire Project: The Rise and Fall of the British World System, 1830–1970* (Cambridge: Cambridge University Press, 2009), p. 476.
145 Darwin, *Britain and Decolonisation*, p. 298.
146 Ronald Hyam, *Britain's Declining Empire: The Road to Decolonisation, 1918–1968* (Cambridge: Cambridge University Press, 2006), p. 397.
147 P. L. Pham, *Ending 'East of Suez': The British Decision to Withdraw from Malaysia and Singapore, 1964–1968* (Oxford and New York: Oxford University Press, 2010), p. 241.

Introduction

148 Colin Cross, *The Fall of the British Empire, 1918–1968* (London: Hodder & Stoughton, 1968), p. 357.
149 J. B. Kelly, *Arabia, the Gulf and the West* (New York: Basic Books, 1991; first published 1980), p. 102.
150 Peter Mangold, *What the British Did: Two Centuries in the Middle East* (London: I. B. Tauris, 2016), p. 263.
151 G. C. Peden, 'Suez and Britain's decline as a world power', *Historical Journal*, 55, 4 (2012), p. 1083.
152 Ibid., p. 1089.
153 Greg Kennedy and Christopher Tuck, 'Introduction', in Greg Kennedy and Christopher Tuck (eds.), *British Propaganda and Wars of Empire: Influencing Friend and Foe, 1900–2010* (Farnham: Ashgate Publishing Limited, 2014), p. 2.
154 Spencer Mawby, *British Policy in Aden and the Protectorates 1955–67: Last Outpost of a Middle East Empire* (London and New York: Routledge, 2005), p. 183.
155 Spencer Mawby, *The Transformation and Decline of the British Empire: Decolonisation after the First World War* (Basingstoke: Palgrave Macmillan, 2015), p. 1.
156 Julia Gallagher, *Britain and Africa under Blair: In Pursuit of the Good State* (Manchester: Manchester University Press, 2011), p. 6.
157 Ashley Jackson, 'Empire and beyond: The pursuit of overseas national interests in the late twentieth century', *English Historical Review*, 123, 499 (2007), pp. 1350–1.
158 Ibid., p. 1351.
159 Ashley Jackson, 'Imperial defence in the post-imperial era', in Greg Kennedy (ed.), *Imperial Defence: The Old World Order, 1856–1956* (London and New York: Routledge, 2008), p. 304.
160 Philip Murphy, 'Britain as a global power in the twentieth century', in Andrew Thompson (ed.), *Britain's Experience of Empire in the Twentieth Century* (Oxford: Oxford University Press, 2011), p. 67.
161 D. George Boyce, *Decolonisation and the British Empire, 1775–1997* (Basingstoke: Palgrave Macmillan, 1999), p. 269.
162 David M. McCourt, 'What was Britain's "East of Suez role"? Reassessing the withdrawal, 1964–1968', *Diplomacy and Statecraft*, 20, 3 (2009), p. 468.
163 Ibid.
164 Michael J. Turner, *Britain's International Role, 1970–1991* (Basingstoke: Palgrave Macmillan, 2010), p. 1.
165 See John Darwin, 'Was there a fourth British Empire?', in Martin Lynn (ed.), *The British Empire in the 1950s: Retreat or Revival* (Basingstoke: Palgrave Macmillan, 2006), p. 28.
166 Turner, *Britain's International Role*, pp. 1–2.
167 Ibid., p. 5.
168 Jackson, 'Imperial defence in the post-imperial era', p. 311.
169 Tore T. Petersen, *Anglo–American Policy Toward the Persian Gulf, 1978–1985: Power, Influence and Restraint* (Brighton: Sussex Academic Press, 2015), p. 2.
170 Ibid., p. 1.
171 Jeffrey Macris, *The Politics and Security of the Gulf: Anglo–American Hegemony and the Shaping of a Region* (London and New York: Routledge, 2010), p. 196.
172 Sato, *Britain and the Formation of the Gulf States*, p. 72.
173 Rob Johnson, 'Out of Arabia: British strategy and the fate of local forces in Aden, South Yemen, and Oman, 1967–76', *International History Review*, 39, 1 (2017), p. 150.
174 Ibid.
175 J. E. Peterson, 'The age of imperialism and its impact on the Gulf', in J. E. Peterson (ed.), *The Emergence of the Gulf States* (London: Bloomsbury, 2016), p. 147.

176 Interview with Sir Alan Munro, 16 May 1996, p. 7, DOHP 13, British Diplomatic Oral History Programme, Churchill Archives Centre, Cambridge.
177 Alan Munro, *Keep the Flag Flying: A Diplomatic Memoir* (London: Gilgamesh Publishing, 2012), p. 132.
178 Worrall, *Statebuilding and Counterinsurgency in Oman*, p. 221.
179 Ibid., p 222.
180 James Worrall, 'Britain's last bastion in Arabia: The end of the Dhofar War, the Labour government and the withdrawal from RAF Salalah and Masirah, 1974–1977', in Tore T. Petersen (ed.), *Challenging Retrenchment: The United States, Great Britain and the Middle East, 1950–1980* (Trondheim: Tapir Academic Press, 2010), p. 140.
181 Worrall, *Statebuilding and Counterinsurgency in Oman*, p. 76.
182 Ibid., p. 228.
183 Ibid., p. 229.
184 Darwin, *The Empire Project*, p. 644.
185 Record of a meeting between the Minister of State, Mr. Roberts and His Highness Sheikh Khalid bin Muhammad al Qasimi, the Ruler of Sharjah, at the Foreign and Commonwealth Office on Thursday, 31 July 1969, at 11.30am, cited in A. L. P. Burdett (ed.), *Records of the Emirates, 1966–1971: Volume 4: 1969* (Slough: Archive Editions, 2002), p. 238.

1 The trials of independence, 1971–1972

In his message to US President Lyndon Baines Johnson relaying the British government's decision to withdraw from East of Suez by 1971, Prime Minister Harold Wilson wrote: 'Believe me, Lyndon, the decisions we are having to take now have been the most difficult and the heaviest of any that I, and I think all my colleagues, can remember in our public life'.[1] However, he went on to insist:

> We are not taking them in a narrow or partisan spirit. We are taking them because we are convinced that, in the longer term, only thus can Britain find the new place on the world stage that I firmly believe the British people ardently desire. And when I say 'the world stage' I mean just that.[2]

Despite Wilson's penchant for extravagant prose, this pledge regarding the continuation of Britain's world role was no mere rhetorical flourish.

In the aftermath of the 1956 Suez crisis, British policy-makers had endlessly debated the degree to which a formal presence in the Gulf was necessary for the maintenance of British interests there.[3] While British officials in the Gulf, and to a lesser extent the Foreign Office itself, made the case for a continuing presence, the cost-conscious Treasury challenged this position, preferring instead to rely on normal commercial processes for the preservation of Britain's economic stake in the region. In many ways, neither side decisively won the argument. Nevertheless, the decision to accelerate the run-down of Britain's presence East of Suez following the devaluation of sterling towards the end of 1967 meant that the Treasury's reasoning would have, ipso facto, to guide British policy-making towards the Gulf. Although the Treasury's approach ultimately prevailed, there was a clear recognition among British decision-makers that Britain could not simply retreat from areas which remained vital to its long-term well-being.

During Cabinet discussions at the beginning of 1968 on withdrawal from East of Suez, Foreign Secretary George Brown intoned: 'Even if we ceased to be a world power, we should continue to retain world interests and to need friends and allies to defend them'.[4] In a subsequent paper for the Cabinet, Brown asserted:

> I believe that a military presence is not the only way to exercise influence. There is still a good deal we can do in the parts of the world from which we

are withdrawing militarily. If we cannot totally replace the degree of protection for our interests which we lose when we withdraw our military presence we can at least mitigate the consequences by maintaining a British presence through non-military means.[5]

Outlining to Parliament on 16 January Britain's intention to withdraw from East of Suez, Harold Wilson declared: 'On the Gulf, we have indicated to the Governments concerned that our basic interest in the prosperity and security of the area remains'.[6] Shortly after this announcement, the Political Resident in the Gulf, Sir Stewart Crawford, emphasized that it would 'remain an important British interest on both political and economic grounds that peace and stability should be maintained in the Gulf in the long term'.[7] Crawford was quick to add that

> it remains important that British firms should do their utmost to earn a substantial share of the sterling which the oil exports of the area will bring to the Gulf States, and that British Government policies should continue to encourage the Governments of the Gulf States to be good holders of sterling.[8]

With similar cold logic, the Foreign and Commonwealth Office observed in May 1968 that

> After we have given up our political position in the Gulf, we shall still depend on the area generally for about half our oil, while access to oil in the Gulf area is a major factor in the contribution which British oil companies make to our foreign exchange earnings through their overseas operations.[9]

Equally, the Permanent Under-Secretary at the FCO, Sir Paul Gore-Booth, remarked:

> It was clear we could not simply retire into our shell once our troops left the regions in question. We had a general interest in the peace, stability and prosperity of the areas and we had also a substantial economic stake, in the form of investments and export markets, which were important for our future solvency and standard of living.[10]

In July 1968, the Foreign Secretary, Michael Stewart, and the Commonwealth Secretary, George Thomson, produced a wide-ranging assessment of the non-military means of maintaining British influence which included the strength of the British economy and of the pound sterling, and what they identified as 'political power' exercised through British membership of the Commonwealth, political alliances, and other associations and informal groupings.[11] The importance, and indeed necessity, of preserving influence was highlighted by the recognition that 'other powers, whether friendly or hostile, compete with us for influence. Reluctance on our side to take part in the competition will not make our competitors slacken their efforts; it will only increase their success'.[12] Stewart and Thomson pragmatically concluded that 'Our political influence will be reduced and the nature of our influence will change from that of a power with a global military role to one with world-wide economic interests. We need to maintain these interests if we are going to restore our economic position'.[13] Indeed, in no real sense was there an acceptance that the end of formal empire would equate with a concomitant abandonment of Britain's global economic interests, represented most explicitly by the £1 billion British investment in Persian Gulf oil production.[14] As the US Ambassador in London, Walter Annenberg, presciently noted:

> The British economic stake on both sides of the Gulf, already immense, is as likely to increase as decrease in the future, and the oil interests and earnings from the Arab side will continue to be vitally important to the UK, just as they are on the Iranian side. The UK may not continue its special political and military relationship with the small Arab states but it will have a strong incentive to work hard through diplomatic and political channels to register its continuing stake in Gulf affairs.[15]

The unexpected defeat of the Labour Party in the June 1970 general election left Edward Heath's Conservative government with the task of shaping British policy towards the Gulf.

Shortly after the Conservatives' victory, the new Foreign Secretary, Alec Douglas-Home, turned his attention to the timetable for Britain's departure from the Gulf and the relinquishment of its formal responsibilities as set out by the previous Labour government. In response to Conservative backbench MP Patrick Wall's suggestion that the existing withdrawal plan should be countermanded,[16] Douglas-Home pointed out that there was 'no harm' in letting the Rulers think that it was continuing since this served to 'encourage them to hasten the process of making the Union of Arab Emirates a working reality'.[17] '[E]ven if we withdraw completely by the end of 1971', Douglas-Home declared, 'we would retain major economic interests in the Gulf area'.[18] Douglas-Home's personal representative in the Gulf, the former Political Resident Sir William Luce, was of a similar opinion.

Following extensive consultations, Luce produced a report towards the end of 1970 on future British policy in the Gulf. Observing that the real threat to stability in the region came from 'subversion and revolution by Arab nationalist and left-wing elements', Luce indicated that 'The presence of a British battalion will not deter the threat, indeed it could encourage it'.[19] Consequently, he recommended that any new agreement reached with the Gulf States should not include any ongoing specific defence commitment and the withdrawal of British units stationed in the Gulf be completed by the end of 1971 as planned. Luce also advocated that the existing exclusive agreements with the Gulf States be terminated by the same date, justifying this stance with the observation that the British announcement in January 1968 had 'generated a firm expectation, and indeed a determination in and around the Gulf, that the nine States will become fully responsible for the conduct of all their affairs in the course of 1971'.[20] Nevertheless, Luce did not envisage that British military withdrawal and the termination of the exclusive agreements would equate with an ending of Britain's involvement in the region.

At the beginning of his report Luce outlined Britain's aims in the Gulf which included preserving 'as much influence as possible' with a view to maintaining regional stability and limiting communist influence to the 'greatest extent possible', sustaining the 'uninterrupted flow of oil on reasonable terms', and increasing British exports in a 'rapidly growing market'.[21] As a result of such considerations, he concluded that

> It would certainly not . . . be in British interests to let it be thought by friends or potential enemies that after 1971 H.M.G. would have no further direct concern with the peace and stability of the Gulf area; on the contrary, it will be very much in our interest to keep as much influence as possible in the area after the withdrawal of our forces. In the conditions of this part of the world I do not believe that this can be done effectively solely by economic and cultural means; for a further period some politico-military manifestation will be a contribution to stability and an important means of maintaining influence.[22]

In particular, Luce recommended that Britain continued to loan officers and other personnel to local forces, to give all possible assistance in training these forces both in the Gulf and the United Kingdom, and to 'facilitate as much as possible the supply of weapons and other equipment'.[23] He also urged that Britain continued to do all it could to assist the build-up, training, and supply of equipment to local police forces, especially their security and intelligence branches.[24] Additionally, he proposed regular visits by Royal Navy ships to the Gulf.[25] 'These proposals', Luce concluded, 'are designed to demonstrate a continuing British politico-military involvement in the Gulf and thus provide some reassurance to the Gulf States'.[26]

Reviewing the Cabinet Defence and Oversea Policy Committee's discussion of Luce's recommendations, the Prime Minister observed that, while pressure should continue to be brought to bear on the Rulers to unite, 'We should make it clear to them that we could not remain in the Gulf on the present footing'.[27] At a subsequent meeting of the same committee, it was agreed that an early statement to the House of Commons should be made to this effect.[28] When discussed by the full Cabinet in February 1971, ministers consoled themselves with the thought that 'By offering training facilities, and other support to the local forces we were making it clear that we did not intend to abandon our friends'.[29] A little earlier, the Political Resident in the Gulf, G. G. Arthur, had predicted:

> we are likely to retain uniquely special opportunities to influence affairs, even after the formal trappings have gone, by virtue of our long political experience and the entrenched position of British subjects in the local security services, in the rulers' administrations (such as they are), in the Trucial States Development Office and in trade, contracting and banking.[30]

Moreover, Secretary of State for Defence Lord Carrington insisted that 'the total abandonment of the Trucial States would be difficult to justify in the context of the Government's policy of maintaining the stability of the Gulf and Indian Ocean areas'.[31] On a similar note, the Head of the FCO's Arabian Department, A. A. Acland, minuted in mid-March 1971: 'Politically, it is desirable that we should demonstrate to the Rulers – and indeed to other countries both friendly and hostile to our interests in the area – that despite our changed relationship we retain a close interest in the development, stability and well-being of the Gulf States'.[32] At the end of the month, Acland impressed upon the Treasury: 'We are all convinced that improvement of the local police forces is vital as a *British* interest, and that if we are to have a chance of making progress we must be in a position to offer some financial help if this proves necessary'.[33] The Treasury subsequently agreed to approve additional expenditure of £125,000 for this purpose in 1971–1972.[34]

During the Commons debate on the Persian Gulf on 1 March 1971, Douglas-Home had informed MPs that Her Majesty's Government were prepared to offer a Treaty of Friendship to the Gulf States, to hand over the Trucial Oman Scouts to form the nucleus of a prospective United Arab Emirates army, to provide training teams for the local security forces, to participate in training exercises involving the British army and air force units, and finally to pledge regular visits to the area by Royal Navy ships.[35] Summing up, the Foreign Secretary maintained that 'arrangements of this kind will form a sound basis for a continuing and effective British contribution to the stability of the area, and a new and up to date relationship between Britain and the States concerned'.[36] The achievement of these aims, however, was threatened by territorial disputes between Iran and the Arabs of the Lower Gulf.

The Shah of Iran's determination to pursue Iranian claims to the Tunbs and Abu Musa,[37] islands also claimed by Ras al Khaimah and Sharjah respectively, served to jeopardize an orderly British withdrawal from the Gulf. To make matters worse, the US State Department was reported to start from the premise that Western interests would 'best be served by the removal of this potential source of friction between the two major riparians, Saudi Arabia and Iran, at almost any cost, even if this amounted to Britain as scapegoat incurring much odium in terms of loss of influence on Gulf littoral as well as providing justifiable grounds for yet another "Arab cause" '.[38] Referring to American policy-makers, J. C. Moberly of the British Embassy in Washington recorded that

> They are bound to feel less keenly than us the undesirability of undermining our future relationship with the Gulf Arabs. Indeed, a reduction of influence, though no doubt regarded by them as regrettable, could seem to them a worthwhile price to pay for an absence of friction between Iran and Saudi Arabia and for maintaining their own relations with both unimpaired.[39]

Moberly was obliquely referencing US policy in the aftermath of Britain's decision to withdraw from East of Suez which identified Iran, and to a lesser extent Saudi Arabia, as the 'twin pillars' of security following Britain's formal departure from the Gulf. Alluding to US hopes that Britain would be prepared to 'coerce' the Gulf Rulers into relinquishing their clams over the disputed islands, Moberly went on to state that the Americans 'would probably regard some damage to our position in the area as a price worth paying for a successful resolution of the Islands' difficulty which, through placing the odium on us, left relations between the Arabs and the Iranians comparatively undisturbed'.[40] In a similar vein, the Head of the FCO's Arabian Department, A. A. Acland, complained that

> The State Department's position recently has been not to put pressure on Saudi Arabia or Iran but to put pressure on us to be prepared to take the blame for settling the Islands question regardless of the effect that this might have on British interests and influence in the Gulf and the rest of the Arab world.[41]

Acland also impressed upon the Chiefs of Staff Committee that 'There would be a strong reaction both in the Arab world and in the United Nations if we were to appear to be imposing a solution on the Arab Rulers and this would have an adverse effect on British interests'.[42]

The dangers to British interests in the Gulf were underlined by Sheikh Zaid of Abu Dhabi's stark warning that 'if Britain handed Abu Musa over unilaterally it would be impossible for [the] proposed Federation of Trucial States to have relations with the UK or to accept British officers in its defence forces'.[43] Against this background, Britain continued negotiations for the remaining months of its treaty obligations while clandestinely preparing for an Iranian occupation should they come to nothing. Douglas-Home recognized the benefits of accelerating British military withdrawal, observing that 'The presence of these forces in the Gulf at the time when the Iranians seize the Islands without opposition will inevitably make it appear that we are colluding with Iran'.[44]

Although the Ruler of Sharjah, Sheikh Khalid, demonstrated a protean frame of mind, accepting generous terms proposed by the Shah which included financial assistance over a nine-year period, the exploitation of oil resources off Abu Musa by a company selected by the Sheikhdom on the basis of a 50/50 division of profits between Iran and Sharjah, and a limited occupation of the island by Iranian forces,[45] the Ruler of Ras al Khaimah, Sheikh Saqr, demonstrated intractability, agreeing neither to voluntary cession of the Tunbs, nor to acceptance of Iranian money for them. The impasse, FCO Minister of State Joseph Godber informed the Cabinet, made it 'virtually certain that the Shah would take control of the islands in his own time'.[46] Against this background, Sir William Luce had already entered into secret discussions with the Shah as regards the timing of an Iranian takeover of the islands,[47] 30 November being set as the date for the landing of Iranian forces on Abu Musa and the Tunbs. Prior to this Kuwait, Saudi Arabia, and the United Arab Republic were to be briefed by Britain on the terms of the islands settlement, a last-ditch effort being made to coax Sheikh Saqr into ceding the Tunbs to Iran and join the United Arab Emirates on 28 November.[48]

The Kuwaiti Foreign Minister, Sheikh Sabah, had previously downplayed the difficulties over the Tunb islands with the remark that 'many Gulf Arabs had traditionally considered it Persian'.[49] Nevertheless, Arab opinion was inflamed by news of a skirmish during the Iranian occupation by the Tunbs which had resulted in the death of a Ras Al Khaimah policeman. While Kuwait did not follow Iraq in severing diplomatic relations with London, the British Ambassador in Kuwait City, A. J. Wilton, admitted that the islands dispute had 'left a residual grievance against ourselves and Iran' which any future difference of opinion was 'likely to exhume'.[50] Despite reporting a rise in British exports to Kuwait in the first three quarters of 1971, Wilton went on to record that 'we, too, have introduced an element of instability into the calculation by our failure to take what the Kuwaiti Government would consider a sufficiently pro-Arab position on the question of the Gulf Islands'.[51] He added that

> Kuwait has found itself feeling more than usually Arab these last few weeks and the attitudes it has struck – at the United Nations, in its Press and radio, and in public demonstrations – have had more in common with those of Iraq and Libya than with those of Egypt and Saudi Arabia, who might be considered its more natural partners and examples in the Arab world of today.[52]

In May 1972, the Kuwaiti and Iraqi Foreign Ministers issued a joint statement 'condemning the Iranian occupation of the Arab islands in the Arabian Gulf and Iran's violation of the Iraqi frontier treaty of 1937, since the islands and the Shatt Al-Arab are an integral part of the Arab homeland'.[53]

In the aftermath of the Iranian seizure of the disputed islands, rioting broke out in Ras al Khaimah and Sharjah.[54] Against the background of heightened tensions, the Deputy Ruler of Sharjah was wounded by an unidentified gunman following the announcement of the agreement over Abu Musa.[55] Taking advantage of the sense of confusion, the former Ruler, Sheikh Saqr, led a coup attempt at the end of January 1972 in which Sheikh Khalid was killed.[56] As if to make matters worse, Sheikh Saqr of Ras al Khaimah was implicated in the Sharjah plot.[57] Although thwarted by other members of the ruling family, the coup contributed to an atmosphere of insecurity following British withdrawal. The Minister for Housing and Reconstruction, Julian Amery, even hypothesized that Sharjah would have seceded from the federation if the coup had been successful.[58] Commenting on what the British had left behind in the Lower Gulf, moreover, Political Resident G. G. Arthur confessed that 'the structure is fragile; and a long experience of the Middle East has left me with a profound pessimism about the ability of Arabs – and for that matter, of Iranians as well – to preserve stability for long without our help'.[59] On a more positive note, Arthur recorded that Britain had parted with the Gulf 'on good terms', adding that 'If we avoid identification with Israel, we should continue for some time to enjoy the confidence of the Gulf Rulers and to exercise greater influence in the area than any non-Arab country'.[60] This aspiration on the part of the British was underlined during Anglo–American talks at the State Department in June 1972.

In advance of these discussions, A. D. Parsons, FCO Under-Secretary of State who was leading the British side, asserted that 'One of our principal objects is to convince the Americans that, although we may have withdrawn our military presence and terminated our protective relationships, we have not cut and run from the Gulf and have no intention of doing so'.[61] 'We still', he continued, 'regard ourselves as having considerable influence in the area and will use it to the best of our ability to protect our and Western interests there'.[62] In many ways, Parsons need not have worried about American attitudes. From the outset, Assistant Secretary of State for Near Eastern Affairs, Joseph Sisco, assured his British guests that 'The State Department welcomed an active British role in the Gulf and did not want to take over in any way from the British'.[63] In response, Parsons informed the Americans that Britain 'intended to play as active and prominent a role in Gulf affairs as possible', going on to state that the 'modernisation of British relations with Gulf States had proceeded smoothly, and instead of the low profile usually adopted by Britain in such post-independence or post-colonial situations, British influence remained strong and visible throughout the area'.[64] During an appearance before the Congressional Foreign Affairs Committee in the aftermath of the Anglo–American discussions, Sisco emphasized that, although Britain's military forces had officially left the region and its special relationship with the Sheikhdoms had ended, 'there was still a strong residual British presence and influence throughout the Gulf'.[65] To illustrate his point, Sisco referred to the presence of British officers and men in the armed forces of the UAE and of the Sultanate of Oman.

As regards the latter, British relations with this nominally independent state had received a fillip by the replacement of the notoriously conservative Sultan Said bin Taimur by his more forward-looking (and for that matter pro-British) son, Sultan Qaboos, on 23 July 1970.[66] Shortly after the coup, the British Consul-General in Muscat, D. G. Crawford, noted: 'The Sultan himself will continue to attach the highest importance to the British connection and, indeed, his own position for some time will be dependent on it'.[67] This was so principally because Qaboos was facing a rebellion in the Dhofar region of Oman. Britain's commitment to defeating the rebellion and to maintaining security throughout the Sultanate in large part reflected Britain's ongoing interests in the Gulf despite impending withdrawal. As the Foreign and Commonwealth Office baldly declared in its brief for Douglas-Home's meeting with Qaboos in mid-1971: 'stability in Oman is important to stability in the Gulf'.[68] Elaborating on this theme in a memorandum for the Cabinet Defence and Oversea Policy Committee, the Secretary of State for Defence, Lord Carrington, remarked that

> Britain has important political, economic and defence interests in ensuring that the present regime in Oman remains in power. Apart from our direct commercial interests in Oman, we could find our wider interests in the region threatened since, if the Sultan's Government failed to control the Communist-supported rebellion in Dhofar, Oman could well become a base for the subversion of the Gulf itself.[69]

In a briefing for the Prime Minister in 1973, moreover, the FCO expressed the fear that a collapse of the Sultan's regime in Oman could 'lead to the disintegration of the United Arab Emirates and the establishment of a radical Arab nationalist or Marxist state in this corner of Arabia'.[70] Britain's ongoing interests in the region were amply demonstrated with respect to Bahrain.

Bahrain's progress towards independent statehood was smoothed by Iran's relinquishment of its traditional claims to the island following the deliberations of a UN mission which visited the Gulf in March–April 1970 and concluded that 'the overwhelming majority of the people of Bahrain wish to gain recognition of their identity in a fully independent and sovereign State free to decide for itself its relations with other States'.[71] Bahraini independence was accompanied by the signing of a Treaty of Friendship with Britain on 3 September 1971 under which the two parties agreed to 'consult together on matters of mutual concern and in time of need'.[72] Although fairly anodyne, the treaty did symbolize Britain's enduring role in Bahrain which survived the end of formal empire on the island. Former Political Agent in Bahrain turned Ambassador, A. J. D. Stirling, noted towards the beginning of 1972 that, although British influence no longer had the weight of a military presence behind it, 'Our apparent position has not significantly changed and our advice is still sought and taken'.[73] Stirling did, however, warn that 'We shall have to work harder than ever and to make the utmost of our non-military means of influence if we are to maintain our political ascendancy and commercial predominance'.[74] In particular, the Ambassador identified the expanded programme of technical assistance as Britain's 'most important instrument', in this regard.[75] In response to Stirling's assessment, Acland recorded: 'Clearly, in spite of all our apprehensions about the effect of military withdrawal the position is at least contained, if not held, for the immediate future'.[76]

Bahraini stability was apparently rocked by a series of strikes and disturbances which broke out on the morning of 13 March 1972. The Manama government deemed the troubles sufficiently serious to deploy the Bahrain Defence Force (BDF), in addition to local police. While critical of the use of the BDF,[77] Stirling was philosophical about events in March, pointing out that they 'would have happened whether or not our troops were here and it was, of course, insignificant beside the series of disturbances which occurred when British forces were firmly ensconced'.[78] He added: 'I have not listed the "effects of the British withdrawal" because I do not believe there were any, thanks to the way the withdrawal was handled'.[79]

Stirling's valedictory despatch before his departure in May 1972 was equally positive regarding Anglo–Bahraini relations. 'We have reached the position', he enthused, 'for which we have been working since 1968. Bahrain has been brought safely through the shocks of losing our apron strings and, tiny though it is, it will repay our continued active attention'.[80] Surveying British assets in the Amirate, Stirling focussed on a 'close relationship with the Bahrain government which allows us to exercise a discreet measure of political influence; 31 per cent of a market which has grown by 30 per cent annually since 1969; and a technical assistance programme which provides both a continuing basis for our favoured standing with the Government and potential commercial rewards'.[81] The Ambassador insisted that 'These advantages are not chance flotsam from the wreck of the Raj but have been painstakingly built up since our withdrawal decision'.[82] Comparing Anglo–Bahraini relations before and after formal withdrawal, Stirling felt able to opine: 'We have, rightly I think, so arranged matters that our involvement in Bahrain is hardly less than it was during the special relationship, except that we have exchanged direct political and military engagement for a sizeable commercial stake which still carries political implications'.[83] While recognizing that 'some attenuation of our close relationship with the Bahrain Government may be inevitable', Stirling concluded that 'our withdrawal brought no cooling of contacts with them or with ordinary Bahrainis'.[84] The new British Ambassador in Bahrain, Robert Tesh's, first impressions of Bahrain, produced in May 1972, were equally positive.

'How very agreeable', remarked Tesh, 'it is to . . . to come to a country which likes the British and did not even bother to celebrate the first anniversary of its independence. The incumbent of this post inherits a large credit balance of past friendships, from the Amir to the casual taxi-driver'.[85] The Ambassador also believed that 'omens' were good:

> The Bahrain economy is thick with Britons in important executive posts in the Big Merchant Houses as well as the foreign enterprises, in the public utilities, in industry and in the security services, and even in the administration; and the Bahrain Government will keep it so if they can and if we will let them.[86]

Tesh underlined that Britain's large share in Bahrain's growing trade and investment, coupled with the advantages from a political and defence point of view of the survival of the existing regime compared with an 'Arab nationalist' one, provided 'two hard-headed reasons for being helpful to Bahrain'.[87] He concluded by stressing the importance of 'reassuring the Bahrainis that the withdrawal of our forces does not mean the end of our sympathetic (if not wholly altruistic) interest in Bahrain and the Gulf'.[88]

Responding to Tesh's despatch, the Head of the FCO's Middle East Department, P. R. H. Wright, was sufficiently encouraged to comment that 'we should be well placed to maintain our interests in Bahrain in the post-1971 period'.[89] Wright had already noted that 'the Bahrainis value their relationship with us highly, and Britain and the British continue to play an important part in the life of Bahrain'.[90] Indeed, during a meeting with Douglas-Home at the Foreign and Commonwealth Office at the beginning of August 1972, the Bahraini Foreign Minister, Sheikh Muhammad bin Mubarak, urged that 'Britain should play a more active role in the region as a whole'.[91]

Towards the end of the year, the FCO's brief for Minister of State Joseph Godber's encounter with the Bahraini Ambassador, Sheikh Sulman bin Da'ij Al-Khalifah, emphasized not only HMG's 'continued interest in the affairs of Bahrain and the whole Gulf region in general', but also its eagerness to maintain 'close relations with the Bahrain Government'.[92] As an indication of this, Godber was authorized to inform the Ambassador that the British government was offering an additional three places on military training courses to Bahraini trainees, in addition to the three staff college courses for Bahraini officers already approved for 1973, and was also pursuing the question of training for the Bahrain police.[93] Britain, in fact, already maintained close links with Bahrain's security services, the local Special Branch being headed by a Briton, Ian Henderson. The Prime Minister of Bahrain, Sheikh Khalifah bin Salman Al-Khalifah, moreover, was reported to favour recruiting more British officers, expressing the view that the Branch would 'collapse without its expatriate officers and would probably be ineffective without Henderson'.[94] In his first impressions of Bahrain mentioned earlier, Ambassador Tesh specifically recorded that the 'Police and Security services are headed by efficient and devoted Britons who have the confidence of the rulers and themselves seem confident'.[95] Nevertheless, Tesh recorded in his annual review for 1972 that 'for all that they ride with a very loose rein', the security services under their British heads were 'beginning to come under attack'.[96] The Ambassador also noted that 'after a spurt in 1970 and 1971, our export performance is declining', going on to speculate that Britain's 'present "natural" percentage of the market might be about 25 per cent'.[97] Far from maintaining its former exclusive position in Bahrain, Tesh reported that the Australians were upgrading their trade mission, the French had installed a Chargé d'Affaires, and the Japanese were planning to open a diplomatic mission.[98] Indeed, Tesh had already expressed the fear that 'The main danger to our position in the next year or so may come not so much from Russians or Iraqis but from the commercial tactics and corrupting influence of some of our Western allies and trade competitors'.[99] Similar concerns were raised in advance of the Deputy Ruler of Qatar, Sheikh Khalifah bin Hamad's, visit to Britain in July 1971.

'Foreign competition in the Gulf States is increasing', warned the Foreign Secretary's Assistant Private Secretary, Ian McCluney, 'and will be given further impetus after 1971 when our major industrial competitors open diplomatic missions in the Lower Gulf'.[100] Against this background, McCluney strongly recommended that the Prime Minister see Sheikh Khalifah while the latter was in London. Reflecting FCO opinion, McCluney argued that Khalifah's impending trip provided the 'opportunity to show that despite our changing relationship with the Gulf, our interest in the development, stability and wellbeing of the region remains'.[101] 'Commercially', concluded McCluney, 'the visit comes at a time when important decisions are being taken about the disposal of Qatar's oil revenues, which have increased very considerably as a result of greater production and the higher prices negotiated at Tehran'.[102] Britain's Political Agent in Qatar, E. F. Henderson, had already stressed that 'Sheikh Khalifah has the complete say in any contract in which the Government is concerned, either directly or as a shareholder'.[103] Against this background Edward Heath readily agreed to meet Khalifah with the comment that 'I know him well'.[104]

In its brief for the Prime Minister's meeting, the FCO was keen to point out that Khalifah's friendship was important since 'real power' in Qatar rested in his hands to the extent that no major political decision was taken or commercial contract let without his prior approval.[105] The FCO also remarked that foreign competition was increasing and that the French had, 'by going out of their way to flatter the Deputy Ruler's ego' when he visited France in 1970, been able to secure an important contract that was about to be awarded to a British firm.[106] Therefore, the FCO suggested that the Prime Minister might wish to mention the strong British interest in Qatar's development plans and express the hope that the long-established commercial links between the UK and Qatar would develop and expand.[107]

In discussing British trade during his encounter with Heath on 28 July 1971, Sheikh Khalifah said that he was 'very pleased' with the British firms operating in Qatar and acknowledged that they were 'co-operating well' with the Qatari authorities.[108] He also extolled the virtues of frequent visits in both directions by British and Qatari merchants, noting that the Japanese had started 'visiting frequently from Kuwait'.[109] Finally, he expressed the hope that 'the traditional links with Britain in all fields would be strengthened'.[110]

In his annual review for 1971, Britain's Ambassador in Doha, E. F. Henderson, dwelt on the agonizing process whereby Qatar opted for separate independence, rather than amalgamation with the other Gulf Sheikhdoms of the Lower Gulf. 'So difficult was it for the Qatari Shaikhs to screw up their courage', recalled Henderson, 'that they had to await the lead of Bahrain and followed them at an interval of a little over two weeks'.[111] In keeping with Bahrain, moreover, Qatar signed a Treaty of Friendship with Britain[112] shortly after the ending of the British position as the protecting power. Henderson also reported that the Amir of Qatar, Sheikh Ahmed, and his Deputy, Sheikh Khalifah, intended to be 'as helpful as possible towards us'.[113] '[T]he general picture for 1971', concluded the Ambassador, 'has been rather more favourable to the honest negotiator with the best proposal than it had been in 1970, when there were some sad disappointments in the case of projects which should by rights have gone to British firms'.[114] Henderson's optimism for the future, however, was threatened by dissension within the Al-Thani ruling family.

'The ultimate political power still rests with the Amir', observed Henderson, 'but his long absences and his great capacity for achieving circumstances appropriate to his single-minded indulgence in idleness, has weakened his control'.[115] The fact that the termination of the existing treaty relations with Britain and the signing of the new treaty of friendship took place in Geneva 'simply because he was too lazy to go back home', lost the Amir further prestige.[116] On 22 February 1972, Doha radio announced that Sheikh Khalifah had assumed the position of head of state and Amir of Qatar in place Sheikh Ahmed who was accused of being concerned only with realizing 'personal benefits at the expense of the homeland'.[117] Later in the day, Khalifah told Henderson that the government would 'continue as before, that he hoped HMG would not regard this as a change of regime which required a new act of recognition, and that business would be as usual'.[118] In Cabinet on 24 February, Douglas-Home told colleagues that he did not consider any formal act of recognition would be necessary following Sheikh Khalifah's assumption of power.[119] Henderson was also instructed to tell Khalifah that HMG proposed to 'conduct business with his government in the normal way'.[120]

As early as 1965, the Political Agent in Qatar, R. H. M. Boyle, declared that 'A country of this size needs only one Ruler in fact and in name, and Sheikh Khalifa is clearly destined to be that man. His outlook is in tune with the age; he is energetic; he has a great capacity for work, and appreciates modern things and modern methods'.[121] Henderson himself reacted positively to Khalifah's seizure of power, describing the new Amir as 'very shrewd' and predicting that the 'chances of his remaining in control are very much greater than the risk that he will lose it'.[122] In view of information he had received that Ahmed's son, Sheikh Abdul Aziz, who had an unenviable reputation for violence and corruption, had been planning his own coup, Henderson applauded Khalifah's actions which, in his judgement, had prevented Qatar from falling under the rule of a 'homicidal maniac'.[123] As regards Anglo–Qatari relations, Henderson highlighted Khalifah's 'devotion to friendship with Britain'.[124] 'The net outcome if we play our cards at all well', summarized Henderson, 'should be a considerable increase in commercial profit to the UK from Qatar, a considerable increase in ties of friendship through individuals and I hope a habit of close and healthy cooperation between the two countries in every field in which we can usefully co-operate'.[125] Sounding a note of caution, however, Henderson warned: 'With a man as impetuous and impatient as Khalifah to deal with there is always the danger that some other power might step in to meet his desires where we have considered it imprudent or impractical to do so'.[126] The first real test of this was provided by Qatari requests for the supply of Jaguar aircraft.

In May 1972, the Ministry of Defence produced a report at the request of the Qatar government on the organization and equipment of the Amirate's security services. The report included a recommendation that, in order to provide Qatar with the capacity to take part in the defence of the region, consideration should be given to the purchase of a Jaguar squadron. In September, the Amir indicated his intention to place a contract for six Jaguar aircraft, with the possibility of an additional six. The sale of Jaguar to Qatar was complicated by the fact that Britain had already refused this aircraft to the Egyptians. Nevertheless, the Head of the FCO's Middle East Department, P. R. H. Wright, warned that

> there is a serious risk that, if we were to refuse to proceed with the Jaguar sale to the Qataris, the French might curry favour with them by claiming that they, unlike us, would have been prepared to sell, and would then offer Mirage in their place. The consequences for the whole re-equipment programme for the Qatar Security Forces, which is estimated to include £40 million worth of orders for the UK, could be serious, not only commercially but also politically. With French influence supplanting ours in the Qatar Security Forces, our special relationship with the Al Thani could be rapidly eroded.[127]

FCO Under-Secretary A. D. Parsons concurred with Wright's analysis of the baleful consequences of a growth of the French presence in Qatar, arguing that 'We should thus lose valuable business as well as much of our general influence and position with the Al Thani'.[128] Summarizing the issue for Prime Minister

Heath, Douglas-Home affirmed that 'There is no doubt that a refusal to supply to either country[129] would create serious political and commercial difficulties for us and, particularly in the case of Qatar, might lead the French to steal a march on us in the defence equipment market'.[130] Douglas-Home's arguments proved persuasive, with Prime Minister Heath agreeing with the recommendation to sell Jaguars to Qatar.[131] Shortly after this decision was relayed to Sheikh Khalifah, Henderson informed the FCO that he had had a 'most wonderful' interview with the Qatari Amir.[132] The Ambassador proceeded to report that Khalifah had 'launched forth on a very extensive and detailed peroration praising HMG and all their works and promising to buy everything he possibly could from "England", provided only that we make it'.[133] 'I usually do not think', concluded Henderson, 'that an Arab goes into lyrical praise unless he wants something; but on this occasion I formed the view that all he wants is for us to continue to help him'.[134] Reacting to Henderson's testimony, Wright remarked: 'It is clear that the positive way in which we have responded to Qatari requests for defence equipment, and in particular Jaguar, has impressed Shaikh Khalifah and led to the somewhat euphoric state of bilateral relations'.[135]

Towards the end of 1972, Henderson specially mentioned that he had been 'impressed by the Amir's determination to buy British'.[136] In his annual review, furthermore, Henderson opined: 'I think that the improvement in the [Qatari] Government's capability since February 1972 has been in our favour; and the Amir, both by what he says and by what he does, has shown himself to be sincerely friendly towards Britain and intends to seek our co-operation in every field where we can help him'.[137] The Ambassador proceeded to note that 'We have gained the position of acting as advisers to the Government in almost every sphere', adding: 'The Amir has said in so many words that had we not proved so willing to provide expertise, he would have gone to the French who have been pressing him very hard indeed to accept their experts'.[138] Henderson did sound a note of caution, though. While accepting that in the fields of defence and development the prospects for British commerce seemed good, he noted that in the consumer field 'several of our firms are making a weak showing and many none at all'.[139] 'What we need for the future', urged Henderson, 'is to find a means to tell our major exporting firms that Qatar is a worthwhile market which, given a little care and thought and choice of the right agent, may well be one of the easiest in the world'.[140] He concluded with the gloomy observation that 'If we cannot get this message through, then I think the Japanese and the French and others will take our place'.[141] An early example of French encroachment on Britain's former exclusive position in the Lower Gulf is provided by defence sales to Abu Dhabi.

In June 1972, the Ruler of Abu Dhabi, Sheikh Zaid, informed the British Ambassador to the United Arab Emirates, C. J. Treadwell, that he was purchasing Puma helicopters and Mirage aircraft from France. Nevertheless, he assured Treadwell that he had only turned to the French because the British supplied 'nothing comparable'.[142] Zaid also promised that he would 'do nothing which could be construed and represented by others as evidence of an anti-British outlook', adding that he needed British support and sympathized with Britain's wish to improve its commercial position in Abu Dhabi.[143] Treadwell concluded that 'Despite the suspicions of certain of his colleagues and advisers – strengthened perhaps by some of his own rather foolish remarks – I believe that Zaid really is anxious to preserve his ties with us'.[144] Following a meeting with the Abu Dhabi ruler earlier in the month, Treadwell had confirmed that Zaid was 'not hostile to the British generally', and would continue to ask for British officers in the Abu Dhabi Defence Force (ADDF) 'for the foreseeable future'.[145]

The positive impression of relations with Britain following the ending of the special treaty relationship was backed up by comments subsequently made by the UAE Foreign Minister, Ahmad Suwaidi. Suwaidi assured Treadwell that Zaid 'made no secret of his attachment to the British' and that there was 'no move to replace British officials working within the Abu Dhabi Government'.[146] The Foreign Minister went on to declare that Zaid wished to 'broaden commercial relations with the British', and that if, in the future, Britain and one other country submitted similar tenders for a project, 'the award was to be made to the British'.[147] Seeking to justify why seemingly unfriendly comments were occasionally expressed in public towards Britain, Suwaidi explained that 'It was vital for the UAE that certain Arab countries should not be antagonised'.[148] As regards relations between the UAE and Iran, Zaid himself informed Treadwell in May 1972 that

> his interests would not be served if he were seen by other Arab countries to be running to the Shah. The islands problem remained a sensitive issue. It was one thing for Arab states to retain long established links with the Iranians. It would be quite another matter for the UAE to be seen to invite the Iranian government to exchange ambassadors at this stage.[149]

When Treadwell tackled Zaid over his Minister of Petroleum, Mana Said Otaiba's, expression of support for Libya's nationalization of British Petroleum's assets,[150] the Abu Dhabi Ruler waved the Ambassador's objections aside, stating: 'The Libyans must not think that the UAE were not fully independent of the UK'.[151]

In addition to incipient pressure from the Arab world on the UAE, British relations with the new entity were also complicated by the structure which had emerged from the former Trucial States. As Treadwell bluntly observed: 'The UAE is a federation of seven[152] disparate States controlled by ruling families whose one common characteristic is an inability to comprehend the meaning of modern political government. Among the seven Rulers there is not to be found a single leader of modern age man'.[153] While recognizing that Sheikhs Zaid of Abu Dhabi and Rashid of Dubai, as President and Vice-President of the UAE respectively, formed the 'cornerstone of the union', Treadwell noted that they were 'unlikely bedfellows' having been briefly at war in 1948 and possessing temperaments which were as different as 'chalk and cheese'.[154]

While seeking to maintain influence and elements of its special relationship with the former protected Gulf Sheikhdoms, Britain was aware of the need to eschew its traditional role, in public at least. As Ambassador Henderson in Doha noted: 'there are obvious dangers if our position were to become too open and all-embracing. . . . They [the Qataris] have for a long time been very conscious of the dangers of appearing to be puppets of the British'.[155] Henderson added that 'the closeness of our relations at the present time is not manifestly apparent outside the walls of the Amir's office in Government House'.[156] Regional powers were also alert to signs of the persistence of the Western presence after formal British withdrawal. As early as January 1968, Iran's Prime Minister, Abbas Hoveyda, warned that 'Britain's exit from one door must not result in American entrance from the other door – or in the British re-entry in another form'.[157] The negative regional response to the US decision in 1970 to retain its meagre naval assets in Bahrain[158] underlined the potential dangers of Western nations appearing to retain too prominent a role into the post-imperial era. As Ambassador Treadwell recognized with respect to Abu Dhabi: 'it might be no bad thing in the long term if a reduction were made in the strength of British officers in the ADDF. This sheer weight of present numbers is something of an embarrassment presentationally'.[159] Indeed, the British were mindful not to lapse into old ways drawing on an imperial past. Even before formal British departure, the British Ambassador in Jedda, Willie Morris, assured King Feisal of Saudi Arabia that 'Britain "would not be returning by the back door"'.[160]

At the end of 1971, Britain's Ambassador in Bahrain, A. J. D. Stirling, counselled: 'Our position here is strong. We can best maintain it by giving help and advice at least as readily in the future as hitherto, but always remembering that the Bahrainis are now fully independent and expect to be treated accordingly'.[161] In a similar vein, Stirling's successor, Robert Tesh, referring to the members of the new Bahraini Parliament, affirmed that his 'main preoccupation will now be to try and educate them without appearing to play old-style British Political Agent'.[162] When Sheikh Zaid flirted with the idea of Soviet representation in the UAE at the beginning of 1972, the Head of the FCO's Arabian Department, Anthony Acland, pragmatically opined:

> I think we have to recognise . . . that our ability to influence the President and his adviser's decisively in matters of this kind is obviously limited. To us it appears that Zaid behaves more and more like the ball in the game of bagatelle, bouncing off each successive obstacle and reacting instinctively, and not always wisely. However much we try to arm him with arguments he is probably going to say and do what is most expedient when he is in a tight corner.[163]

Acland's observations were confirmed by Ambassador Treadwell who noted in February 1972: 'It is the first time since my arrival in Abu Dhabi nearly four years ago that he [Zaid] has failed to accept our advice on a matter of real substance'.[164] Arguably, it was pressure from Zaid's more powerful conservative neighbours, as well as from within the UAE itself, that persuaded Zaid to suspend the exchange of ambassadors with the Soviet Union,[165] rather than British counsel.

Responding later in the year to requests from US State Department officials for Britain to place pressure on Sheikh Zaid over long-standing territorial disputes

42 *The trials of independence, 1971–1972*

with Saudi Arabia, British diplomats in Washington adopted a correct approach, pointing out that 'our ability to influence Shaikh Zaid was now strictly limited and that HMG no longer had a *locus standi* in the dispute'.[166] In a similar vein, when the Iranian Ambassador in London, Amir Khosrow Afshar, criticized Britain for not ensuring that Zaid 'behaved properly', the Head of the FCO's Middle East Department, P. R. H. Wright, retorted: 'our influence with Zaid is by no means what it was under the old relationship. This was not to say that we had no influence anymore; but it was a mistake to think that we could get Zaid to do what we wanted'.[167] Although British policy-makers strongly supported rapprochement between the UAE and Iran, it was not until the Secretary General of the Arab League, Mahmoud Riad, informed Zaid towards the end of September 1972 that 'there need be no further obstacle to the UAE's establishment of relations with Iran', that concrete moves towards this took place.[168] In response to Zaid's request for advice about the timing of the exchange of ambassadors with Iran, Riad counselled 'before the end of the year'.[169] Despite some last minute hitches regarding the nomination of the UAE's candidate for ambassador to Iran,[170] the announcement of the exchange duly took place on 24 December 1972.[171]

Despite British satisfaction at the warming of relations between the UAE and Iran, there was a palpable sense of instability in the Gulf following the British withdrawal decision. This was underlined by the growth of political assassinations in Kuwait, the most significant of which was the murder of former Vice-President of Iraq, General Hardan al-Takriti, outside the Amiri Hospital on 30 March 1971. Ruminating on this dramatic event, Ambassador Wilton stressed:

> Political assassinations, unknown in Kuwait since the Sabah stopped murdering each other in 1896, has reappeared on the scene at a time when political stability is, as our withdrawal from the Gulf approaches, a particularly vital commodity. It has been demonstrated how very easy it is to stage such a crime in Kuwait, making appropriate use of her easily penetrable frontiers; and the fear that 'once this sort of thing starts it won't be easy to stop' is voiced by many Kuwaitis.[172]

The limits on Britain's residual influence in the Gulf, and the applicability of the concept of 'informal empire' to characterize British relations with the Gulf States after the dissolution of 'formal empire', were underscored by the events in 1973, especially the use of the 'oil weapon' by Arab producers. This will be examined in Chapter 2.

Notes

1 Message from Wilson to Johnson, 15 January 1968, LBJ Library, NSF, Head of State Correspondence File, Box 11, M.O.D. 1968, no 5.
2 Ibid.
3 See Simon C. Smith, 'Britain's decision to withdraw from the Persian Gulf: A pattern not a puzzle', *Journal of Imperial and Commonwealth History*, 44, 2 (2016), pp. 330–6.
4 Cabinet conclusions, 4 January 1968, CAB 128/43, CC (68), 1st conclusions.

5 'Foreign policy', Memorandum by Brown, 23 February 1968, cited in S. R. Ashton and Wm. Roger Louis (eds.), *East of Suez and the Commonwealth, 1964–1971: Part II: Europe, Rhodesia, Commonwealth* (London: TSO, 2004), p. 75.
6 Cited in Farzad Cyrus Sharifi-Yazdi, *Arab-Iranian Rivalry in the Persian Gulf: Territorial Disputes and the Balance of Power in the Middle East* (London: I. B. Tauris, 2015), p. 175.
7 Despatch from Crawford to Brown, 27 January 1968, cited in S. R. Ashton and Wm. Roger Louis (eds.), *East of Suez and the Commonwealth: Part I: East of Suez* (London: HMSO, 2004), p. 145.
8 Ibid.
9 Cited in Sharifi-Yazdi, *Arab-Iranian Rivalry in the Persian Gulf*, p. 192.
10 Minutes of a meeting of the Defence and Oversea Policy (Official) Committee, 10 June 1968, CAB 148/83, OPDO(68) 4th meeting.
11 'Non-military means of influence in the Persian Gulf, South East Asia and Australasia', Memorandum by Secretary of State for Foreign Affairs and Secretary of State for Commonwealth Affairs, 24 July 1968, CAB 148/37, OPD(68)44(revise).
12 Ibid.
13 Ibid.
14 Minutes of a meeting of the Defence and Oversea Policy Committee, 26 July 1968, in Ashton and Louis, *East of Suez and the Commonwealth, 1964–1971: Part II*, p. 95.
15 Telegram from American Embassy, London (Annenberg), to the Secretary of State, No. 4351, 4 June 1970, RG 59, Subject-Numeric Files, 1970–1973, Box 2381, POL IRAN-UK. A little over a year later, Annenberg noted: 'HMG hopes [to] retain greatest possible degree of influence in lower Gulf after withdrawal' (Tore Petersen, 'Anglo–American relations over Aden and the United Arab Emirates, 1967–71', *Middle Eastern Studies*, 53, 1 (2017), p. 107).
16 'Report on a visit to the Gulf', by Wall, 20 September 1970, Hull History Centre, Papers of Sir Patrick Wall, U DPW/59/103. At the beginning of 1968, Wall impressed upon the Ruler of Bahrain, Sheikh Isa, 'how much I and my friends deplore the decision to withdraw British forces precipitately from the Arabian Gulf' (Letter from Wall to His Highness Sheikh Isa, 25 January 1968, Hull History Centre, Papers of Sir Patrick Wall, U DPW/59/32). Wall subsequently prophesied that 'If . . . the Labour government's withdrawal plans are carried out in full, attempts will almost certainly be made to overthrow the Rulers under the banner of democratic Arab Socialism' (Patrick Wall, 'The Persian Gulf – Stay or Quit?', in *Brassey's Annual: Defence and the Armed Forces 1971* (London: William Clowes & Sons Limited, 1971), p. 132). He consequently called for a delay in British withdrawal and the maintenance of British military presence (ibid., pp. 133–4).
17 Letter from Douglas-Home to Wall, 13 October 1970, Hull History Centre, Papers of Sir Patrick Wall, U DPW/59/103.
18 James Worrall, *Statebuilding and Counterinsurgency on Oman: Political, Military, and Diplomatic Relations at the End of Empire* (London: I. B. Tauris, 2014), p. 79.
19 'Policy in the Persian Gulf', Report by Sir William Luce, pp. 6–7, 4 December 1970, CAB 148/102, DOP (70) 44. Britain's Political Resident in the Gulf, Sir Stewart Crawford, had already opined: 'The presence of British forces in the Gulf has always in the past been a steadying element and has never attracted local hostility. It would be preferable for them to leave while this is the case, rather than risk their overstaying their welcome' (Letter from Crawford to the Secretary of State for Foreign and Commonwealth Affairs, 3 August 1970, cited in A. L. P. Burdett (ed.), *Records of the Emirates, 1966–1971: Volume 5: 1970* (Slough: Archive Editions, 2002), p. 33).
20 'Policy in the Persian Gulf', Report by Sir William Luce, p. 5, 4 December 1970, CAB 148/102, DOP (70) 44.
21 Ibid., p. 4.
22 Ibid., p. 8.
23 Ibid., p. 11.

44 *The trials of independence, 1971–1972*

24 Ibid.
25 Ibid., p. 8.
26 Ibid., p. 9.
27 Minutes of a meeting of the Defence and Oversea Policy Committee, 11 December 1970, CAB 148/101, DOP (70) 12th meeting.
28 Minutes of the Cabinet Defence and Oversea Policy Committee, 24 February 1971, CAB 148/115, DOP (71) 6th meeting.
29 Cabinet Conclusions, 25 February 1971, CAB 128/49 Part 1, CM (71) 11th conclusions.
30 Tore T. Petersen, *Richard Nixon, Great Britain and the Anglo–American Alignment in the Persian Gulf and Arabian Peninsula: Making Allies out of Clients* (Brighton and Portland: Sussex Academic Press, 2009), p. 55.
31 M. W. Daly, *The Last of the Great Proconsuls: The Biography of Sir William Luce* (San Diego: Nathan Berg, 2014), p. 287.
32 'Visits of Gulf Rulers to Britain', Minute by Acland, 15 March 1971, FCO 8/1731.
33 Letter from Acland to H. S. Lee (Treasury), 31 March 1971, cited in A. L. P. Burdett (ed.), *Records of the Emirates, 1966–1971: Volume 6: 1971* (Slough: Archive Editions, 2002), p. 406. The Deputy Political Resident in the Gulf, P. R. H. Wright, had already stressed that 'our aim in assisting with Police and Special Branches will be to protect the area as a whole (whether its component States are in a Union or not) from subversive influences which could severely harm remaining British interests' (Letter from Wright to J. M. Edes (Arabian Department, FCO), 9 February 1971, cited in ibid., p. 402).
34 Letter from C. H. W. Hodges (Treasury) to Acland, 20 May, 1971, ibid., p. 419.
35 *Parliamentary Debates (Commons), 1970–1, Volume 812*, col. 1228, 1 March 1971.
36 Ibid., col. 1229.
37 Khalid S. Z. Al-Nahyan, *The Three Islands: Mapping the UAE-Iran Dispute* (London: Royal United Services Institute, 2013), pp. 39–43. Referring to the Tunbs and Abu Musa, the Iranian Minister of Court, Asadollah Alam, informed Foreign Secretary Michael Stewart in May 1969 that 'Britain had gained unlawful possession of these islands and handed them as a benighted inheritance to the Sheikhs of Sharjah and Ras al-Khaimah whom his government now supports against Iran' (Asadollah Alam, *The Shah and I: The Confidential Diary of Iran's Royal Court, 1968–77* (London: I. B. Tauris, 2008), p. 70).
38 Letter from S. L. Egerton (Arabian Department) to J. C. Moberly, 11 March 1971, FCO 8/1573.
39 Letter from Moberly (Counsellor, British Embassy, Washington) to Egerton, 17 March 1971, FCO 8/ 1573.
40 Letter from Moberly to A, A. Acland, 6 May 1971, FCO 8/1573.
41 'American help over Gulf affairs', Minute by Acland, 14 July 1971, FCO 8/1573.
42 Chiefs of Staff Committee: COS 18th Meeting/71, 2 June 1971, cited in Burdett, *Records of the Emirates, 1966–1971: Volume 6: 1971*, p. 371.
43 Telegram from Department of State (Irwin) to American Embassies, London and Tehran, No. 172104, 18 September 1971, RG 59, Subject-Numeric Files 1970–73, Box 1996, POL 33 Persian Gulf.
44 'Gulf policy and the islands', Minute from Douglas-Home to the Secretary of State for Defence, FCS/71/71, 12 October 1971, T 225/3542.
45 Telegram from American Embassy, Tehran, to the Secretary of State, No. 6452, 15 November 1971, RG 59, Subject-Numeric Files 1970–73, Box 1996, POL 33 Persian Gulf.
46 Conclusions of a meeting of the Cabinet, 18 November 1971, CAB 128/49 Part 2, CM (71) 56th Conclusions.
47 Telegram from American Embassy, Tehran, to the Secretary of State, No. 6452, 15 November 1971, RG 59, Subject-Numeric Files 1970–73, Box 1996, POL 33 Persian Gulf.

48 Telegram from Department of State (Irwin) to American Embassy, Tel Aviv, No. 214109, 26 November 1971, RG 59, Subject-Numeric Files 1970–73, Box 1996, POL 33 Persian Gulf.
49 Telegram from American Embassy, Tehran, to Secretary of State, No. 901, 11 March 1970, RG 59, Subject-Numeric Files 1970–73, Box 1774, DEF 1 Near East.
50 Letter from Wilton to the Secretary of State for Foreign and Commonwealth Affairs, 6 January 1972, FCO 8/1834.
51 Ibid.
52 Ibid.
53 Telegram from Kuwait to the Foreign and Commonwealth Office, No. 285, 4 May 1972, FCO 8/1837.
54 Conclusions of a meeting of the Cabinet, 2 December 1971, CAB 128/49 Part 2, CM (71) 61st Conclusions.
55 Telegram from American Embassy, London (Annenberg) to Secretary of State, No. 10982, 1 December 1971, RG 59, Subject-Numeric Files 1970–73, Box 2640, POL 7 UAE.
56 Ibid.; 'Death of Shaikh Khalid bin Mohammed al Qasimi, Ruler of Sharjah', Minute by Acland, 25 January 1972, FCO 8/1925.
57 'Persian Gulf: coup and countercoup in Sharjah', Intelligence Note: Bureau of Intelligence and Research, 4 February 1972, RG 59, Subject-Numeric Files 1970–73, Box 2640, POL 7 UAE; Letter from Walker to Treadwell, 1 February 1972, FCO 8/1925. See also Brandon Friedman, 'From union (ittihad) to united (muttahida): The United Arab Emirates, a success born of failure', *Middle Eastern Studies*, 53, 1 (2017), p. 129.
58 Letter from Julian Amery to Douglas-Home, 17 February 1972, FCO 8/1925.
59 Letter from Arthur to Douglas-Home, 24 January 1972, FCO 8/1804.
60 Ibid.
61 'Talks with the Americans about the Arabian Peninsula', Minute by Parsons, 9 May 1972, FCO 8/1806.
62 Ibid.
63 Record of Anglo–United States talks on the Persian Gulf and Arabian Peninsula held in the State Department, 26 June 1972, FCO 8/1806.
64 Ibid.
65 Letter from M. R. Melhuish to D. G. Allen, 14 August 1972, FCO 8/1806.
66 D. F. Hawley, who served as Britain's Ambassador to Oman from 1971 to 1975, stated in his memoirs that the ousting of Said and his replacement with Qaboos took place with the 'discreet connivance of the British Government' (Donald Hawley, *Desert Wind and Tropic Storm: An Autobiography* (Wilby: Michael Russell, 2000), p. 160). He adds that Said 'had been unable after the arrival of oil revenues in 1967 to abandon the habits of economy and careful husbandry, developed over a lifetime, and to initiate development schemes at a speed sufficient to satisfy his people' (Ibid., p. 173).
67 Letter from Crawford to the Political Resident, 4 January 1971, FCO 8/1669.
68 Brief for the Secretary of State's visit with His Majesty the Sultan of Oman, attached to Acland's minute, 9 June 1971, FCO 8/1681
69 'Defence assistance to the Sultanate of Oman', Memorandum by the Secretary of State for Defence, 22 May 1972, CAB 148/122, DOP(72)25 (revised).
70 Kristian Coates Ulrichsen, *Insecure Gulf: The End of Certainty and the Transition to the Post-Oil Era* (London: Hurst and Company, 2011), p. 23.
71 Roham Alvandi, 'Muhammad Reza Pahlavi and the Bahrain question, 1968–1970', *British Journal of Middle Eastern Studies*, 37, 2 (2010), p. 175. The influential Minister of Court in Iran, Asadollah Alam, had already told the Shah with respect to the Gulf that 'We cannot sacrifice our interests there for the sake of an antiquated claim to Bahrain' (Alam, *The Shah and I*, p. 142).

72 *Treaty of friendship Between the United Kingdom of Great Britain and Northern Ireland and the State of Bahrain*, 3 September 1971 (London: HMSO, 1972), Cmnd. 4828.
73 Letter from Stirling to Douglas-Home, 15 February 1972, FCO 8/1826.
74 Ibid.
75 Ibid.
76 Letter from Acland to Stirling, 22 February 1972, FCO 8/1826.
77 Letter from Stirling to D. G. Allen, 22 March 1972, FCO 8/1822.
78 Letter from Stirling to P. R. H. Wright, 9 May 1972, FCO 8/1822.
79 Ibid.
80 Letter from Stirling to the Secretary of State for Foreign and Commonwealth Affairs, 23 May 1972, FCO 8/1824.
81 Ibid.
82 Ibid.
83 Ibid.
84 Ibid.
85 Letter Tesh to Secretary of State for Foreign and Commonwealth Affairs, 29 August 1972, FCO 8/1822.
86 Ibid.
87 Ibid.
88 Ibid.
89 Letter from Wright to Tesh, 1 September 1972, FCO 8/1822.
90 Miriam Joyce, *Bahrain from the Twentieth Century to the Arab Spring* (New York: Palgrave Macmillan, 2012), p. 51.
91 Record of a conversation between the Foreign and Commonwealth Secretary and Sheikh Muhammad bin Mubarak, Foreign Minister of Bahrain, at the Foreign and Commonwealth Office at 3.45pm on Wednesday, 2 August 1972, FCO 8/1825.
92 Brief for Minister of State's meeting with Shaikh Sulman bin Da'ij Al-Khalifah, Ambassador of Bahrain, on Friday, 24 November 1972, FCO 8/1825.
93 Ibid.
94 Letter from Stirling to Wright, 9 May 1972, FCO 8/1822.
95 Letter Tesh to Secretary of State for Foreign and Commonwealth Affairs, 29 August 1972, FCO 8/1822.
96 Letter from Tesh to Douglas-Home, 31 December 1972, FCO 8/1974.
97 Ibid.
98 Ibid.
99 Letter Tesh to Secretary of State for Foreign and Commonwealth Affairs, 29 August 1972, FCO 8/1822.
100 Letter from McCluney to P. J. S. Moon, 29 April 1971, PREM 15/531.
101 Ibid.
102 Ibid. McCluney is referring to the Tehran agreement of 14 February 1971 which ditched the old 50/50 profit-sharing principle between oil companies and host governments in favour of minimum government take of 55 per cent, as well as raising the price of a barrel of oil by 35 cents with the possibility of further annual increases (Daniel Yergin, *The Prize: The Epic Quest for Oil, Money and Power* (London: Simon and Schuster, 1991), p. 582; F. Gregory Gause, *The International Relations of the Persian Gulf* (Cambridge: Cambridge University Press, 2010), p. 27).
103 Letter from Henderson to J. L. Bevan, 9 March 1971, FCO 8/1731.
104 Note by Heath, 30 April 1971, on McCluney's letter to Moon, 29 April 1971, PREM 15/531.
105 Brief for the Prime Minister's meeting with Shaikh Khalifah bin Hamad Al Thani, Deputy Ruler and Prime Minister of Qatar (undated), by the Arabian Department, Foreign and Commonwealth Office, PREM 15/531.

106 Ibid.
107 Ibid.
108 Letter from Moon to McCluney, 28 July 1971, PREM 15/531.
109 Ibid.
110 Ibid.
111 Letter from Henderson to the Secretary of State for Foreign and Commonwealth Affairs, 4 January 1972, FCO 8/1890.
112 *Treaty of friendship Between the United Kingdom of Great Britain and Northern Ireland and the State of Qatar*, 3 September 1971 (London: HMSO, 1972), Cmnd. 4850.
113 Letter from Henderson to the Secretary of State for Foreign and Commonwealth Affairs, 4 January 1972, FCO 8/1890.
114 Ibid.
115 Ibid.
116 Ibid.
117 Telegram from American Consul General (Dinsmore) to the Secretary of State, No. 368, 23 February 1972, RG 59, Subject-Numeric Files 1970–73, Box 2560, POL 23–9 Qatar.
118 Letter from Henderson to J. L. Beaven (Arabian Department, FCO), 29 February 1972, FCO 8/1892.
119 Cabinet conclusions, 24 February 1972, CAB 128/50, CM(72)10th conclusions.
120 Telegram from the Foreign and Commonwealth Office to Kuwait, No. 56, 24 February 1972, PREM 15/1085.
121 Letter from Boyle to Sir William Luce, 14 July 1965, cited in Anita L. P. Burdett (ed.), *Records of Qatar, 1961–1965: 1965* (Slough: Archive Editions, 1997), p. 254.
122 Letter from Henderson to Beaven, 29 February 1972, FCO 8/1892.
123 Letter from Henderson to the Secretary of State for Foreign and Commonwealth Affairs, 7 March 1972, FCO 8/1892.
124 Ibid.
125 Ibid.
126 Ibid.
127 'Jaguar for Qatar', Minute by Wright, 4 October 1972, FCO 8/1896.
128 'Jaguar for Qatar and Saudi Arabia', Minute by Parsons, 6 October 1972, FCO 8/1896.
129 Saudi Arabia was also trying to secure a contract for Jaguars.
130 'Supply of Jaguar for Qatar and Saudi Arabia', Minute by Douglas-Home, PM/72/47, 24 October 1972, FCO 8/1896.
131 Letter from Tom Bridges to M. O'D. B. Alexander, 25 October 1972, FCO 8/1896.
132 Letter from Henderson to Wright, 21 November 1972, FCO 8/1895.
133 Ibid.
134 Ibid.
135 'Qatar/UK relations', Minute by Wright, 24 November 1972, FCO 8/1895.
136 Letter from Henderson to Peter Britain (Ministry of Defence), 17 December 1972, FCO 8/1896.
137 Letter from Henderson to Douglas-Home, 8 January 1973, FCO 8/2079.
138 Ibid.
139 Ibid.
140 Ibid.
141 Ibid.
142 Letter from Treadwell to Wright, 25 June 1972, FCO 8/1934.
143 Ibid.
144 Ibid.
145 Letter from Treadwell to Wright, No. 10/49, 17 June 1972, FCO 8/1934.
146 Letter from Treadwell to Wright, 18 June 1972, FCO 8/1934.

48 *The trials of independence, 1971–1972*

147 Ibid.
148 Ibid.
149 Telegram from Abu Dhabi to the Foreign and Commonwealth Office, No. 247, 8 May 1972, FCO 8/1929. In a similar vein the UAE Foreign Minister, Ahmad Suwaidi, told Ambassador Treadwell that the Shah 'should not . . . expect a new country like the UAE to establish formal relations, particularly when other Arab states disliked the idea' (Letter from Treadwell to Wright, 18 June 1972, FCO 8/1929). Referring to the Iranians, Suwaidi also declared that 'He was not . . . prepared to seek their friendship if the UAE lost the goodwill of certain Arab countries in the process' (Letter from Treadwell to A. Reeve, 31 July 1972, FCO 8/1930).
150 Telegram from Tripoli to the Foreign and Commonwealth Office, No. 584, 3 May 1972, FCO 8/1929. The Libyan government's nationalization of BP's assets in Libya on 7 December 1971 had ostensibly been in response to Britain's failure to prevent Iran's seizure of the disputed Gulf islands (G. Winthrop Haight, 'Libyan nationalization of British Petroleum Company assets', *International Lawyer*, 6, 3 (1972), p. 541).
151 Telegram from Abu Dhabi to the Foreign and Commonwealth Office, No. 249, 8 May 1972, FCO 8/1929.
152 On 10 February 1972, Ras al-Khaimah became the seventh state in the UAE having been assured of equal treatment with Qasimi member, Sharjah (David Commins, *The Gulf States: A Modern History* (London and New York: I. B. Tauris, 2012), p. 193).
153 Letter from Treadwell to Douglas-Home, 11 May 1972, FCO 8/1923.
154 Ibid.
155 Letter from Henderson to the Secretary of State for Foreign and Commonwealth Affairs, 7 March 1972, FCO 8/1892.
156 Ibid.
157 Joyce, *Bahrain*, p. 37.
158 Telegram from American Embassy, Tehran (MacArthur), to the Secretary of State, No. 279, 15 January 1972, Telegram from American Embassy, Manama (John Newton Gatch), to Secretary of State, No. 229, 3 April 1972, NARA, RG 59, Subject-Numeric Files 1970–73, Box 1690, DEF 15-4 BAHRAIN-US; Letter from Stirling to Allen, 25 April 1972, FCO 8/1806. See also Michael A. Palmer, *Guardians of the Gulf: A History of America's Expanding Role in the Persian Gulf, 1833–1992* (New York: The Free Press, 1992), p. 90.
159 Treadwell to Wright, No. 10/49, 17 June 1972, FCO 8/1934.
160 Telegram from Morris to the Foreign and Commonwealth Office, No. 647, 23 August 1971, FCO 8/1741.
161 Stirling to the Secretary of State for Foreign and Commonwealth Affairs, 31 December 1971, FCO 8/1823.
162 Joyce, *Bahrain*, p. 55.
163 Letter from Acland to Treadwell, 13 January 1972, FCO 8/1927.
164 Letter from Treadwell to Acland, 7 February 1972, FCO 8/1927.
165 Mordechai Abir and Aryeh Yodfat, *In the Direction of the Persian Gulf: The Soviet Union and the Persian Gulf* (London: Frank Cass, 1977), p. 73.
166 Letter from Moberly to Acland, 10 April 1972, FCO 8/1806.
167 'Iran/UAE', Minute by Wright, 31 July 1972, FCO 8/1930. Iranian suspicions of Britain, however, continued. Towards the end of October 1972, the Shah's Minister of Court, Asadollah Alam, noted in his diary: 'Reported yet another visit from Mahdi al-Tajer, presently ambassador of the UAE in London, who was received yesterday by HIM [His Imperial Majesty]. He wanted to tell me that during his audience he had forgotten to mention that he can persuade Ahmad al-Suwaidi, the UAE's Foreign Minister, to adopt a less hostile attitude towards Iran. "Tell him to go ahead", said HIM. "All these people are under the influence of the British; he's only doing his

master's bidding". HIM's suspicions of the British are quite incredible; but on this occasion he's got even me wondering whether he may not be correct' (Alam, *The Shah and I*, p. 249).
168 Telegram from the Foreign and Commonwealth Office to Tehran, No. 505, 29 September 1972, FCO 8/1931.
169 Ibid.
170 'Iran-UAE', Minute by Wright, 8 November 1972, FCO 8/1931.
171 Telegram from Abu Dhabi to the Foreign and Commonwealth Office, No. 526, 24 December 1972, FCO 8/1931.
172 Letter from Wilton to Douglas-Home, 7 April 1971, cited in Richard Schofield (ed.), *Arabian Boundaries: New Documents, 1966–75: Volume 12, 1971* (Cambridge: Cambridge University Press, 2009), p. 9. Wilton also reported that 'Public opinion in Kuwait takes it for granted that the killing was the work of the General's enemies in the Iraqi Ba'ath Party and the favourite candidate for instigator is Saddam [Hussein] al Takriti' (Ibid., p. 4).

2 The oil revolution, 1973

In their celebrated article, 'The imperialism of decolonization', William Roger Louis and Ronald Robinson contend that 'It should be a commonplace . . . that the post-war Empire was more than British and less than an imperium. As it survived, so it was nationalized and internationalized as part of the Anglo–American coalition'.[1] Drawing on Louis and Robinson's interpretation, P. J. Cain and A. G. Hopkins argue that 'As the United States began to intervene in imperial affairs in the interest of the Cold War, the empire became part of a joint Anglo–American global venture'.[2] Focussing specifically on Anglo–American policy towards the Gulf and Arabian Peninsula during the Nixon presidency, Tore Petersen depicts the region as 'for practical purposes, an exclusive British and American domain'.[3] He also goes so far as to insist that the 'Persian Gulf was to all intents and purposes an Anglo–American lake during the Heath and Nixon era'.[4] He concludes that British and American polices towards the Gulf were 'closely aligned and mutually supportive'.[5] Certainly the Nixon White House valued Britain's continued involvement in the region, in many ways seeing it as the 'third pillar' of stability along with the pro-Western orientation of Saudi Arabia and, more especially, Iran.[6]

During discussions in July 1970 with the British Ambassador in Washington, John Freeman, Acting US Secretary of State, U. A. Johnson articulated his hope that 'the new [Conservative] government would plan to keep its political presence in the Gulf and that removal of troops did not mean removal of its political presence'.[7] From his vantage point in London, US Ambassador Walter Annenberg opined towards the beginning of 1971: 'I think that the USG may have to play a more active role in moving Gulf affairs in a reasonably orderly manner through a rough transition period this year. However, I believe we should continue to let UK take the lead'.[8]

At the time of Britain's formal departure in December 1971, the US Secretary of State, William Rogers, expressed his satisfaction that 'the transition in the Gulf has taken place in a manner permitting a continuing British role in support of the security of the region'.[9] In August 1972, a National Security Decision memorandum, signed by Henry Kissinger,[10] on US policy towards the Lower Gulf States asserted that 'a continuing British role should be encouraged'.[11] Secretary of State for Defence Lord Carrington, moreover, reported at the beginning of

April 1973 that 'Mr Elliot Richardson, the new Secretary for Defense in Washington, impressed upon me the importance which his Government attach to our maintaining British influence in the Gulf and the Arabian peninsula'.[12] Earlier the Deputy Assistant Secretary of Defense for Near Eastern, African, and South Asian Affairs, James Noyes, had told a subcommittee hearing of the House of Representatives that the US had 'no intention of seeking or appearing to replace the British in the Gulf'.[13] During Anglo–American talks at the US State Department in September 1973, moreover, Assistant Secretary for Near East Affairs, J. J. Sisco, told his British guests that the Americans 'welcomed the British decision to play a continuing role in the Gulf' and emphasized that 'The US had no desire to supplant the British role in the Gulf and in Oman'.[14] The US Embassy in London had already assured the FCO that 'The Administration were . . . particularly anxious to avoid "treading on British toes" and did not wish to complicate the role of British advisers in Oman'.[15]

While American policy-makers undoubtedly welcomed the fact that formal British military withdrawal from the region had not coincided with the termination of a tangible British presence in the region, it would perhaps be an exaggeration to suggest that British and American policies were 'closely aligned', still less that the Gulf formed an 'Anglo–American lake'. President Nixon's signing of a presidential determination on 17 January 1971 affirming that arms sales to Kuwait would 'strengthen the security of the United States and promote world peace',[16] for instance, foreshadowed a strengthening of the US role in Kuwait at the expense of Britain. In November 1971, the US Ambassador to Kuwait, John Walsh, reported that 'In the course of the past two years there has been a remarkable reversal of GOK attitudes toward the United States. Starting from a position of bristling antagonism they have come full circle to a position of intimacy and basic trust'.[17] By contrast, Walsh remarked that 'No one should misunderstand the bitterness of the Kuwaitis in respect to their past contracts with the British. They are absolutely convinced that they have been consistently cheated'.[18] Referring to US defence contractors, moreover, Walsh noted that the 'throttles are down and the companies are swarming in',[19] a situation which stood in marked contrast to Britain's former monopoly on arms supplies to Kuwait.

While Anglo–American policies were not always 'closely aligned', the notion that the Gulf become an 'Anglo–American lake' is equally suspect. Not only did Britain and America's Western allies, most notably France and Japan, encroach on the region to exploit the commercial opportunities which presented themselves, but also neither Washington nor London could prevent the intrusion of Arab influences into the Gulf. The differing responses of Britain and America to the Arab use of the 'oil weapon' at the time of the Yom Kippur War towards the end of 1973, furthermore, served to underline the limits of Anglo–American 'alignment' in the region. The beginning of the year, however, witnessed some positive signs for the preservation of British interests in the Gulf. With respect to Kuwait, it was renewed Iraqi pressure which presaged closer Anglo–Kuwaiti alignment.

Reflecting at the beginning of 1973 on the dilemma which Kuwait faced in its relations with its neighbours, the British Ambassador, A. J. Wilton, noted:

> For a score of reasons of domestic political prudence, emotional commitments over Palestine, a desire to stand well with everybody and a realistic assessment of the inability of the conservative regimes in the Arab world to help her in time of trouble, Kuwait has seen the best hope of political survival, at home and abroad, to lie in the espousal of the 'progressive' line whether this emanates from Algiers, Tripoli, Cairo, Damascus or Baghdad. But her most 'progressive' neighbour, Iraq, constitutes the only real threat to her continued independent existence.[20]

Towards the beginning of 1973, the Iraqis attempted to foist a treaty on Kuwait under which Iraq would be granted the right to 'build, operate and maintain one or more pipelines on Kuwaiti territory extending to a terminal on the Arabian Gulf'.[21] Unsurprisingly, the Kuwaiti government rejected the treaty out of hand. In response, Iraqi forces expelled 20 armed Kuwaiti police from the border post at al Samita on 20 March. This recrudescence in Kuwaiti–Iraqi tension prompted the government of Kuwait to order a complete mobilization of its armed forces.[22]

Within days, the Head of the FCO's Middle East Department, P. R. H. Wright, recorded that 'we have received a stream of requests for arms for the Kuwaiti Armed Forces'.[23] The Minister of State at the FCO, Lord Balniel, soon wrote to the Ministry of Defence in support of a positive response. 'The continued independence of Kuwait', insisted Balniel, 'is vital to the oil consuming countries of the western world, and in particular Britain, and it is in our interests that she should be as strong militarily as her limited human resources allow'.[24] The Minister of State added that Britain's political position in Kuwait would be 'seriously eroded if the Kuwaitis had to turn elsewhere for major imports of arms, or if they felt that they could no longer turn to us for helpful advice'.[25] Balniel also stressed that it was not simply that British arms sales were at risk. 'Any imports on a large scale from other countries', he explained, 'would require instructors and advisers from the same source and our whole defence connection, including the Kuwait Liaison Team which is playing a valuable role in Kuwait, would be seriously damaged'.[26] Balniel also advocated a visit by a senior British general to discuss defence planning with the Kuwaitis. 'Our aim', he concluded, 'must be to show the Kuwaitis that we really care about their defence problems and this personal touch will in my view achieve this aim, provided we can also be forthcoming on their arms requests'.[27]

The Minister of State for Defence, Ian Gilmour, assured Balniel that he fully endorsed 'all you say about the importance of doing all we can to meet the needs of the Kuwaitis'.[28] As a result of such considerations, the Commander-in-Chief Near East Land Forces, Major General Butler, visited Kuwait in mid-April to provide a preliminary survey of Kuwait's defence planning needs.[29] The Ministry of Defence also consented to meeting the Amirate's immediate needs, which required an airlift by fourteen RAF Hercules transport aircraft. R. M. Hunt of the FCO's Middle East Department dismissed the possibility of political embarrassment stemming from this overt display of British support for Kuwait. 'It is widely known that Britain has provided many of Kuwait's defence requirements in the past and it would not be unnatural for us to be seen to be strengthening their Armed Forces at this time', he noted.[30] FCO Under-Secretary of State A. D. Parsons was in full agreement, observing: 'If the Kuwaitis are prepared to accept any political consequences, which they are, it is not for us to be more sensitive than them'.[31]

Kuwaitis' sense of vulnerability against the background of the renewed Iraqi threat also opened the prospect of major arms deals for Britain. In April 1973, they expressed interest in purchasing Chieftain tanks. R. M. Hunt emphasized that 'We should miss no opportunity to bolster the independence of a country on which we rely for 20% of our oil imports and which holds 10% of all sterling reserves'.[32] In a similar vein, Parsons remarked:

> Kuwait is a harmless State which needs all the military equipment it can get in view of the Iraqi threat. Apart from our commercial, financial and oil interests, we have a strong political obligation to help the Kuwaitis. Furthermore, we know that the Americans are trying to sell the M60 tank to the Kuwaitis: hence there is no reason why we should not try to sell them Chieftains.[33]

P. R. H. Wright, moreover, pragmatically noted that 'A negative reply now would not only lose (probably to the Americans) the prospect of substantial tank sales but also prejudice our future arms prospects generally and undermine the position of the Kuwait Liaison Team'.[34] As a result of such considerations, the FCO told the British Ambassador in Kuwait, A. J. Wilton: 'Ministers agree that, in view of the initiatives which our competitors have already taken and the difficulties they may now be experiencing, you should take discreet steps to get us back in the running on arms sales'.[35] Wilton concurred that the time was 'ripe' for a renewal of Britain's arms sales effort in Kuwait.[36]

In response to Kuwait's request for ammunition to replace what was sent by the Kuwaitis to their forces in Syria and Egypt, Wright pointed out that

> We are a traditional supplier of arms and military equipment to Kuwait and a refusal to supply might not only cause a considerable set-back to our prospects for further arms sales to Kuwait ... but could sour the Kuwait Government's attitude towards us over a whole range of questions, including oil.[37]

In a reassertion of Britain's traditional approach to Kuwait, Parsons underlined that 'Kuwaiti independence and integrity is an extremely important British interest both in terms of Kuwait and in terms of the security of the whole Gulf'.[38] The revival of Britain's role in Kuwait was to some extent mirrored in Bahrain.

In January, former Political Agent in Bahrain A. D. Parsons, visited the Amirate at the invitation of the Bahraini government. Britain's Ambassador in Manama, Robert Tesh, recalled in his annual report for 1973 that 'The year began well with a visit by Mr Parsons . . . a legendary figure, for whom scores of Bahrainis turned out in my garden on a Friday morning'.[39] On his return, Parsons himself wrote:

> I came away with the firm impression that Anglo–Bahraini relations have never been better. The Bahrainis are determined to maintain an intimate and uninhibited dialogue with us on all subjects and still look to us for help and advice before all others. Even the Emir is reconciled to the removal of our protection and the withdrawal of our forces and I was struck by the growing confidence and maturity of the leading members of the regime, including the Emir himself.[40]

The Permanent Under-Secretary of State, Sir Denis Greenhill, enthused: 'This is encouraging, if it is to be lasting'.[41] In a major report on the outlook for the Gulf up to 1978 generated in May 1973, the Joint Intelligence Committee (JIC) noted that Bahrain's long association with the United Kingdom had been one of 'trust and friendship' and that the large British expatriate community had become 'integrated'.[42] The JIC concluded that 'the traditionally strong commercial ties have survived independence, challenged only by the competitiveness of other trading nations, notably Japan'.[43] In order to maintain the momentum for close post-imperial Anglo–Bahraini relations, a series of meetings between British ministers and members of the Al Khalifah ruling family were arranged.

Taking advantage of the Amir of Bahrain, Sheikh Isa's, visit to London for medical treatment in May, the Minister of State at the FCO, Lord Balniel, called on him at the Dorchester Hotel on the 30th. In its brief for the encounter, the FCO stressed that 'We wish to assure Sheikh Isa of HMG's continuing interest in the affairs of Bahrain and the Gulf region in general. We wish to see Bahrain, as one of the centres of commerce and communications in the Gulf, maintain her stability and independence'.[44] The FCO also prevailed on No. 10 Downing Street to arrange a Prime Ministerial lunch for Isa, the Head of the Middle East Department, P. R. H. Wright, justifying this request with the observation that 'Although Bahrain is not a leading actor on the world stage, the Bahrainis value their relationship with us highly, and Britain and the British continue to play an important part in the life of Bahrain'.[45] A lunch with Edward Heath was duly organized for Sheikh Isa on 4 June, the FCO brief for the occasion emphasizing that 'Bahrain's stability and independence are important elements in the political and commercial development of the Gulf region. We shall endeavour to deepen the close and friendly relationship between Britain and Bahrain which is characterised by the complete absence of problems, political or otherwise'.[46] Shortly after Isa's departure, Heath wrote to the Amir telling him: 'I greatly value Britain's relations with Bahrain and sincerely believe that your visit has done much to strengthen the links between our countries'.[47]

A further opportunity to cement Britain's relations with Bahrain in the aftermath of formal British withdrawal was provided by the visit of the Bahraini Crown Prince and Minister of Defence, Sheikh Hamad bin Isa. In its brief for Lord Balniel's meeting with Hamad at the end of July, the FCO underlined that

'Although our special treaty relationship with Bahrain has ended, we are willing to help Bahrain in any fields we can, including the development of her defensive capacity'.[48] At the beginning of October, moreover, Balniel met Sheikh Khalifah bin Salman, the Bahraini Prime Minister, during the latter's visit to London. Responding to Balniel's query about the state of Anglo–Bahraini relations, Khalifah noted that they were 'better now than when British troops had been in Bahrain' and that a 'better basis for dealing with Britain had now been established'.[49] He also counselled that Britain 'must not dessert the Gulf area' and 'must try to support her friends there'.[50] The Amir of Qatar expressed similar views during his visit to London in September 1973.

When the possibility of a trip to Britain was first mooted in April, the British Ambassador in Qatar, Edward Henderson, recommended that Heath see Sheikh Khalifah, arguing that the effect of failure to organize this would be 'disastrous'.[51] Supporting his case, Henderson noted: 'I do not think . . . that there will be much movement on major equipment matters until Khalifah has visited England, and in this context a call on the Prime Minister may be worth millions of pounds'.[52] In its approach to 10 Downing Street over a possible meeting between Khalifah and Heath, the FCO pointed out that 'We enjoy at present the lion's share of Qatar's commercial market (about 30%) and want to keep it thus. The Amir retains personal responsibility for many of the major decisions affecting commercial contract'.[53] Although Heath readily agreed to a meeting, Henderson subsequently reported that Khalifah would not visit Britain without a formal invitation. The Ambassador made a hard-headed case for the issuing of such an invitation, pointing out that Khalifah was coming under 'strong French pressure' to purchase military hardware and participate in industrial projects in Qatar.[54] 'Opportunities for British concerns to take the lead in this field', he concluded, 'will be lost if he were to visit France without a compensating visit to Britain. The field is at the moment open and large prizes are to be won'.[55] Henderson's arguments proved persuasive and he was authorized to issue an open invitation to the Amir.[56] Khalifah's visit was eventually confirmed for September, Heath not only hosting talks with the Qatari Amir, but also offering him lunch.

During the initial talks held on 18 September, Khalifah spontaneously described British relations with Qatar as 'very good' and that cooperation between the two countries was 'very satisfactory'.[57] In keeping with the views of Bahraini Prime Minister Sheikh Khalifah bin Salman, the Amir of Qatar firmly stated that 'As Britain was a friend of the Gulf States, and the rulers paid attention to the advice given by the British Government, he felt that the British had an obligation to promote the prosperity of the people in the region, and to improve their cooperation and political stability'.[58] In particular, Khalifah expressed concern about the ongoing insurgency in Oman which prompted Heath to remark that 'Sultan Qaboos was doing a good job and we would continue to support him'.[59] During discussions with Foreign Secretary Sir Alec Douglas-Home the following day, Khalifah again returned to the situation in the Sultanate. He observed that 'Oman was not only defending herself but also defending the whole Gulf against infiltration', sentiments with which Douglas-Home 'agreed strongly'.[60] Despite the apparent unity of purpose, some fault lines in post-imperial Anglo–Qatari relations started to be revealed.

In a paper on the oil industry in Qatar produced by the Department of Trade and Industry towards the beginning of 1973, the DTI commented that 'HMG's relations with Qatar are very cordial and the Amir appears genuinely to want to strengthen his links with Britain, especially in the commercial field'.[61] The scale of Britain's continuing involvement in Qatar was demonstrated at Sheikh Khalifah's accession day parade on 22 February 1973. When Ambassador Henderson congratulated him on the event, the Amir whispered: 'It was all thanks to British training'.[62] In its report on the outlook for the Gulf up to 1978, the JIC made the point that Qatar's 'internal affairs depend very largely upon the advice and help of the United Kingdom, a dependence which the new Amir has been happy to see increase'.[63] With reference to Qatar, the JIC proceeded to note that 'It is paradoxical that the Gulf State in which our past presence made perhaps the least local impact seems likely to be the scene of our greatest future involvement'.[64]

In a wide-ranging survey of Anglo–Qatari relations produced in June 1973, Henderson underlined that the government in Doha had been 'markedly sympathetic towards Britain in many fields' and that the Amir had shown himself 'ready to turn to us for help in most aspects of Qatar's development'.[65] Nevertheless, Henderson pointed out that

> The most prominent characteristic of our relationship with Shaikh Khalifah over much of the last ten years has been that when we have made a proposal which appealed to him, or whenever we have agreed to help him with one of his own schemes, the result has invariably been successful; but when we have nothing to offer he turns to someone else and our stock declines.[66]

The Ambassador also admitted that he feared a 'descent' from the peak in relations with Khalifah which had been reached by the beginning of 1973. The principal reason for this was that 'Although the Amir himself seems as well-disposed as ever in the echelons below him there are experts and advisers who do not share his sympathies'. 'As a result', lamented Henderson, 'he does seem at times to be a little less able than before to take action on our side when the inevitable Egyptian expert in a key position in a Ministry deftly swings a contract away from us, on specious grounds, towards one of our competitors'.[67] The Ambassador concluded that 'like Alice we need to run in order to keep in the same place in Qatar'.[68]

Commenting on Henderson's portrayal of Anglo–Qatari relations, J. R. Young of the FCO's Middle East Department bemoaned that 'A "good deed" keeps our stock at roughly the same (high) level but one misdeed puts us in the doghouse.... Is this really a proper basis for a mature bilateral relationship?'[69] Young also pointed out that 'we cannot regard Qatar as a "chasse gardée" any longer and while many firms have adapted to the new situation, we must expect that some will sink now that the flood gates have been opened'.[70] In his formal response to

The oil revolution, 1973 57

Henderson's despatch, the Head of the Middle East Department, P. R. H. Wright, mused:

> We have all been at times victims of Qatari sensitivities. I agree with you that we have had to run in order to keep in the same place. Our relationship with Qatar sometimes reminds me of a game of snakes and ladders in which the ladders are horizontal and the snakes all too numerous. It is unfortunate that the Amir should take our response to each individual request as an earnest of our relationship as a whole.[71]

In his approach to oil matters, Sheikh Khalifah was ostensibly moderate. Of the two 'British' oil companies operating in Qatar, Shell and British Petroleum, the former was the more important being the sole foreign investor in Qatar Shell and, in keeping with BP, holding a 23.75 per cent stake in the Qatar Petroleum Company.[72] In April 1972, the Qatar government established a national oil company, the Qatar National Petroleum Company (QNPC). Following in the wake of other producers, Qatar began the process of participating in the producing companies' concessions, the QNPC obtaining a 25 per cent share on 1 January 1973.[73] In the course of discussions with Henderson in April 1973, nevertheless, Khalifah emphasized the 'need for the Arab oil producing countries to keep things in perspective and not press the companies too hard'.[74] Henderson also opined that the Amir did 'not intend anything nasty for the oil companies'.[75] In the wake of news that Kuwait intended to achieve 51 per cent participation in the oil companies operating there, Khalifah informed the Ambassador that 'he himself would be at the very end of the queue for this as he did not want any change'.[76] Nevertheless, he did admit that 'he could not do less than a good Arab must and he might be forced to negotiate a similar agreement if the Saudis did so'.[77]

A similar duality in the Amir's approach to oil matters can be detected with respect to the use of the 'oil weapon'. In response to a question from a *Daily Express* reporter regarding Khalifah's attitude towards the view of more extreme Arab countries that oil was a legitimate weapon to use in the fight against Israel, the Amir replied to the effect that 'oil was trade and he did not wish to mix this with politics'.[78] Nonetheless, Khalifah confessed that if the Arab League or OPEC insisted on all members taking a particular stance, 'of course he would go along with it', adding 'He would never go against the wishes of Arab countries as a whole'.[79] The FCO's brief for Edward Heath's lunch with Sheikh Khalifah on 18 September, moreover, warned that 'if Saudi Arabia decided to cut back production or boycott certain oil-producing [sic] countries, Qatar would be under strong pressure to follow suit'.[80] During Anglo–American talks on the Middle East later in the month, Brooks Wrampelmeir of the State Department's Office of Arabian Affairs ominously referred to Saudi Arabia's 'growing oil revenues and increasing realization of the power of the oil weapon'.[81] The JIC had already recorded that 'Growing oil revenues may tempt some producer countries to use the interruption of oil supplies as a political weapon'.[82]

58 *The oil revolution, 1973*

The level of concern in London (and Washington) over oil matters is a controversial issue. In the opinion of Tore Petersen, 'oil does not seem to have been a major Anglo–American interest in the Nixon administration and the Heath government'.[83] As regards the former, he contends that 'oil was clearly a subsidiary concern, a means to achieve other and evidently more important policy ends'.[84] Certainly, the US Secretary of State, William Rogers, took a robust line in discussions with FCO Under-Secretary of State, A. D. Parsons, in June 1973. He dismissed talk of the Arabs using their oil as a political weapon as 'nonsense as far as the US was concerned', adding that he had 'left the Arabs in no doubt that the US would be perfectly prepared to apply the necessary conservation measures or develop alternative methods or both if the Arabs showed unwillingness to sell them their oil at bearable prices'.[85] While the Nixon administration might have been bullish about Arab use of the oil weapon, the Heath government, and in contrast with Petersen's interpretation, was seriously concerned and did not share Washington's views on the 'unimportance of oil'.[86]

As early as December 1970, Heath impressed upon US Vice-President Spiro Agnew that 'the British are keenly concerned with the situation in the Persian Gulf, because of oil interests there which are vital both to the UK and the US'.[87] In March 1973, Deputy Head of the FCO's Energy Department, Nicholas Fenn, observed: 'We need the oil more than the producers need to sell it'.[88] In a wide-ranging despatch on the Middle East written a month later, Britain's Ambassador in Washington, Lord Cromer, gloomily predicted that 'if full-scale war were to break out again between the Arabs and Israelis as in 1967, the Saudi Arabians and the Gulf States generally . . . would no doubt as in 1967 have to follow the dictates of emotional Arab nationalism rather than economic self-interest'.[89] Having remarked upon the 'near monopoly position' of Middle Eastern oil producers, Permanent Under-Secretary of State at the FCO Sir Denis Greenhill went on to state that their 'vast wealth' meant they would be able to 'restrict additional production or even to interrupt supplies – steps for which they might have either commercial or political motives'.[90] In mid-June 1973, Edward Heath presciently warned President Nixon of an impending energy crisis. 'We in the West', elaborated the British Premier, 'are all becoming increasingly dependent on Arab oil as well as increasingly exposed to the problems resulting from the movements of vast oil revenues. All the signs are that this situation is going to get worse, not better, and that unless we can do something about the Arab/Israel problem our whole industrial power and progress many be threatened'.[91] Heath's fears were soon confirmed.

On 6 October 1973, Egyptian and Syrian forces launched surprise attacks on their Israeli foes, enjoying considerable initial success. As early as August, King Feisal of Saudi Arabia, in response to a request from Egyptian President Anwar Sadat, agreed to use the oil weapon if Egypt went to war with Israel.[92] Shortly after the Egyptian offensive began, Feisal reiterated his pledge.[93] On 17 October, a conference of Arab oil ministers meeting in Kuwait agreed to cut production by a recurrent monthly rate of 5 per cent from September levels 'until such time as total evacuation of Israeli forces from all Arab territory occupied during the

June 1967 war is completed, and the legitimate rights of the Palestinian people are restored'.[94] This blow to Western economies came on top a 70 per cent rise in posted oil prices agreed by OPEC a day earlier.[95] The Arab oil ministers, nevertheless, declared that 'the countries that support the Arabs actively and effectively or that take important measures against Israel to compel its withdrawal shall not be prejudiced by this production cut and shall continue to receive the same oil supplies that they used to receive prior to the reduction'.[96] Those countries deemed to be hostile to the Arab cause, such as the US which provided Israel with much-needed financial and military assistance during the October war, were embargoed altogether. On a wider level, Francesco Petrini argues that the increase in oil prices in the autumn of 1973 'was the outcome of a long-standing duel between the oil-exporting countries and the oil companies, whose ultimate stake was the control of the international oil market'.[97]

Even before the wielding of the oil weapon, Anthony Parsons, responding to a request for an appreciation of British objectives in the Middle East crisis, urged that 'We must . . . avoid saying or doing things which are unlikely to produce results and which will only serve to alienate the Arabs, thus increasing the risk to our oil supplies'.[98] Although the exploitation of North Sea oil raised the prospect of reducing British dependence on Arab oil, it was estimated at the beginning of 1973 that it would take until 1980 before half of Britain's requirements could be met from this source.[99] At the time of the 1973 Arab–Israeli conflict, Cabinet Secretary Sir John Hunt recorded that between 65 and 70 per cent of Britain's oil supplies came from Arab sources. 'This suggests', he averred, 'that for the time being we should avoid action which might produce undue concern, and hence increased demand, at home or which would provoke the Arabs to turn off the tap'.[100] An FCO telegram to British missions in the Arab world stressed: 'The Prime Minister has warned that nothing should be done or said that might imperil our oil supplies'.[101]

In a message to President Nixon on 15 October, Edward Heath confessed that he was 'seriously concerned about the grave situation which we are all facing over oil supplies and prices'.[102] He went so far as to suggest that these developments served to 'threaten the stability of the world economic system', estimating that OPEC demands on price alone would result in an immediate drain on the resources of European Economic Community (EEC) countries to the tune of $10 billion a year.[103] *The Times* Political Editor, David Wood, remarked upon 'the personal determination of the Prime Minister that the British economy should not be placed at risk by antagonizing Arab suppliers', adding that the 'preservation of Britain's oil supplies appears to have become a crucial feature of the Government's diplomacy'.[104] However, the legacies of empire, and more specifically Britain's attempts to cultivate its former imperial charges in the Gulf following formal withdrawal in 1971, did little to protect Britain from the dual challenges of rises in oil prices coupled with threats to supply.

From his vantage point in Doha, Ambassador Henderson observed: 'I think that as in the past Qatar will tend to follow the example of Saudi Arabia and they will also be more afraid of appearing out of line with the Arabs than of upsetting their friends'.[105] Sheikh Khalifah himself told Henderson that, while he was being as 'gentle as possible', he could 'not step too far out of line'.[106] While Khalifah deprecated the use of the oil weapon in private, Henderson pointed out that 'the Qatar government is not going to say anything on the record which is far out of line with Arab thinking'.[107] Kuwait proved particularly incorrigible so far as the British were concerned.

The issue of Palestine had impinged on Kuwait's political life as early as October 1936 when a public meeting was called in the Sheikhdom to draw attention to, and raise funds for, the strike of Palestinians protesting against increasing Jewish immigration.[108] The following year a group calling itself *Shabab al Kuwait* (the Youth of Kuwait) was established which sent telegrams to the League of Nations, the House of Commons, and to the Secretary of State for Colonies challenging the Peel Commission's proposed partition of Palestine.[109] Rosemarie Said Zahlan points out that 'The ties that bound them to an Arab cause proved stronger to the people of the Gulf than those that restricted them by virtue of their treaty relationship with Britain'.[110] The immediacy of the fate of Palestine was heightened by the growing Palestinian population in the Gulf. In the aftermath of the 1967 Arab–Israeli conflict, for instance, some 400,000 Palestinians resided in Kuwait alone.[111] The potential for Palestine to encroach upon Anglo–Kuwaiti relations was reflected by the British Ambassador to Kuwait, Geoffrey Arthur. In August 1967, he confessed that Kuwait had always been sensitive to events in Palestine and that this sensitivity had 'grown with her increasing involvement in the Arab world'.[112] He lugubriously added that 'In every crisis in Palestine we lose something here, and this time we have lost a lot'.[113]

As conflict loomed once more, early indications of Kuwait's approach were provided on 9 January 1972 when the Minister of State for Cabinet Affairs told a press conference that 'Kuwait was ready to go back to the tent life we lived before oil' and cease completely the production and export of oil 'if the Arab oil producing countries agreed unanimously on using oil as a weapon in the liberation struggle'.[114] A few months later, the Under-Secretary in the Kuwaiti Ministry of Foreign Affairs explained that Kuwait had 'for long been applying the principle of using oil as a weapon in the Arab battle against Israel'.[115] The Amir of Kuwait himself declared that his state's support for the Palestinians was 'unlimited' and that oil would be used as a weapon in the struggle for their rights.[116]

Kuwait's preparedness to use oil as a political weapon was borne out at the time of the 1973 Arab–Israeli conflict. On 24 October, Britain's Ambassador to Kuwait, A. J. Wilton, reported that

> We have . . . had, over the past few days, a classical display of Kuwaiti technique in such a situation. When bearded about the intention to use the rest of the world as a whipping-boy for the United States the Prime Minister [Sheikh Jabir Al-Ahmad] made reassuring noises but entered into no commitment.[117]

Referring to the Kuwaiti Cabinet's decision three days earlier to increase the cut in oil production to 10 per cent in response to President Nixon's announcement of a $2 billion credit for Israel, Wilton ironically remarked: 'So much for the Prime Minister's assurance that Kuwait had no wish to hurt her friends'.[118] Wilton concluded that

> it is clear enough that it [the oil weapon] will continue to be brandished at us at every stage of the peace negotiations to enforce the sort of settlement the Arabs want. And the greatly increased income all the producing states voted themselves on 16 October vastly extends their ability to keep up the squeeze.[119]

In a subsequent assessment, Wilton warned that 'we may expect all the Arabs to be watching our actions like hawks and to be ready to use any supposed straying from the path of purity as a reason for not being able to continue to give us preferential treatment in the face of criticism by their brethren'.[120] Wilton added that 'Kuwait have given no directives to the [oil] companies about "preferred" destinations and appear in no hurry to do so. They have indicated that they fully recognise that even preferred customers will go short this winter'.[121]

The Head of the FCO's Middle East Department, P. R. H. Wright, described Kuwait's attitude towards Britain over oil supplies as 'unhelpful' and treatment of so-called 'friendly' countries as 'ambivalent'.[122] Summing up, he underlined that 'Kuwait has not in practice shown any disposition to treat Britain favourably over oil supplies'.[123] This was all the more alarming given that Britain relied on Kuwait for nearly 20 per cent of its crude oil imports.[124] Douglas-Home admitted to being 'disturbed by the unhelpful attitude which Kuwait is currently displaying towards Britain over oil supplies'.[125] He proceeded to tell Wilton that 'I have been surprised to note that, although the Kuwaiti Prime Minister told you on 17 October that it was not the wish or intention of the Kuwait government to hurt their friends, the situation has in practice proved very different'.[126] When Wilton tackled the Kuwaiti Foreign Minister, Sheikh Sabah al-Ahmad, the latter claimed that 'the measures were not aimed at their friends as only a partial cut had been imposed except on the US and Holland'.[127] Wilton retorted that 'a partial cut on a large proportion of one's imports was a more severe measure than a total cut on a small proportion'.[128] Moreover, he bluntly told Sheikh Sabah that 'Kuwait was not in fact doing anything for her friends'.[129] Within the confines of Whitehall, the Head of the FCO's Energy Department, S. L. Egerton, expostulated: 'Ever since the OAPEC meeting in Kuwait on 17 October, the Kuwaitis have been noticeably unhelpful in their attitude to supplies for the UK. They have not even placed us yet in the "friendly" category of states'.[130]

Edward Heath himself wrote to the Amir of Kuwait, Sheikh Sabah Salim, emphasizing that his government had 'tried consistently to work towards a just settlement' of the Arab–Israeli conflict.[131] He also stressed that the effectiveness of the European Community in fostering peace in the region would be 'diminished if our economies continue to be weakened by the present cutbacks in oil supplies'.[132] In response, the Amir of Kuwait stated that 'despite his own personal feelings and Kuwait's long and valued relationship with us it was difficult for Kuwait to stand out against decisions taken by Arab countries generally'.[133] Ambassador Wilton subsequently pointed out that Kuwait engaged in an 'arbitrary system of cuts which reflected the consuming country's pattern of oil imports rather than its political attitudes'.[134] Indeed, despite ostensibly enjoying a 'favoured' status among Arab oil producers, Britain did not secure all the oil it needed. A US National Intelligence Estimate concluded that at best Britain would forfeit growth and at worst would suffer a drop in GNP and employment.[135] Britain's difficulties over supply were intensified by pressure from its EC partners to share oil.[136] In addition, the precipitous rise in oil prices exacerbated Britain's acute inflation and balance of payments problems.[137] Britain's heavy reliance on Arab oil not only shaped its approach to the 1973 crisis, but also exposed marked differences with American policy-makers.

Shortly after the renewal of armed conflict in the Middle East, A. D. Parsons noted: 'We are of course taking care not to identify ourselves in any way with the Israeli war effort, or with apparently pro-Israeli American policies or actions and to express as much sympathy as possible with the Arab side in our public statements'.[138] US Secretary of State Henry Kissinger's request for a Security Council resolution calling for a cease-fire and a return to the cease-fire line was consequently rejected by the British, Cromer informing the US Secretary of State that 'we do not want a resolution which called for the Arabs to withdraw from territory which was their own'.[139] Kissinger responded by declaring that the Americans would 'would pour in supplies to Israel and see what the battle brought'.[140] Britain, by contrast, made it clear that it would in no way be involved in US operations to resupply the embattled Israelis[141] and observed a strict arms embargo on Israel and 'frontline' Arab states (Egypt, Syria, Jordan, Iraq, and Libya). The embargo, nonetheless, was not applied to all Arab states. Accounting for this apparent anomaly, the Minister of State at the FCO, Lord Balniel, emphasized that it was done 'for reasons of Gulf security, to protect our major arms sales interests in Saudi Arabia, Kuwait and the Gulf, and above all to protect our oil interests'.[142]

The American efforts to resupply the Israelis took place against the background of 'fierce opposition from the British and Japanese, both largely dependent on Middle East oil'.[143] Equally, the approach of Britain (and its European partners) to the renewal of the Arab–Israeli conflict exasperated policy-makers in Washington. The US Under-Secretary of State for Economic Affairs, William J. Casey, observed that 'The disarray of the Europeans and the general scramble to appease the Arabs and take care of themselves has made the oil weapon successful more than anything else'.[144] The US Secretary of State for Defence, James R. Schlesinger, went so far as to tell his UK counterpart, Lord Carrington, 'the [Anglo–American] special relationship was being placed under a severe strain by recent events and we could not count on its being maintained'.[145] At the end of 1973, Kissinger himself stated that the special relationship was 'collapsing'.[146] He also lamented that Britain's entry into Europe 'should have raised Europe to the level of Britain. Instead it had reduced Britain to the level of Europe'.[147] Earlier in the crisis, the US Secretary of State informed Cromer that 'As far as the President was concerned, he could not recall any crisis in the last three years when the British had been with the Americans when the chips were down'.[148]

During discussions with Cromer in mid-November 1973, Schlesinger referred to Europe's 'overt acquiescence in Arab bullying' which, he believed, would merely 'increase the strength of the Arabs' whip-hand'.[149] At the beginning of 1974, the British Ambassador recalled that 'Tendentious phrases like "giving in to blackmail" became all too common here and retain some currency even now'.[150] Cromer proceeded to remark:

> The fact that Dr Kissinger found it necessary to swallow his pride and embark on his mediation efforts without first having secured a relaxation of the oil embargo, does not apparently strike him as inconsistent with his own strictures that the Europeans should stand firm with the United States and not dance to the Arab tune, regardless of the consequences.[151]

Cromer also recorded that the Americans were

> unable to comprehend that the Europeans, with their overwhelming dependence on Arab oil, saw their interests in the Middle East rather differently ... the US interpreted European policies towards the Arabs, which in most cases stemmed from careful diplomacy, as sudden capitulation to Arab blackmail; and saw themselves alone in the Western world as holding high the star-spangled banner of freedom against the Arab hordes bearing armour embossed with hammer and sickle.[152]

Cromer went so far as record that the war 'laid bare differences of perception and attitude towards the Middle East situation and to the Alliance itself which resulted in deeper cleavages within it than any since 1956'.[153] The lack of consultation prior to the US decision on 25 October to place American bases on nuclear alert, in response to general secretary of the Soviet Communist Party Leonid Brezhnev's threat unilaterally to send Soviet forces to Egypt, had rankled especially with the British.[154] 'We have to face the fact that the American action has done immense harm', expostulated Edward Heath. 'An American President in the Watergate position apparently prepared to go to such lengths at a moment's notice without consultation with his allies ... without any justification in the military situation at the time'.[155]

From his vantage point in London, US Ambassador to Britain, Walter Annenberg, noted that the 1973 Middle East crisis had produced strains in the Anglo–American relationship which had been 'as evident as they had been deplorable'.[156] He also reported that 'the British have reacted with acute sensitivity to US criticism of their attitude and performance: they considered our rebukes unjustifiably harsh and lacking in recognition of the difficult position in which Britain found itself, especially with respect to Arab oil on which the country's industrial life depends'.[157] During a meeting at the FCO towards the beginning of 1974 with a

64 *The oil revolution, 1973*

US delegation led by Counselor for the State Department Helmut Sonnenfeldt, Deputy Under-Secretary of State J. O. Wright sought to explain the contrasting approach which Europe had taken to the recent crisis in the Middle East:

> Europe was much closer to the Middle East; it was also far more dependent on oil than the US. Europe was about 75% dependent on Middle East oil (80% in the case of some individual European countries), whereas the US was only 10–15% dependent, and approaching a state of self-sufficiency. The US could therefore afford to take a more detached view of Middle East affairs. In the Yom Kippur war, when the Arabs deployed the oil weapon, Europe was at much greater risk than the US.[158]

In contrast with Tore Petersen's claim that London shared Washington's views on the 'unimportance of oil', British policy-makers were acutely concerned to preserve and protect oil supplies from Arab producers and sought to shape policies on the Arab–Israeli conflict to facilitate these objectives. In so doing they clashed with their counterparts in Washington to a degree which also calls into question Petersen's contention that Anglo–American polices in the region were 'closely aligned and mutually supportive'. The fact that Britain enjoyed limited success in influencing the oil policies of its former imperial charges among the Gulf States casts doubt on its ability to exercise effective influence following formal withdrawal. While the threat of radical pan-Arabism had been reduced by the defeat of its most charismatic advocate, Gamal Abdel Nasser, in the 1967 Six-Day War,[159] the Gulf States could not ignore the blandishments of the Arab world, especially on the emotive issue of the ongoing Arab–Israeli conflict. Indeed, oil producers such as Kuwait and Qatar were reluctant to adopt policies which were out of line with the rest of the Arab world and with respect to the use of the oil weapon were prepared to offer Britain relatively little in the way of mitigation.

The wielding of the oil weapon also sheds light on Shohei Sato's somewhat contradictory interpretation. On the one hand, he argues that the events of 1973 demonstrated that the Gulf States were 'no longer mere clients of the former imperial metropole but had become capable and independent players in international affairs'.[160] On the other hand, he contends that the process of decolonization in the Gulf 'entailed only a rearrangement of the collaborative relationship that had developed during the period of Britain's informal empire'.[161] As regards the first part of his argument, the Gulf States' acquiescence in the use of the oil weapon reflected the growing regional influences on them, not least those emanating from the Arab world, rather than their emergence as 'capable and independent players' on the international scene. Equally, Britain's limited influence on its former imperial charges in the wake of the 1973 Arab–Israeli conflict demonstrates that the shift from dependence to independence in the Gulf involved far more than a mere 'rearrangement of the collaborative relationship' stemming from imperial times. Indeed, it was much more profound and far-reaching, reflecting the end of Britain's exclusive role in the region and its ability to shape the policies of the Gulf States. Referring to the new dynamic after 1973, Rory Miller appositely notes: 'What was not in doubt was that since the oil crisis the Arab Gulf States had established themselves as regional political powers and global economic powers of the first rank'.[162]

Britain also found its commercial position undermined by the encroachment of other Western industrial nations into the Gulf. As Edward Henderson reported from Doha: 'I am very anxious about the French influence here which is increasing and I fear will increase a great deal more at our expense. The Amir's eyes almost sparkle when he mentions them nowadays'.[163] In his annual report for 1973, moreover, Britain's Ambassador to the United Arab Emirates, D. J. McCarthy, underscored that 'There is growing competition, especially in Abu Dhabi, from other nations, considerable investment interest from Japan, and increasing efforts by the Arabs on the one hand and Japan, Pakistan and France on the other towards joint projects, either in the UAE or employing Abu Dhabi money outside it'.[164] McCarthy proceeded to lament that 'Our prices are now right, the product is often right, and the habit of buying British is still a factor: but we get worse rather than better on slow delivery promises and even slower performance'.[165] As regards Britain's military relationship with the UAE, the Ambassador remarked that it 'remained friendly and at a working level close, but the benefits of this were being eroded politically by the Pakistanis and others and commercially by the French'.[166] He concluded with the observation that 'I can hardly claim . . . that British involvement in the Emirates is scarcely less apparent than in pre-independence days or that Zaid still looks to us for advice'.[167] McCarthy's ruminations also cast doubt on William Roger Louis' claim with respect to the UAE that the new union remained 'informally within the British imperial system'.[168] The extent to which Britain was able to reverse some of the trends identified by McCarthy and Henderson, or at least hold its position in the Gulf, will be examined in the next chapter.

Notes

1. Wm. Roger Louis and Ronald Robinson, 'The imperialism of decolonization', *Journal of Imperial and Commonwealth History*, 22, 3 (1994), p. 494.
2. P. J. Cain and A. G. Hopkins, *British Imperialism, 1688–2015*, third edition (London and New York: Routledge, 2016), p. 717.
3. Tore T. Petersen, *Richard Nixon, Great Britain and the Anglo–American Alignment in the Persian Gulf and Arabian Peninsula: Making Allies out of Clients* (Brighton and Portland: Sussex Academic Press, 2006), p. 28.
4. Ibid., p. 60. See also Tore T. Petersen, 'Richard Nixon, Great Britain, and the Anglo–American strategy of turning the Persian Gulf into an allied lake', in Jeffrey R. Macris and Saul Kelly (eds.), *Imperial Crossroads: The Great Powers and the Persian Gulf* (Annapolis: Naval Institute Press, 2012), p. 78.
5. Petersen, *Richard Nixon, Great Britain and the Anglo–American Alignment in the Persian Gulf and Arabian Peninsula*, p. 133.
6. For an examination of the 'tilt' towards Iran during the Nixon presidency, see Roham Alvandi, 'Nixon, Kissinger, and the Shah: The origins of Iranian primacy in the Persian Gulf', *Diplomatic History*, 36, 2 (2012), pp. 337–72.
7. Review of Persian Gulf Policy by Health Government: Memorandum of Conversation, 2 July 1970, RG 59, Subject-Numeric Files1970–73, Box 2656, POL UK-US.

66 *The oil revolution, 1973*

8. Tore Petersen, 'Anglo–American relations over Aden and the United Arab Emirates, 1967–71', *Middle Eastern Studies*, 53, 1 (2017), p. 105.
9. 'Persian Gulf': Memorandum for the President from William P. Rogers, 16 December 1971, RG 59, Subject-Numeric Files 1970–73, Box 1774, DEF 1 Near East.
10. Assistant to the President for National Security Affairs, 1969–1975; US Secretary of State, September 1973 to January 1977.
11. 'US military supply policy for the Lower Gulf States and Oman', National Security Decision Memorandum 186 from Kissinger to the Secretary of State, the Secretary of Defense, and the Chairman of the NSC Under Secretaries Committee, 18 August 1972, RG 273, Records of the National Security Council: National Security Decision Memorandum, Box 1.
12. 'Oman', Note by the Secretary of State for Defence, 2 April 1973, CAB 148/130, DOP (73)26.
13. Shohei Sato, *Britain and the Formation of the Gulf States: Embers of Empire* (Manchester: Manchester University Press, 2016), pp. 87–8. The hearing took place on 2 February 1972. Noyes later wrote that 'post-Vietnam American public feelings alone virtually ruled out a direct U.S. military role in which our forces would replace the British' (F. Gregory Gause, 'British and American policies in the Persian Gulf, 1968–1973', *Review of International Studies*, 11, 4 (1985), p. 260).
14. Record of the Anglo–US talks on the Middle East held at the State Department, 28 September 1973, FCO 8/1950.
15. 'The US and Oman', Minute by P. R. H. Wright, 1 July 1973, FCO 8/2010.
16. Memorandum for the Secretary of State from Nixon, Presidential Determination No. 71–6, 17 January 1971, RG 59, Subject-Numeric Files 1970–73, Box 1762, DEF 12–5 KUW.
17. Telegram from Walsh to the Secretary of State, No. 1293, 17 November 1971, RG 59, Subject-Numeric Files 1970–73, Box 2432, POL 23 KUW.
18. Ibid.
19. Ibid.
20. Letter from Wilton to the Secretary of State for Foreign and Commonwealth Affairs, 8 January 1973, FCO 8/1987.
21. J. B. Kelly, *Arabia, the Gulf and the West* (New York: Basic Books, 1991; first published 1980), p. 283.
22. 'Kuwait/Iraq border incident', Minute by R. M. Hunt, 20 March 1973, FCO 8/1991; Cabinet Conclusions, 22 March 1973, CAB 128/ 51, CM(73) 18th conclusions.
23. 'Arms for Kuwait', Minute by Wright, 30 March 1973, FCO 8/2000.
24. Letter from Balniel to Ian Gilmour, 4 April 1973, FCO 8/2000.
25. Ibid.
26. Ibid.
27. Ibid.
28. Letter from Gilmour to Balniel, 9 April 1973, FCO 8/2000.
29. 'Arms for Kuwait', Minute by Hunt, 11 April 1973, FCO 8/2000.
30. Ibid.
31. Minute by Parsons, 11 April 1973, FCO 8/2000.
32. 'Chieftain tanks for Kuwait', Minute by Hunt, 25 April1973, FCO 8/2001.
33. Minute by Parsons, 25 April 1973, FCO 8/2001.
34. 'Tanks for Kuwait', Minute by Wright, 28 June 1973, FCO 8/2001.
35. Telegram from the Foreign and Commonwealth Office to Kuwait, No. 351, 21 November 1973, FCO 8/2002.
36. 'Arms for Kuwait', Minute by Wright, 21 November 1973, FCO 8/2002.
37. 'Replacement ammunition for Kuwait', Minute by Wright, 21 November 1973, FCO 8/2002.
38. Minute by Parsons, 22 November 1973, FCO 8/2002.
39. Letter from Tesh to Douglas-Home, 30 December 1973, FCO 8/2181.
40. 'Bahrain', Minute by Parsons, 15 January 1973, FCO 8/1979.

41 Minute by Greenhill, 15 January 1973, FCO 8/1979.
42 'The outlook for the Persian Gulf up to 1978', Report by the Joint Intelligence Committee, 11 May 1973, CAB 186/15, JIC (A) (73) 10.
43 Ibid.
44 'Brief for Lord Balniel's call on Shaikh Isa bin Sulman al Khalifah, Amir of Bahrain, on Wednesday, 30 May', attached to Wright's minute 24, May 1973, FCO 8/1981.
45 'Visit of the Amir of Bahrain', Minute by Wright, 9 May 1973, FCO 8/1981.
46 'Brief for the Prime Minister's lunch for HH Shaikh Isa bin Sulman al Khalifah, Amir of Bahrain, on Monday, 4 June 1973', attached to A. A. Acland's letter to Lord Bridges, 1 June 1973, FCO 8/ 1981.
47 Letter from Heath to His Highness Sheikh Isa, 27 June 1973, FCO 8/1981.
48 'Brief for the Minister of State's meeting with His Excellency Shaikh Hamad bin Isa al Khalifah, Crown Prince and Minister of Defence and Commander of the Bahrain Defence Force, at 12.15pm on Monday, 30 July', attached to Wright's minute, 27 July 1973, FCO 8/1980.
49 Record of a call by the Minister of State on Sheikh Khalifah bin Sulman, Prime Minister of Bahrain, at 51 Hyde Park Gate at 11am on Tuesday, 2 October 1973, FCO 8/1976.
50 Ibid.
51 Letter from Henderson to Wright, 17 April 1973, FCO 8/2088.
52 Ibid.
53 Letter from P. H. Grattan to Bridges, 4 May 1973, FCO 8/2088.
54 Telegram from Henderson to the Foreign and Commonwealth Office, No. 237, 8 July 1973, FCO 8/2088.
55 Ibid.
56 Telegram from the Foreign and Commonwealth Office to Doha, No. 156, 10 July 1973, FCO 8/2088.
57 Record of a conversation between the Prime Minister and Sheikh Khalifah of Qatar at 12.30 on Tuesday 18 September 1973, FCO 8/2088.
58 Ibid.
59 Ibid.
60 Record of a meeting between the Foreign and Commonwealth Secretary and the Amir of Qatar at the Hilton Hotel at 4pm on 19 September 1973, FCO 8/2088.
61 'The oil industry in Qatar', Paper by the Petroleum Division of the DTI, attached to letter from A. D. Harris to R. D. Gordon (Doha), 15 February 1973, FCO 8/2086.
62 Letter from Henderson to the Secretary of State for Foreign and Commonwealth Affairs, 6 March 1973, FCO 8/2080.
63 'The outlook for the Persian Gulf up to 1978', Report by the Joint Intelligence Committee, 11 May 1973, CAB 186/15, JIC (A) (73) 10.
64 Ibid.
65 Letter from Henderson to the Secretary of State for Foreign and Commonwealth Affairs, 11 June 1973, FCO 8/2085.
66 Ibid.
67 Ibid.
68 Ibid.
69 'British policy towards Qatar', Minute by Young, 20 June 1973, FCO 8/2085. In an undated note on Young's minute, A. D. Harris (First Secretary, FCO) opined: 'I see little joy in trying to "educate" the Qataris to be more reasonable'.
70 'British policy towards Qatar', Minute by Young, 20 June 1973, FCO 8/2085.
71 Letter from Wright to Henderson, 29 June 1973, FCO 8/2086.
72 Ragaei El Mallakh, *Qatar: Development of an Oil Economy* (London: Croom Helm, 1979), p. 33.
73 'The oil industry in Qatar', Department of Trade and Industry paper attached to letter from A. D. Harris (FCO) to R. D. Gordon (Doha), 15 February 1973, FCO 8/2086.
74 Letter from Henderson to Wright, 17 April 1973, FCO 8/2088.

68 *The oil revolution, 1973*

75 Ibid.
76 Letter from Henderson to R. M. Hunt, 2 July 1973, FCO 8/2086.
77 Ibid.
78 Letter from Henderson to Harris, 9 June 1973, FCO 8/2086.
79 Ibid.
80 Brief for the Prime Minister's lunch for His Highness, Sheikh Khalifah bin Hamad al Thani, Amir of the State of Qatar, on 18 September 1973, FCO 8/2088.
81 Record of the Anglo–US talks on the Middle East held at the State Department, Friday 28 September 1973, FCO 8/1950.
82 'The outlook for the Persian Gulf up to 1978', Report by the Joint Intelligence Committee, 11 May 1973, CAB 186/15, JIC (A) (73) 10.
83 Petersen, *Richard Nixon, Great Britain and the Anglo–American Alignment in the Persian Gulf and Arabian Peninsula*, p. 47.
84 Ibid., p. 42.
85 'The United States and Arab Oil', Minute by Parsons, 12 June 1973, cited in Keith Hamilton and Patrick Salmon (eds.), *Documents on British Policy Overseas: Series III, Volume IV: The Year of Europe: America, Europe and the Energy Crisis, 1972–1974* (Routledge: London and New York, 2006), document 122.
86 For Petersen's interpretation, see Richard Nixon, *Great Britain and the Anglo–American Alignment in the Persian Gulf and Arabian Peninsula*, pp. 29–47.
87 'The Vice President's meeting with British Prime Minister Heath', Memorandum of conversation, 18 December 1970, RG 59, Subject-Numeric Files, 1970–73, Box 2657, POL UK-US.
88 Francesco Petrini, 'The British Government, the Oil Companies and the First Oil Crisis, 1970–3', in John Fisher, Effie G. H. Pedaliu, and Richard Smith (eds.), *The Foreign Office, Commerce and British Foreign Policy in the Twentieth Century* (Basingstoke: Palgrave Macmillan, 2017), p. 456.
89 Letter from Cromer to Sir Alec Douglas-Home, 17 April 1973, cited in Hamilton and Salmon, *The Year of Europe*, document 66.
90 'Energy policy', Minute by Greenhill, 26 April 1973, cited in ibid., document 76.
91 Telegram from the Foreign and Commonwealth Office to Washington, No, 1269, 15 June 1973, cited in ibid., document 127.
92 James Bamberg, *British Petroleum and Global Oil, 1950–1975: The Challenge of Nationalism* (Cambridge: Cambridge University Press, 2000), p. 474.
93 Alexei Vassiliev, *King Faisal of Saudi Arabia: Personality, Faith and Times* (London: Saqi Books, 2012), p. 376.
94 Jordan J. Paust and Albert P. Blaustein, *The Arab Oil Weapon* (New York: Oceana Publications, 1977), p. 43.
95 Bamberg, *British Petroleum and Global Oil, 1950–1975*, p. 477.
96 Paust and Blaustein, *The Arab Oil Weapon*, p. 45.
97 Francesco Petrini, 'Eight squeezed sisters: The oil majors and the coming of the 1973 oil crisis', in Elisabetta Bini, Giuliano Garavini, and Frederico Romero (eds.), *Oil Shock: The 1973 Crisis and its Economic Legacy* (London and New York: I. B. Tauris, 2016), p. 89.
98 'Our objectives in the Middle East', Minute by Parsons, 11 October 1973, cited in Hamilton and Salmon, *The Year of Europe*, document 259.
99 Report on oil by policy for Cabinet Ministerial Committee on energy strategy, 8 February 1993, ibid., document 23.
100 'Oil', Minute by Hunt, 9 October 1973, PREM 15/1837.
101 Telegram from FCO to Jedda, No. 345, 12 October 1973, cited in Hamilton and Salmon, *The Year of Europe*, document 268.
102 Telegram from the Foreign and Commonwealth Office to Washington, no. 2081, 15 October 1973, cited in Hamilton and Salmon, *The Year of Europe*, document 288.
103 Ibid.

104 David Wood, 'Mr Heath is determined not to antagonize Arab oil suppliers', *Times*, 6 November 1973, http://find.galegroup.com/ttda/infomark.do?&source=gale&prodId=TTDA&userGroupName=unihull&tabID=T003&docPage=article&searchType=AdvancedSearchForm&docId=CS17135974&type=multipage&contentSet=LTO&version=1.0 [accessed 5 December 2016].
105 Telegram from Henderson to the Foreign and Commonwealth Office, No. 321, 20 October 1973, FCO 8/1970.
106 Telegram from Henderson to the Foreign and Commonwealth Office, No. 358, 12 November 1973, FCO 8/1971.
107 Telegram from Henderson to the Foreign and Commonwealth Office, No. 370, 21 November 1973, FCO 8/1971.
108 Rosemarie Said Zahlan, *Palestine and the Gulf States: The Presence at the Table* (New York: Routledge, 2009), p. 17.
109 Rosemarie Said Zahlan, 'The Gulf States and the Palestine problem, 1936–48', *Arab Studies Quarterly*, 3, 1 (1981), p. 7.
110 Ibid., p. 21.
111 Zahlan, *Palestine and the Gulf States*, p. 39.
112 Ibid., p. 42.
113 Ibid.
114 Telegram from Wilton to the Foreign and Commonwealth Office, No. 18, 10 January 1972, FCO 8/1843.
115 Telegram from Wilton to the Foreign and Commonwealth Office, No. 518, 5 August 1972, FCO 8/1843.
116 Rory Miller, *Desert Kingdoms to Global Powers: The Rise of the Arab Gulf* (New Haven and London: Yale University Press, 2016), p. 26.
117 Letter from Wilton to Wright, 24 October 1973, FCO 8/1970.
118 Ibid.
119 Ibid.
120 Telegram from Wilton to the Foreign and Commonwealth Office, No. 1086, 8 November 1973, FCO 8/1971.
121 Ibid.
122 'Arab oil and Kuwait', Minute by Wright, 19 November 1973, FCO 8/1971.
123 Ibid.
124 Ibid.
125 Telegram from the Foreign and Commonwealth Office (Douglas-Home) to Kuwait, No. 345, 19 November 1973, FCO 8/1971.
126 Ibid.
127 Telegram from Wilton to the Foreign and Commonwealth Office, No. 1148, 20 November 1973, FCO 8/1971.
128 Ibid.
129 Ibid.
130 'Approaches to Arab oil producers', Minute by S. L. Egerton, 6 December 1973, FCO 8/1969.
131 Letter from Heath to the Amir of Kuwait, 6 December 1973, FCO 8/1972.
132 Ibid.
133 Telegram from Wilton to the Foreign and Commonwealth Office, No. 1226, 8 December 1973, FCO 8/1969.
134 Letter from Wilton to Douglas-Home, 6 January 1974, FCO 8/2188.
135 National Intelligence Estimate, 5 December 1973, *Foreign Relations of the United States, 1969–76: Volume XXXVI: Energy Crisis, 1969–74* (Washington, DC: United States Government Printing Office, 2011), p. 740.
136 Ibid., p. 743.
137 Memorandum from the Under Secretary of State for Economic Affairs (William P. Casey) to Secretary of State Kissinger, 3 November 1973, ibid., p. 669. See also

70 *The oil revolution, 1973*

Dominic Sandbrook, *State of Emergency: The Way We Were: Britain, 1970–1974* (London: Allen Lane, 2010), p. 537.
138 'Our objectives in the present Middle East crisis', Minute by Parsons, 11 October 1973, PREM 15/1765.
139 Telegram from Washington to FCO, No. 3118, 6 October 1973, FCO 93/254.
140 Telegram from Washington to Foreign and Commonwealth Office, No. 3201, 13 October 1973, FCO 93/260.
141 Telegram from American Embassy, London, to Secretary of State, No. 12022, 16 October 1973, RG 59, Electronic Telegrams, 1973, https://aad.archives.gov/aad/createpdf?rid=117619&dt=2472&dl=1345 [accessed 13 November 2016].
142 Letter from Balniel to Ian Gilmour, 29 October 1973, FCO 93/291.
143 Craig Daigle, *The Limits of Détente: The United States, the Soviet Union, and the Arab–Israeli Conflict, 1969–1973* (New Haven and London: Yale University Press, 2012), p. 309.
144 Memorandum from the Under Secretary of State for Economic Affairs (Casey) to Secretary of State Kissinger, 3 November 1973, cited in *Foreign Relations of the United States, 1969–76: Volume XXXVI*, p. 668.
145 Discussion between the Defence Secretary and the US Secretary of Defense held over lunch at HM Ambassador's house in The Hague, 7 November 1973, PREM 15/1767.
146 Catherine Hynes, *The Year That Never Was: Heath, the Nixon Administration and the Year of Europe* (Dublin: University College Dublin Press, 2009), p. 203.
147 Alex Spelling, '"Recrimination and reconciliation": Anglo–American relations and the Yom Kippur War', *Cold War History*, 13, 4 (2013), p. 499.
148 Telegram from Washington to the Foreign and Commonwealth Office, No. 3208, 13 October 1973, FCO 93/260.
149 Letter from Cromer to Douglas-Home, 15 November 1973, PREM 15/1767.
150 Letter from Cromer to Douglas-Home, 9 January 1974, cited in Hamilton and Salmon, *The Year of Europe*, document 496.
151 Ibid.
152 Letter from Cromer to Douglas-Home, 2 January 1974, FCO 82/409.
153 Letter from Cromer to Douglas-Home, 9 January 1974, FCO 82/432.
154 Letter from Cromer to Douglas-Home, 15 November 1973, PREM 15/1767. In mid-1974, the Head of the FCO's North American Department, Lord N. Gordon Lennox, recorded that there had been indications of the Americans taking greater care to keep the UK informed about their policies, if not actually consulting Britain in advance of their formulation. He also noted that 'There are still instances in which they have kept us (as well as most of the Alliance) wholly in the dark' ('The US performance on consultation', Minute by Gordon Lennox, 7 June 1974, FCO 8/2157).
155 Spelling, '"Recrimination and reconciliation"', p. 497.
156 Telegram from American Embassy, London, to Secretary of State, No. 13970, 29 November 1973, RG 59, Electronic Telegrams, 1973, https://aad.archives.gov/aad/createpdf?rid=98000&dt=2472&dl=1345 [accessed 13 November 2016].
157 Ibid.
158 Record of a meeting between the Foreign and Commonwealth Secretary and the Counselor for the State Department, Mr. Sonnenfeldt, at the Foreign and Commonwealth Office, 15 March 1974, cited in Hamilton and Salmon, *The Year of Europe*, document 568.
159 Bruce Maddy-Weitzman, *A Century of Arab Politics: From the Arab Revolt to the Arab Spring* (Lanham, MD: Rowman & Littlefield, 2016), pp. 102–5.
160 Sato, *Britain and the Formation of the Gulf States*, p. 142.
161 Ibid., p. 143.
162 Miller, *Desert Kingdoms to Global Powers*, p. 45.

163 Letter from Henderson to P. R. H. Wright, 4 December 1973, FCO 8/2088.
164 Letter from McCarthy to Douglas-Home, 31 December 1973, FCO 8/2354.
165 Ibid.
166 Ibid.
167 Ibid.
168 Wm. Roger Louis, 'The British withdrawal from the Gulf, 1967–71', *Journal of Imperial and Commonwealth History*, 31, 1 (2003), p. 102.

3 Challenges and opportunities, 1974–1977

In the immediate aftermath of the 1973 Yom Kippur conflict, Britain's Ambassador to Qatar, Edward Henderson, made a passionate plea for a tilt towards the Arab cause. While Henderson admitted that it was 'irritating to see Zionism equated with imperialism and both lumped at our doorstep as our responsibility in Arab propaganda', he insisted that 'unless positive steps are taken to publicise to the British people where their interests lie, the present economic crisis created by the Israeli problem may make this question one which could prove lethal to our economic development'.[1] He went on to argue: 'the delusion that we can afford the luxury of protecting little Israel presents a huge danger to the future of this country as an industrial nation'.[2] Although Prime Minister Harold Wilson admitted during a meeting with the Ruler of Abu Dhabi, Sheikh Zaid, in September 1974 that he had 'close personal relations with the Israeli leadership', he also stressed he was 'anxious to have good relations with all the Arab states'.[3] He proceeded to opine that 'no solution to the Palestine problem was possible without a solution to the position of the Palestinians themselves'.[4]

The risks which the Arab–Israeli conflict could pose to Britain had already been exposed by the use of the 'oil weapon' during the Yom Kippur War. Britain's ongoing economic travails, moreover, served to expose its vulnerability to regional developments beyond its control. The hike in oil prices contributed to Britain's record monthly trade deficit of £383 million by February 1974 which prompted the financier Siegmund Warburg to declare that Britain was facing the 'most serious economic crisis in its history'.[5] Nevertheless, swollen oil revenues, not least among Gulf producers, provided Britain with an opportunity to exploit new economic opportunities. As Richard Smith observes: 'Britain's survival . . . would rest on the very countries responsible for pushing Britain into its balance of payments predicament in the first place – the oil-producing nations, now awash with petro-dollars'.[6]

Following a visit to Arab countries in early November 1973, the Under-Secretary at the Department of Trade and Industry, S. W. Spain, urged that 'We should consider how the UK's special relationship with the Gulf producing states can be capitalised for the UK and Europe in the new pattern of relationships now emerging'.[7] Responding to Spain's exhortation, the Head of the Foreign and Commonwealth Office's Middle East Department, P. R. H. Wright, produced a series of proposals for strengthening Britain's relations with the Gulf States.[8] Observing that many Gulf VIP's regarded London as a 'bolt-hole to which they can escape and be out of the public eye', Wright recommended that 'we should try to profit from private visits when appropriate by arranging calls and entertainment'. He also urged that 'More individual Arab businessmen of prominence should be encouraged to visit this country and more middle-ranking or up-and-coming officials should be invited here'. Technical training in the UK, suggested Wright, would not merely help to ease the shortage of skilled manpower in the Gulf, but also to bring commercial returns, not least with respect to defence sales. Finally, he emphasized that 'We should explore every opportunity for developing economic links with the Gulf States that will serve to make them more dependent upon us'.

At the beginning of 1974, Ambassador Henderson provided a sober counterpoint to Wright's optimism.[9] On the one hand, he pointed out that in the previous year British industry had maintained its 25 to 30 per cent share of the Qatar market. On the other hand, he was critical of the modus operandi of some British enterprises operating in Qatar. '[A] few British firms', he intoned, 'seem to be politically deaf and dumb and are still not trying as hard as I think they could to make their faces fit. Firms enter contracts which will cover long periods and involve tens of millions of pounds and still not engage a single Arab-speaking member of their management staff'. Henderson reserved particular criticism for the British firm Power Gas which was over five months late in completing the £25 million Natural Gas Liquids plant contract and over eighteen months late in completing the £28 million fertilizer plant contract. 'Leaving aside problems of late delivery of materials which are common to British industry', he explained, 'the Power Gas team have lacked sufficiently competent middle management both on site and in London. Their failure has damaged our reputation severely in this small but important market'. Despite the failings of Power Gas, Henderson recorded that 'The Amir continues to declare his preference for British goods and for cooperation with British industry'. 'This built-in advantage', he concluded, 'will only continue if we are successful in stimulating British companies to take an interest in this small but growing market and in keeping those companies which are here up to the mark'. On reading Henderson's' despatch, A. D. Harris of the FCO's Middle East Department concurred that 'We cannot rely on goodwill to maintain our place in Qatar'.[10] Writing in April 1974, Henderson himself recognized the growing international competition faced by Britain in Qatar, noting in particular that the French had 'made some impact'.[11]

During talks with Henderson in June, the Amir noted that 'In the Middle East he saw America followed by France taking the lead in industrialisation and Britain lagging far behind'.[12] He expressed particular incredulity that 'Britain, who was leading the technological world, was unwilling to construct a petrochemical plant in Qatar'.[13] He also admitted that the Japanese bid to construct a steel plant was 'a very strong one'.[14] Subsequently, he told Henderson that Tokyo was 'strongly behind' the proposal for a steel plant and wished to make it a 'government to government affair'.[15] By the beginning of July, Henderson reported that the Japanese firm Kobe Steel would soon be signing up with the Qatar government. Accounting for British Steel's failure to land the contract, the Ambassador remarked that the poor performance of Power Gas in producing a fertilizer plant one-and-a-half years late had 'weighed very heavily with the Amir against another big British project at this moment'.[16] More generally, Henderson posited that, although 'in the old days our special position gave us an enormous advantage . . . we cannot use our historical influence to offset high prices nor will it offset major weaknesses such as the appearance of a company which is made up of separate parts whose managers are not even in agreement when proposals are made'.[17] Towards the end of August 1974, Henderson lamented that 'We have had a bad summer, either by letting things go by default to the Japanese or the French or losing contracts through pricing our goods too high'.[18] He added that 'We lost the BSC bid after a good fight, but in other fields we hardly tried'.[19]

Some hope for British industry was provided by Sheikh Khalifah's comment during a visit to London in August 1974 that he 'wished to give Britain the first option on future industrial development in Qatar'.[20] In his report on a mission to Abu Dhabi, Kuwait, and Qatar in November 1974, moreover, the Co-ordinator of Industrial Advisers in the Departments of Trade and Industry, Stephen Baker, recorded that 'The climate for British firms to operate in the Gulf, particularly the Lower Gulf, is clearly very favourable. The number to times the mission was told that people in the Gulf would much prefer to work with British firms seemed to go beyond mere politeness'.[21] In the wake of a visit to Qatar in February 1975, however, Treasury Deputy Secretary F. R. Barratt observed:

> I got very much the usual story. . . . A great desire to buy from the UK. The problem is not price, but marketing and delivery dates. German firms outsell us, though their products are more expensive, partly because of their greater energy in marketing and partly because they can deliver.[22]

Despite the problems which Britain faced in the industrial field, the provision of loan service personnel for the Qatari armed forces offered opportunities for the maintenance of British influence in the Amirate.

At the beginning of 1974, Henderson reported that the Deputy Commander-in-Chief of the Qatar Security Forces, Brigadier Attiyah, had requested news of progress on his request for a loan service signals officer. The Ambassador immediately impressed upon the FCO the need to nominate a suitable candidate as soon as possible while the Deputy Commander-in-Chief's request remained alive. 'If there is a delay', warned Henderson, 'he will soon blow cold and we should have lost an important opportunity to introduce a serving British officer into the QSF in a key position particularly in regards to arms purchases'.[23] Although the Ministry of Defence undertook to identify a suitable candidate, Henderson baulked at the Ministry's suggested cost for such an officer of some £10,400 per annum. 'A British army signals officer', stressed the Ambassador, 'should hold the key to sales of British signals equipment worth well over £1 million, and probably should be in a good position to influence sales of other equipment as well. With this in mind

I believe we should tailor the cost to suit the customer'.[24] In a further missive, Henderson commented that 'We are at a crucial stage in our relations with Qatar and it essential that we do everything possible to strengthen our influence in the armed forces. The cost to us politically and commercially if we do not is incalculable and it is in our interests that the MoD should make the offer of a loan service officer as attractive as possible'.[25] In a final appeal, Henderson asserted that 'We are facing a danger of decline in political/commercial influence and I would have thought that we should try to strengthen rather than weaken our position at a vital point when we can still do so'.[26]

The Ambassador's appeals fell on deaf ears in Whitehall. The Ministry of Defence did not acquiesce in Henderson's suggestions primarily on sales grounds, expressing the view that a signals officer would not be in a position to influence the £1 million signals equipment deal under negotiation since the matter was a straight commercial proposition between the Qataris and a consortium of British manufacturers with no government-to-government involvement.[27] Bearing in mind Qatar's inflated income deriving from the dramatic increase in oil prices, as well as Britain's own difficult economic circumstances, the FCO questioned the wisdom of providing a subsidy for a loan service officer.[28] Nevertheless, the dangers of being undercut in the defence field were soon exposed with respect to the secondment of officers from other countries to the QSF. In March 1974, Henderson reported that Pakistan was imminently sending a 'high grade' military mission to Qatar.[29] He confessed: 'I now fear that the Pakistanis will do as in Abu Dhabi and offer immediate secondment at cheap rates for pilots and possible senior officers and staff officers. They could quickly gain control of the force. This would have very serious effects as regards our defence sales'.[30] The weakening of the British position in Qatar reflected in the encroachment of other powers into the defence field was matched by the Amirate's growing responsiveness to pressures from the Arab world, not least in oil matters.

At the beginning of 1974, Sheikh Khalifah told Henderson that in view of Kuwait's intention to increase its participation in the oil companies operating there to 60 per cent, it would be 'very difficult for him not to do the same thing'.[31] By February, Henderson was reporting the signature of a 60/40 agreement in Qatar with respect to both Shell and QPC.[32] Although the Amir disavowed nationalization on the grounds that oil enterprises could not be 'Arabised' very quickly, Henderson warned that 'If Kuwait were to nationalise her companies, and Abu Dhabi and Saudi Arabia were to do the same, then obviously it would be difficult for Qataris not to follow suit'.[33] The Ambassador's prophesy was borne out with the Qatari decision at the end of 1974 to take over the remaining 40 per cent equity in Shell and QPC following the failure of the Kuwaiti Majlis to ratify the 60/40 participation agreement in favour of 100 per cent nationalization.[34] The FCO had already noted that 'The traditional method of determining oil prices and regulating supply is likely to change. With the rapid increase in producer government participation, less and less oil is owned by the companies'.[35]

It is with considerable justification that James Bamberg, summarizing developments in the crucial period 1973–1975, has argued that 'The OPEC countries were in control of the commanding heights of the world oil industry, and the once-dominant oil majors would have to find new roles in the new order of global oil'.[36] Nevertheless, Sheikh Khalifah was quick to reassure the new British Ambassador in Doha, D. G. Crawford, that 'Qatar was inevitably influenced by the actions of the other Arab members of OPEC and the recent decisions should not be regarded as a change in her traditional policy of friendship towards the West, particularly towards the United Kingdom', adding that he wished to see commercial relations with Britain grow.[37] During Crawford's formal presentation of credentials, Sheikh Khalifah specifically referred to the importance he attached to his friendship with Britain and to the British presence in Qatar.[38] He proceeded to assure the new Ambassador that he relied on Britain to assist him with his plans to develop Qatar 'as in the past his predecessors had depended on British support and guidance'.[39] In his annual review for 1974, however, Crawford painted a sobering picture.

Although Crawford reported that Britain's traditional ties with Qatar remained strong, he warned that 'there is no room for complacency since they are being increasingly challenged by our Western competitors'.[40] He went on to record that the Amir had 'complained several times last year about the slowness of British industry to accept his invitations to take part in the development of and industrialisation of Qatar'.[41] Referring to Qatar's conclusion of multi-million–pound projects with the Japanese (steel mill) and the French (petrochemicals), Crawford lamented that 'British industry was unable to compete successfully in either field despite the Amir's preference to do so'.[42] The net result was that Britain lost its position in 1974 as the leading exporter to Qatar, statistics indicating that Japan had captured 17 per cent of the market compared with Britain's 15 per cent. This stood in marked contrast with the position just three years earlier when Britain held some 37 per cent of Qatar's imports.[43] Crawford himself stressed the fierce competition from other industrial countries, a development which was matched in the diplomatic field with France appointing its first resident ambassador in February 1974, and Germany, Japan, and the United States opening diplomatic missions in the course of the year.[44] In response to Crawford's observations, Richard Kinchen of the FCO's Middle East Department concluded: 'Relations with the UK remained cordial but have become a degree or two less special as Qatar's foreign relations have become more diverse'.[45]

A concerted effort to revive British fortunes in Qatar, especially in the industrial and commercial spheres, was made in the course of 1975. This was spearheaded by a series visits to Qatar by both ministers and officials. The most significant of these was Minister of State at the FCO, David Ennals', sojourn in Doha in February. During a meeting with the Amir on the 13th, Ennals emphasized his wish to promote the role of British industry and technology in the 'exciting development' taking place in Qatar, to which Sheikh Khalifah encouragingly replied: 'this subject was perpetually in his thoughts'.[46] F. R. Barratt of the Treasury, who visited Qatar shortly before Ennals, had already reported that the Amir welcomed 'impartial developmental advice from the UK'.[47] The Minister quickly suggested the visit of two experts for discussions on technological cooperation leading to the secondment of a permanent adviser in the field to which Sheikh Khalifah responded positively, inviting Crawford to examine the matter with the Qatari Industrial Development Technical Centre.[48] 'Clearly the attachment of British project officers to the IDTC in positions of direct involvement in Qatar's development plan', enthused Crawford, 'would be of enormous advantage to us in respect of our commercial interests'.[49]

The prospects for commercial cooperation were enhanced during the talks with Ennals by Sheikh Khalifah's support for joint ventures, British participation in Qatari enterprise being matched by Qatari participation in complementary enterprises in the United Kingdom.[50] During his visit to the United Kingdom in the summer of 1974, moreover, the Amir had expressed his desire to give Britain 'the first option on future industrial development in Qatar',[51] a sentiment he reiterated in welcoming members of a British industrial and technical mission to Qatar in November 1974.[52] The Foreign Secretary, James Callaghan, had already commented that 'Our relations with Qatar are based on a close and long-standing historical connection, and formalised by a Treaty of Friendship. This represents an advantage for us on which we should certainly capitalise'.[53]

When Qatar's Minister of Finance, Sheikh Abdul Aziz, suggested the formation of a joint Anglo–Qatari Committee to make proposals for cooperation between the two countries,[54] it was taken up with alacrity by the British. The Agreement on Cooperation was initialled in London by Sheikh Abdul Aziz and the Secretary of State for Trade, Peter Shore, on 1 August 1975.[55] Among the matters the Committee was charged with studying were opportunities for joint ventures in the industrial and agricultural fields, as well as cooperation between the two countries on the exchange of experts.[56] A UK/UAE Committee was established along similar lines a year later. In 1981, K. J. Passmore of the FCO's Middle East Department observed that the Committee was 'valuable for making the UAE side feel we care about them and for reminding their ministers and officials who have, as far as we can tell, no paper-keeping or paper-retrieving methods where we stand on the various projects in which we try to obtain decisions from them'.[57]

Britain's efforts to revivify its commercial position in Qatar appeared to yield tangible results. In his annual report for 1975,[58] Crawford reported that unofficial customs figures to October indicated that Britain had regained its position as market leader with the United States and Japan in second and third places respectively. He also predicted that British visible exports would in all likelihood reach the target of £50 million for the year. Nevertheless, he did sound a note of caution, pointing out that with the exception of a £30 million desalination project awarded to the British firm Weir Westgarth, no major contract had featured in this 'happy outcome'. He also observed that the growth in British exports was due principally to the efforts of Britain's traditional suppliers of manufactured goods and of many small and medium-sized firms which had come to Qatar, some for the first time. 'If only GEC, and other major concerns had shown a similar enthusiasm we might have hit the jackpot', lamented Crawford.[59] The Ambassador had earlier been highly critical of the electronics, communications, and engineering giant, remarking that 'We share Abu Dhabi's impression that GEC are "sluggish" and not prepared to take an aggressive approach to large contracts invariably preferring caution to risk taking'.[60] He also noted that GEC's negotiations for a new power station at Umm Said and Taylor Woodrow's proposals for industrialized building did not constitute the 'breakthrough both the Amir and we are looking for allowing our mutual cooperation to compare favourably with the major projects on which the Japanese and French are now engaged'.[61]

The Anglo–Qatari Cooperation Agreement, moreover, did not provide a panacea for promoting British commercial interests in Qatar. Just three days after the initialling of the agreement on 1 August 1975, Britain's Head of Chancery and Consul in Doha, R. D. Gordon, reported that the British company Airwork Limited, which specialized in providing defence support services, had lost its contract with the Qatar Armed Forces.[62] Towards the beginning of 1976, moreover, Crawford noted that the 'traditional preference' for British goods and services had evaporated and that Japanese equipment in particular was 'pouring in'.[63] 'After observing the Japanese at work in Umm Said recently', he continued, 'I find it difficult to see how we can prevent them becoming the market leaders here and the predominant contractors'.[64] Sheikh Khalifah himself conveyed to Crawford his disappointment that 'British industry had failed to share in the development of his country to the extent that we would wish'.[65]

The Anglo–Qatari Cooperation Agreement was formally signed on behalf of Britain by the Parliamentary Under-Secretary for Trade, Michael Meacher, in Doha on 19 June 1976. Although the Amir was reported to be 'genuinely pleased' with the agreement, Crawford observed: 'I am sure that we and not he will have to work the harder if it is to have substance'.[66] Referring to Meacher's visit to Qatar, the Ambassador commented that it was a 'further demonstration to the Qataris of the increasing importance Her Majesty's Government attach to their country and its growing economy'.[67] In his own summary of his Qatari odyssey, Meacher recorded that in discussions with local businessmen, both Qataris and expatriate British, 'it was apparent that our presence is so well established that we should have a head start over our competitors'.[68] However, he also noted that there were 'plenty of complaints' about the service received from British suppliers, typically late delivery, occasionally the supply of inappropriate products such as non-air-conditioned cars, and, conversely, the inadequate supply of those products which had a strong local demand, most notably Land Rovers and Range Rovers. 'It was also apparent', lamented Meacher, 'that British companies were not being as successful as they might expect in securing the large contracts for major public works projects and heavy industry'.[69] In the course of a business seminar held at the British Embassy during Meacher's time in Doha, the conclusion was reached that although Britain finished first in Qatar's export stakes in 1975, it should have 'won by several lengths instead of only by a head'.[70] On the eve of Meacher's visit, furthermore, Crawford stressed that 'The United Kingdom press is regularly read or quoted in Qatar and Qataris have numerous British business contacts both here and in London. These sources continue to utter a gloomy prognostication on Britain's economic future tending to make this Embassy a lonely optimistic voice'.[71] Indeed, Meacher's trip occurred against the background of renewed economic crisis in Britain.

In the estimation of Kathleen Burk and Alec Cairncross, two fundamental weaknesses in the British economy – in reserves and competitive power – resulted in the government not being able to maintain a stable exchange rate.[72] Convinced that the pound was over-valued, investors began selling sterling. Shortly after entering 10 Downing Street in April 1976, James Callaghan discovered that the Bank of England had spent $2 billion since January, one third of its total currency reserves, trying unsuccessfully to prop up the pound.[73] With considerable justification, *The Economist* quipped that holders of sterling 'put no more value on a British pound than on an ice-cream sundae'.[74] By 3 June, sterling had fallen to $1.70, a decline of more than 10 per cent since early March. Two days later, Crawford emphasized that 'A vitally important purpose of Mr Meacher's visit should therefore be to give a candid but confidence building assessment putting into perspective the decline in sterling'.[75] The Parliamentary Under-Secretary's presentation to the Amir evidently fulfilled Crawford's expectations, Sheikh Khalifah commenting that 'he wanted to see the UK become the leading trading nation in the Gulf, replacing the Japanese'.[76] He also made clear his 'strong friendship' for the United Kingdom and his hope that the Co-operation Agreement would strengthen the ties between the two countries and, in particular, 'bring about a still closer involvement by the UK in Qatar's industrial development programme'.[77] While the Amir's dominant position in Qatar[78] was undoubtedly an asset for the former imperial power, in Bahrain the maintenance of British interests and influence was challenged by the emergence of new political forces beyond the direct control of the Al-Khalifah ruling family.

Following labour disorders in March 1972, the Bahraini government committed itself to the creation of some form of Parliament at which the issue of permitting trade unions could be discussed.[79] As a prelude to this, a Constituent Assembly was elected at the beginning of December 1972 charged with the task of drafting a constitution. Britain's Ambassador to Bahrain, Robert Tesh, reassuringly reported that the elected members looked like a 'fairly moderate body'.[80] On 9 June 1973, the Assembly finalized its proposals,[81] a Parliament being duly elected towards the end of the year. Tesh was quick to point out that

> The results of the voting . . . came as a surprise, and caused alarm among the conservatives in Bahrain and among neighbouring traditionalist regimes. Only a third of the members of the Constituent assembly were re-elected. The loose Nationalist group which had occupied the Left of the Assembly and provided the main opposition to the Government were largely swept away, and of the four who survived, three were among the regime's most ardent critics. The Right Wing is filled with six 'Religious' Shia, who represent the villages. On the Left we now find eight new faces in Bahraini politics – lawyers and clerks in their early thirties with long security records, Marxist sympathies, PFLOAG and Iraqi connections, and, some of them, training in subversion and militancy.[82]

Tesh went on to point out that these left-wing radicals, who styled themselves as the 'People's Bloc', had campaigned on a common election manifesto calling for nationalization of foreign firms, Bahrainization, freedom for trade unions, curbs on police powers, and opposition to foreign military bases.[83] The Ambassador also warned that 'What the Government will have to watch is attempts by the Left to organise support and subversion from behind the protection of parliamentary privilege. The power of the Police and Special Branch will be a crucial factor'.[84] Both were run by Britons, Jim Bell filling the position of Director-General of Police while Ian Henderson headed Special Branch. In the wake of the first Parliamentary elections in Bahrain, A. D. Harris of the FCO's Middle East Department remarked: 'We can now expect the [Bahraini] Government to come under strong pressure to get rid of these two key figures'.[85] Tesh had already reported that Bahrain's 'efficient and loyal Police and Security Branch are run by Britons, because no Bahraini could do it. These are now coming under attack'.[86]

The Bahraini Prime Minister, Sheikh Khalifah bin Salman, admitted to Tesh that he 'wasn't happy with "the democracy we got"'.[87] Disenchantment reached Iran where the Shah told British Ambassador Peter Ramsbotham of his concerns over the turn of events in Bahrain and, especially, the election of left-wing elements.[88] From his vantage point in Manama, nevertheless, Tesh asserted that 'It would be wrong to suppose that Bahrain has gone Communist and that the Al-Khalifah are doomed'.[89] He also consoled himself with the thought that 'The bees in the Assembly's bonnet about Bahrainisation and nationalisation will buzz ineffectually against the shortage of qualified Bahrainis and the need for foreign capital and enterprise'.[90] As regards the former, the Ambassador noted that the British labour adviser to the Minister of Labour, Bill Berry, 'has been an extremely useful source of experienced advice to his Minister'.[91] Overall, Tesh opined that 'Our main contribution to Bahrain is the widespread activities of the British Council, our teachers and experts, and our well-behaved and self-reliant British community of, I imagine, over 4,000 who help us hold, just about, our share of an expanding market'.[92]

Bahrain's imports for the first ten months of 1974 totalled BD144 million, 30 per cent higher than for the previous year. Britain's market share in this ten-month period, nonetheless, was only 12.7 per cent, as compared with 18.9 per cent in 1973. The United Kingdom, moreover, had slipped behind the US and Japan which enjoyed a 19.2 per cent and 14.5 per cent share in the Bahrain market respectively. This disappointing result was achieved despite the fact that, as Tesh pointed out, there was much in Britain's favour, including 'goodwill, the ever-increasing number of British engineers and managers in key positions, and the preference for British consulting engineers'.[93] In keeping with Qatar, one of the main reasons for Britain's poor relative performance was traced by Tesh to problems with delivery dates.[94] 'I have been disappointed', he added, 'by the lack of follow-up to the successful Exhibition of British Quality Consumer Goods in February and by the failure of exporters to visit regularly and frequently. Subsidised missions from Chambers of Commerce . . . still consist mainly of people whose firms do business here already or people who are never seen here again'.[95]

Challenges and opportunities, 1974–1977 81

As regards Anglo–Bahraini relations more generally, Tesh confessed that 'the Bahrainis feel that on our side the "special relationship" has cooled'.[96] Tesh proceeded to record that 'they express regret that it is the French who of the Europeans are the most visibly and successfully active in the Arab world'.[97] In response, Richard Kinchen of the FCO's Middle East Department observed: 'It is sad but, I suppose inevitable, that relations with the UK should already be becoming less special. Our endeavour to maintain an even-handed policy in the Middle East dispute is clearly one of the reasons behind this trend'.[98] In his valedictory despatch produced shortly before his departure from Bahrain in July 1975, Tesh specifically noted: 'It is regretted that the French, for whom the Bahrainis have no natural feeling, should have forged ahead of us in Arab favour'.[99] Reflecting the changes to Bahrain's geo-political alignments since 1971, moreover, the outgoing Ambassador predicted that 'In a new rift between the Arabs and the West they [the Bahrainis] could only be on the Arab side'.[100]

The immediate prospects for the preservation of British interests appeared to receive a boost in August 1975 by the formation of a new government under Sheikh Khalifah bin Salman and his request for the dissolution of the Bahrain Parliament with a view to establishing a new assembly 'more representative of the people of Bahrain'.[101] These events were foreshadowed by a series of arrests of around forty individuals whom the Ministry of the Interior depicted as 'a real danger to the security and stability of the country'.[102] The new British Ambassador in Bahrain, E. F. Given, made a strong case for maintaining Britain's close ties with the regime of the ruling family:

> The Al Khalifah, whether Ministers or not, are accessible and friendly, as are the non-shaikhly members of the Government and administration, and it would be foolish to throw away the advantages which flow from their confidence for the sake of contacts with an opposition which will no doubt have to be reckoned with one day, but which, whether under its present leaders or under new ones, is likely to remain aloof from us.[103]

Nevertheless, Given finished on a positive note, observing that Britain's position in Bahrain was 'due to the achievements of our predecessors, to the welcome which Bahrainis have always had in Britain, and to honest dealing by British business, and not to a covert continuation of colonialism'.[104]

At the beginning of 1976, Given's optimism appeared to be justified by the news that Britain had in all likelihood regained its position as Bahrain's biggest supplier.[105] The Ambassador also pointed out that 'The number of British subjects living in Bahrain has continued to grow. Some of these make a quantifiable contribution to our export drive'.[106] Responding to his predecessor's observation that Bahrainis felt that the 'special relationship' with Britain had cooled, Given noted the positive impression that visits to Bahrain by David Ennals, Peter Shore, and James Callaghan in the course of 1975 had produced.[107] Given himself sought to promote British commerce by reassuring business visitors that Bahrain was a safe place to invest or locate a regional office.[108] Although the Head of the FCO's

Middle East Department, Ivor Lucas, expressed satisfaction that Britain had regained its market lead in Bahrain, he admitted that it was 'niggling' that several important contracts had been lost by small margins.[109]

As regards the approach which Britain should adopt towards Bahrain more generally, Given made a strong case for non-interference in the island's internal affairs. On the one hand, the Ambassador indicated that British diplomats knew less about what went on under the surface since they were reliant upon information passed on by officials whose first loyalty was to the Bahrain government. 'In this state of ignorance', he declared, 'I do not think we are qualified to try and move the Bahrain government in one direction or another'.[110] On the other, he noted: 'I have the impression that the Political Agents here nannied the local authorities more than their counterparts elsewhere in the Gulf; however that may be, I do not think the results were particularly successful in the political field'.[111] Responding on behalf of the FCO, Lucas stressed: 'we entirely endorse the philosophy of "non-interference". . . . "Responsibility without power" got us into enough difficulties prior to 1971, and we are even less well-placed now to proffer our advice. I think that this goes for the other Gulf States too'.[112] Although Kuwait turned to the British first for help and advice following the Iraqi attack on the border police post at al Samita in March 1973,[113] the Kuwaitis persistently demonstrated a predilection for independent policy-making which often clashed with British interests.

In April 1974, the Kuwaitis concluded an arms deal with the Soviet Union.[114] In his valedictory despatch produced in the same month, Ambassador Wilton noted that 'in 1971 the Kuwaitis' faults and foibles were very largely their own affair; now they can, and increasingly may, cause acute difficulties to half mankind'.[115] Elaborating on this point, Wilton mused:

> as a country which can vary her [oil] production upwards or downwards by a million or more barrels a day without any serious practical or financial constraints, is in a position to exercise a very great influence on supplies and prices whenever she wishes. She has so far chosen to exert her pressures to increase the price and I expect her to continue to do so.[116]

The Ambassador went on to lament that

> the weakness of the government, the bletherings of the Assembly, the acid tongue of the Finance and Oil Minister, the indecision of the Defence Minister, the bland myopia of the civil service and the breathtaking self-centredness of the Kuwait population at large give rise to a disquieting sensation of insecurity among those who are in any measure dependent upon Kuwait. The position of a dependent is seldom agreeable.[117]

Referring to news that Kuwaitis were to take over the industrialization and development of their economy, Wilton waspishly remarked: 'It would be difficult to see where all the necessary talent could come from even if the Kuwaitis were exceptionally gifted and exceptionally talented. They are neither'.[118] On reading Wilton's despatch, the Assistant Head of the FCO's Middle East Department, T. J. Clark, admitted: 'I find little comfort in this account of contemporary Kuwait with too much money, too few capable people to administer it and no clear ideas, except harmful retrogressive ones, about what to do with it'.[119]

Wilton's successor, A. T. Lamb, was equally critical of Kuwait, claiming that 'hypocrisy and double standards' were practised 'as an art'.[120] In particular, he contrasted Kuwait's insistence that Western governments maintained a free, capitalist system, unthreatened by nationalization, for profitable ventures by Kuwaitis, who, at the same time, approved of Kuwait state ownership, or majority participation in it, and the local means of production and distribution. He also bemoaned the fact that 'Western countries must provide an open-door for Kuwaitis and their investments and property acquisitions but no foreigner may trade independently or own property in Kuwait'.[121] Nevertheless, Lamb went on to speculate that the restoration of relations between Britain and Iraq might make the Kuwaiti government friendlier towards its former guardian as an insurance against renewed Anglo–Iraqi accord weakening Britain's attachment to Kuwait. As the Ambassador colourfully put it: 'I doubt that Kuwait wants to lose an old flame even if not much attention has been paid to her in recent times'.[122] 'A resurgence of affection', continued Lamb, 'could also help us commercially, especially in the consulting and contracting fields where the big money is spent'.[123] In conclusion, Lamb emphasized that 'we cannot afford not to try hard to influence Kuwait's oil, oil-pricing and financial policies and their political and other dimensions'.[124] In recognition of this, the Governor of the Bank of England, Gordon Richardson, visited the Amirate in November 1974, impressing upon his hosts that 'his very presence in Kuwait on a special visit showed that we were giving Kuwait special consideration'.[125] Britain's new Ambassador in Abu Dhabi, D. J. McCarthy, also made the case for greater British prominence in the UAE.

Shortly before his stepping down in June 1973 as Britain's Ambassador to the UAE, C. J. Treadwell reported a conversation with the UAE Foreign Minister, Ahmad Suwaidi, in which he told the latter:

> I was not still a Political Agent but was conscious that the old easy relationship had not disappeared with the revision of political patterns and the arrival of diplomatic missions in the UAE, and it might be to our mutual advantage if we could continue to exchange views without regard to the limitations usually observed in discussions between Foreign Minister and Ambassador.[126]

In response, Suwaidi 'agreed warmly' and reminded Treadwell that Sheikh Zaid considered his relationship with the Ambassador 'had not changed'.[127] In his valedictory despatch, Treadwell recorded that Zaid had 'always insisted that the British representative should have special rights of access to him'.[128]

Referring to his predecessor, McCarthy observed that 'Jim Treadwell had successfully bridged from Political Agent to Ambassador while retaining his personal intimacy despite the transition'.[129] Sheikh Zaid himself told Prime Minister

Edward Heath in September 1972 that 'He habitually received the advice from the British Ambassador before that proffered from any other quarter'.[130] Two years later, nevertheless, McCarthy explained: 'I had little doubt that [Sheikh] Zaid would watch me, a post-independence arrival, against any presumptive tendencies reminiscent of the former role'.[131] The Ambassador went on to point out that although Zaid 'never said anything to us that he wished to weaken the British connection . . . in practice he was diminishing it in ways some of which constituted the undermining of his own security'.[132] In an effort to reverse this trend, McCarthy proposed to raise Britain's profile in the UAE. He was quick to point out, however, that 'I mean raising the profile within the context of Independence, and not expecting to get back to the pre-Independence relationship'.[133] The recognizably post-imperial relationship that Britain was forging with the Gulf was demonstrated by the resolution of the long-running border dispute between Abu Dhabi and Saudi Arabia[134] in 1974.

Towards the end of 1969, D. F. McCarthy, then Head of the FCO's Arabian Department, lamented: 'the mentality of these rulers is such that they are prepared to dispute a barren sand dune till judgement day'.[135] He proceeded to remark: 'if, after twenty years' effort, we have been unable to settle these particular boundaries it seems unlikely that we shall be able to do so in the next year or so, having reduced our leverage by announcing withdrawal'.[136] The Parliamentary Under-Secretary of State at the FCO, Evan Luard, nonetheless, asserted: 'we ought to do everything within our power to bring about the resolution of as many as possible of these conflicts within the next two years before our withdrawal'.[137] Seeking to justify this stance, Luard stressed:

> if we do not do so, I am afraid that they may re-emerge, possibly in far more acute form, at a later stage. We should then have no capacity to influence events. In some cases they could lead even to armed conflict: it is well known that the readiness to go to war over these issues bears no relation to the intrinsic value of the territory concerned. This could in turn lead to threats to our oil supplies. It might lead to serious intervention by larger powers of the region such as Saudi Arabia and Iran. And it could certainly provide an opportunity for revolutionary forces to take control in certain areas.[138]

While Britain did make 'strenuous efforts' to settle the Abu Dhabi–Saudi boundary in the years 1970–1971, it remained unresolved at the time of British formal withdrawal.[139] At the end of 1971, Ambassador Treadwell wearily remarked: 'let both these independent states get on with it. Active mediation would certainly at some stage injure our reputation with one or the other, or both'.[140] In August 1972, moreover, Foreign Secretary Douglas-Home mused: 'So far as Abu-Dhabi/Saudi relations are concerned, having failed to persuade Zaid to come to an agreement with Saudis while we were still responsible for his foreign relations, we have no illusions that we can influence him to do so now'.[141] In response to the Saudi Minister for Foreign Affairs, Omar Saqqaf's, request for information about the advice that Britain was giving Sheikh Zaid regarding the Abu Dhabi–Saudi Arabian frontier, FCO Under-Secretary A. D. Parsons bluntly stated: 'We were no longer acting as Abu Dhabi's lawyer. We had no intention of re-involving ourselves in the dispute'.[142] The Saudis, however, continued to look to Britain to intercede with Zaid. For instance, in May 1973 the Saudi Second Deputy Prime Minister, Prince Fahd bin Abdul Aziz, specifically requested that both the Foreign Secretary and the Prime Minister use their influence with Zaid to achieve a settlement.[143] 'Our long association with this problem', countered the Head of the FCO's Middle East Department, P. R. H. Wright, 'has convinced us that that there is little profit to be gained from playing the role of honest brokers'.[144] Foreign Secretary Alec Douglas-Home, furthermore, expressed the fear that any further British involvement would 'achieve nothing except further recriminations from both sides'.[145]

During discussions at the beginning of July 1974 with the US Ambassador to the UAE, Michael Sterner, Ambassador McCarthy reported that although the Qataris, Bahrainis, and Kuwaitis were trying to use their good offices to move matters forward, the British were 'right out of it'.[146] McCarthy also pointed out that none of the parties had tried to involve Britain and that when he had broached the border question with Sheikh Zaid a couple of months earlier, the Abu Dhabi ruler had 'not even hinted at our taking a hand'.[147] The FCO concurred with McCarthy's approach, emphasizing its 'unwillingness to become involved in the UAE/Saudi dispute'.[148]

In mid-July, Sultan Qaboos informed the British Ambassador to Oman, D. F. Hawley, that 'very secret' negotiations were taking place between Saudi Arabia and the UAE and that they appeared to be 'getting somewhere'.[149] Following a visit to the UAE by Prince Fahd, a communiqué was issued on 29 July announcing the solution of the outstanding differences between Saudi Arabia and the UAE.[150] P. R. H. Wright underlined that the Amir of Qatar, Sheikh Khalifah, had 'played an important role in bringing the two sides together'.[151] Providing more detail on Khalifah's role, the British Ambassador in Doha, E. F. Henderson, remarked that the Qatari ruler had managed to allay the Saudis' fears about making territorial concessions by reassuring them that 'Zaid was worth treating with and that the government of the UAE was reasonably stable'.[152] The border agreement itself was formally signed by the Saudi King, Feisal bin Abdul Aziz, and Sheikh Zaid on 21 August 1974 during the latter's official visit to Saudi Arabia.[153] H. B. Walker (Counsellor, British Embassy, Jedda) reported that the visit had 'gone off very well indeed' and that the Saudis had 'rolled out the largest of red carpets (literally and figuratively)'.[154] The communiqué which was issued at the conclusion of Zaid's sojourn referred to discussions between the two sovereigns having been 'conducted in an atmosphere characterised by a spirit of love, brotherhood and a sincere desire for complete cooperation'.[155] Although Prime Minister Harold Wilson sent congratulatory messages to both Sheikh Zaid and King Feisal,[156] Britain had played no role in the settlement of the border dispute. This should perhaps not be surprising, however. As McCarthy presciently observed: 'I think it fair to say that the dispute could never have been solved so long as concessions appeared to be under Western aegis. It had to be settled – and to be seen to be settled – among the Arabs concerned'.[157]

By comparison with the apparent weakening of British ties with Sheikh Zaid, those with the Ruler of Dubai and Vice-President of the UAE, Sheikh Rashid, remained robust to the extent that the Pakistani Ambassador to the UAE observed, with only a little exaggeration, that Dubai was a 'British colony'.[158] McCarthy pointed out that following the termination of formal British protection in 1971, Rashid still saw British expatriates as providing the 'sinew of his state'.[159] He also departed from the practice of Kuwait and Abu Dhabi in employing 'hordes of Egyptians, Iraqis and Palestinians, or even Lebanese', declaring that he would only Arabize as and when nationals of his own state were qualified to assume responsibility. In these circumstances, McCarthy reported a 'remarkable continuum', in which the 'key positions in the government and around it which the British held before independence remain in their hands'.[160] One important example of this was Jack Briggs who retained his position as Commandant of Police in Dubai. Nonetheless, by 1974 his position was threatened by the non-cooperation of senior Arab officers under him who started refusing to carry out his orders. In these circumstances, he offered his resignation. Although Sheikh Rashid persuaded him to reverse this decision, McCarthy gloomily predicted that Briggs would almost certainly cease to be Commandant of Police before long. 'In a deeper sense', continued the Ambassador, 'Briggs' departure would be the beginning of the end of an era. Shaikh Rashid would lose the best of his intimate British advisers as well as an outstanding Chief of Police. Those hoping or working for an overall change would be enormously encouraged to push for it in other respects'.[161] McCarthy concluded that Shaikh Rashid would be 'forced . . . to move faster than his judgement or the optimum pace of Arabisation would dictate'.[162] The loosening of ties with Britain implied by Arabization was paralleled in the military sphere. Here, however, the impetus for change came from British economic stringency rather than local pressure.

In common with most government departments, the FCO was called upon by the Treasury to reduce its expenditure from the 1975–1976 financial year onwards. In these circumstances, one of the FCO commitments which became vulnerable was the British Military Advisory Team for the United Arab Emirates, based in Sharjah. The team was established towards the end of 1971 as a consequence of HMG's offer to station British forces in the UAE after the termination of Britain's special treaty relationship with the former Trucial States. In practice, it was discovered that the only function of the team was to provide assistance to British units which occasionally visited the UAE for training purposes.[163] Although reduced from ninety-two to fifty personnel in 1973, the team still cost the FCO some £311,000 per annum. Since there was also no specific requirement by UAE forces for the facilities available from MAT, the decision was made to withdraw it in the first half of 1975.[164] McCarthy, however, comforted himself with the thought that the Rulers concerned would be 'relieved rather than upset' by the British decision.[165] Although the withdrawal of MAT proved uncontroversial, the vexed question of Palestine threatened to disrupt British relations with the UAE. In mid-1974, McCarthy reported 'a fresh round of private expressions of regret that Britain seemed to be following the United States over the Palestine problem

Challenges and opportunities, 1974–1977 87

and that we are, in this, both more subservient to the US and less constructive than France'.[166] Although US Deputy Assistant Secretary of State for Near Eastern Affairs Roger P. Davies, during Anglo–American talks in May 1974, had declared that the two countries' interests were 'parallel from the northern end of the Gulf to Oman',[167] the dangers of too close an association with the United States were underscored in relation to the continuing US military presence in Bahrain.

At the end of 1971, stationing and facilities agreements had been reached between the US and Bahrain which permitted the US Navy access to the Amirate. The arrangement attracted controversy in Washington since it had been made under an Executive Agreement to which the Senate objected. On 6 March 1972, a resolution was passed by a vote of 50–6 calling on the administration to submit as treaties to the Senate the recent agreements with Bahrain.[168] Such wrangling between the executive and legislature ensured that the question attracted wide media attention. As early as January 1972, the Bahrain government felt obliged to issue a statement regretting the manner in which international news agencies and the American press had treated the nature of Bahraini–American relations and emphasizing that Bahrain's sovereignty and independence were not compromised by the recent agreements.[169] During discussions with America's Chargé d'Affaires in Manama, John Newton Gatch, the Bahraini Foreign Minister, Sheikh Muhammad, confessed that unwelcome publicity was making the Bahraini government 'more and more uncomfortable and exposed not only with Arab neighbors but also with Bahraini people'.[170] As if to underline this point, he referred to Kuwaiti Foreign Minister Shaikh Sabah's advice to cancel the agreements. 'If you really need 600,000 dollars a year', he said dismissively, 'Kuwait will give it to you'.[171]

Against the backdrop of the 1973 Yom Kippur War, the Bahraini government invoked the one-year termination clause in the 1971 Executive Agreement. As US–Arab relations thawed, America secured the continuation of the military presence not only by addressing certain Bahraini concerns about the exercise of criminal jurisdiction over US Navy personnel, but also by increasing the rent for the Middle East Force facilities from $600,000 to $4 million per annum. This proved to a temporary reprieve, however. Responding to domestic and regional pressure, the government of Bahrain indicated in August 1975 its intention to secure the departure of the US Navy by 30 June 1977. Reflecting the potential for controversy and ill-feeling that the issue could engender, Ambassador Given reported in October 1976 that the Amir of Bahrain, Sheikh Isa, 'delivered himself of a very angry outburst against the Americans for trying to put pressure on him to renew the lease of the US naval base here for a further three years'.[172] Nonetheless, the government of Bahrain signalled its willingness to accept a new arrangement under which Americans would keep their logistic support facilities with some seventy-five Department of Defense personnel and allow the Commander Middle East Force and his flagship to visit Bahrain at least four months per year, provided the 1971 agreement were terminated and Bahrain ceased being the homeport for the Command and flagship.[173] Subsequently, the Bahraini Ministry of Foreign Affairs issued an official statement to the effect that the 1971 agreement would be terminated on 30 June 1977, but pointing out that some ships of the US Navy of the Middle East would, 'from time to time, visit Bahrain in the same way as they visit the ports of other friendly countries in the region'.[174] The Bahraini Minister of Foreign Affairs informed Given that a reduced rent would henceforth be payable but added that the government of Bahrain had been less concerned about this than with the Amirate's image in the Arab world and with the resentment that some Bahrainis felt towards the American presence.[175] Sheikh Muhammad added that 'No-one is likely to notice the extent of the storage facilities which the Americans will keep, but the stigma of having an American "base" will be removed'.[176]

As regards Anglo–Bahraini relations, 1977 started on a positive note with Ambassador Given being able to report that Britain had retained its position as Bahrain's leading supplier with over 18 per cent of the market.[177] During a brief visit to the UK in February 1977, however, Sheikh Isa told the Head of the FCO's Middle East Department, Ivor Lucas, that 'the British are too slow in promoting trade with Bahrain; the Bahrainis valued their traditional relationship with Britain, and wanted more goods and people . . . from the UK'.[178] Given also reported in his annual review for 1976 that 'There were the usual complaints that British firms were not keen enough in going after such big contracts as were on offer'.[179] Lucas admitted that the 'failure to go for the big contracts has been echoed elsewhere in the Gulf'.[180] In response, Given resignedly stated: 'I doubt if there is much you or DOT could do to persuade British contractors, whose lack of keenness in certain cases was due to inability to produce the equipment required'.[181] The Ambassador also pointed out that 'Our commercial rivals are now tending to send politico/business missions headed by a Minister, which secures them attention at high levels which is not open to ordinary business visitors'.[182] Lucas, however, stressed that the delicate political situation in the UK, centring on uncertainty over how long the Parliamentary alliance between the Labour government and the Liberal Party would last, made any arrangements for visits by ministers or MPs 'subject to disruption'.[183]

British business in Bahrain also laboured under what Given characterized as an 'under-current of nationalism'.[184] 'Bahraini Ministers may in theory be willing to tolerate the presence of many British', he expatiated, 'but their Egyptian advisers get them so tangled up in laws which on their face are perfectly reasonable that the effect is a squeeze'.[185] No doubt in an effort to counteract such disadvantages, the Ambassador made a passionate plea for setting aside scruples regarding sales to the Bahraini Defence Force. He warned that if Britain declined to sell the Bahrainis proven equipment on the grounds that they had neither any real use for it, nor the ability to maintain it, 'we shall merely be handing the business to the French'.[186] Indeed, the penetration of the Bahrain market since 1971 by Britain's industrial competitors was graphically demonstrated by the fact that the building of a $340 million dry dock capable of accommodating tankers of 500,000 tons was completed at the end of 1977 by Hyundai Construction Company of Korea. Although the design for the dock was produced by an Anglo–Portuguese consortium, Gibb Profabril, Ambassador Given pointed out that Hyundai Construction, 'by doing a first-class job and finishing ahead of time', had put itself in a 'good position' to get more work in the area.[187] In his annual

Challenges and opportunities, 1974–1977 89

review for 1977, moreover, Given emphasized that although Britain remained 'on the friendliest of terms' with Bahrain, this did not mean that it automatically got the 'inside track' where it really mattered, namely in trade.[188] He also pointed out that British contractors and consultants had been 'heavily criticized for various shortcomings' and that Britain had 'lost ground' to competitors in work for the Bahraini government.[189]

Britain also faced strong competition in Abu Dhabi. In a March 1973 interview with Salim Lawzi, the editor-in-chief of the Arabic publication, *al-Hawadeth*, Sheikh Zaid proclaimed with reference to the British: 'We told them frankly that we are not to blame if we find suitable weapons at lower prices from other sources. We are free to buy arms from any source we wish'.[190] This was soon confirmed. At the beginning of 1974, P. A. Raftery of the FCO's Middle East Department recorded that 'the French have been very successful with the sale of Mirage aircraft to Abu Dhabi; they are now engaged in direct competition with us to secure the lucrative contract for a surface to air missile defence system there (ie: Rapier v. Crotale)'.[191] He expatiated: 'There are no holds barred in the arms sales business and . . . the French in Abu Dhabi have engaged in a knocking job over Rapier during the last two months'.[192] R. W. Renwick, First Secretary at the British Embassy in Paris, pointed out that the appointment of French Ambassadors to the Gulf States was part of a 'long-term French effort' to ensure that they were as well placed as possible to win commercial and arms sales contracts in the region.[193] 'There is no doubt that we can expect increasingly fierce competition from them', he concluded.[194] There were also British concerns that the Paris government was illegally subsidising French arms sales to achieve an unfair advantage.[195] In September 1974, moreover, B. R. Pridham of the British Embassy in Abu Dhabi reported that the French approach had included the 'denigration of Rapier in specific and unfounded terms'.[196] In an increasingly rare victory for British commerce, a contract for the supply of Rapier missiles was signed on 17 November 1974, smoothed in part by the manufacturers, the British Aircraft Corporation's, agreement to a reduction in price of some 4 per cent.[197]

In Qatar, Ambassador Crawford conceded at the beginning of 1977 that a slowing in the Amirate's development would mean 'reduced opportunities' for British participation in major contracts, particularly since those for the main industrial projects had already been awarded to Japanese and other foreign companies.[198] A further challenge to British business prospects in Qatar was dealt by the Amir's naming of his son, Sheikh Hamad, as crown prince. Although Lucas stressed that Hamad was a graduate of Sandhurst and admired the UK, the new crown prince launched an unexpected tirade during a demonstration of the British-made Blindfire air defence system in July 1977, declaring that 'all Englishmen hated Arabs and that he and his fellow countrymen respected the way in which President Amin had dealt with the British in Uganda'.[199] E. A. Mohan of the British Embassy in Qatar, however, described Hamad's outburst as 'a bit of customer one-upmanship and an attempt to put the air defence negotiators on the defensive from the start'.[200] The visit of the Amir of Qatar to Britain in the autumn of 1977, however, provided an opportunity to bolster British relations with Hamad's father.

On hearing of Sheikh Khalifah's impending trip, Ivor Lucas stressed that a meeting with Prime Minister James Callaghan would 'do much to promote our interests in Qatar'.[201] Lucas went on to point out that 'We are keen to go on increasing our exports' and that Qatar remained Britain's fifth most significant supplier of oil.[202] He also noted that Britain was facing strong competition from France in the sale of modern fighter aircraft to Qatar. When the Amir met Foreign Secretary Callaghan in Doha in 1975, he had made clear the importance he attached to his links with Britain, but questioned whether this feeling was reciprocated. Consequently, the arrangement of a meeting with Callaghan in London would, according to Lucas, serve to reassure Khalifah on this point.

When the two men finally met on 1 November 1977, the Amir indicated that although he was 'very pleased' with the development of economic and cultural relations between Qatar and the United Kingdom, 'the Japanese were proving very strong competitors with the Europeans in the Arabian Gulf'.[203] He also referred to 'misconduct' on the part of British consultants in Qatar, mentioning in particular 'serious errors' made with respect to a water distillation project which had resulted in a 'great deal of expense'.[204] The Amir added that the episode had 'given rise to doubts about the competence of British firms'.[205] In an effort to mitigate any potential ill-feeling, Callaghan offered personally to look into the Amir's complaints. Investigations revealed that the fault was not attributable to the British firm concerned, Ewbanks, but to the contractors, an Italian firm which had admitted responsibility. In his formal response to the Amir, Callaghan reflected this and also the fact that error was 'rapidly and effectively' corrected. In conclusion, the Prime Minister assured Sheikh Khalifah of his 'friendship and support', as well as expressing his wish that British firms would continue to co-operate 'fully and efficiently' with Qatar in its social and economic development.[206] The potential for disputes in the commercial (and defence) fields to disrupt British relations with the Gulf States was also demonstrated with respect to British tank sales to Kuwait.

In the aftermath of the renewal of tensions along the Kuwait-Iraq border in early 1973, the Kuwaitis had expressed interest in purchasing British-made Chieftain tanks. Interminable wrangling over price and delivery times, however, had led Ambassador Lamb at the beginning of 1975 to describe the Chieftain deal as 'abortive'.[207] The Kuwaiti Minister of State for Cabinet Affairs, Abdulaziz Hussein, chided Lamb for Britain's 'apparent reluctance to push the Chieftain tank deal' which, he felt, illustrated British 'failure' to work hard for its interests in the Gulf.[208] He went on to inform Lamb that Britain had had a strong commercial position in Kuwait but had allowed it 'to slip away to foreigners'.[209] Despite Abdulaziz Hussein's downbeat message, the Kuwaiti Minister of Defence, Sheikh Sa'ad al-Abdullah, told Lamb that the 'door was not closed' to further negotiations on the sale of Chieftains to Kuwait.[210] The Ambassador himself attempted to breathe new life into the prospective deal, warning that if it fell through it 'would not improve our chances of being counted among the ranks of the "friendly nations" should another Arab/Israel war break out'.[211] 'After all', he concluded, 'a decline in the

Challenges and opportunities, 1974–1977 91

attachment of Kuwait to Britain represents far more of a risk to the [British] taxpayer than could the Chieftain deal'.[212]

As the negotiations over the purchase of Chieftains appeared to reach deadlock, especially on the key question of price, Lamb once more entered the debate, indicating that the issue was becoming 'a central one in Anglo–Kuwaiti relations. In their eyes it is much more than a commercial arms transaction and they now profess to see it as a test case of British willingness to help Kuwait meet what she regards as her essential defence requirements'.[213] Summing up, he observed that 'a breakdown of the Chieftain negotiations will have repercussions going beyond the defence sales field . . . spilling over into other areas of Anglo–Kuwaiti relations'.[214]

Précising the dilemma in which the British found themselves, the Head of the FCO's Middle East Department, Ivor Lucas, minuted: 'The argument boils down to balancing a real and tangible risk of loss to the British taxpayer which it would be difficult to defend in the context of a deal with an oil-rich country, against potential but intangible effects on Kuwaiti attitudes to other aspects of our political, commercial and financial relations with them'.[215] Displaying clear signs of exasperation, Minister of Defence Sheikh Sa'ad al-Abdullah expostulated in October 1975 that he 'did not want to hear the word "Chieftain" again and had not liked the way the negotiations had been conducted'.[216] Nevertheless, before the end of the year agreement was finally reached to supply 165 Chieftain tanks at a total cost of £105 million. 'The British military connection will therefore be maintained through a reinforced Kuwait Liaison Team', enthused Ambassador Lamb.[217] The Chieftain deal, moreover, offset to some extent the Kuwaiti decision to purchase American-built Skyhawk attack aircraft rather than British-made Jaguars.[218] Nonetheless, Lamb's summary of Britain's commercial performance in Kuwait for 1976 was decidedly downbeat. 'Regrettably', he intoned, 'British traders and manufacturers failed in 1976 to take full advantage of the new boom and to maintain, let alone improve the rate of increase in British exports to Kuwait'.[219] Providing tangible evidence for this, the Ambassador noted that British exports for the year amounted to £140 million, an improvement of only £40 million in value over 1975 which, in view of inflation, suggested very little improvement by volume. The glow from the tank contract, moreover, was dimmed by the failure of the Ministry of Defence and the British Embassy in Kuwait successfully to arrange a visit by representatives of the Kuwait army to Britain and Germany to inspect Chieftain repair facilities.[220] While recognizing that part of the explanation for this rested with the Kuwaitis providing only one month's notice, Lamb noted that the French had required only twenty-four hours to organize a similar visit.[221] 'We all regret', bemoaned Ivor Lucas, 'that the Kuwaitis are not coming and the French look like cashing in'.[222]

In 1977, some ostensibly positive news came in the form of British attempts to meet Kuwait's requirements for fast patrol boats. Initially, a complaint by Sheikh Sa'ad al-Abdullah at the beginning of the year regarding Britain's supply of nine-year-old ammunition for Chieftain tanks appeared to jeopardize the successful

92 *Challenges and opportunities, 1974–1977*

conclusion of a deal on patrol boats.[223] The Kuwaitis were apparently pacified by the commitment by the Ministry of Defence to replace any ammunition with which they were unhappy.[224] Moreover, in response to Sheikh Sa'ad al-Abdullah's concern about past problems in the pricing of British military products, Prime Minister James Callaghan personally assured him that the price in this case was 'reasonable' and that Britain could also offer training and other support facilities associated with the sale.[225]

Sheikh Sa'ad subsequently confirmed that on 4 April 1977 the Kuwaiti Supreme Defence Council had decided to award the contract to Britain, specifically for craft manufactured by Vosper Thorneycroft.[226] During the Kuwaiti Minister of Defence's visit to Britain towards the end of May, a Memorandum of Understanding was signed covering the support and training which the Ministry of Defence would provide on the conclusion of a formal contract for the supply of the fast patrol boats.[227] This was something of a pyrrhic victory, nevertheless. In 1980, the Kuwaitis finally decided to place the order for patrol boats with Lürrsens of Germany.[228] The acting Kuwaiti Chief of Staff, Major General Abdullah Faraj Al Ghanim, and Brigadier Abdul Aziz Radha Al Sayegh who chaired the Naval Purchasing Committee, made it clear that the contract went to the Germans because it was 'very much cheaper'.[229]

Lamb reported, shortly before stepping down as Ambassador towards the end of 1977, that Britain, far from being Kuwait's principal supplier, was in fact 'languishing in fourth place behind the US, Japan and West Germany'.[230] Similar disappointments were noticeable as regards British trade with the United Arab Emirates. In his annual review for 1975, Ambassador McCarthy gave the ostensibly good news that British exports to the UAE were likely to total £196 million representing an increase in sterling terms of well over 100 per cent over the previous year.[231] Nevertheless, he noted that this improvement should be placed in the context of a quintupling of the UAE's income in just two years. He added that 'our performance could have been better had our traders and manufacturers alike not lost on price and delivery in all too many cases'.[232] Equally worrying, he remarked that 'there were whole sectors of the market which British industry virtually could not touch, whether because of price or the absence of product'.[233] 'British exports', he lamented, 'should do much better in a market which is still biased in our favour provided that other things are equal'.[234] McCarthy's review for 1976 hardly made for better reading.

On the one hand, the Ambassador highlighted that Britain's visible exports totalled around £202 million for the year, an increase of some 53 per cent over the 1975 figure. On the other hand, he pointed out some 'disquieting truth' behind these figures.[235] After earlier improvement, he expatiated, 'the year ended with a chorus of complaint about our late deliveries and accompanying cost increases'.[236] Warming to his theme, McCarthy stressed that Britain remained 'virtually unrepresented' in the automotive market and had lost major contracts which it should have secured, even though in one case the deadline had been extended for over a month to enable the submission of an improved offer. The Ambassador expressed particular concern that British trade with Abu Dhabi was 'slipping'. Reflecting wider fears about British commerce in the UAE, McCarthy concluded:

> The British managers drive Mercedes. Their heavy transport is Japanese, German, or Swedish; their earth movers are American. They often install Japanese or German steel and other foreign content in their projects.... American technology (and the beginnings of Japanese) still monopolise those oil related operations and construction which are not under British management.[237]

Despite the Gulf States' swollen oil revenues, British commerce proved incapable of either exploiting fully the new opportunities, or meeting the challenge presented by rivals from the industrialized world. Britain's domestic travails, moreover, served to erode confidence in the British economy. In July 1974, for instance, the Kuwaiti Minister of Finance and Oil, Abdul Rahman Atiqi, bluntly informed Ambassador Lamb that his government 'wished to keep as much of its money as possible in Britain but were frightened by the twin spectres of devaluation and inflation'.[238] Following his visit to the Gulf in February 1975, moreover, the Minister of State at the FCO, David Ennals, underlined that 'Everywhere there were complaints about slow deliveries of goods from Britain',[239] something that Secretary of State for Trade Peter Shore also encountered during his own tour of the region a few months later.[240] Further damage to British commercial (and geopolitical) interests was provided by chronic instability in Iran, culminating in the Iranian Revolution and the overthrow of the Shah in 1979. This will be the subject of the next chapter.

Notes

1 Letter from Henderson to P. R. H. Wright, 3 December 1973, FCO 8/2158.
2 Ibid.
3 Summary record of a conversation between the Prime Minister and His Highness, Sheikh Zaid, President of the United Arab Emirates and Ruler of Abu Dhabi at dinner at No. 10 Downing Street, 9 September 1974, FCO 8/2360.
4 Ibid.
5 Dominic Sandbrook, *Seasons in the Sun: The Battle for Britain, 1974–1979* (London: Allen Lane, 2012), p. 9. Siegmund Warburg had founded the London-based investment bank, S. G. Warburg, in 1946.
6 Richard Smith, '"Paying our way in the world": The FCO, export promotion and Iran in the 1970s', in John Fisher, Effie G.H. Pedaliu, and Richard Smith (eds.), *The Foreign Office, Commerce and British Foreign Policy in the Twentieth Century* (Basingstoke: Palgrave Macmillan, 2017), p. 490. Britain faced a balance of payments deficit for 1974 of £3317 million (Ibid., p. 487).
7 Report of a visit to certain Arab countries to discuss oil supplies and other matters (1–9 November 1973), by Spain, 14 November 1973, FCO 8/2163.
8 The following is based on 'UK relations with Gulf States', Minute by Wright, 30 November 1973, FCO 8/2163.
9 The following is based on Letter from Henderson to Sir Alec Douglas-Home, 9 January 1974, FCO 8/2290.

10 'Qatar annual review for 1973', Minute by Harris, 30 January 1974, FCO 8/2290.
11 Letter from Henderson to Harris, 1 April 1974, FCO 8/2293.
12 Letter from Henderson to Wright, 2 June 1974, FCO 8/2295.
13 Ibid.
14 Ibid.
15 Telegram from Doha to the Foreign and Commonwealth Office, No. 179, 20 June 1974, FCO 8/2295.
16 Letter from Henderson to S. Baker (Department of Trade and Industry), 8 July 1974, FCO 8/2296.
17 Letter from Henderson to Baker, 15 July 1974, FCO 8/2296.
18 Letter from Henderson to Baker, 25 August 1974, FCO 8/2296.
19 Ibid.
20 'Inward investment from Qatar', Minute by Peter Shore (Secretary of State for Trade), 10 September 1974, T 317/2403.
21 Report of the reconnaissance mission to Abu Dhabi, Kuwait, and Qatar, 11–21 November 1974, T 317/2404.
22 'Qatar, 3–6 February 1975', Minute by Barratt, 10 February 1975, T 317/2404.
23 Telegram from Henderson to the Foreign and Commonwealth Office, No. 1, 1 January 1974, FCO 8/2298.
24 Telegram from Henderson to the Foreign and Commonwealth Office, No. 7, 7 January 1974, FCO 8/2298.
25 Telegram from Henderson to the Foreign and Commonwealth Office, No. 16, 14 January 1974, FCO 8/ 2298.
26 Telegram from Henderson to the Foreign and Commonwealth Office, No. 22, 24 January 1974, FCO 8/2298.
27 'Signals officer for the Qatar Security Forces', Minute by P. A. Raftery, 22 January 1974, FCO 8/2298.
28 Ibid.
29 Telegram from Henderson to the Foreign and Commonwealth Office, No. 103, 30 March 1974, FCO 8/2298.
30 Ibid.
31 Telegram from Henderson to the Foreign and Commonwealth Office, No. 9, 7 January 1974, FCO 8/2300. QPC was owned by British Petroleum (23.75 per cent), Royal Dutch Shell (23.75 per cent), Compagnie Francaise des Petroles (23.75 per cent), Standard Oil of New Jersey (11.875 per cent), Mobil Oil (11.875 per cent), Participations and Exploration Corporation (5 per cent).
32 Letter from Henderson to the Foreign and Commonwealth Office, 24 February 1974, FCO 8/2300.
33 Ibid.
34 Telegram from Henderson to the Foreign and Commonwealth Office, No. 92, 17 March 1974, FCO 8/2300; Letter from D. G. Crawford to S. L. Egerton, 30 December 1974, FCO 8/2300. The remaining 40 per cent of the Qatar Petroleum Company and the Shell Company Qatar was formally turned over to the Qatari government in September 1976 and February 1977 respectively (Ragaei El Mallakh, *Qatar: Development of an Oil Economy* (London: Croom Helm, 1979), pp. 34–5).
35 Telegram from the Foreign and Commonwealth Office to Washington, No. 1723, 16 August 1974, FCO 8/2360.
36 James Bamberg, *British Petroleum and Global Oil, 1950–1975: The Challenge of Nationalism* (Cambridge: Cambridge University Press, 2000), p. 499.
37 Letter from D. G. Crawford to S. L. Egerton, 30 December 1974, FCO 8/2300.
38 Letter from Crawford to Wright, 19 November 1974, FCO 8/2304.
39 Ibid.
40 Letter from Crawford to the Secretary of State for Foreign and Commonwealth Affairs, 20 January 1974, FCO 8/2524.
41 Ibid.

Challenges and opportunities, 1974–1977 95

42 Ibid.
43 Letter from E. F. Henderson to Sir Alec Douglas-Home, 8 January 1973, FCO 8/2079.
44 Letter from Crawford to the Secretary of State for Foreign and Commonwealth Affairs, 20 January 1974, FCO 8/2524.
45 'Qatar annual review', Minute by Kinchen, 3 February 1975, FCO 8/2524.
46 Record of a conversation between the Minister of State for Foreign and Commonwealth Affairs and the Amir of Qatar, Doha, 13 February 1975, T 317/2404.
47 Letter from J. C. Rowley to Crawford, 8 February 1975, FCO 8/2528.
48 Telegram from Doha to the Foreign and Commonwealth Office, No. 49, 13 February 1975, FCO 8/2528; Telegram from Doha to the Department of Trade, No. 40, 31 March 1975, FCO 8/2528.
49 Telegram from Doha to the Department of Trade, No. 40, 31 March 1975, FCO 8/2528.
50 Record of a conversation between the Minister of State for Foreign and Commonwealth Affairs and the Amir of Qatar, Doha, 13 February 1975, T 317/2404.
51 'Inward investment from Qatar', Minute by Peter Shore, 10 September 1974, T 317/2403.
52 Agreed record of a meeting between His Highness the Amir, Sheikh Khalifah bin Hamad al Thani, and the members of the British industrial and technical mission, 19 November 1974, T 317/2404.
53 Minute by Callaghan, FCS/74/68, 12 September 1974, T 317/2403.
54 Telegram from Doha to the Department of Trade, No. 44, 7 April 1975, FCO 8/2530.
55 Telegram from the Foreign and Commonwealth Office to UK Representative, Brussels, No. 838, 31 July 1975, FCO 8/2530.
56 Agreement on Cooperation between the Government of the United Kingdom and Northern Ireland and Government of the State of Qatar, undated, FCO 8/2530.
57 'UAE/UK Joint Committee', Minute by Passmore, 28 April 1981, FCO 8/3911. Similarly, writing three years earlier the British Ambassador to the UAE, D. A. Roberts, remarked: 'I have to confess . . . to having been a bit sceptical in the past about the value of Joint Committees. I no longer am. Not only do they force a government which hardly has a filing system, let alone a "bring-up" system, to review a range of problems twice a year, but they also ensure contact twice a year between Ministers in the two governments' (Letter from Roberts to David Owen, 15 March 1978, FCO 8/3142).
58 Letter from Crawford to Callaghan, 18 January 1976, FCO 8/2770.
59 Ibid.
60 Letter from Crawford to H. V. B. Brown (Department of Trade), 18 May 1975, FCO 8/2529.
61 Letter from Crawford to I. T. M. Lucas, 10 February 1975, FCO 8/2528.
62 Letter from Gordon to Jones, 4 August 1975, FCO 8/2531.
63 Letter from Crawford to Lucas, No. 090/1, 23 February 1976, FCO 8/2775.
64 Ibid.
65 Letter from Crawford to the Secretary of State for Foreign and Commonwealth Affairs, 18 January 1967, FCO 8/2623.
66 Letter from Crawford to Lucas, 10 July 1976, FCO 8/2771.
67 Letter from Crawford to the Secretary of State for Foreign and Commonwealth Affairs, 26 June 1976, FCO 8/2772.
68 Report by Michael Meacher on his visit to Qatar, 6 July 1976, FCO 8/2772.
69 Ibid.
70 Letter from Crawford to the Secretary of State for Foreign and Commonwealth Affairs, 26 June 1976, FCO 8/2772.
71 Letter from Crawford to Lucas, 5 June 1976, FCO 8/2776.
72 Kathleen Burk and Alec Cairncross, *'Goodbye, Great Britain': The 1976 IMF* Crisis (New Haven and London: Yale University Press, 1992), p. 169.
73 Sandbrook, *Seasons in the Sun*, p. 467.
74 Ibid., p. 470.
75 Letter from Crawford to Lucas, 5 June 1976, FCO 8/2776.

96 *Challenges and opportunities, 1974–1977*

76 Note of Mr Meacher's audience with His Highness, Shaikh Khalifah bin Hamad Al Thani, the Amir of Qatar, 19 June 1976, FCO 8/2772.
77 Report by Michael Meacher on his visit to Qatar, 6 July 1976, FCO 8/2772.
78 At the beginning of 1975, Ambassador Crawford reported that 'The most striking feature of Government was the unflagging energy of the Amir himself which outshone the efforts, and indeed showed up the shortcomings, of most of his Ministers and officials' (Letter from Crawford to the Secretary of State for Foreign and Commonwealth Affairs, 20 January 1975, FCO 8/2524).
79 Letter from R. M. Tesh to the Secretary of State for Foreign and Commonwealth Affairs, 24 December 1972, FCO 8/1822.
80 Ibid.
81 Letter from Tesh to the Secretary of State for Foreign and Commonwealth Affairs, 12 June 1972, FCO 8/1975.
82 Letter from Tesh to Sir Alec Douglas-Home 28 December 1973, FCO 8/2180.
83 Ibid.
84 Ibid.
85 'Bahrain's first Parliament', Minute by Harris, 14 January 1974, FCO 8/2180.
86 Letter from Tesh to Douglas-Home, 30 December 1973, FCO 8/2181.
87 Letter from Tesh to Wright, 9 April 1974, FCO 8/2180.
88 Letter from N. W. Browne to P. K. Williams, 30 January 1974, FCO 8/2180.
89 Letter from Tesh to Douglas-Home, 30 December 1973, FCO 8/2181.
90 Letter from Tesh to Wright, 9 April 1974, FCO 8/2180.
91 Letter from Tesh to Wright, 10 June 1974, FCO 8/2180.
92 Letter from Tesh to Douglas-Home, 30 December 1973, FCO 8/2181.
93 Letter from Tesh to the Secretary of State for Foreign and Commonwealth Affairs, 2 January 1975, FCO 8/2414.
94 Ibid.
95 Ibid.
96 Ibid.
97 Ibid.
98 'Bahrain annual review', Minute by Kinchen, 15 January 1975, FCO 8/2414.
99 Letter from Tesh to James Callaghan, 3 July 1975, FCO 8/2416.
100 Ibid.
101 'Bahrain: internal situation', Minute by T. J. Clark, 9 September 1975, FCO 8/2415.
102 Letter from E. H. Noble (First Secretary, British Embassy, Bahrain) to Lucas, 26 August 1975, FCO 8/2415.
103 Letter from Given to Callaghan, 18 December 1975, FCO 8/2415.
104 Ibid.
105 Letter from Given to the Secretary of State for Foreign and Commonwealth Affairs, 5 January 1976, FCO 8/2644.
106 Ibid.
107 Ibid.
108 Letter from Given to the Secretary of State for Foreign and Commonwealth Affairs, 5 July 1976, FCO 8/2643.
109 Letter from Lucas to Given, 26 January 1976, FCO 8/2644.
110 Letter from Given to the Secretary of State for Foreign and Commonwealth Affairs, 5 July 1976, FCO 8/2643.
111 Ibid.
112 Letter from Lucas to Given, 29 October 1976, FCO 8/2643.
113 Letter from A. J. Wilton to Douglas-Home, 6 January 1974, FCO 8/2188.
114 J. B. Kelly, *Arabia, the Gulf and the West* (New York: Basic Books, 1991), p. 172. Three years later, the Kuwaitis purchased further Soviet weaponry which elicited a strong US response. The British Ambassador to Kuwait remarked: 'Although, as you

know, I think that American diplomacy has been rather inept in raising this matter with the Kuwaitis after the event, I still think that we must keep an eye on Kuwait's foreign and defence policies and speak confidently to them whenever we see the possibility of their contemplating action which could, in American words, introduce a "destabilising influence"' (Letter from A. T. Lamb to Lucas, 27 April 1977, FCO 8/2931).
115 Letter from Wilton to Callaghan, 22 April 1974, FCO 8/2192.
116 Ibid.
117 Ibid.
118 Ibid.
119 Minute by Clark, 30 April 1974, FCO 8/2192.
120 Letter from Lamb to Callaghan, 1 August 1974, FCO 8/2192. In his memoirs, Lamb remarked: 'I saw my job as Ambassador to Kuwait as being to conduct harmonious relations with Kuwait, harmonious because the two governments were not playing the same tune and could not be in unison: in musical terms the Kuwaiti tune was in the pentatonic Arab tradition whilst ours was based on the octave. The best the Ambassador could do was to produce a harmony' (Sir Archie Lamb, *A Long Way from Swansea: A Memoir* (Clunderwen: Starborn Books, 2003), p. 142).
121 Letter from Lamb to Callaghan, 1 August 1974, FCO 8/2192.
122 Ibid. The FCO subsequently commented that 'In recent years, because of nationalist pressures, the Kuwaitis have played down their British connection' (Brief attached to 'Call of Kuwait Ambassador, His Excellency Sayyid Ahmad Abdul Wahhab al-Naqib, at 10.30am on Friday, 23 August', Minute by Wright, 22 August 1974, FCO 8/2195).
123 Letter from Lamb to Callaghan, 1 August 1974, FCO 8/2192.
124 Ibid.
125 Letter from Lamb to Wright, 24 November 1974, FCO 8/2200.
126 Letter from Treadwell to Wright, 27 December 1972, FCO 8/2126.
127 Ibid.
128 Letter from Treadwell to the Secretary of State for Foreign and Commonwealth Affairs, 10 June 1973, FCO 8/2126.
129 Letter from McCarthy to Wright, 21 April 1974, FCO 8/2359.
130 Record of a conversation between the Prime Minister and the President of the United Arab Emirates at Chequers at 12 noon on Tuesday 12 September 1972, PREM 15/1086.
131 Letter from McCarthy to Wright, 21 April 1974, FCO 8/2359.
132 Ibid.
133 Ibid.
134 For a detailed analysis of the origins of the dispute, see Michael Quentin Morton, *Buraimi: The Struggle for Power, Influence and Oil in Arabia* (London and New York: I. B. Tauris, 2013).
135 'Territorial disputes in the Persian Gulf', Minute by McCarthy, 12 November 1969, cited in Richard Schofield (ed.), *Arabian Boundaries: New Documents, 1966–75: Volume 10, 1970* (Cambridge: Cambridge University Press, 2009), p. 51.
136 Ibid., p. 52. A few months earlier, A. F. Goulty of the FCO's Arabian Department had commented: 'Although the present position leaves a lot to be desired we do not think that we should take the initiative in attempting to clear up outstanding frontier problems at this stage, since any such attempt would probably arouse more disputes than it would solve. Indeed if British effort were the answer the frontiers would have already been settled' (Letter from Goulty to G. P. Wall (Residency, Bahrain), 5 August 1969, cited in Richard Schofield (ed.), *Arabian Boundaries: New Documents, 1966–75: Volume 8, 1969* (Cambridge: Cambridge University Press, 2009), p. 486).
137 Minute from D. E. T. Luard to McCarthy, 27 November 1969, cited in ibid., p. 55.

98 Challenges and opportunities, 1974–1977

138 Ibid.
139 Letter from R. N. Dales (Assistant Private Secretary to the Secretary of State for Foreign and Commonwealth Affairs) to Lord Bridges (Private Secretary (Overseas Affairs) to the Prime Minister), 1 August 1974, in Richard Schofield (ed.), *Arabian Boundaries: New Documents, 1966–75: Volume 15, 1974* (Cambridge: Cambridge University Press, 2009), p. 190. In early 1972, the British Ambassador in Jedda, Willie Morris, had reported that during discussions with Prince Fahd, the latter had launched into 'lengthy criticism' of Britain's failure to secure a border settlement with Abu Dhabi before terminating its responsibilities (Record of a conversation between HM Ambassador Jedda and Prince Fahd bin Abdul Aziz, Second Deputy Prime Minister and Minister of the Interior at the latter's office in Jedda, 26 February 1972 at 1.00pm, in Richard Schofield (ed.), *Arabian Boundaries: New Documents, 1966–75: Volume 13, 1972* (Cambridge: Cambridge University Press, 2009), p. 111). Fahd's remarks, noted Morris, 'only confirmed . . . that our failure to arrange a settlement of the Abu Dhabi border problem remains the real bone in the throat of Anglo–Saudi relations. The sense of grievance on this now looms larger than our "betrayal" on Aden and is of course historically more deeply rooted' (Telegram from Jedda to the Foreign and Commonwealth Office, No. 129, 28 February 1972, ibid., p. 109). Richard Schofield contends that 'While Britain had throughout the late 1960s tried to marginalise the debilitating effects for the regional political map of messy, localised traditional territorial claims, it ended up bequeathing a complex, contradictory, and essentially unworkable equation with which the two local disputants have struggled ever since' (Richard Schofield, 'The crystallisation of a complex territorial dispute: Britain and the Saudi-Abu Dhabi borderland, 1966–71', *Journal of Arabian Studies*, 1, 1 (2011), p. 50).
140 Letter from Treadwell to W. Morris, 13 December 1971, cited in Richard Schofield (ed.), *Arabian Boundaries: New Documents, 1966–75: Volume 12, 1971* (Cambridge: Cambridge University Press, 2009), p. 518.
141 Telegram from the Foreign and Commonwealth Office (Douglas-Home) to Amman, No. 348, 10 August 1972, FCO 8/1930.
142 'Abu Dhabi-Saudi frontier', Minute by A. D. Parsons, 23 February 1973, cited in Richard Schofield (ed.), *Arabian Boundaries: New Documents, 1966–75: Volume 14, 1973* (Cambridge: Cambridge University Press, 2009), p. 319.
143 Telegram from Jedda to the Foreign and Commonwealth Office, No. 228, 13 May 1973, in Schofield, *Arabian Boundaries: Volume* 14, p. 354; Letter from Lord Denman (Chairman, Committee for Middle East Trade) to Douglas-Home, 17 May 1973, in Schofield, *Arabian Boundaries: Volume* 14, p. 355.
144 'Saudi-UAE relations', Minute by Wright, 23 May 1973, cited in Schofield, *Arabian Boundaries: Volume* 14, p. 359.
145 Letter from Douglas-Home to Denman, 24 May 1973, cited in Schofield, *Arabian Boundaries: Volume* 14, p. 362.
146 Letter from McCarthy to Wright, 7 July 1974, cited in Schofield, *Arabian Boundaries: Volume* 15, p. 172.
147 Ibid.
148 Letter from Wright to McCarthy, 23 July 1974, cited in Schofield, *Arabian Boundaries: Volume* 15, p. 176.
149 Letter from Hawley to Wright, 15 July 1974, cited in Schofield, *Arabian Boundaries: Volume* 15, p. 174.
150 'Settlement of the Saudi/UAE dispute', Minute by Wright, 30 July 1974, in Schofield, *Arabian Boundaries: Volume* 15, p. 186.
151 Ibid., p. 187.
152 Letter from Henderson to Wright, 15 August 1974, cited in Schofield, *Arabian Boundaries: Volume* 15, p. 229. The Saudi Ambassador to Qatar had told his British counterpart, E. F. Henderson, that 'one of the things which inhibited the King [Feisal] from making further progress towards a solution was the fear that Shaikh Zaid's government of the UAE was very precarious, that it might topple and something of

Challenges and opportunities, 1974–1977 99

a PDRY/Dhofari kind take its place' (Letter from Henderson to A. D. Harris, 6 May, 1974, cited in Schofield, *Arabian Boundaries: Volume 15*, p. 168).
153 Telegram from Jedda to the Foreign and Commonwealth Office, No. 598, 23 August 1974, in Schofield, *Arabian Boundaries: Volume 15*, p. 242.
154 Letter from Walker to T. J. Clark, 24 August 1974, cited in Schofield, *Arabian Boundaries: Volume 15*, p. 245.
155 Translation of joint communiqué issued at Jedda on 21 August 1974, cited in Schofield, *Arabian Boundaries: Volume 15*, p. 247.
156 Telegram from the Foreign and Commonwealth Office to Tunis, No. 50, 2 August 1974, in Schofield, *Arabian Boundaries: Volume 15*, p. 194; Telegram from the Foreign and Commonwealth Office to Cairo, No. 436, 2 August 1974, in Schofield, *Arabian Boundaries: Volume 15*, p. 195.
157 Letter from McCarthy to the Secretary of State for Foreign and Commonwealth Affairs, 7 August 1974, cited in Schofield, *Arabian Boundaries: Volume 15*, p. 207.
158 Letter from Treadwell to the Secretary of State for Foreign and Commonwealth Affairs, 10 June 1973, FCO 8/2126.
159 Letter from McCarthy to Wright, 24 June 1974, FCO 8/2359.
160 Ibid.
161 Ibid.
162 Ibid.
163 Letter from J. A. Thomson (Assistant Under-Secretary of State, FCO) to A. P. Hockaday (Deputy Under-Secretary of State, MoD), 6 May 1974, FCO 8/2370.
164 Telegram from the Foreign and Commonwealth Office to Washington, No. 2652, 31 December 1974, FCO 8/2370.
165 Telegram from McCarthy to the Foreign and Commonwealth Office, No. 216, 6 December 1974, FCO 8/2370.
166 Letter from McCarthy to Lucas, 1 June 1975, FCO 8/2409.
167 Anglo–US talks on the Gulf and the Arabian Peninsula at the State Department, 23 May 1974, FCO 8/2157.
168 Letter from Senator Clifford P. Case to Rogers, 6 March 1972, RG 59, Subject-Numeric Files 1970–73, Box 1690, DEF 15-4 BAHRAIN-US.
169 Telegram from American Embassy, Manama, (Gatch) to American Embassy, Tehran, No. 60, 23 January.1972, RG 59, Subject-Numeric Files 1970–73, Box 2113, POL BAHRAIN IS-A [POL BAHRAIN-US].
170 Telegram from American Embassy, Manama, (Gatch) to Secretary of State, No. 229, 3 April 1972, RG 59, Subject-Numeric Files 1970–73, Box 1690, DEF 15-4 BAHRAIN-US.
171 Ibid.
172 Letter from Given to Lucas, 26 October 1976, FCO 8/2623.
173 Action Memorandum from the Acting Director of the Bureau of Politico-Military Affairs (Reginald Bartholomew) and the Assistant Secretary of State for Near Eastern and South Asian Affairs (Alfred L. Atherton) to Secretary of State Vance, 2 May 1977, *Foreign Relations of the United States, 1977–80: Vol. XVIII: Middle East Region; Arabian Peninsula* (Washington, DC: United States Government Publishing Office, 2015), p. 14.
174 Letter from Given to Lucas, 30 June 1977, FCO 8/2842.
175 Ibid.
176 Ibid.
177 Letter from Given to the Secretary of State for Foreign and Commonwealth Affairs, 5 January 1977, FCO 8/2873.
178 'Transit visit of His Highness the Amir of Bahrain', Minute by Lucas, 10 February 1977, FCO 8/2876.
179 Letter from Given to the Secretary of State for Foreign and Commonwealth Affairs, 5 January 1977, FCO 8/2873.
180 Letter from Lucas to Given, 11 February 1977, FCO 8/2873.

100   *Challenges and opportunities, 1974–1977*

181 Letter from Given to Lucas, 15 March 1977, FCO 8/2873.
182 Ibid.
183 Letter from Lucas to Given, 1 April 1977, FCO 8/2873.
184 Letter from Given to Lucas, 15 February 1977, FCO 8/2875.
185 Ibid.
186 Letter from Given to W. J. Jones (Ministry of Defence), 21 June 1977, FCO 8/2877.
187 Letter from Given to Lucas, 20 December 1977, FCO 8/2878.
188 Letter from Given to the Secretary of State for Foreign and Commonwealth Affairs, 2 January 1978, FCO 8/3091.
189 Ibid.
190 Interview with Sheikh Zaid bin Sultan by Salim Lawzi (translation), *al-Hawadeth*, p. 3, 2 March 1973, FCO 8/2126.
191 Letter from Raftery to R. W. Renwick (British Embassy, Paris), Ref: NBT 10/6, 17 January 1974, FCO 8/2366.
192 Ibid.
193 Letter from Renwick to Raftery, 25 January 1974, FCO 8/2366.
194 Ibid.
195 Letter from McCarthy to Wright, 9 June 1974, FCO 8/2367.
196 Telegram from Abu Dhabi to the Foreign and Commonwealth Office, No. 261, 21 September 1974, FCO 8/2368.
197 Telegram from Abu Dhabi to the Foreign and Commonwealth Office, No. 308, 18 November 1974, FCO 8/2369.
198 Letter from Crawford to Anthony Crosland, 13 January 1977, FCO 8/3001.
199 Telegram from Doha to the Ministry of Defence, No. 070700Z, 7 July 1977, FCO 8/3002.
200 Teleletter from Doha to the Foreign and Commonwealth Office, No. 072, 25 July 1977, FCO 8/3002.
201 'Visit by Amir of Qatar', Minute by Lucas, 28 October 1977, FCO8 /3003.
202 Ibid.
203 Letter from Bryan Cartledge (Private Secretary to the Prime Minister) to W. K. Prendergast, 2 November 1977, FCO 8/3003.
204 Ibid.
205 Record of a conversation between the Prime Minister and the Amir of Qatar, Sheikh Khalifah, at No. 10 Downing Street, 1 November 1977 at 16.30, PREM 16/1425.
206 Message from Callaghan to HH the Amir, in telegram from Foreign and Commonwealth Office to Doha, No. 138, 8 December 1977, PREM 16/1425.
207 Letter from Lamb to the Secretary of State for Foreign and Commonwealth Affairs, 2 January 1975, FCO 8/2440.
208 Letter from Lamb to T. J. Clark, 26 January 1973, FCO 8/2446.
209 Ibid.
210 Letter from Lamb to M. S. Weir, 21 January 1973, FCO 8/2447.
211 Ibid.
212 Ibid.
213 Telegram from Kuwait to the Foreign and Commonwealth Office, No. 236, 11 May 1973, FCO 8/2447.
214 Ibid.
215 'Kuwait: Sale of Chieftain tanks', Minute by Lucas, 20 May 1975, FCO 8/2447.
216 Telegram from Kuwait to the Foreign and Commonwealth Office, No. 518, 6 October 1975, FCO 8/2449.
217 Letter from Lamb to the Secretary of State for Foreign and Commonwealth Affairs, 4 January 1975, FCO 8/2673. By the end of 1977, the Kuwait Liaison Team numbered some 150 regular officers and NCOs drawn from Her Majesty's armed forces

Challenges and opportunities, 1974–1977 101

(Letter from Lamb to the Secretary of State for Foreign and Commonwealth Affairs, 9 November 1977, FCO 8/2915).
218 Letter from Sheikh Sa'ad al-Abdulla al-Sabah to R. Anderson (Ministry of Defence), 16 November 1974, FCO 8/2204.
219 Letter from Lamb to the Foreign and Commonwealth Office, 1 January 1977, FCO 8/2914.
220 'Chieftain base overhaul facilities – Kuwaiti study visit', by H. G. Hogger (British Embassy, Kuwait), FCO 8/2677.
221 Letter from Lamb to Lucas, 5 January 1976, FCO 8/2677.
222 Letter from Lucas to Lamb, 20 January 1976, FCO 8/2677.
223 Letter from Lamb to Lucas, 10 January 1977, FCO 8/2930.
224 Letter from Hogger to B. Major (Middle East Department, FCO), 12 March 1977, FCO 8/2930.
225 Telegram from the Foreign and Commonwealth Office to Kuwait, No. 6, 18 February 1977, FCO 8/2927.
226 Telegram from Kuwait to the Foreign and Commonwealth Office, No. 128, 7 April 1977, FCO 8/2927.
227 Letter from Lucas to Lamb, 20 June 1977, FCO 8/2928.
228 Letter from S. J. G. Cambridge to the Secretary of State for Foreign and Commonwealth Affairs, 5 January 1981, DEFE 24/2679.
229 Letter from Christopher Prentice (Third Secretary, British Embassy, Kuwait) to H. D. A. C. Miers, 18 May 1980, DEFE 24/2679.
230 Letter from Lamb to the Secretary of State for Foreign and Commonwealth Affairs, 9 November 1977, FCO8/2915. See also letter from S. J. G. Cambridge to the Secretary of State for Foreign and Commonwealth Affairs, 1 January 1978, FCO 8/3154.
231 Letter from McCarthy to the Secretary of State for Foreign and Commonwealth Affairs, 10 January 1976, FCO 8/2659.
232 Ibid.
233 Ibid.
234 Ibid.
235 Letter from McCarthy to the Secretary of State for Foreign and Commonwealth Affairs, 5 January 1977, FCO 8/2888.
236 Ibid.
237 Ibid.
238 Letter from Lamb to Wilton, 16 July 1974, FCO 8/2195.
239 Letter from Ennals to Peter Shire, 19 February 1975, FCO 8/2399.
240 Letter from McCarthy to James Callaghan, 14 April 1975, FCO 8/2400; 'Mr Peter Shore reports concerns over delivery dates', Press Notice: Department of Trade, 9 May 1975, FCO 8/2400.

4 Revolution and reaction, 1978–1979

Against the background of the war in Vietnam, President Nixon's Assistant for National Security Affairs, Henry Kissinger, remarked: 'It is beyond the physical and psychological capacity for the U.S. to make itself responsible for every part of the world'.[1] In these circumstances, the value of allies, such as the Shah of Iran, who were willing to take on the burdens of defending areas of the world vital to Western interests, increased. Reviewing Iran's position and importance to America in April 1971, the US Ambassador in Tehran, Douglas MacArthur II, observed that it was the 'only strong, stable asset we possess between Europe and Japan'.[2] In May 1972, President Richard Nixon journeyed to Tehran and while there signed an arms deal which permitted the Shah, excepting nuclear technology, to purchase any US weapons systems in any quantity.

For Stephen McGlinchey, the Nixon presidency 'completed the transformation of Iran from a client state into a major American partner'.[3] In a similar vein, Roham Alvandi argues that 'Although President Johnson and his advisers had seen regional stability as resting on a balance of power between Iran and Saudi Arabia as the "twin pillars" of the Gulf, between 1969 and 1972 the shah convinced Nixon and Kissinger to abandon this policy and tilt in favor of Iran'.[4] As J. E. Peterson points out, 'Iran was militarily the more significant partner in this arrangement, due to its much larger population, relatively more developed economy, and more powerful armed forces'.[5] Moreover, Ben Offiler contends that 'In light of Britain's intention to have completed its withdrawal from East of Suez by the end 1971, the Nixon administration gradually chose to embrace the Shah's willingness to adopt a leading role in maintaining the stability of the Persian Gulf'.[6] Michael Palmer puts things even more bluntly. In his interpretation, the 1969 Nixon Doctrine, which exhorted the nations of Asia to take greater responsibility for their own defence, 'was actually little more than an Iranian policy eagerly embraced by an administration caught in the morass of the Vietnam War'.[7] Equally, Pierre Razoux observes: 'Bogged down in the Vietnam War, the American government openly banked on the Shah and promised him significant military assistance. Richard Nixon and Henry Kissinger considered the Iranian monarch to be the West's best rampart against Soviet activism in the Middle East'.[8] Furthermore, Andrew J. Bacevich asserts: 'By selling top-line American weapons to Iran, now flush with cash due to booming oil exports, President Nixon was counting on the Shah to ensure stability in the gulf'.[9] For Salim Yaqub, America's embrace of the Shah 'would bind Washington to an Iranian regime whose vulnerabilities it underestimated and whose eventual collapse would scramble the politics of the Arab world'.[10] Problems associated with the Nixon administration's approach to Iran soon began to surface.

Jack Miklos, the Iranian Country Director in the US State Department who had accompanied Nixon on his trip to Iran, ominously admitted that he had been 'struck by the level of internal discontent, even at fairly high levels, and at the degree of disillusion with corruption in government'.[11] Miklos added that he had also heard 'many critical comments about the increasing isolation and megalomania of the shah and his unwillingness to listen to criticism'.[12] Despite such concerns with the Shah's regime, President Jimmy Carter, who entered the White House in January 1977, largely followed his predecessors' policy. As Tore Petersen observes: 'for all his emphasis on human rights[13] and limiting arms sales, the president and his advisors failed to develop an alternative policy towards Iran, being saddled with Nixon's policy of making Iran into an American pillar in the Persian Gulf'.[14] Stephen McGlinchey and Andrew Moran, moreover, point out that, if anything, President Gerald Ford had deepened the arms relationship with Iran, cementing 'a momentum that became near impossible for a successor to break'.[15] Indeed, McGlinchey, writing with Robert W. Murray, emphasizes that Ford's support for the established Iran-arms regime 'left Carter with no alternative short of a wholesale regional policy rethink – for which there was negligible appetite in Washington'.[16]

During a visit to Tehran at the very end of 1977, Carter characterized Iran as 'an island of stability in one of the most troubled areas of the world'.[17] Addressing the Shah directly, the President declared: 'This is a great tribute to you, Your Majesty, and to your leadership and to the respect and the admiration and love which your people give to you'.[18] Referring to the two leaders' toasting the New Year with French champagne, Robert Strong notes that 'to an Iranian audience it would have been odd, perhaps even offensive, to see the shah commemorate a Western holiday that Iranians do not observe with the consumption of an alcoholic beverage forbidden to the faithful under Islamic law'.[19] Within days of Carter's eulogy, demonstrations in the holy city of Qom were met with excessive force by the police, resulting in a number of deaths.[20] In his reminiscences of his time as Britain's Ambassador to Iran, Sir Anthony Parsons[21] noted: 'The whole country was rocked and staggered by the incident and a crisis developed between the Muslim religious leadership and the government'.[22]

Shortly after the Qom riots in January 1978, Parsons observed that Islamic radicals' grievance had been that 'in the headlong rush for economic development and an independent national defence capability, the country had become over-Westernised, if not colonised, to the detriment of the traditions of Islam'.[23] He added that

> Apart from the grievances of the particular sectors of society . . . there is a general malaise in the country stemming from the failure of the Government

to solve economic and developmental problems arising from Iran's over-rapid expansion in recent years and above all from the failure to fulfil people's still steeply rising expectations.[24]

Nevertheless, Parsons concluded on an upbeat note, recording that 'There will be ups and downs, but in the short term I think the Shah will not be forced to make any radical alterations to his policies and will be able to govern, as he is at present, without any genuinely dangerous opposition from any quarter'.[25]

Shortly before going on leave towards the end of May 1978, Parsons produced a similarly optimistic assessment, opining:

> I do not believe there is a serious risk of an overthrow of the regime while the Shah is at the helm. He has gained vast experience of ruling the country over the past 37 years and I see no reason to think the Armed Forces, the basic prop of the regime, would be likely to judge that their own and their country's interests would be better served by getting rid of the Pahlavis.[26]

In his memoirs, nonetheless, Parsons admitted that on his return to Tehran in early September, 'it was glaringly obvious that there had been a qualitative change for the worse and the whole Pahlavi apparatus was in danger'.[27] When the Shah appealed to Parsons to 'influence the moderate mullahs to a more tractable frame of mind', the Ambassador replied that 'because of his suspicions of us, I and my immediate predecessors had avoided all contact with the religious classes'.[28] 'As we know from reporting from Tehran', commented Counsellor at the British Embassy in Washington, R. J. Carrick, 'the risk of offending the Shah by consorting with the opposition was a high one'.[29] In a post-mortem on British policy towards Iran in the lead-up to the revolution commissioned by Foreign Secretary David Owen, the FCO admitted that 'After 1963. . . British contacts with the opposition to the Shah lapsed and British policy increasingly focussed on keeping the Shah happy'.[30] In a similar vein, the Head of the Middle East Department at the time of the Iranian Revolution, Alan Munro, recalled that 'we put all our effort, as did our main Western partners, into sustaining our precious relationship with the Shah and with his system. We did not seek to evaluate, let alone have contact with the Opposition'.[31]

Britain's lack of information on the local opposition to the Shah was mirrored by US intelligence failures. Donette Murray points out that the US had 'no decent intelligence about Iran, hampered as it was by an inability to develop contacts with opposition figures for fear of risking the wrath of the Shah'.[32] Moreover, Robert Strong asserts that 'the president and his entourage missed whatever signs there may have been of the shah's underlying weakness and political vulnerability'.[33] Referring to opposition to the Shah, Jimmy Carter admitted in his memoirs that 'We knew little about the forces contending against him'.[34] Gary Sick, the White House's principal aide during the Iranian Revolution, recalled that the concentration on the Shah and his immediate circle had meant that 'US intelligence capability to track the shah's domestic opposition had been allowed to deteriorate almost to vanishing point'.[35] At the time, Sick had exclaimed: 'this has been an intelligence disaster of the first order'.[36] Subsequently, however, Sick admitted that 'Only in retrospect is it obvious that a good intelligence organization should have focussed its attention on the religious schools, the mosques and the recorded sermons of an aged religious leader living in exile for fourteen years'.[37]

Despite the growing enfeeblement of the Pahlavi regime, highlighted by its inability to deal effectively with a series of strikes which began at the end of September 1978 and progressively paralyzed the country, Parsons impressed upon David Owen that 'even the gloomier predictions do not mean that it would be in the British interest to abandon the Shah, since the alternatives, chaos or a military take-over, are each likely to be disadvantageous for us'.[38] During a private audience with the Shah on 16 September, Parsons told the Iranian monarch that 'We supported him and sincerely hoped that the present difficulties would be overcome. I assured him that we were not hedging our bets and were not trying to reinsure'.[39] Justifying this stance in his memoirs, Parsons insisted that 'If we were to seen to be wavering in our support for the Shah, we would lose this asset and gain only the contempt of the opposition. The effect would be to compound the troubles of the regime'.[40] Highlighting the many positives which flowed from the Shah's regime, not least the fact that Iran between 1974 and 1978 had become Britain's largest export market in the Middle East, Parsons insisted that 'had we adopted a more equivocal attitude towards the Shah in the light of a more pessimistic assessment of his chances of survival, many of these benefits would not have accrued to us. To sum up, we gambled on the Shah and, for many years, our gamble paid off'.[41]

In an FCO review of British policy towards Iran in the years preceding the Shah's ouster, Parsons stressed that 'we must never forget how well we did out of the Shah's regime for a number of years'.[42] In a similar vein, the Head of the FCO's Middle East Department, I. T. M. Lucas, recalled that 'Iran had become not only a significant source of oil but a major export market, not least for defence equipment. In short, we had a good thing going with the Shah. . . . The prescription therefore tended to be "support the Shah, warts and all"'.[43] '[N]ot for the first time in Britain's relationships in the Middle East', concurred Alan Munro, 'the wish to see a successful and valuable alliance endure became father to the thought. To search out and establish contact with the emerging centres of opposition would have put Britain's political and economic stake at risk'.[44] 'Tedious at times though it may be to have to keep smoothing the peacock's feathers', remarked Rex Hunt of the FCO's Middle East Department in 1973, 'we realise that the potential rewards are worthwhile'.[45] Referring to the Shah two years later, Parsons emphasized: 'the "national security" element in his foreign policy by and large serves our interests too, because it is helping to preserve from disorder an area which is still of great importance to us'.[46] As late as mid-November 1978, the Minister of State at the FCO, Frank Judd, told UAE Minister of State for Foreign Affairs, Rashid Abdullah al-Naimi, that 'the British Government firmly believed that there was no positive alternative to the Shah in sight'.[47] In his memoirs, David Owen was less charitable about British policy, remarking that 'We failed to remember how weak he [the Shah] was before he took on the airs of an autocrat. We were far too deferential before his charade of leadership while he vacillated month by month'.[48]

In his annual review for 1978, written on New Year's Eve, Parsons was forced to concede that the events of the previous four months had brought the Pahlavi regime to the 'point of collapse'.[49] 'Whatever the outcome', he continued, 'monarchical, republican or military dictatorship, the Shah's vision of Iran as a modernised, Westernised, industrialised country separated only by the accident of geography from Western Europe, is shattered'.[50] On 16 January 1979, the Shah went into exile, and two weeks later Ayatollah Khomeini returned to Iran after an absence of fourteen years, paving the way for the creation of an Islamic Republic. Two days after the Iranian monarch's flight from Tehran, Parsons confessed:

> I always thought and still do that, thanks mainly to the loyalty of the Armed Forces, the Shah could have survived until the chosen moment of handover to his son, say in the mid-1980s, provided that he maintained his dictatorial political system while at the same time delivering a reasonable amount of the goods to his people.[51]

Referring to the Shah's decision in early 1977 to liberalize his regime, Parsons observed that he 'could not have chosen a worse moment'.[52] 'If he had been a student of history', elaborated Parsons, 'he would have known from the experiences of pre-revolutionary France and Tsarist Russia that the period of liberalisation is one which poses the most mortal danger to a dictatorial regime'.[53] The FCO's P. J. Westmacott, who had served as Second Secretary at the British Embassy in Tehran in the mid-1970s, drew similar historical parallels, remarking that 'Louis XVI and Nicholas II lost their thrones because, although both had at last been forced to give way to pressure for reform, neither had been able to do so before the movements that eventually swept them away had built up their own momentum'.[54] Summarizing the reasons for the Shah's downfall in discussions with Sheikh Rashid of Dubai, Parsons highlighted a number of factors,

> chiefly, his vision of Iran as a historic centre of Aryan civilisation, which clashed with Islamic beliefs and traditions, the widespread corruption, the lack of contact between the Shah and his people and the insulation of the Shah from unpleasant facts, by advisers who would not tell him the truth.[55]

Rashid, however, assured Parsons that 'the Rulers in the Arab countries of the Gulf were in much closer contact with their peoples'.[56]

Despite the shock produced by the collapse of the Pahlavi monarchy, British policy-makers sought to mitigate damage to Britain's interests and to establish a working relationship with the new regime in Tehran. Even before the fall of the Shah, the Assistant Head of the FCO's Middle East Department, D. E. Tatham, remarked: 'While our commercial interests and the size of our community could be suddenly reduced by a hostile government, the new regime would still need western technology, goods and markets and we could settle down to an uneasy but profitable relationship like that we enjoy with Iraq'.[57] In October 1979, Tatham's colleague in the Middle East Department, D. H. A. Hannay, urged that it was in Britain's 'interest to begin to seek a political dialogue with post-revolutionary Iran'.[58] Attempting to justify this recommendation, Hannay proceeded to stress that

> The public foreign policy stance of post-revolutionary Iran is fiercely nationalistic and both anti-Western and anti-Soviet. But behind the rhetorical flourishes there has also been a realisation that the facts of world economic interdependence imply a degree of continuing co-operation with the West and thus a need to talk to and do business with us. From our side Iran remains important for its oil, for its strategic position and as an important market.[59]

Even the hostage crisis, precipitated by the seizure of US Embassy staff in Tehran on 4 November 1979 by students professing loyalty to Ayatollah Khomeini, did not, at least in the short term, fundamentally alter the British approach. The new British Ambassador to Iran Sir John Graham, emphasized that

> we do not believe that it would be in the interests of the American hostages, let alone of our own communities and interests here, to be seen to be participating in joint action with the Americans against Iran, e.g. over the blocking of funds or the non-purchase of Iranian oil.[60]

Moreover, the FCO, while recognizing that the seizure of the hostages and their subsequent treatment was 'undoubtedly an outrage', went on to argue that 'further escalation of the crisis could have very far-reaching effects on the world economy, on relations between the West and the principal oil producers, and on East–West relations'.[61]

Despite British policy-makers' concern to reach a modus vivendi with the new regime in Tehran, which in some respects mirrors Britain's earlier efforts to establish working relations with the revolutionary government in Baghdad following the overthrow of the Hashemite monarchy in 1958,[62] the fall of the Shah and the rise of the Islamic Republic posed a palpable threat to British interests on the Arab side of the Gulf. Even before the Shah's ouster, an interdepartmental group of officials charged with the task of producing an assessment of the potential implications for the UK of the deteriorating situation in Iran, posited that

> One of the most dangerous side-effects of the Shah's downfall . . . would be a loss of confidence by the other traditional regimes in the area. Saudi Arabia would be highlighted as the remaining pillar of stability and pro-Western alignment in the area and the fragile smaller Gulf States . . . would find themselves confronting an unstable and possibly unfriendly neighbour. The danger of interruption of all oil supplies from the Gulf . . . would increase significantly.[63]

At the end of 1978, Ambassador Brant reported that 'Like the other Gulf States, Qatar was surprised and alarmed by the tide of events in Iran after Ramadan, though there was little that they could do about it except to work on improving security co-operation'.[64] Moreover, Brant's US counterpart, Andrew Killgore, observed that

> The Shah is not really liked and neither are Iranians as a whole. But Iran is by far the biggest and most populous country in the Gulf and the Shah, whatever his pretensions to grandeur, is perceived here as representing stability and legitimacy. The Qataris fear that with the Shah gone an uncertain and fearsome future would lie ahead. A conservative Islamic regime would superficially be not so frightful. But politically sophisticated Qataris realize that such a regime would stir latent prejudices between the two main branches of Islam.[65]

Reporting from Kuwait, the US Ambassador there, Frank E. Maestrone, noted that the government had been

> Deeply concerned about instability in Iran and the possibility that Iran's role as a strong, conservative, friendly neighbour to Kuwait might be upset. Kuwaitis generally probably expect that if the Shah falls from power or becomes only a figurehead, Iran's traditional policy with respect to its neighbors may be called in question. In short they have historically relied upon the Shah as a bulward [sic] of stability in the Gulf area and, implicitly, as a restraining influence with respect to possible Iraqi designs on Kuwait. They are not certain that the Shah's departure would mean disaster, but they see his continuation in power as the optimal situation where their own interests are concerned.[66]

Writing shortly after the fall of the Shah at the beginning of 1979, I. T. M. Lucas predicted that the shadow of Iran was 'likely to lengthen in the coming months'.[67] Lucas' prophecy was soon confirmed. On 11 February 1979, Ayatollah Khomeini announced: 'We will export our revolution to the four corners of the world: and the struggle will continue until the cry of "There is no God but Allah and Muhammad is his Prophet" prevails throughout the world'.[68] Khomeini also made his view clear that monarchical and secular-nationalist forms of governance were incompatible with the requirements of 'Islamic governance'.[69] With considerable justification, F. Gregory Gause has contended that 'The sense of threat felt by the rulers of Iraq and the Arab monarchies of the Gulf in the wake of the revolution was exacerbated by the clearly stated intention of the new Iranian regime, in particular Ayatollah Khomeini, to "export" the revolution to neighbouring states'.[70] Kristian Coates Ulrichsen has gone even further, arguing that the threat from Iran was 'multifaceted and operated at the trans-national and inter-cultural, as well as at the traditional inter-state level'.[71] For J. E. Peterson, the upheavals of the Iranian Revolution 'excited passions on both sides of the Gulf and raised the possibility of political agitation and even revolutionary sentiment among the population – especially the Shi'a elements – of the Arab littoral'.[72] In his memoirs, Alan Munro recalled that the Gulf States were 'unsettled by the potential for subversion presented by Iran's new mood of sectarian zealotry and the pledge by Ayatollah Khomeini to "export revolution"'.[73] Khomeini himself ominously declared: 'The Iranian revolution is not exclusively that of Iran, because Islam does not belong to any particular people . . . we will export our revolution throughout the world because it is an Islamic revolution'.[74]

Arguably, the Iranian Revolution and the fall of the Shah at the beginning of 1979, a catastrophe which the British signally failed to predict or plan for, represented a greater blow to British interests than the relatively peaceful military withdrawal from the region a little over seven years earlier. 'The changes in Iran', lamented the FCO, 'are likely to mean her withdrawal from the role, willingly assumed by the Shah, of seeking to protect, by diplomatic and military means the political status quo in the Gulf and, by extension, Western access on favourable terms to major oil resources and a massive trading market'.[75]

By 1978, Britain's exports to Iran had reached the unprecedented annual figure of £751 million.[76] In January 1979, however, the *Financial Times* gloomily reported that 'The outlook for British trade in Iran is deteriorating daily'.[77] Events in Iran also posed a significant risk to the small Gulf States themselves. In his memoirs, Parsons recalled that 'co-operation with Iran was essential to the maintenance of the status quo in the independent states of the Persian Gulf in the years immediately following our withdrawal at the end of 1971'.[78] The Islamic Republic, by contrast, sought to 'export' revolution to the Arab side of the Gulf.[79] The presence of large Shia minorities, especially in Kuwait[80] and Bahrain,[81] and fears that Iran would seek to use them as agents of subversion, presented further potential challenges to the stability of the Gulf.[82]

In the course of discussions with British Premier Margaret Thatcher during her brief stopover in Manama on 2 July 1979, the Bahraini Prime Minister, Sheikh Khalifah bin Salman Al-Khalifah, 'repeatedly expressed his deep concerns over recent developments in Iran and the present situation there'.[83] Nevertheless, Sheikh Khalifah informed Thatcher that he 'particularly valued' the services of Jim Bell (Director-General of Police) and Ian Henderson (Head of Special Branch), as well as the 'other assistance' that Britain provided in the security field.[84]

Qatar's stability was also under threat. As early as December 1977, Britain's Ambassador to Qatar, D. G. Crawford, had remarked that 'Events elsewhere could easily sweep the Al Thani aside'.[85] As regards Qatar's internal problems, Crawford added that 'undoubtedly the Amir, confronted by greedy relatives and quarrelsome and corrupt officials, faces an increasingly complex task'.[86] Nevertheless, he predicted that Sheikh Khalifah would 'muddle through' and 'continue to regard Britain as one of Qatar's closer friends'.[87] Indeed, the Ambassador pointed out that 'Through history, familiarity and the widespread use of English we maintain an influential, but unobtrusive, position'.[88] Crawford recorded that Britain's visible trade from January to October 1977 was worth £97 million, representing an increase of 40 per cent over the same period the previous year. Nonetheless, he warned that the US, West Germany and France were beginning to make 'significant inroads' into the Qatari market.[89]

Writing in May 1978, Crawford's successor, C. T. Brant, was able to report that Britain's visible sales to Qatar had risen from £7.5 million in 1970 to £116 million in 1977.[90] The new Ambassador identified three 'trump cards' in Britain's hands, all mutually reinforcing its commercial advantage in Qatar. First, Brant pointed out that the historical links with Britain had 'accustomed the older generation of Qataris to doing business with us'.[91] Second, he stressed that from these earlier associations, and from Qatar's newfound wealth, a British community had grown up 'of serious, respected and highly competent company representatives and expatriate British professional men and businessmen, guiding and advising the inexperienced Qataris in almost every field'.[92] Brant concluded that 'the combination of history and experience seems to have induced in the Qataris a feeling of affinity with Britain and the British which defies analysis'.[93]

In response to Brant's upbeat assessment, P. J. Parramore of the FCO's Middle East Department underlined that 'over the last few years we have lost first place to Japan in Qatar's import market (we stand at 17% against their 29%) despite all that we have going for us'.[94] In his reply to Brant's message, I. T. M. Lucas expressed disappointment that Britain had lost its position as Qatar's leading supplier, but also hope that the close ties of history, language, goodwill, and mutual trust between the two countries could be used to improve Britain's share of the lucrative Qatari market.[95] The joint Anglo–Qatari Committee, however, did not prove to be a suitable instrument for the promotion of British interests.

The Committee, established under the Co-operation Agreement with Qatar in June 1976 (see Chapter 3), provided for possible joint ventures in the development of light industry, the training of personnel, and the provision of experts. The first formal meeting took place in Doha in January 1977. The second, due to have been held the following year, was linked with a short visit to the United Kingdom by Sheikh Abdul Aziz, second son of the Amir of Qatar and Minister of Finance and Petroleum. After several postponements, the Committee meeting, along with the Abdul Aziz visit, were cancelled.[96] Commenting on the failure of the meeting to take place, Brant noted: 'the whole project foundered on Abdul Aziz's insistence on being met by someone of a least equal rank in our hierarchy'.[97] Nevertheless, the Department of Trade was insistent that there was no question of Britain taking the initiative in winding up the Committee since to do so risked harming Anglo–Qatari relations, not least as the Amir himself was its 'original begetter'.[98]

While the British relationship with Qatar was to some extent smoothed by the Amirate's relative cohesion under Sheikh Khalifah's rule, British relations with the UAE were complicated by its internal divisions and contradictions. As early as May 1973, the British Ambassador to the UAE, C. J. Treadwell, had emphasized that the partnership between Sheikh Zaid of Abu Dhabi and Sheikh Rashid of Dubai had 'never been a really confident one and Abu Dhabi's overbearing ways cause much bitterness in Dubai'.[99] Treadwell went on to record that 'The recent unsuccessful attempt by the Ministry of the Interior to coerce Rashid into handing over responsibility for port and airport immigration control to the UAE authorities ... did much to inflame passions'.[100] In its brief for Foreign Secretary Alec Douglas-Home's London meeting with Sheikh Zaid on 18 September 1973, the FCO set down that 'There is no sign of any lessening of inter-state rivalries within the UAE. The relationship between Sheikhs Zaid and Rashid (on which the stability of the UAE continues to rest) and some of the other Rulers is characterised by distrust and lack of communication'.[101] Four years later, the situation had scarcely improved. In his annual review for 1977 produced at the beginning of the following year, Britain's Ambassador to the UAE, D. A. Roberts, described it as a 'dismal year' with 'no Federal achievement'.[102] Indeed, he indicated that 'in the armed forces there was a distinct move the other way'.[103] If anything, the fissiparous tendencies increased in the course of 1978.

On 31 January Sheikh Zaid issued a decree abolishing the three existing regional commands of the UAE Armed Forces and putting all units under the direct control of the Federal Military Command in Abu Dhabi. In a separate decree, Zaid appointed his own son, Sultan, Commander-in-Chief of the re-organized Federal Armed Forces. Sheikh Rashid and Sheikh Saqr of Ras al Khaimah subsequently refused to recognize the decrees on the grounds that they had been issued without consultation and were, therefore, unconstitutional. Rashid's senior adviser, Mahdi Al-Tajir, emphasized that Dubai 'wanted to see a strong UAE but a union of partners not overlords and underlings'.[104] I. T. M. Lucas was quick to point out that Britain had a 'strong interest' in backing the Federation, not least because in the event of its collapse the individual Rulers would be 'vulnerable to a scramble for influence, if not territory, by their powerful neighbours, and also to subversion supported from places like Iraq and the PDRY'.[105] Nevertheless, Lucas added that

> As regards our historical relationship with the UAE, it seems to me only realistic to recognise that this must become less exclusive as time goes on. When the country achieved full independence in 1971, its people hardly knew that any country existed in the outside world other than Britain; the UAE now has diplomatic relations with a large number of foreign countries, many of whom are energetically promoting their trade.[106]

On 9 May, Rashid informed HM Ambassador Abu Dhabi and HM Consul-General in Dubai that he intended withdrawing from the UAE.[107] The former British Ambassador to the UAE, D. J. McCarthy, noted that Rashid was

> clearly trying to make our flesh creep by dragging us in as though it were still the days of the Political Resident and the Political Agent. Those days were ended by the decision of Sir Harold Wilson's Government in February [sic] 1968. The local resentment of that decision is one reason among many why we can no longer revert to the status quo ante. The very Arab nature of the mess, moreover, suggests to me that we cannot in fact influence its outcome greatly. . . . My instinct and judgment alike suggest therefore that we should not get mixed up in this any further.[108]

Indeed, the political fix which foreclosed Rashid's threats to withdraw from the UAE and involved his assuming the role of the country's Prime Minister, essentially stemmed from local initiative,[109] rather the pervasive influence of the former protecting power. Rashid's elevation, however, provided no panacea for the problems and contradictions of the UAE.

In July 1978, B. A. Major of the FCO's Middle East Department, having noted that the unification of the UAE's armed forces had always been 'something of a fiction', went on to observe that 'Central procurement has broken down completely now and is in the hands of the individual commands'.[110] Worse still, he remarked that 'With the French dominant in Abu Dhabi and ourselves in Dubai and the Northern Emirates we have always had a nagging fear of fuelling an arms race between the French and ourselves and between the Emirates'.[111] Summarizing the invidious position in which Britain found itself, Ambassador Roberts commented:

> We must accept that we have to walk a political tightrope. If we supply arms to Dubai as well as Abu Dhabi we shall sooner or later incur Abu Dhabi's resentment. . . . Conversely, Dubai will have far greater grounds for resentment if we refuse to supply arms to it while making them available to Abu Dhabi.[112]

Musing on the merits and demerits of adopting a more interventionist stance towards the UAE, Roberts remarked:

> Expediency . . . suggests and morality . . . dictates that we should seek to help the rulers and peoples of the Emirates in their predicament. Yet we must recognise not only that a special uncertainty pervades the politics of this region, but also that history and the nature of the people conspire to load the dice against any such enterprise.[113]

The Consul-General in Dubai, D. K. Haskell, was equally doubtful about the prospects of British intervention in the UAE, noting that 'everyone here tacitly acknowledges that Rashid will listen to disinterested outside advice, but Zaid will not'.[114] 'Since responsibility for the present state of affairs lies at least partly with Zaid', Haskell continued, 'this means that while our further exhortations may be impartial in spirit they cannot be so in effect, as one only one side is likely to pay attention to them'.[115]

Reviewing the parlous condition of the UAE, Ambassador Roberts observed: 'It should not surprise us that the Federation has sunk into its present state. British federations in the Third World do not seem to have much success anyway: nor can I think of any Arab federation or Union which has lasted for any length of time'.[116] The Minister of State at the FCO, Frank Judd, encountered tensions and contradictions within the UAE at first hand during a meeting with the Ruler of Dubai, Sheikh Rashid, in February 1979. In the course of discussions, the UAE Ambassador to the UK and senior adviser to Sheikh Rashid, Mahdi Al-Tajir, emphasized that 'Whilst there should be federal laws, the local rulers ought to be able to retain within their prerogative the means of enforcement within their area'.[117] Al-Tajir went on to lament that 'when Dubai said that she wanted proper local government there was a tendency for others to accuse her of seeking independence from the Federation'.[118] Drawing his own conclusions, Judd observed:

> In the UAE we must face up to the weakness of the Federation. It was disturbing to be told in Dubai that the real reasons why they wanted arms was their fear of Abu Dhabi. Of course we should do all we can to keep the concept of an effective federation alive but we need to be realistic and have our discreet direct links with the individual emirates.[119]

The visit of the Queen and Prince Philip to the UAE between 24 and 26 February, part of a royal tour of the Gulf in early 1979, served to highlight the inherent divisions within the UAE. The British Ambassador, D. A. Roberts, reported that Mahdi Al-Tajir was denied a place in the Queen's flight from Abu Dhabi to Jebel Dhanna on the grounds that Sheikh Zaid would not to travel in the same aeroplane as him.[120] Mahdi Al-Tajir subsequently returned to Dubai and took no further part in the proceedings in Abu Dhabi. In Dubai, the Abu Dhabian Head of the Delegation of Honour, Sheikh Sarour bin Mohammed, was affronted by Dubai's parading a Guard of Honour for the Queen's arrival as it implied the Emirate was a separate country.[121] Referring to the rivalry between Abu Dhabi and Dubai, the Head of the FCO's Middle East Department, A. G. Munro, observed that 'The squabble over the guard of honour and Shaikh Zaid's refusal to travel in the same plane as Mahdi Al-Tajir would be laughable, if they did not reflect the incorrigible nature of this feud'.[122] Ambassador Roberts himself admitted that 'the infant Federation is vexed by tribal and dynastic vendettas from the past, compounded by rivalry in the markets of the modern world'.[123] Nevertheless, there was palpable British reluctance to intervene in the affairs of the UAE. As Sir Anthony Parsons told his American hosts during US–UK talks in Washington on the Middle East in mid-March 1979: 'The UAE Federation was admittedly not working well and this could be a source of instability; but attempts from the outside to make it work better might well lead to its total collapse'.[124]

Internal divisions on the Arab side of the Gulf were undoubtedly exacerbated by the Iranian Revolution. As regards Kuwait, the US Ambassador there, Frank E. Maestrone, commented that the Amirate's own Shia community was 'generally considered insulated by prosperity from Khomeini's fervor'.[125] Nevertheless, the Ambassador proceeded to observe that 'the future course of Iraq's majority Shi'ite population – traditionally dissatisfied with its lot under the Sunni-controlled government in Baghdad – is a major preoccupation of Kuwaitis'.[126] An early example of the potential which the Iranian Revolution had to destabilize the Arab Gulf in a more direct sense was soon demonstrated by events in Qatar.[127]

As many 60,000 Iranians lived in the Amirate. Shortly after the Shah's departure from Iran, a crowd of some 7,000 demonstrated in front of the Iranian embassy to threaten the Ambassador in the (mistaken) belief that he was a SAVAK agent.

Qatari counsels were divided, the Amir's third son, Sheikh Abdullah, favouring the use of force to disperse the crowd, while Commandant of Police, Sheikh Hamad bin Jassim, argued for a softer approach. Hamid, who knew the ringleaders, prevailed and succeeded in persuading the crowd to leave peacefully.[128] The danger of the situation, however, was recognized by Brant who remarked: 'had the Army's tough methods been tried, and some shooting ensued, it would not have taken long for the 60,000 or so Iranian population to have come out on the streets to raise Cain'.[129] The Amir was confident that events in Iran would not repeat themselves in Qatar, comforting himself with the thought that the Iranian Revolution was in essence founded on the discontent of the urban poor whereas no such class existed in Qatar since all ranks of Qatari society were 'adequately cushioned against real life' by the country's oil revenues and the Amir's methods of 'dispensing them down' through the social structure.[130]

Demonstrations also occurred in Bahrain in the wake of the Iranian Revolution. On 17 August 1979, several hundred of Shias marched from the Manama Suq to the PLO Office and back in response to Khomeini's call for action in support of the recovery of Jerusalem.[131] Although the Amir was reported to be 'totally relaxed' about the situation, events took a turn for the worse during the last days of Ramadan towards the end of August. Ambassador H. B. Walker recorded that 'sermons by Shia Mullas reached new levels of bitterness in their attacks on the Amir's ministers'.[132] The Shia leader Mohammed Al-Akri also made an 'offensive' radio broadcast during a visit to Iran, in response to which the Bahraini authorities arrested him on his return along with four other prominent Mullas.[133] A call for demonstrations in favour of the release of a fifth, who had in fact been released shortly after his arrest, was responded to on 23 August by a protest by some 200 people carrying such slogans as 'Our watchword is the rule of Islam'.[134] Although Walker described such demonstrations as 'no more than a pin-prick in the fabric of Bahraini stability', he expressed concern that the Mullas' 'apparent determination to continue them, apart from giving heart to the now dormant non-religious opposition groups, increases the risks that some unforeseen incident may occur that might ... spark off sectarian disturbances'.[135] 'The nub of the situation', stated Walker, 'remains that the authorities and the Shia leaders are confronting each other with apparently irreconcilable positions'.[136] The Bahraini Minister of the Interior, Mohamed bin Khalifah Al-Khalifah, however, downplayed the protests, arguing that they had not been on the scale portrayed by the press, especially the Western press.[137]

During discussions with Sir Anthony Parsons in June 1979, the Amir of Qatar also professed 'no great anxiety about the current situation', expressing 'full confidence in his ability to cope with his own Iranian community'.[138] He was more concerned about the Egyptian–Israeli peace process since he saw the 'tide of events bearing the moderate Arab States nearer and nearer towards the Iraqis and farther and farther away from the United States, Europe and Egypt' all of which were their 'natural allies'.[139] He also told Prime Minister Margaret Thatcher in the course of talks at 10 Downing Street on 11 September 1979 that it was 'not at all impossible that President [Anwar] Sadat would go the same way as the

Shah' since there was 'no true compact between President Sadat and the Egyptian people'.[140] As regards events in Iran, the Amir described them as 'highly regrettable' which stimulated Thatcher to interject: 'they were a tragedy'.[141] In response to the Prime Minister's request that the Amir should get in touch with her if he thought that the UK was being in any way 'less active' than was desirable, Sheikh Khalifah noted that 'Britain had given up her bases in the Gulf but that it would certainly be possible to re-establish at least some of them'.[142] The sense of threat to regional stability which underpinned the warming of Anglo–Qatari relations was reinforced by events in Saudi Arabia.

On 20 November 1979, a group of Islamic fundamentalists stormed and occupied the Grand Mosque in Mecca. There were two attempts to regain control on the following day, the first being repulsed with heavy losses. While Saudi security forces managed to gain access to the tunnels beneath the mosque in the course of the second attempt, the infiltrators continued to resist. It was not until 4 December that the last ones were finally flushed out. Ruminating on these events, Britain's Ambassador to Saudi Arabia, James Craig, noted: 'the attack, the time it took to deal with it, the many causalities suffered by the security forces and the possibility that some elements of the National Guard were involved with the dissidents, all of this has shaken the government's confidence that "it could not happen here"'.[143]

The US Secretary of State, Cyrus Vance, identified two 'disquieting' factors in the Mecca affair: first, the 'religious fanatics' were more widespread than had originally been envisaged; secondly, the Saudi authorities had been 'taken unawares' which, given the 'comprehensive nature' of their regime, boded 'ominously for the future'.[144] In a similar vein, the FCO argued that the occupation of the Grand Mosque had made Saudi Arabia's Arab neighbours 'jumpy' and suspicious of the kingdom's internal stability.[145] Moreover, the Head of the FCO's Middle East Department, H. D. A. C. Miers, remarked that while Gulf Rulers had made 'every effort' to keep in step with religious opinion, their private lives were often 'far from Islamic' and the scale of corruption was 'immense'.[146] Miers concluded that 'Fanatical religious groups, which were discounted as a political threat until the Mecca outrage, will now be taken more seriously'.[147] A simultaneous outbreak of violence among alienated Shiites in Saudi Arabia's oil-rich Eastern Province[148] merely exacerbated the Gulf Rulers' security fears and focussed their minds on regime survival.[149] Reflecting the seriousness of the situation in Saudi Arabia, James Craig remarked: 'It was to be feared that Mecca in November and Qatif in December might start a fashion for violent outbursts against the regime'.[150]

Against the background of events in Saudi Arabia, the Amir of Qatar impressed upon Ambassador Brant that HMG could 'count on firm support' for British policies in the Middle East and elsewhere.[151] He added that he had the 'highest regard' for Prime Minister Thatcher and would be happy to cooperate with Britain in trying to 'bring stability wherever necessary'.[152] The closer alignment of Britain and Qatar in the course of 1979 was ostensibly mirrored in the economic sphere. Brant was able to report that 'for one heady moment, the import figures for February 1979 showed that we had regained our long-lost top place in the import league table here'.[153] In keeping with his earlier analysis, the Ambassador opined that

> British firms selling here enjoy advantages and assistance from the basic strength of our relations with Qatar. In turn, that strength derives from our historic ties with this small country, the support given to the Amir and his Government by the policies of HM Government, and the vital role of members of the British community in Qatar's national life.[154]

Following the healthy February trade figures, nevertheless, Brant reported that 'massive' payments to Japanese and German firms for generating equipment had pushed Britain back into third place by March.[155] Indeed, Britain's commercial position in Qatar continued to come under pressure from its industrial competitors.

In mid-1979, Brant reported that the contract for building a new university had been given to the Japanese company Fujita, while a Korean firm had been engaged to complete the Sheraton Hotel and Conference Centre.[156] Underlining the erosion of Britain's former exclusive role in Qatar, furthermore, the French succeeded in establishing a joint Franco–Qatari Commission which mirrored the Anglo–Qatari Committee set up in 1976. Brant also pointed out in June 1979 that the French had fielded a senior minister for recent meetings of the Franco–Qatari Commission held in France.[157] A month earlier the Ambassador had referred to the opening of a Franco–Qatari petrochemical plant in Dunkirk. He proceeded to lament that the French had picked up the project after ICI, having procrastinated for two years following the original Qatari request for assistance, had 'turned them down with a terse two paragraph letter'.[158] To make matters worse, Brant reported that the Amir had 'always held it against us since then that "Britain would not help us"'.[159]

As regards commercial relations with the UAE, Ambassador Roberts reported in his annual review for 1978 that Britain remained the second largest supplier after Japan. Nevertheless, he did inject a note of caution. '[W]hen the boom in construction ends and the Costains and the Laings depart', he mused, 'I wonder whether we shall do as well in cars, refrigerators, and the like, where prices and dates of delivery are more important than our inheritance of two centuries of skill in engineering'.[160] A somewhat more positive picture emerged in Bahrain where Britain, with a 20 per cent share of the Bahraini market in both 1978 and 1979, remained the Amirate's largest supplier of goods and services.[161] During discussions with Margaret Thatcher on 2 July 1979, the Prime Minister of Bahrain, Sheikh Khalifah bin Salman Al-Khalifah, spoke 'very warmly' of Anglo–Bahraini relations, adding that 'Bahrain found it easier to get along with the U.K. than with any other country'.[162] In his annual review for 1979, however, Ambassador Walker admitted that Bahraini merchants 'complained about price increases caused by the strength of sterling, about our failure to keep to delivery dates, and on occasion about our failure to innovate'.[163]

In Kuwait, British commerce suffered a setback when a £200-million order for ten fast patrol boats fell through, partly on grounds of cost. '[O]ur influence here is no longer very considerable', bemoaned the British Ambassador to Kuwait, S. J. G. Cambridge.[164] In his annual review for 1979, Cambridge confessed that, although the British could 'still count on a special affection' in Kuwait, they could not rely on this traditional friendship to give them influence, still less commercial advantage.[165] 'All that has to be worked for', he intoned.[166] He also reported that the value of British visible exports to Kuwait was likely to drop to £250 million for 1979 from the record figure of £332 million for the previous year, due largely to the fact that 1978 witnessed the last payments for ships ordered from Govan Shipyards some five years earlier.[167] In conclusion, Cambridge remarked that 'In the political fields too, we do not have the same degree of influence with the Kuwaitis as with other Gulf States. . . . This last year, though too polite to say so, Kuwait probably regarded us as not much use and too tied to the USA'.[168]

The decline of British influence in Kuwait, and the growth of commercial competition from industrial rivals, belie the notion that Britain seamlessly made the transition from formal to informal empire in the Gulf, still less that it successfully achieved the status of a neo-colonial power. Equally, British policy-makers were decidedly wary about raising Britain's military profile in the region in the aftermath of the Iranian revolution. In its report for the Chiefs of Staff Committee on the defence options for the UK in the Gulf, produced in April 1979, the Defence Policy Staff insisted:

> heavy-footed military activities can be counter-productive. Those which are too large in scale can be construed as bullying, and those in support of regimes which are likely to fall of their own accord may – if they fail in their buttressing action – seal the door to the West in that country for many years to come.[169]

More specifically, the Defence Policy Staff stressed:

> Assistance to the Gulf States is intended to help their defence forces to operate efficiently until they can assume full responsibility for their own defence. However care will be necessary, if the UK wishes even to retain its present level of military involvement to prevent the susceptibilities of the Gulf States from being upset.[170]

Explaining British policy towards the Gulf, the Head of the FCO's Middle East Department, A. G. Munro, minuted: 'Our approach is based on fostering self-help, and mutual prophylaxis among the states of the area, backed by continued discreet assistance over security'.[171] The outbreak of the Iran–Iraq War in 1980 provided Britain with an opportunity to strengthen links with the Gulf States in the fields of security and defence. This will be examined in the following chapter.

Notes

1 Cited in Osamah F. Khalil, *America's Dream Palace: Middle East Expertise and the Rise of the National Security State* (Cambridge, MA: Harvard University Press, 2016), p. 214.
2 'Political–military affairs/Iran', Memorandum of conversation, 8 April 1971, RG 59, Subject-Numeric Files 1970–73, Box 2377, POL IRAN.
3 Stephen McGlinchey, *US Arms Policies Towards the Shah's Iran* (London and New York: Routledge, 2014), p. 61.
4 Roham Alvandi, *Nixon, Kissinger, and the Shah: The United States and Iran in the Cold War* (Oxford and New York: Oxford University Press, 2014), p. 29.
5 J. E. Peterson, *Defending Arabia* (London and New York: Routledge, 2017; first published in 1986), p. 146.
6 Ben Offlier, *US Foreign Policy and the Modernization of Iran: Kennedy, Johnson, Nixon, and the Shah* (Basingstoke: Palgrave Macmillan, 2015), p. 139.
7 Michael A. Palmer, *Guardians of the Gulf: A History of America's Expanding Role in the Persian Gulf, 1833–1992* (New York: The Free Press, 1992), p. 88.
8 Pierre Razoux, *The Iran–Iraq War* (Cambridge, MA: Belknap Press, 2015), p. 53.
9 Andrew J. Bacevich, *America's War for the Greater Middle East: A Military History* (New York: Random House, 2017), p. 13.
10 Salim Yaqub, *Imperfect Strangers: Americans, Arabs, and U.S.–Middle East Relations in the 1970s* (Ithaca and London: Cornell University Press, 2016), p. 53.
11 Letter from P. R. H. Wright to M. R. Melhuish, 14 June 1972, FCO 8/1884.
12 Ibid.
13 Shortly after Carter entered the White House, the State Department impressed upon US diplomatic posts that 'Throughout his campaign President Carter placed priority among his concerns that of human rights, not only for the American people but for the peoples of the world. A human rights theme flowed through the President's inaugural address, as exemplified by his statement that "The world itself is now dominated by a new spirit. Peoples more numerous and more politically aware are craving and now demanding their place in the sun – not just for the benefit of their own physical condition, but for basic human rights"' (Telegram from the Department of State to multiple Diplomatic posts, 3 February 1977, cited in *Foreign Relations of the United States, 1977–80: Volume II, Human Rights and Humanitarian Affairs* (Washington, DC: United States Government Printing Office, 2013), pp. 23–4).
14 Tore T. Petersen, *Anglo–American Policy Toward the Persian Gulf, 1978–1985: Power, Influence and Restraint* (Brighton: Sussex Academic Press, 2015), p. 54.
15 Stephen McGlinchey and Andrew Moran, 'Beyond the blank cheque: Arming Iran during the Ford administration', *Diplomacy and Statecraft*, 27, 3 (2016), p. 523.
16 Stephen McGlinchey and Robert W. Murray, 'Jimmy Carter and the sale of AWACS to Iran in 1977', *Diplomacy and Statecraft*, 28, 2 (2017), p. 256.
17 Petersen, *Anglo–American Policy toward the Persian Gulf*, p. 60.
18 Ibid.
19 Robert A. Strong, *Working in the World: Jimmy Carter and the Making of American Foreign Policy* (Baton Rouge: Louisiana State University Press, 2000), p. 58.
20 Michael Axworthy, *Revolutionary Iran: A History of the Islamic Republic* (London: Penguin, 2014), pp. 95–6.
21 Sir Anthony (Derrick) Parsons (1922–1996): HM Forces, 1940–1954; Assistant Military Attaché, Baghdad, 1952–1954; Foreign Office, 1954–1955; HM Embassy: Ankara, 1955–1959; Amman, 1959–1960; Cairo, 1960–1961; FO, 1961–1964; HM Embassy, Khartoum, 1964–1965; Political Agent, Bahrain, 1965–1969; Counsellor, UK Mission to UN, NY, 1969–1971; Under-Secretary, FCO, 1971–1974; Ambassador to Iran, 1974–1979; FCO, 1979; UK Permanent Representative to UN, 1979–1982; Special Adviser to PM on foreign affairs, 1982–1983.

22 Anthony Parsons, *The Pride and the Fall: Iran, 1974–1979* (London: Jonathan Cape, 1984), p. 61.
23 Letter from Parsons to the Secretary of State for Foreign and Commonwealth Affairs, 31 January 1978, FCO 8/3183. See also Ivor Lucas, *A Road to Damascus: Mainly Diplomatic Memoirs from the Middle East* (London: The Radcliffe Press, 1997), p. 165.
24 Letter from Parsons to the Secretary of State for Foreign and Commonwealth Affairs, 31 January 1978, FCO 8/3183.
25 Ibid.
26 Letter from Parsons to the Secretary of State for Foreign and Commonwealth Affairs, 10 May 1978, PREM 16/1719. A copy of the letter can also be found in FCO 8/3194.
27 Parsons, *The Pride and the Fall*, p. 67.
28 Ibid., p. 71.
29 Letter from Carrick to I. T. M. Lucas, 31 January 1979, FCO 8/3360.
30 'British policy on Iran, 1974–1978', Report by N. W. Browne, p. 71, FCO 8/4029.
31 British Diplomatic Oral History Programme: Alan Gordon Munro, interviewed 16 May 1996, DOHP 13, Churchill Archives Centre, University of Cambridge.
32 Donette Murray, *US Foreign Policy and Iran: American-Iranian Relations Since the Islamic Revolution* (London and New York: Routledge, 2010), p. 7.
33 Strong, *Working in the World*, p. 58.
34 Jimmy Carter, *Keeping the Faith: Memoirs of a President* (London: Collins, 1982), p. 440.
35 Gary Sick, *All Fall Down: America's Tragic Encounter with Iran* (Lincoln, NE: iUniverse, 2001), p. 193.
36 Ibid., p. 104.
37 Ibid., p. 193. Sick is referring here to Ayatollah Khomeini.
38 Letter from Parsons to the Secretary of State for Foreign and Commonwealth Relations, 9 October 1978, BT 241/3045.
39 Telegram from Parsons to the Foreign and Commonwealth Office, No. 588, 16 September 1978, BT 241/3045.
40 Parsons, *The Pride and the Fall*, p. 77.
41 Ibid., p. 140.
42 Cited in Richard Smith, '"Paying our way in the world": The FCO, export promotion and Iran in the 1970s', in John Fisher, Effie G. H. Pedaliu, and Richard Smith (eds.), *The Foreign Office, Commerce and British Foreign Policy in the Twentieth Century* (Basingstoke: Palgrave Macmillan, 2017), p. 501.
43 Lucas, *A Road to Damascus*, p. 170.
44 Alan Munro, *Keep the Flag Flying: A Diplomatic Memoir* (London: Gilgamesh Publishing, 2012), p. 124.
45 Richard Smith, '"Paying our way in the world"', p. 500. The value of UK export to Iran rose from £66.3 million in 1970 to £510.9 by 1976 (Ibid., p. 496).
46 Letter from Parsons to the Secretary of State for Foreign and Commonwealth Affairs, 1 May 1975, cited in Richard Schofield (ed.), *Arabian Boundaries: New Documents, 1966–75: Volume 16, 1975* (Cambridge: Cambridge University Press, 2009), p. 715.
47 Record of a meeting of the UAE/UK Joint Committee in the Foreign and Commonwealth Office on 14 November 1978 at 10.30am, FCO 8/3143.
48 David Owen, *Time to Declare* (London: Penguin, 1992), pp. 386–7. In September 1979, Owen had told the Cabinet that 'It was difficult to foresee how events would develop, but he was inclined to believe that the armed forces would remain loyal to the Shah and would restore law and order and that the country, which had been through similar crises in the past, would return to stability' (Cabinet conclusions, 14 September 1978, CAB 128/ 64, CM(78) 31st conclusions).
49 Letter from Parsons to the Secretary of State for Foreign and Commonwealth Affairs, 31 December 1978, FCO 8/3359.

120 *Revolution and reaction, 1978–1979*

50 Ibid.
51 Letter from Parsons to the Secretary of State for Foreign and Commonwealth Affairs, 18 January 1979, FCO 8/3377.
52 Ibid.
53 Ibid.
54 'Iran – What price democracy?' Minute by Westmacott, 15 March 1978, FCO 8/3184.
55 Record of a call on HH Sheikh Rashid bin Sa'id Al-Maktoum, Vice-President and Prime Minister of the UAE and Ruler of Dubai, on Monday 11 June at 11am 1979, FCO 8/3287.
56 Ibid. In the course of Anglo–American talks held in Washington in March 1979, Sir Anthony Parsons informed his hosts that on the whole the Rulers of the Gulf States were 'in closer contact with their own people than the Shah had been and received enough feedback to pre-empt discontent' (Anglo–US official talks on the Middle East, Washington, 15–16 March 1979, B3: Oman, FCO 8/3283).
57 'Iran: The future', Minute by Tatham, 13 June 1978, FCO 8/3193.
58 'Iran: Ministerial visits', Minute by Hannay, 26 October 1979, FCO 8/3375.
59 Ibid.
60 Telegram from Tehran to the Foreign and Commonwealth Office, No. 1182, 11 November 1979, FCO 8/3363.
61 'Iran: Possible action and British interests', Foreign and Foreign Office paper, attached to draft minute from Minister of State (Douglas Hurd) to the Secretary of State (Lord Carrington), undated, FCO 8/3375.
62 Nigel John Ashton, *Eisenhower, Macmillan, and the Problem of Nasser: Anglo–American Relations and Arab Nationalism, 1955–59* (Basingstoke: Palgrave Macmillan, 1996), p. 196.
63 'Iran: Economic and political implications: Annex A', pp. 7–8, Note by officials, 10 November 1978, CAB 134/4215, EY(78) 45.
64 Letter from Brant to Owen, 31 December 1978, FCO 8/3397.
65 Telegram from the American Embassy, Doha, to the Secretary of State, Washington, No. 01577, 6 December 1978, RG, Electronic Telegrams, https://aad.archives.gov/aad/createpdf?rid=304279&dt=2694&dl=2009 [accessed 16 November 2016].
66 Telegram from the American Embassy, Kuwait, to the Secretary of State, Washington, No. 06669, 17 December 1978, RG 59, Electronic Telegrams, https://aad.archives.gov/aad/createpdf?rid=315802&dt=2694&dl=2009 [accessed 18 November 2016].
67 Letter from Lucas to Brant, 25 January 1979, FCO 8/3397.
68 Rob Johnson, *The Iran–Iraq War* (Basingstoke: Palgrave Macmillan, 2010), p. 39.
69 Kristian Coates Ulrichsen, 'The Gulf States and the Iran–Iraq War: Cooperation and confusion', in Nigel Ashton and Bryan Gibson (eds.), *The Iran–Iraq War: New International Perspectives* (London: Routledge, 2014), p. 113.
70 F. Gregory Gause, *The International Relations of the Persian Gulf* (Cambridge: Cambridge University Press, 2010), p. 48.
71 Kristian Coates Ulrichsen, *Qatar and the Arab Spring* (London: Hurst and Company, 2014), p. 22.
72 Peterson, *Defending Arabia*, p. 216.
73 Munro, *Flying the Flag*, p. 128.
74 Rory Miller, *Desert Kingdoms to Global Powers: The Rise of the Arab Gulf* (New Haven and London: Yale University Press, 2016), p. 51.
75 'UK policy Towards Arabia and the Gulf in the wake of the Iran crisis', FCO paper (undated), FCO 8/3301.
76 Telegram from the Foreign and Commonwealth Office to certain missions and dependent territories, No. 17, 13 February 1979, FCO 8/3374.
77 *Financial Times*, 8 January 1979, FCO 8/3374.
78 Parsons, *The Pride and the Fall*, p. 140.

79 'British policy on Iran, 1974–1978', Report by N. W. Browne, p. 65, FCO 8/4029. See also David E. Long, 'The impact of the Iranian Revolution on the Arabian Peninsula and the Gulf States', in John L. Esposito (ed.), *The Iranian Revolution: Its Global Impact* (Miami: University of Florida Press, 1990), pp. 105–06; David Commins, *The Gulf States: A Modern History* (London and New York: I. B. Tauris, 2012), p. 227; Kristian Coates Ulrichsen, *Insecure Gulf: The End of Certainty and the Transition to the Post-Oil Era* (London: Hurst and Company, 2011), p. 27.
80 Jill Crystal points out that 'When the revolution erupted, Kuwait's 30, 000 Iranians received it with joy' (Jill Crystal, *Oil and Politics in the Gulf: Rulers and Merchants in Kuwait and Qatar* (Cambridge: Cambridge University Press, 1990), p. 100). Claire Beaugrand points out that 'Shiite political Islam represented the main threat to the rule of the Al-Sabah throughout the 1980s' (Claire Beaugrand, 'Deconstructing minorities/majorities in parliamentary Gulf States (Kuwait and Bahrain)', *British Journal of Middle Eastern Studies*, 43, 2 (2016), p. 241).
81 The Bahraini Shia formed 72 per cent of the population. Vanessa Martin argues that Shia grievances were 'compounded by elite frustration at not having a larger share of government responsibilities' (Vanessa Martin, *Creating an Islamic State: Khomeini and the Making of a New Iran* (London and New York: I. B. Tauris, 2010), p. 194).
82 Gause, *The International Relations of the Persian Gulf*, pp. 47–8.
83 Letter from Bryan Cartledge (Private Secretary [Overseas Affairs] to the Prime Minister) to Paul Lever (FCO), 2 July 1979, PREM 19/2021.
84 Telegram from Bahrain to the Foreign and Commonwealth Office, No. 142, 3 July 1979, PREM 19/2021.
85 Letter from Crawford to the Secretary of State for Foreign and Commonwealth Affairs, 20 December 1977, FCO 8/3221.
86 Ibid.
87 Ibid.
88 Ibid.
89 Ibid.
90 Letter from Brant to David Owen, 1 May 1977, FCO 8/3222.
91 Ibid.
92 Ibid.
93 Ibid.
94 'First impressions of Qatar', Minute by Parramore, 22 May 1978, FCO8/3222.
95 Letter from Lucas to Brant, 24 May 1978, FCO 8/3222.
96 'Cancellation of UK/Qatar Joint Committee and the Abdul Aziz visit', Minute by M. W. Hunt, 30 June 1978, FCO 8/3223.
97 Letter from Brant to Hunt, 3 August 1978, FCO 8/3223.
98 Letter from O. H. Kemmis (Department of Trade) to Brant, 25 September 1978, FCO 8/3223.
99 Letter from Treadwell to P. R. H. Wright, 8 May 1973, FCO 8/2126.
100 Ibid.
101 Brief for the Secretary of State's meeting with Sheikh Zaid, President of the United Arab Emirates on 18 September 1973 at 4.30pm: UAE Internal affairs, attached to 'Shaikh Zaid's call on the Secretary of State', Minute by Wright, 14 September 1973, FCO 8/2141.
102 Letter from Roberts to the Secretary of State for Foreign and Commonwealth Affairs, 1 January 1978, FCO 8/3139.
103 Ibid.
104 Teleletter from H. St. John B. Armitage to the Foreign and Commonwealth Office, 5 February 1978, FCO 8/3140.
105 'United Kingdom diplomatic representation in the UAE', Minute by Lucas, 21 April 1978, FCO 8/3140.

106 Ibid.
107 'United Arab Emirates: Internal', note attached to Lucas' minute, 17 May 1978 FCO 8/3140.
108 'The UAE mess', Minute by McCarthy, 15 June 1978, FCO 8/3141.
109 Letter from D. K. Haskell to Carrington, 1 January 1980, FCO 8/3507.
110 Letter from Major to Lt. Col. R. Jury, 14 July 1978, FCO 8/3101.
111 Ibid.
112 Letter from Roberts to Lucas, 25 July 1978, FCO 8/3101.
113 Letter from Roberts to Owen, 20 July 1978, FCO 8/3141.
114 Letter from Haskell to David Tatham, 24 August 1978, FCO 8/3141.
115 Ibid.
116 Letter from Roberts to Owen, 20 July 1978, FCO 8/3141.
117 Record of a meeting between Frank Judd and His Highness Sheikh Rashid bin Said Al-Maktoum, 26 February 1979, FCO 8/3299.
118 Ibid.
119 Minute from Judd to the Secretary of State, 5 March 1979, FCO 8/3299.
120 Letter from Roberts to Owen, 10 March 1979, FCO 8/3300. In his valedictory despatch on stepping down as British Ambassador to the UAE, Roberts remarked upon the 'perennial tension between Abu Dhabi and Dubai, whose relations are roughly those of Rangers and Celtic' (Letter from Roberts to Carrington, 25 April 1981, FCO 8/3910).
121 Letter from Roberts to Owen, 10 March 1979, FCO 8/3300.
122 Letter from Munro to Roberts, 23 March 1979, FCO 8/3300.
123 Letter from Roberts to Owen, 10 March 1979, FCO 8/3300.
124 Anglo–US official talks on the Middle East, Washington, 15–16 March 1979, B2: The Gulf Sheikhdoms, FCO 8/3283.
125 Telegram from Maestrone to the Secretary of State, Washington, No. 00829, 17 February 1979, RG 59, Electronic Telegrams, 1979, https://aad.archives.gov/aad/createpdf?rid=93710&dt=2776&dl=2169 [accessed 13 November 2016].
126 Ibid.
127 In early 1979, the US Ambassador to Qatar, Andrew Killgore, reported that 'Qatar is deeply concerned over collapse of the Shah's regime and apprehensive about stability of Gulf area in wake of the cataclysm in Iran' (Telegram from Killgore to the Secretary of State, Washington, No. 00141, 4 February 1979, RG 59, Electronic Telegrams, 1979, https://aad.archives.gov/aad/createpdf?rid=80568&dt=2776&dl=2169 [accessed 13 November 2016]).
128 Letter from Brant to Tatham, 5 March 1979, FCO 8/3398.
129 Ibid.
130 Letter from Brant to Munro, 25 March 1979, FCO 8/3398.
131 Telegram from Bahrain to the Foreign and Commonwealth Office, No. 188, 18 August 1979, FCO 8/3307.
132 Telegram from Bahrain to the Foreign and Commonwealth Office, No. 192, 28 August 1979, FCO 8/3307.
133 Ibid.
134 Ibid.
135 Ibid.
136 Letter from Walker to D. E. Tatham, 9 September 1979, FCO 8/3307.
137 Telegram from Bahrain to the Foreign and Commonwealth Office, No. 204, 15 September 1979, FCO 8/3307. Walker himself admitted that it was 'inconceivable to me that any combination of malcontents in Bahrain could topple the government. They have not got the necessary numbers, weapons, unity, membership in the police/Bahrain Defence Force etc' (Telegram from Walker to the Foreign and Commonwealth Office, No. 208, 17 September 1979, FCO 8/3307).

138 Teleletter from Brant to Tatham, 6 June 1979, FCO 8/3398.
139 Letter from Brant to Lord Carrington, 16 June 1979, FCO 8/3398.
140 Record of the Prime Minister's talk with the Amir of Qatar at 10 Downing Street, 11 September 1979, FCO 8/3399.
141 Ibid.
142 Ibid.
143 Telegram from Jeddah to the Foreign and Commonwealth Office, No. 688, 5 December 1979, FCO 8/3419.
144 Telegram from Washington to the Foreign and Commonwealth Office, No. 3891, 25 November 1979, FCO 8/3364.
145 'Iran: Western options', FCO paper attached to Tatham's minute to Douglas Hurd, 23 November 1979, FCO 8/3375.
146 'Iran: Risk of retaliation in the Middle East against Britain', Minute by Miers, 20 December 1979, FCO 8/3376.
147 Ibid.
148 For an account of the 1979 uprising, see Toby Matthiesen, *The Other Saudis: Shiism, Dissent and Sectarianism* (New York: Cambridge University Press, 2015), pp. 104–08.
149 Ulrichsen, 'The Gulf States and the Iran-Iraq War', p. 113.
150 Telegram from Jedda (Craig) to the Foreign and Commonwealth Office, No. 117, 6 February 1980, PREM 19/1126.
151 Telegram from Doha to the Foreign and Commonwealth Office, No. 284, 23 December 1979, FCO 8/3399.
152 Ibid.
153 Letter from Brant to Lord Carrington, 16 June 1979, FCO 8/3398.
154 Ibid.
155 Ibid.
156 Letter from Brant to Lord Carrington, 16 June 1979, FCO 8/3398.
157 'UK–Qatar relations', Minute by Brant, 19 June 1979, FCO 8/3399.
158 Teleletter from Brant to Munro, 20 May 1979, FCO 8/3400.
159 Ibid.
160 Letter from Roberts to the Secretary of State for Foreign and Commonwealth Affairs, 1 January 1979, FCO 8/3319.
161 Letter from E. F. Given to the Secretary of State for Foreign and Commonwealth Affairs, 10 January 1979, FCO 8/3305; Letter from H. B. Walker to the Secretary of State for Foreign and Commonwealth Affairs, 8 January 1980, FCO 8/3490.
162 Letter from Bryan Cartledge (Private Secretary (Overseas Affairs) to Prime Minister) to Paul Lever (FCO), 2 July 1979, PREM 19/43.
163 Letter from Walker to the Secretary of State for Foreign and Commonwealth Affairs, 8 January 1980, FCO 8/3490.
164 Letter from Cambridge to the Secretary of State for Foreign and Commonwealth Affairs, 20 January 1979, FCO 8/3322.
165 Letter from Cambridge to the Secretary of State for Foreign and Commonwealth Affairs, 12 January 1980, FCO 8/3523.
166 Ibid.
167 Ibid.
168 Ibid.
169 'Defence options available to the United Kingdom in contributing to stability in the Gulf and former CENTO areas', Report by the Defence Policy Staff, 23 April 1979, Annex A, p. 9, FCO 8/3292.
170 Ibid, p. 12.
171 'Mr Schlesinger's views on US strategic interests in the Middle East', Minute by Munro, 3 August 1979, FCO 8/3292.

5   War and peace, 1980

In retirement, the former Head of the FCO's Arabian Department, Anthony Acland, noted with respect to efforts to encourage the creation of the United Arab Emirates following the 1968 decision to withdraw from East of Suez: 'It was a British responsibility, we didn't have to consult with our European allies, we told the Americans what we were doing, they backed us up but it really was a British operation'.[1] In the following decade and beyond, however, Britain's exclusive position in the Gulf, as we have already seen, was significantly eroded as other powers encroached on the region. In June 1974, for instance, the EEC sent an aide-memoire to the Arab League suggesting a new mechanism for cooperation between Europe and the Arab world to be known as the Euro–Arab Dialogue.[2] Although the EAD foundered on Arab insistence on raising the issue of Palestine,[3] it did indicate a willingness on the part of the Europeans to play a more prominent role in the region. Despite the failure of the EAD, German Foreign Minister Hans-Dietrich Genscher at the beginning of 1980 floated the idea of an EEC–Gulf Dialogue, which, perhaps unsurprisingly, drew a sceptical response from the FCO, not least because of the recognition that the Gulf States would 'inevitably raise the Arab/Israel dispute in the context of the dialogue'.[4]

The heightening of a sense of regional crisis in the aftermath of the Soviet invasion of Afghanistan in December 1979 also served to sharpen the US commitment to the Gulf. Commenting on the Soviets' actions to British Premier Margaret Thatcher, President Carter declared: 'They have in effect changed a proper nation into a puppet nation and I think it will have profound strategic consequences on the stability of that entire region'.[5] Seeking to respond to the new challenges, Carter told both Houses of Congress during his State of the Union address on 23 January 1980:

> Let our position be absolutely clear: An attempt by any outside force to gain control of the Persian Gulf region will be regarded as an assault on the vital interests of the United States of America, and such an assault will be repelled by any means necessary, including military force.[6]

Carter proceeded to delineate the steps the United States would be making to fulfil what became known as the Carter Doctrine, including improvements in capabilities to deploy US forces rapidly to the region and strengthening the US naval presence in the Indian Ocean. In the judgement of Jeffrey Macris, 'The annunciation of the Carter Doctrine marked a radical break from previous policy, and laid to rest for good the Nixon Doctrine's reliance on outside powers to safeguard the West's interests in the Gulf'.[7] Similarly, Amitav Acharya argues that, in response to the situation in Iran and Afghanistan, Washington set about fashioning a 'long-term military strategy to replace the defunct "twin pillar" doctrine as the basic framework of US policy in the Gulf. This involved increased emphasis on building a direct US force projection capability to deal with possible contingencies in the region'.[8]

During Anglo–American talks towards the end of January 1980, Assistant Under-Secretary of State at the FCO, P. H. Moberly, welcomed President Carter's statement as contributing to the stability of the region in general and to individual countries in particular. Nevertheless, he stressed that Arab states would 'find it difficult to welcome publicly an increased US presence so long as there was no movement in settling the Palestinian problem'.[9] He also opined that 'Arab states in the Gulf area could probably live with a large expansion of US presence on Diego Garcia as being preferable to bases on Arab territory'.[10] So far as British policy was concerned, Moberly remarked that while Britain would continue its existing naval deployments, there was 'no intention to restore a permanent UK military presence East of Suez'.[11] 'We have to recognise, depressing though it is', ruminated the Assistant Head of the FCO's Middle East Department, D. E. Tatham, 'that super power confrontation has reached the Gulf and in preparing to counter a Soviet invasion of Iran or Pakistan the Americans are planning for a contingency which cannot be excluded and which only they can meet'.[12] Nevertheless, in further Anglo–American talks in April the Director of Politico-Military Affairs at the State Department, Reginald Bartholomew, assured the British delegation that the US 'did not intend to make the Middle East a purely US show. They wished to work with the allies particularly the UK whose expertise and relationship in the area were valued'.[13]

For its part, the government of Margaret Thatcher exhibited a marked degree of pragmatism in its response to the regional crisis. On the one hand, the Prime Minister, following a recommendation from Foreign Secretary Lord Carrington,[14] informed Carter that Britain would 'accelerate negotiations over the sales of British defence equipment to Oman, Saudi Arabia and the other States in the Gulf'.[15] On the other hand, there was recognition of the real limits of British influence over the Gulf States. As K. J. Passmore of the FCO's Middle East Department noted: 'The Gulf rulers' future is very much what they (not we) make of it. Our strongest asset used to be our ability to "advise" them. Even if we tried to do that, they would not now listen'.[16] Passmore also observed that 'Whatever might be our policy on strengthening our military connections with the area, I do not believe that the Gulf States would wish to refer to military assistance by name'.[17] Reporting for the Chiefs of Staff Committee, the Directors of Defence Policy similarly argued that 'too sudden an increase in deployments might raise fears of intervention in Gulf states'.[18] D. H. Gillmore of the FCO's Defence Department, furthermore, asserted that

> If either Iran or Iraq were to launch an all-out attack by land or sea on the Gulf States, UK resources would not be sufficient by themselves to repel such an attack. Moreover it would be impossible for the UK alone to put troops on the ground in sufficient numbers in a short time-scale.[19]

Gillmore also indicated that the Ministry of Defence was 'deeply concerned at the risk of giving an open-ended commitment which would add to the already marked overstretch of our defence resources'.[20]

Concerns about an over-extension of British commitments in the region also arose from the UAE Ambassador to the UK, Mahdi Al-Tajir's, grandiose plans to oversee a Pahlavi restoration in Iran.[21] While admitting that there were 'good reasons why the Gulf shaikhs would like to see an end of the present regime in Iran', Passmore mused that 'the Gulf states, like the Iranians, are inclined to have extremely exaggerated ideas about British ability to influence events in the area'.[22] What is more, the Head of the FCO's Middle East Department, H. D. A. C. Miers, observed that 'The Revolutionary leaders still command fanatical enthusiasm in Iran from many. We have carefully avoided giving any expressions of support to any of the exile groups. I believe we should maintain this line with Madhi Tajir'.[23] The decline in Britain's capacity to 'influence events in the area', was compounded by the intrusion of commercial competitors.

In March 1980, French President Valéry Giscard d'Estaing, accompanied by a posse of ministers – Foreign Affairs, Industry, Trade, and Education – visited the Gulf. Shortly before Giscard's departure for the region, the British Ambassador in Doha, Colin Brant, lamented: 'Clearly the wall has been breached by the French in a big way.... With President Giscard's visit coming up, they will be riding the crest of a wave, and will doubtless exploit this situation to the full'.[24] Indeed a host of agreements resulted covering cooperation in energy development, environmental, industrial, cultural, and agricultural matters.[25] Even before the French President's arrival, Miers noted the 'inroads the French (and others)' were making and pledged to 'watch with interest how Giscard goes down and what he manages to sweep into his enormous carpet bag'.[26] In the aftermath of Giscard's visit, Brant, emphasized: 'On the commercial front, I was left in no doubt of the French Government's hopes and intentions of seeing French industry and commerce expand here – even if such operations were described as "a matter for the companies"'.[27] He also reported that 'it is clear that the French energy industry . . . has its sights firmly fixed on the "treasure-house" . . . of the immense North-West Dome gas deposits'.[28]

Reflecting on Giscard's Gulf tour, Passmore confessed that 'In the Gulf, traditionally our chasse gardée, the enemy, as far as our posts are concerned, is the French, and this is despite their inferior commercial performance to both the Germans and the Japanese. It is not hard to see why. I suspect the French have made no secret that they wish to rival our position, in the linguistic and cultural as well as the commercial fields'.[29] As regards arms sales, Passmore went on to point out that the French had made

> good progress at our expense, not only because their delivery times are better and their arms are more suited to what many Gulf shaikhs (rather than their military advisers) think they need, but also because of the good relations established at the highest level. This is particularly true of Qatar and the UAE (Abu Dhabi).[30]

Miers concurred that 'we can expect the French to reinforce their successes at our expense in the field of defence sales amongst others. They are undoubtedly trying hard, and with the advantage of good "fixers" and sales technique they can be expected to follow up determinedly'.[31] Brant himself regretted that 'we should . . . be elbowing in the line-out with the French at every turn in the game'.[32] He concluded resignedly that 'while the French are so clearly set on such spoiling tactics, with the aim of profiting at our expense, there seems to be little we can do except keep our end up as far as possible'.[33]

To make matters worse for the British, France's standing in the Gulf also reached something of a peak in the aftermath of Giscard's visit. For instance, the Qatari Minister of Defence and Heir Apparent, Sheikh Hamad bin Khalifah, told Brant that 'for the first time ever, the Qataris felt themselves to be in close relations with the French as a result of Giscard's visit here'.[34] Referring specifically to the defence field, Brant proceeded to comment: 'In the course of time, with the Qataris having established a French language training school of a size equal to the English language training school, it may be increasingly difficult for us to break in here on the basis of longstanding ties as well as excellent quality'.[35] Moreover, in conversations with Assistant Under-Secretary of State at the FCO, J. C. Moberly, the Bahraini Foreign Minister, Sheikh Muhammad bin Mubarak, declared that

> the French were now regarded in the Gulf as the real friends of the Arabs in the West. He was sorry to say this, bearing in mind our own long associations with the Gulf States. However, it was the French who were seen as taking the lead in pointing Europe towards support for a just and comprehensive Middle East settlement and they would reap the benefits in the area accordingly.[36]

In his annual review, the British Ambassador to Bahrain, H. B. Walker, observed that 'Among the Western powers 1980 might have to be conceded as France's year'.[37] In a similar vein, Ambassador Brant remarked: 'The French, in particular, have made a major effort this year to achieve a substantial position in Qatar in all fields – political, industrial and military'.[38] Although Britain remained preeminent in the Qatari market for helicopters and communications equipment, Brant noted: 'In every other aspect of defence sales, we were undercut by the advantages which the French enjoy: manufacturing arms specifically for export, and the ability to offer quicker deliveries and lower prices'.[39] 'The combination', he reported, 'proved irresistible here'.[40]

Quite apart from its inability to prevent the intrusion of other external powers into the Gulf, Britain found its capacity to foster cooperation among the states of the Arab Gulf, a long-standing aim, strictly limited. In the aftermath of the 1972 coup which brought Sheikh Khalifah to power, D. G. Allen of the FCO's Middle East Department recorded that 'Relations between the UAE and Qatar have never been worse, mainly because the former Ruler of Qatar chose to seek refuge with his father-in-law, Shaikh Rashid of Dubai'.[41] Equally, Allen pointed out that 'the UAE's relations with Saudi Arabia are severely strained by Shaikh Zaid's continuing boundary dispute with King Feisal'.[42] While advocating the formation of a regional council to facilitate cooperation among the new states of the Gulf, Allen conceded that 'the present state of relations between Bahrain, Qatar and the UAE is such that there can be little hope of any of them agreeing to this'.[43]

As regards Kuwait, the British Ambassador there, S. J. G. Cambridge, reported:

> After a flurry of activity at the end of 1979, when Sheikh Sa'ad[44] visited the other Gulf States, the Kuwaitis seem to have lost interest in Gulf cooperation. They pay lip service to the idea, and beaver away in a number of technical fields. But in the important areas of defence and political cooperation, I detect no keenness to engage in serious discussions.[45]

Seeking to explain this attitude, Cambridge declared: 'The Kuwaitis cannot afford to antagonise the Iraqis. This means there are limits to which they feel able to cooperate in arrangements that exclude the Iraqis'.[46] The Ambassador also stressed that 'At best, their progress towards regional cooperation will be low, and they will not thank the Saudis (or the West, if our hand is manifest) for trying to rush them or seeming to teach them their business'.[47] While there was general agreement among British diplomatic posts in the region that Saudi Arabia should take the lead in measures of Gulf cooperation, the British Ambassador to Bahrain, H. B. Walker, perceived difficulties in pressing upon the Saudis individual ideas on the grounds that 'we risk being snubbed if we offer gratuitous advice on matters that we cannot know all that much about, eg peninsula cooperation on technical subjects, and on which we are not in a position to offer a contribution in the shape of finance or technical assistance'.[48] Indeed, Britain tended to favour entering into bilateral discussions with the Gulf States themselves.

At the beginning of 1980 the Minister of State at the FCO, Douglas Hurd, visited Bahrain, Qatar, and the UAE. Although during Hurd's talks in Doha the Amir 'opened with his standard lecture on the Arab–Israel problem' and also opined that the British withdrawal from Aden had 'encouraged Soviet expansionism', Brant was able to report that the Minister of State had 'tapped to [the] full the underlying cordiality of Anglo–Qatari relations'.[49] The Ambassador also reported that Sheikh Khalifah 'seemed receptive to our offers to help with the development of the North-West Dome gas field'.[50] Hurd was also able to reassure him that the British government was 'in no way contemplating the cessation of British Council operations in Qatar'.[51]

Following the signature in 1971 of a Memorandum of Understanding, the British Council had established an office in Doha a year later to promote the UK's cultural and educational relations with Qatar.[52] In 1974, the British Ambassador in Doha, E. F. Henderson, remarked upon the 'Egyptianisation of the Department of Education, especially on the English language teaching side'.[53] Despite this worrying development, Henderson was able to record that 'under the patient and skilful guidance of the Council Director, both the Council itself, and the increased number of Council-recruited teachers have improved their position greatly throughout the year. They are making a strong impact on the teaching of English in Doha through the secondary and primary schools'.[54] In his annual report for 1974–1975, the Director for Qatar, M. R. W. Dexter, asseverated that the Council was 'now definitely part of the general scene in Doha and enjoys the most cordial relations with the Government and with wide sectors of the Qatari, and multinational, general public'.[55]

On 26 January 1976, new Council offices were opened by Sheikh Jassim bin Hamad Al-Thani, the Qatari Minister of Education.[56] In his annual report for 1976–1977, the new Director of the British Council in Qatar, W. H. Jefferson, enthused that the recruitment of teachers had been 'one of the main factors contributing to the Council's special relationship with the Ministry'.[57] He also remarked upon the first meeting of the UK–Qatar Joint Committee for Economic Cooperation in Doha in January 1977, at which the British Council was represented. '[O]ne of the more concrete things to emerge', Jefferson recorded,

> was an agreement between the Ministry of Education and the Council paving the way to future cooperation in training, exchange of persons, technology and recruitment and acknowledging two important principles; that of payment for Council services and that of the Council's role in the promotion of British commercial interests. We now work closely with the commercial section of the Embassy and have ensured since the agreement that appropriate British firms and consortia are invited to tender for Ministry contracts and that the Ministry is made aware of British capability and expertise over a wide area.[58]

Referring to the British Council's activities in Qatar, the Director of its Middle East Department, G. A. Tindale, reported on 5 April 1979 that 'The Council has a position of immense influence in ELT and is known and respected in all areas of Government'.[59] Despite the evident success of the British Council in promoting British interests overseas, it was not immune from the Thatcher government's determination to rein in public expenditure following its election in May 1979. In August 1979, Foreign Secretary Lord Carrington informed the Director-General of the British Council that the government had decided the Council would have to find savings of £3 million from the FCO grant-in-aid for the financial year 1980–1981.[60] Reflecting the esteem with which the British Council was held in Qatar, the new Minister of Education, Sheikh Mohammed bin Hamad Al-Thani, urged Secretary of State for Education Mark Carlisle, during a visit to London in January 1980, that 'every effort be made to maintain the Council operation in Qatar at its present level of activity'.[61] On his return to Doha, Sheikh Mohammed was instrumental in arranging for the government of Qatar to meet the rent of the Council's offices to the tune of £36,000 per year.[62] In July 1980, moreover, D. F. B. Edye, First Secretary and Consul at the British Embassy in Qatar, stated: 'Both politically and commercially Britain stands to gain from the success of the Council activities'.[63]

Reflecting on Anglo–Qatari relations in 1980, nevertheless, the British Council itself observed:

> While a special relationship with Britain continues, Qatar has made efforts since independence in 1971 to widen its circle of non-Arab friends, and the visit earlier this year of the French President with an entourage of four ministers can be seen as part of that process. Most of the new industrial projects are in non-British hands.[64]

As an indication of growing European influence in the Gulf, and the erosion of Britain's exclusive position since 1971, the Qatari Minister of Defence and Heir apparent, Sheikh Hamad bin Khalifah, informed Douglas Hurd in January 1980 that 'it was necessary for the Gulf States to co-operate with the European Community'.[65] While Hurd pointed out the Community was not a defence organization, Hamad insisted that 'it could nevertheless be of help'.[66]

Hurd's visit to the Gulf took place against the background of the Soviet invasion of Afghanistan in December 1979. The UAE, in particular, condemned Soviet actions as 'conspicuous meddling in the internal affairs of the Afghan Muslim people'.[67] Referring to Hurd's visit to the UAE, the British Ambassador there, D. A. Roberts, remarked that the 'timing could hardly have been more opportune, in view of events in Iran and Afghanistan'.[68] 'A common theme in all discussions', reported Roberts, 'was that the UK still had a role to play in the area based on its long experience of the Gulf'.[69] Nevertheless, he proceeded to note that 'Mr Hurd's offer of British help to plug any gaps which the Gulf States might find when reviewing their collective defence effort was welcomed but evoked no specific response'.[70]

In March, Hurd returned to the Gulf, holding a series of meetings with leading Kuwaiti ministers and officials. While the encounters revealed the warmth of Anglo–Kuwaiti relations, they also underlined that the links between the two countries had entered a palpably post-imperial phase. For instance, Sheikh Jabir al Ali, the Kuwaiti Deputy Prime Minister and Minister of Information, informed Hurd that 'while Kuwait would like to depend much more on British expertise, the British could not be specially favoured in modern market conditions'.[71] Referring to the Gulf, moreover, the Kuwaiti Minister of Defence, Sheikh Salim Al-Sabah, informed Hurd that 'security was more likely to be maintained if there was no outside interference', adding that it would 'create instability, clashes and international problems'.[72] In a similar vein, the Minister of State for Cabinet Affairs and Acting Foreign Minister, Abdul Aziz Hussain, insisted that there should be no foreign bases in the Gulf and that the existence of such bases would 'cause instability which would affect the production of oil'.[73] On the vexed question of Palestine, Abdul Aziz expressed his appreciation that Britain had supported Giscard d'Estaing's backing for Palestinian self-determination 'within the framework of a just and lasting peace'.[74] Indeed, shortly before Hurd's visit to Kuwait he had stated that the Palestinians had rights which went 'well beyond' those addressed in UN Security Resolution 242 and that Britain considered 'there was a case for the Security Council to recognise those rights'.[75] Crown Prince Sheikh Sa'ad also impressed upon Hurd that the Kuwaitis were 'very pleased by Britain's statement on the future of the Palestinians'.[76] As regards Gulf cooperation, Sheikh Sa'ad admitted that recent events 'were a warning of the need for the Gulf states to come much closer together' to which Hurd responded: 'we agreed that the Gulf states should not seek pacts with the West but if after they came together the states founds gaps on the defence side, we would be happy to help'.[77]

During his time in Kuwait, Hurd expressed HMG's eagerness to 'increase the visibility of British policy in the Middle East eg through more ministerial visits'.[78] Indeed, Hurd's tour was followed towards the end of March by the Parliamentary Under-Secretary of State for Trade, R. E. Eyre. Eyre's visit to Cairo was blighted by what the British Ambassador to Oman, I. T. M. Lucas, referred to as 'a malady not uncommon in those who have just visited Cairo for the first time'.[79] Having recovered sufficiently to continue on to Oman, Eyre fared little better, Lucas recording that the minister came across as 'something of an innocent abroad'.[80] Lucas' critique proceeded with the following observations: 'His idea of trade promotion in general, and in this area in particular, seemed superficial and rudimentary; and his attempts to express admiration of the Sultanate's progress came across as patronising and ingratiating'.[81] The Ambassador added that during his meeting with Omani Deputy Prime Minister Sayyid Fahr, Eyre 'was immediately placed on the defensive as His Highness bowled a series of fast and all too accurate balls on the subject of the shortcomings of British Leyland and other vehicle manufacturers . . . giving the poor PUSS little chance to do any trade promotion'.[82] The visit to the UAE by Eyre's superior, Minister for Trade Cecil Parkinson, a month later proved altogether more successful.

Reporting from Abu Dhabi, Ambassador Roberts emphasized that the visit demonstrated to the authorities of the UAE that HMG had a 'lively interest in the area', adding that it received 'admirable publicity' through the press, radio, and television.[83] In Dubai, Parkinson was the guest at a lunch provided by the Chamber of Commerce there and had a formal meeting afterwards, while in Abu Dhabi he met five leading local businessmen in the company of the British Embassy's Commercial Secretary.[84] Summing up, Roberts declared: 'All in all the visit was a great success and left an excellent impression on the authorities of the UAE and the British business community'.[85] The Head of the FCO's Middle East Department, H. D. A. C. Miers, agreed that both politically and commercially Parkinson's sojourn had 'strengthened still further' Britain's 'good relations' with the UAE.[86] The Trade Minister's subsequent trip to Kuwait was an equal success.

During his four days in Kuwait, Parkinson called on no less than five Kuwaiti ministers, the President of the Chamber of Commerce, and the Acting Chairman of the Municipality. In addition, he gave an address to some sixty senior Kuwaiti merchants and financiers at the Chamber, visited a joint venture factory, and attended three major receptions at which he met a large number of Kuwaiti and local British businessmen. Summing up, the British Ambassador to Kuwait, S. J. G. Cambridge, observed:

> Mr Parkinson's achievements in this visit, apart from the obviously important one of extending our range of direct inter-ministerial contacts, were to present a favourable impression of Britain as a trading partner, to demonstrate the keen interest which HMG and British industry take in Kuwait as an important export market for our goods, and to promote certain items of current business.[87]

Parkinson's visit was followed up by Health Minister Dr Gerald Vaughan who travelled to Kuwait in early June as the guest of Dr Awadhi, his Kuwaiti counterpart. 'From the point of view of reinforcing Anglo–Kuwaiti relations', reported Cambridge, 'the visit was an outstanding success. It received considerable publicity and there was a marked atmosphere of friendliness throughout'.[88] The Ambassador was particularly impressed by the 'close personal relationship' Vaughan established with Awadhi which, he posited, would be 'of immense value to us in continuing and developing cooperation with the Kuwaitis in the heath field'.[89]

Despite the apparent success of Parkinson and Vaughan's ministerial visits, they did expose some underlying problems in British relations with the Gulf, especially in the economic field. Referring to Parkinson's experiences in Kuwait, Ambassador Cambridge remarked that 'we were subjected to the usual grumbles about high prices, missed delivery dates and the absence of British contractors from this market'.[90] Assistant Head of the FCO's Middle East Department D. E. Tatham, moreover, observed: 'While Dr Vaughan clearly got on well with his Kuwaiti opposite number and others whom he met, they took pains to point out, in the usual hardheaded Kuwaiti fashion, that goodwill could not compensate for high prices and long delivery'.[91]

In Qatar, the Royal tour of the Gulf in early 1979 ostensibly produced long-term benefits for both Qatar and Britain.[92] Writing at the very end of the year, Ambassador Brant claimed that the Queen's visit had 'subtly but markedly given the Amir and his Government a new self-confidence in their dealing with others'.[93] In addition, he reported that the 'Amir has privately instructed his administration to look to Britain first and foremost for the supply of military equipment and industrial plant – and only go elsewhere if our prices and delivery dates prove manifestly unacceptable'.[94] Sheikh Khalifah's visit to London in September, added Brant, had left him a 'fervent admirer' of Prime Minister Thatcher. Brant also informed Carrington that his 'spectacular success' in achieving a settlement of the long-running crisis in Rhodesia had encouraged the Amir to pledge his assistance to British policies 'wherever and whenever it may be of use to us'.[95] He went on to describe the Thatcher administration as 'in a class by itself'.[96] Nevertheless, Brant warned that the happy state of Anglo–Qataris relations 'must not blind us to the fact that the French are making rapid strides, particularly among the younger Al Thani (including Shaikh Hamad, the Heir Apparent, and his two brothers) and the Armed forces'.[97] The Qatari Air Force's order for six French Alpha-Jet advanced trainer/ground attack aircraft to replace its ageing fleet of British-built Hunter aircraft, served to justify Brant's fears. The fact that British Aerospace could only deliver twenty-four months from signature of contract for its rival the Hawk trainer, whereas the French, whom Brant charged with entertaining 'fewer scruples about retrieving aircraft and equipment from their own armed forces for sale abroad', could offer delivery times of between six and twelve months, was also crucial in French success.[98] Following a visit to Qatar in October 1980, the Director of the UK's Military Assistance Office, Major General K. Perkins, confessed that 'The French have beaten us so far in terms of defence sales'.[99] High-level visits by Qatari ministers to the UK, moreover, did not always produce positive results.

Towards the beginning of 1980, the Qatari Minister of Petroleum and Finance, Sheikh Abdul Aziz bin Khalifa Al-Thani, arrived in London along with an entourage of bodyguards carrying firearms. He subsequently refused to surrender the weapons unless Metropolitan Police could provide similar protection. Only after six hours of discussions involving the police, the FCO, and the Qatar Embassy in London, did Sheikh Abdul Aziz agree to hand over the guns.[100] On receiving this news, Brant admitted to being 'somewhat dismayed'.[101] 'My dismay', he added, 'was the greater because of the contrast between the warm official reception which Abdul Aziz had been given by the French (the French Minister of Industry was at the steps of his aircraft to meet him when he arrived in Paris!) and our own strictly official approach'.[102] 'I quite realise', expatiated Brant,

> how rough, tough and ungracious the leading Al Thani must seem in London. Indeed, just as this letter was being drafted, I was forcibly reminded by a couple of British officials how little removed in manners they can sometimes be from their pirate forebears. . . . The only trouble is that with all this, they are so stinking rich. . . ![103]

In response, Miers stressed that 'We are all agreed upon the importance of Qatar from the sales point of view and of doing everything we reasonably can to flatter the sensitivities of the Al Thani (however irritating this may be) so as to keep the climate sweet for orders'.[104]

The potential for Al-Thani 'sensitivities' to impact on commercial relations was underlined by the Qatari Assistant Deputy Commander-in-Chief, Sheikh Abdullah bin Khalifah Al-Thani's, decision to place in abeyance negotiations with the British firm, Westland, for the supply of helicopters and defence systems worth £50 million until his security concerns during his stay in London had been addressed to his satisfaction.[105] There were also fears that other contracts, including British Aerospace's Rapier air defence system worth £250 million, might be in jeopardy.[106] Indeed, Abdullah specifically refused to attend demonstrations of Rapier firings until the matter of his security had been resolved.[107] There were particular fears that the French defence industry could potentially benefit from any deterioration in British relations with the Al-Thani ruling family.[108] As a result of such considerations, Abdullah was subsequently offered armed protection from Special Branch during his time in the UK.[109] Brant had already urged that 'Since his [Abdullah's] importance to us will obviously increase, as he comes to take over more and more of the GHQ decisions on defence orders, it becomes all the more advantageous to find a solution to this wretched gun business'.[110]

Despite efforts to smooth the ruffled Qatari feathers, Brant's roundup of defence sales to Qatar at the end of 1980 made for gloomy reading. Indeed, he went so far as to describe the French as having achieved a 'near monopoly'.[111] Examining the reasons for this phenomenon, the Ambassador pointed out that in a number of cases Britain did not have the equipment to offer which the Qataris wanted, whereas the French did. This was especially so with the decision in September 1980 to purchase 12 French-made Mirage aircraft which fulfilled Qatar's requirement for a supersonic interceptor to protect its airspace. The British alternatives – the Harrier, the Jaguar, and the Tornado – were seen as inappropriate in this role. '[W]here we could compete', lamented Brant, 'we were up against "France Incorporated", and especially the close Government-Industry co-ordination orchestrated in support of defence sales'.[112] By contrast, he noted that support from HMG as whole for Britain's defence effort in Qatar could 'hardly be described as overwhelming', with only one British minister (Douglas Hurd) having visited the Amirate between the royal tour of February 1979 and the arrival of the Secretary of State for Social Services, Patrick Jenkin, in October 1980.[113] Brant also recalled that Britain had 'scored something of an "own goal" ' earlier in the year by having a row with Sheikhs Abdullah and Abdul Aziz over personal protection while in the UK.[114] In addition, the Ambassador emphasized that the French had 'somehow or other been able to beat us substantially on prices and delivery dates for their weapons systems'.[115] Finally, Brant conceded that

> we must give credence to the charge by the (British) Commander of the Qatar Air Force . . . that the sales methods and representations of major British firms are distinctly poor when compared with the show which the French put on when they are after an order. The French firms, when called for negotiations with GHQ here, send out a team of 20, including directors armed with sufficient authority to take major decisions on the spot, (and a hired Lebanese TV "personality" to do the presentation in Arabic!). By contrast . . . our own people seem pretty low-level and low calibre – even bucolic.[116]

The advent of the Iran–Iraq War in September 1980 provided Britain with an opportunity to re-establish defence links with Qatar and the other Gulf States.

Shortly after the outbreak of hostilities, Foreign Secretary Lord Carrington told his Cabinet colleagues that 'The crisis had . . . revealed alarmingly how little the minor Gulf States seemed to be aware of the vulnerability of their position. It was to be hoped that greater realism would now develop'.[117] Against this background, Assistant Under-Secretary of State at the FCO, J. C. Moberly, was despatched to the Gulf for consultations. Belying Carrington's observations, the Qatari Heir Apparent, Sheikh Hamad, was quick to express his 'grave concern about the vulnerability of Qatar, like the other smaller states in the Gulf, in the light of Iranian threat to take action against them should they be perceived as helping Iraq'.[118] He also seemed 'anxious to establish an understanding with Britain about the reaction to any attack', adding that 'it would be too late . . . to concert measures after the event'.[119] The Iran–Iraq conflict also provided an opportunity to solidify relations between Britain and the UAE.

Having previously served as Political Agent in Dubai in the 1960s, D. A. Roberts stressed that 'When I returned as Ambassador based in Abu Dhabi in 1977 it was borne in on me that they [the Rulers and people] felt we had lost interest in them since 1971 and were content to let others make the running'.[120] An example of this was provided on 1 October 1980 when the French told the UAE that they would be prepared to come to the UAE's aid in case of an attack. Shortly after this, the UAE Minister of Petroleum, Mana al Otaiba, summoned Roberts and requested a similar undertaking from Britain. On 10 October, Roberts was authorized by Lord Carrington to pledge: 'in the spirit of the treaty of friendship, we stand ready in principle to provide such assistance if requested'.[121] The Ambassador also extended a British offer to send a small Ministry of Defence team to the UAE to advise on the country's likely needs. During his visit to the UAE towards the end of the month, however, Moberly told Sheikh Zaid that while Britain would be willing to consider new areas of assistance 'any request likely to involve the movement of British units would need time both for operational planning and for seeking ministerial approval for any specific proposal'.[122] For his part, Zaid created an atmosphere which was 'markedly friendly and relaxed', making a point of 'contrasting the depth of the UAE's ties with the UK with the position of newcomers such as the French and the Americans'.[123]

Hard on the heels of Moberly's visit came a tour of the Gulf by the Director of the UK's Military Assistance Office, Major General K. Perkins. First, Perkins called on Sheikh Hamad of Qatar. The latter quickly underlined that he 'did not want to become involved with overt Western military assistance as this would prejudice Qatar's position but he felt that we could help in a covert manner'.[124] In particular, he asked the UK to undertake a 'strategic survey' covering all aspects of Qatar's armed services, which Perkins himself agreed to lead. Within the confines of Whitehall, he declared: 'The report will point to their glaring deficiency in air defence and should surely ease the way for a deal to be concluded on Rapier'.[125] Perkins concluded on an upbeat note, opining that although the French had 'beaten us so far in terms of defence sales', the proposed comprehensive review of Qatar's armed services would 'maintain our influence and also help future sales'.[126] Ambassador Brant concurred, arguing that 'We have an excellent and unrepeatable opportunity to press the sale of Rapier here in Qatar'.[127] Whilst in the UAE, Perkins also tried to point up the merits of Rapier.

Perkins' mission took place, as Miers pointed out, 'against a background of a persistent, if undefined feeling in Abu Dhabi that we had to some extent lost interest in the UAE'.[128] He held high-level talks with Sheikhs Zaid and Rashid, but the most detailed discussions took place with the Deputy Commander-in-Chief of UAE armed forces, Sheikh Khalifa bin Zaid, and the Chief of Staff, Aqeed Mohammed bin Said. In the course of his visit, Perkins made two specific suggestions: the despatch of a military advisory team and the deployment of British units, especially those related to air defence. The UAE view was that, as the immediate danger had 'somewhat receded', there was no need for the deployment of forces, but that the team would be welcome.[129] '[I]t would not be to the prejudice of the team's report as a whole', asserted Perkins, 'if it helps push Rapier along'.[130] He ended on a congratulatory note, observing: 'I believe that by providing an air defence team and by demonstrating our ability to discuss in some detail all levels of assistance, we have played a better card than either the Americans or the French'.[131] Miers also described Perkins' mission as a 'positive and timely development in our relations with Abu Dhabi'.[132] Ambassador Roberts, furthermore, reported: 'Shaikh Zaid himself and others stated that we had restored in their eyes our old position, which our withdrawal from the Gulf had seemed to diminish if not extinguish'.[133]

As regards the Kuwaitis, they were arguably the most vulnerable to the fallout from the Iran–Iraq war due to their proximity to the main theatres of conflict and their support for the Iraqi war effort. The Kuwaiti Minister of Defence, Sheikh Salim Al-Sabah, told J. C. Moberly during the latter's visit to the Gulf in October 1980 that 'in the last resort Kuwait would be bound to side with Iraq', prophetically adding: 'Saddam Hussein's ambition to be the new Nasser could pose as much of an eventual threat to Kuwait as the pretensions of Iran'.[134] In the aftermath of his tour of the Gulf, Moberly informed the US Deputy Assistant Secretary of State for Near Eastern and South Asian Affairs, Joseph Twinam, that he had found the Kuwaitis 'very nervous about the repercussions for them of the Iran–Iraq War'.[135] Twinam expressed little surprise in this, pointing out that in the past the Kuwaitis had 'relied for their security on an Iraq–Iran balance and also e.g. in 1961 on Egypt, which was now out of the picture owing to the Camp David split'.[136] Kuwait's vulnerability was underlined in November 1980 when Iranian planes violated Kuwaiti airspace and fired rockets in the vicinity of the Abdali border post.[137] Ambassador Cambridge immediately sought a meeting with the Under-Secretary at the Kuwaiti Ministry of Foreign Affairs, Rashid Abdulaziz al-Rashid. Reporting the outcome of the encounter, Cambridge remarked:

> Whether or not the Kuwaitis specifically want a dialogue with us on maintaining the freedom of navigation in the Gulf, Rashid made quite clear their interest in seeing us more involved in affairs out here. He spoke scathingly of the Japanese: 'they were like bees' and interested only in trade. We, on the other hand, were ready to take on our share of responsibilities in this part of the world, and the Kuwaitis appreciated that.[138]

It was not merely the repercussions of the Iran–Iraq War that threatened the stability of the Gulf, but also the continuing revolutionary fervour emanating from Tehran. Responding in April 1980 to Iranian radio broadcasts following the execution in Iraq of the Shia cleric Saqr Badr, disturbances broke out among Shia villages in Bahrain which soon spread to Manama.[139] A month later, the death in police custody of Jamil Ali,[140] a Shia accused of beating up two Bahraini intelligence officers, provoked two separate protests by around 1,000 Shia, during the first of which ritual swords were carried indicating that a revenge killing would take place.[141] Despite the ostensible closeness of Anglo–Bahraini relations, the British were largely dependent for information on the troubles on informal channels, most notably the Director of Bahrain's Security and Intelligence Service, Ian Henderson.[142] Equally, it was the Bahraini authorities, albeit assisted by Henderson, which took the leading role in containing the disorders, whereas in the 1950s and 1960s it was the British themselves who did so. In 1956, and again in 1965, for instance, British forces were called in to suppress Bahraini disturbances which threatened the Al-Khalifah ruling family.[143]

In keeping with Bahrain, Kuwait, with its large Shia population, found itself vulnerable to pressure from the Islamic Republic. 'While Khomeini remains', remarked Head of Chancery at the British Embassy in Kuwait Ian McCluney, 'there will always be some anxiety about his personal hold on the Shia in Kuwait and sensitivity to his accusations of un-Islamic practices and subservience to the USA'.[144] McCluney proceeded to note that 'Kuwait's conspicuous public criticism of the superpowers and careful observance of Islamic forms are both, in part, reactions to Iran's aggressive criticisms'.[145]

Kuwait's concern to keep the superpowers, especially the US, at arm's length, was mirrored to some degree by the other Gulf States. Towards the end of 1980, the British Ambassador in Bahrain, H. B. Walker, emphasized that the 'local governments and peoples are deeply suspicious of US policies and actions'.[146] From this, Walker concluded that 'it would not be in our national interests in the area, or indeed in long-term UK–US interests, for us to be seen locally as invariably supporting the Americans right or wrong'.[147] In the immediate aftermath of the outbreak of the Iran–Iraq War, moreover, D. H. Gillmore of the FCO's Defence Department predicted that 'Both because of their historical ties with us and because they fear the involvement of both superpowers if they were to turn to the Americans, the Gulf Rulers are likely to look first to the UK for help'.[148] Indeed, he noted that the Ruler of Ras al Khaimah and the UAE Minister of Petroleum had both spoken in these terms.[149]

Despite the geo-political incentives for a re-establishment of close British relations with the Gulf States, Britain continued to face strong commercial pressure from its industrial rivals. In his annual review for 1980, Ambassador Walker pointed out that, although Britain remained Bahrain's principal trading partner, its market share had dropped from 20 per cent to less than 18 per cent, with the US and Japan 'coming up fast behind us'.[150] By 1980, Britain's share of the Kuwaiti market had slipped to 10 per cent, considerably behind the Japanese (18 per cent) and the US (14 per cent).[151] Referring to the UAE, moreover, Ambassador Roberts conceded that 'British firms have won a number of major contracts, but with increasing international competition, they will have to fight very hard to maintain their share of the market'.[152] An example of this was provided by defence sales to the UAE.

In mid-October 1980, reports were received that Sheikh Zaid was about to rule in favour of thirty French-built Alpha jets for the UAE air force, rather than the fifteen to eighteen British-made Hawk aircraft which his own military had favoured. The change of heart appeared to be because President Giscard D'Estaing, on a stopover in Abu Dhabi en route to China, had persuaded Zaid of the merits of purchasing the larger number of French aircraft.[153] Ambassador Roberts, however, strongly advised against mixing General Perkins' visit to the UAE with the sale of Hawk aircraft. 'To tie it to the purchase of specific UK equipment', he warned, 'would lead Zaid to conclude and his advisers to conclude that our only interest in helping the UAE was for what we could obtain in commercial terms'.[154] On the other hand, Miers insisted that 'the connection has to be made somehow unless we are to sit back and see the French snatch a contract from under our nose'.[155] In a similar vein, K. J. Passmore of the FCO's Middle East Department emphasized:

> we are happy that there should be the link in Zaid's mind between British military help and the buying of British military equipment. . . . The French make no secret of their interest in selling arms. I do not see why we should be so coy, and take comfort that Zaid loves us the best while he gives the French the money.[156]

During discussions in London with Douglas Hurd, the UAE Minister of Defence, Mohammed bin Rashid, bluntly declared: 'Britain was too often losing out. British firms and the British government sometimes responded slowly and did not show enough flexibility, when arranging credit terms, to take account of the difficulties of timing payments in view of the UAE's budgetary system'.[157] Hurd responded robustly, stating that 'it would be very disappointing if, when we did offer equipment which we believed met the UAE's requirements . . . a few hours' conversation between Giscard and Zaid were sufficient to deprive us at the last moment of a valuable contract'.[158]

By the end of the year, J. C. Moberly conceded that 'We have clearly reached a very critical moment in BAe's efforts to secure this contract, which may have a significant effect on BAe's efforts to hold off the challenge of the French Alpha Jet elsewhere'.[159] In a similar vein, D. B. Omand, Private Secretary to the Secretary of State for Defence, informed Margaret Thatcher's Principal Private Secretary, C. A. Whitmore, that British Aerospace were 'determined' to sell Hawk to the Abu Dhabi air force.[160] 'They believe', he expatiated, 'and we, the Foreign Office and our Embassy all share this view, that this is the place where the French Alpha-Jet bandwagon must be stopped'.[161] As a result of such considerations, Britain's Chargé d'Affaires was authorized by Lord Carrington to inform Zaid that both he and Prime Minister Thatcher attached 'great importance' to BAe securing the

Hawk contract and that the Ministry of Defence was prepared to offer some training free of charge additional to that contained in BAe's proposals.[162] The Chargé was requested to relate that this represented 'a very conscientious effort our part to provide what the UAE needs, and is of course only available as part of the Hawk package'.[163] In a personal message to Sheikh Zaid, the Prime Minister also stressed that

> the best way to meet the challenge to stability in the Gulf posed by the Soviet occupation of Afghanistan and the present Iran–Iraq War is for the Gulf States to increase their level of co-operation amongst themselves and thus to develop suitable structures for greater mutual security. . . . Meanwhile, pending the development of such arrangements we remain ready to co-operate with you in the defence and security fields by equipping and training your armed forces in ways which will make that co-operation most effective.[164]

In keeping with her hands-on approach to Gulf affairs, Thatcher called a meeting to discuss the sale of Hawks to the UAE attended by the Lord Privy Seal (Sir Ian Gilmour), the Chief Secretary (John Biffen), the Minister of State at the Ministry of Defence (Lord Strathcona), Sir Robert Armstrong (Secretary to the Cabinet), and Sir Frank Cooper (Permanent Under-Secretary at the Ministry of Defence). Thatcher began by stating that she was 'completely unhappy' about the way in which the efforts to secure the order for Hawks had been handled.[165] She expressed concern that the French had 'probably stolen a march on us' and criticized the attitude of officials and the British mission in Abu Dhabi for being 'too casual'.[166] Although it was pointed out that the British Embassy in Abu Dhabi had in fact been 'extremely active' and that efforts to secure the contract had been hampered by the elusiveness of leading Sheikhs, including Sheikh Zaid, Thatcher indicated that she was 'unimpressed' by these arguments and made clear her determination to see that 'whatever was necessary to win the order was done'.[167] In particular, she advocated the despatch of a three-man team to Abu Dhabi to make the case for Hawks. The three selected for this task were Douglas Hurd, Sir Ronald Ellis (head of defence sales at the Ministry of Defence), and Sir Freddie Page (Chief Executive, Aircraft Group, British Aerospace).[168] Thatcher also sent a further missive to Sheikh Zaid in which she candidly acknowledged that 'this contract is extremely important to us not just as a matter of trade but for the contribution it will make to the development of our defence industry and therefore to our ability to help you in the future'.[169] She also pleaded for Douglas Hurd to be given a 'sympathetic hearing'.[170]

Hurd's party duly arrived in Abu Dhabi at the beginning of 1981. During a meeting with the Deputy Commander-in-Chief of UAE armed forces, Sheikh Khalifa bin Zaid, on 6 January, Hurd emphasized that while Britain did not seek a monopoly of supply, 'it might become difficult for us to pursue ideas and cooperation if he felt that all the UAE's main procurement policies were directed to other countries and we were left with nothing substantial'.[171] In response, Khalifa declared that the UAE was 'also very keen that bilateral cooperation should

140 *War and peace, 1980*

continue in all fields, especially military'.[172] In a subsequent letter to Khalifa, Hurd underlined that 'the UK wishes to enhance defence cooperation with the UAE and other Gulf States in order to make an effective long-term contribution to stability'.[173] He also offered the assistance of Royal Air Force and British Aerospace specialists in setting up an air training school in Abu Dhabi.[174]

In his own report of the visit to the UAE, Sir Ronald Ellis lamented that 'BAe and ourselves had been working patiently for a number of years without, until recently, political support, whereas the French had fielded Valery Giscard D'Estaing three times in twelve months'.[175] It was left to Margaret Thatcher, despite her free market ideology, to provide the necessary political support during her visit to the Gulf in April 1981. This will be explored in the final chapter.

Notes

1. British Diplomatic Oral History Project: Sir Anthony Acland interviewed by Liz Cox, 23 April 2001, pp. 21–2, DOHP 57, Churchill Archives Centre, Cambridge.
2. See Rory Miller, 'The Euro–Arab Dialogue and the limits of European external intervention in the Middle East, 1974–77', *Middle Eastern Studies*, 50, 6 (2014), pp. 936–59.
3. Ibid., p. 953.
4. Teleletter from G. E. Fitzherbert to I. T. M. Lucas, undated, FCO 8/3442. See also Letter from Lucas to H. D. A. C. Miers, 10 February 1980, FCO 8/3442.
5. Telephone conversation between the Prime Minister and President Carter on Friday 28 December 1979, www.margaretthatcher.org/document/112219 [accessed 11 July 2016].
6. Address by President Carter on the State of the Union Before a Joint Session of Congress, 23 January 1980, cited in *Foreign Relations of the United States, 1977–1980: Volume I: Foundations of Foreign Policy* (Washington, DC: United States Printing Office, 2014), p. 695.
7. Jeffrey R. Macris, *The Politics and Security of the Gulf: Anglo–American Hegemony and the Shaping of a Region* (London and New York: Routledge, 2010), p. 210.
8. Amitav Acharya, *U.S. Military Strategy in the Gulf: Origins and Evolution under the Carter and Reagan Administrations* (Abingdon and New York: Routledge, 2013), p. 107.
9. Anglo–US talks on the Indian Ocean 26 January 1980: Summary Record, FCO 8/3469. The Kuwaiti Minister of State for Cabinet Affairs referred to President Carter's pledge to use force if necessary to protect the Gulf as an 'interference in the affairs of the Gulf States', adding that they were 'capable of looking after their own security and stability' (Telegram from Kuwait to the Foreign and Commonwealth Office, No. 46, 26 January 1980, FCO 8/3488).
10. Anglo–US talks on the Indian Ocean 26 January 1980: Summary Record, FCO 8/3469. Moberly subsequently reported that the American had drawn up plans for a further expansion of the Diego Garcia base in the period 1982–1985 to the tune of over $1 billon ('US defence plans in the Indian Ocean', Minute from Moberly to A. A. Acland, 17 April 1980, FCO 8/3469).
11. Anglo–US talks on the Indian Ocean 26 January 1980: Summary Record, FCO 8/3469.
12. Letter from Tatham to Lucas, 27 April 1980, FCO 8/3469.
13. Anglo–US talks on the Indian Ocean, 16–17 April 1980, FCO 8/3469.
14. Minute from Carrington to Thatcher, 19 January 1980, in Richard Smith, Patrick Salmon and Stephen Twigge (eds.), *The Invasion of Afghanistan and UK–Soviet Relations, 1979–82* (London and New York: Routledge, 2012), p. 94.
15. Letter from Thatcher to Carter, 26 January 1980, cited in ibid. p. 99.

16 'Strengthening our ties in Arabia and the Gulf', Minute by Passmore, 5 March 1980, FCO 8/3443.
17 Letter from Passmore to Alyson Bailes (Ministry of Defence), 28 July 1980, FCO 8/3443.
18 'Defence options in the Gulf, Red Sea and North West Indian Ocean', Report by Directors of Defence Policy, Annex A to DP 7/80, p. 15, 9 October 1980, DEFE 69/1390.
19 'Iran/Iraq: Military aid to the Gulf States', Minute by Gillmore, 9 October 1980, FCO 8/3443.
20 Ibid.
21 Telegram from Abu Dhabi to the Foreign and Commonwealth Office, No. 273, 19 August 1980, FCO 8/3445.
22 'Restoring the ancient regime in Iran', Minute by Passmore, 4 September 1980, FCO 8/3445.
23 Minute by Miers, 5 September 1980, FCO 8/3445.
24 Letter from Brant to W. J. Jones (Ministry of Defence), 27 January 1980, FCO 8/3674.
25 Letter from S. J. G. Cambridge to Miers, 3 March 1980, FCO 8/3447; Letter from Colin Brant to Carrington, 10 March 1980, FCO 8/3447; Charles Hargrove. 'Giscard visit leads to closer Franco-Qatar industrial links', *Times*, 7 March 1980, http://find.galegroup.com/ttda/infomark.do?&source=gale&prodId=TTDA&userGroupName=unihull&tabID=T003&docPage=article&searchType=AdvancedSearchForm&docId=CS118195815&type=multipage&contentSet=LTO&version=1.0 [accessed 7 December 2016].
26 Letter from Miers to Brant, 25 February 1980, FCO 8/3668.
27 Letter from Brant to Miers, 15 March 1980, FCO 8/3447.
28 Ibid.
29 'Gulf tour of President Giscard d'Estaing', Minute by Passmore, 18 March 1980, FCO 8/3447.
30 Ibid.
31 Letter from Miers to Brant, 21 March 1980, FCO 8/ 3447.
32 Letter from Brant to Miers, 14 April 1980, FCO 8/3447.
33 Ibid.
34 Letter from Brant to Miers, 24 March 1980, FCO 8/3671.
35 Letter from Brant to Miers, 17 March 1980, FCO 8/3673.
36 'Call on the Foreign Minister of Bahrain', Minute by Moberly, 10 March 1980, FCO 8/3447.
37 Letter from Walker to the Secretary of State for Foreign and Commonwealth Affairs, 10 February 1980, FCO 8/3894.
38 Letter from Brant to the Secretary of State for Foreign and Commonwealth Affairs, 8 January 1981, FCO 8/4107.
39 Ibid.
40 Ibid.
41 'Possibility of a regional council in the Gulf', Minute by Allen, 11 September 1972, FCO 8/1805.
42 Ibid.
43 Ibid.
44 Prime Minister of Kuwait.
45 Telegram from Kuwait to the Foreign and Commonwealth Office, No. 80, 10 February 1980, FCO 8/3449.
46 Ibid.
47 Ibid.
48 Telegram from Walker to Miers, 24 March 1980, FCO 8/3449.
49 Telegram from Doha to the Foreign and Commonwealth Office, No. 16, 21 January 1980, FCO 8/3454.
50 Ibid.
51 Ibid.

52 A note for the Director-General's meeting with Mr Brant Ambassador-designate to Qatar, 16 December 1977, BW 180/4.
53 Letter from Henderson to James Callaghan, 16 June 1974, BW180/2.
54 Ibid.
55 Director's Annual Report, 1974–1975, 30 April 1975, BW 180/15.
56 Qatar situation report no. 3 by W. H. Jefferson (Director, Qatar), 21 March 1976, BW180/4.
57 Qatar annual report 1976–1977: Main statement, by Jefferson, BW 180/4.
58 Ibid.
59 Note from Director, Middle East Department, to Controller Overseas, 5 April 1979, BW 180/4.
60 Frances Donaldson, *The British Council: The First Fifty Years* (London: Jonathan Cape, 1984), p. 310.
61 The British Council: Country Brief for Qatar 1979–1980: Section I, The work of the Council, BW 180/4.
62 Ibid.
63 Letter from Edye to J. E. C. Macrae (Cultural relations Department, FCO), 28 July 1980, BW 180/15.
64 The British Council: Country brief for Qatar 1979–1980: Section II, Background information, BW 180/4.
65 Record of a meeting between Mr Hurd, Minister of State, and HH Shaikh Hamad bin Khalifa, Qatari Minister of Defence and Heir apparent, in Doha, 20 January 1980, FCO 8/3454.
66 Ibid.
67 Panagiotis Dimitrakis, *The Secret War in Afghanistan: The Soviet Union, China, and the Role of Anglo–American Intelligence* (London: I. B. Tauris, 2013), p. 99.
68 Telegram from Abu Dhabi to the Foreign and Commonwealth Office, No. 38, 29 January 1980, FCO 8/3508.
69 Telegram from Abu Dhabi to the Foreign and Commonwealth Office, No. 32, 24 January 1980, FCO 8/3454.
70 Ibid.
71 Record of a meeting between Mr Hurd, Minister of State, and the Deputy Prime Minister and Minister of Information of Kuwait, at the Ministry of Information, 11 March 1980, FCO 8/3455.
72 Record of a conversation between the Minister of State for Foreign and Commonwealth Affairs and the Minister of Defence of Kuwait, 12 March 1980, FCO 8/3455.
73 Record of a meeting between Mr Hurd, Minister of State, and the Kuwaiti Minister of State for Cabinet Affairs and Acting Foreign Minister, Mr Abdul Aziz Hussain in Kuwait, 11 March 1980, FCO 8/3455.
74 Ibid.; Rory Miller, *Inglorious Disarray: Europe, Israel and the Palestinians Since 1967* (London: Hurst and Company, 2011), p. 83.
75 Miller, *Inglorious Disarray*, p. 84.
76 Record of a meeting between Mr Hurd, Minister of State and HH Sheikh Sa'ad, Crown Prince and Prime Minister of Kuwait in Kuwait, 11 March 1980, FCO 8/3455.
77 Ibid.
78 Record of a conversation between the Minister of State for Foreign and Commonwealth Affairs and the Minister of Defence of Kuwait, 12 March 1980, FCO 8/3455.
79 Letter from Lucas to Miers, 2 April, 1980, FCO 8/3457.
80 Ibid.
81 Ibid.
82 Ibid.
83 Letter from Roberts to Carrington, 20 April 1980, FCO 8/3458.
84 Ibid.

85 Ibid.
86 Letter from Miers to Roberts, 1 May 1980, FCO 8/3458.
87 Teleletter from Cambridge to Miers, 21 April 1980, FCO 8/3458.
88 Letter from Cambridge to D. E. Tatham, 5 June 1980, FCO 8/3458.
89 Ibid.
90 Teleletter from Cambridge to Miers, 21 April 1980, FCO 8/3458.
91 'Dr Vaughan's visit to Kuwait', Minute by Tatham, 10 June 1980, FCO 8/3458.
92 Referring to the Queen's tour, Foreign Secretary David Owen wrote: 'The timing of the visit, as it turned out, could not have been better, for it allowed us to demonstrate our support for the Gulf States in the wake of events in Iran in a way which they found acceptable' ('Iran, the Gulf and the Middle East', Minute from Owen to the Prime Minister, PM/79/18, 22 February 1979, DEFE 70/631). In his memoirs, the former Head of the FCO's Middle East Department, I. T. M. Lucas, remarked: 'in the aftermath of the Shah's fall, the Rulers on the Arab side of the Gulf were left wondering who their friends now were. Within weeks of the Iranian revolution, the royal tour took place: there could have been no more appropriate answer to the question nor a better ambassador to convey it' (Ivor Lucas, *A Road to Damascus: Mainly Diplomatic Memoirs from the Middle East* (London: The Radcliffe Press, 1997), p. 161).
93 Letter from Brant to Carrington, 31 December 1979, FCO 8/3668.
94 Ibid.
95 Ibid.
96 Ibid.
97 Ibid.
98 Letter from Brant to Carrington, 10 March 1980, FCO 8/3674. See also Letter from Brant to Jones, 24 March 1980, FCO 8/3674.
99 'Visit DMAO to Qatar 28–29 October 1980', Minute by Perkins, 3 November 1980, FCO 8/3670.
100 Telegram from the Foreign and Commonwealth Office to Doha, No. 7, 24 January 1980, FCO 8/3671.
101 Letter from Brant to O. Paget, 2 February 1980, FCO 8/3671.
102 Ibid.
103 Letter from Brant to Miers, 24 March 1980, FCO 8/3671.
104 Letter from Miers to Brant, 3 April, FCO 8/3671.
105 Minute from R. H. Pavely to Paget, 29 April 1980, FCO 8/3671. Earlier in the year, Qatar had cancelled an order for thirteen Westland Lynx helicopters once it was discovered that they could not undertake the maritime strike role which the Qataris had envisaged (Letter from Brant to Carrington, 10 March 1980, FCO 8/3674).
106 Minute from R. H. Pavely to Paget, 29 April 1980, FCO 8/3671.
107 Telegram from Brant to the Foreign and Commonwealth Office, No. 58, 13 April 1980, FCO 8/3671.
108 Minute from R. H. Pavely to Paget, 29 April 1980, FCO 8/3671.
109 Telegram from the Foreign and Commonwealth Office, No. 39, 8 May 1980, FCO 8/3671.
110 Letter from Brant to Jones, 24 March 1980, FCO 8/3674.
111 Letter from Brant to P. H. Moberly, 11 November 1980, FCO 8/3674.
112 Ibid.
113 Ibid.
114 Ibid.
115 Ibid.
116 Ibid.
117 Cabinet conclusions, 2 October 1980, CAB 128/68, CC(80)34th conclusions.
118 Telegram from Doha to the Foreign and Commonwealth Office, No. 145, 11 October 1980, FCO 8/3453.

119 Ibid.
120 Letter from Roberts to Carrington, 16 November 1980, FCO 8/3509.
121 Ibid.
122 Telegram from Abu Dhabi to the Foreign and Commonwealth Office, No. 354, 27 October 1980, FCO 8/3453.
123 Ibid.
124 'Visit of DMAO to Qatar 28–29 October 1980', Minute by Perkins, 3 November 1980, FCO 8/3453.
125 Ibid.
126 Ibid.
127 Letter from Brant to P. H. Moberly, 11 November 1980, FCO 8/3674.
128 'British relations with the United Arab Emirates', Minute by Miers, 9 December 1980, FCO 8/3509.
129 'Visit DMAO to the United Arab Emirates 23–30 October 1980', Minute by Perkins, 3 November 1980, FCO 8/3453.
130 Ibid.
131 Ibid.
132 Letter from Miers to Roberts, 9 December 1980, FCO 8/3509.
133 Letter from Roberts to the Secretary of State for Foreign and Commonwealth Affairs, 31 December 1980, FCO 8/3908.
134 Telegram from Kuwait to the Foreign and Commonwealth Office, No. 472, 7 October 1980, PREM 19/813. Iraqi President, Saddam Hussein, ordered the invasion of Kuwait in August 1990.
135 Letter from Moberly to M. J. E. Fretwell, 26 November 1980, FCO 8/3452.
136 Ibid. Twinam was referring to the agreements between Israel and Egypt, signed on 17 September 1978 that paved the way for a peace treaty between the two countries the following year.
137 Telegram from Kuwait to the Foreign and Commonwealth Office, No. 722, 17 November 1980, FCO 8/3453.
138 Telegram from Kuwait to the Foreign and Commonwealth Office, No. 782, 25 November 1980, FCO 8/3453.
139 Telegram from Bahrain to the Foreign and Commonwealth Office, No. 77, 24 April 1980, FCO 8/3489.
140 Jamil Ali was also known as Jamil al-Thawr.
141 Letter from C. E. J. Wilton to Passmore, 14 May 1980, FCO 8/3489.
142 'Bahrain internal', Minute by Passmore, 3 December 1980, FCO 8/3489.
143 Simon C. Smith, *Britain's Revival and Fall in the Gulf: Kuwait Bahrain, Qatar, and the Trucial States, 1950–1971* (London: Routledge, 2004), p. 13, p. 22. Miriam Joyce, *Bahrain from the Twentieth Century to the Arab Spring* (New York: Palgrave Macmillan, 2012), p. 24, p. 27.
144 Letter from McCluney to Miers, 30 October 1980, FCO 8/3485.
145 Ibid.
146 Letter from Walker to J. C. Moberly, 2 December 1980, FCO 8/3452.
147 Ibid.
148 'Iran/Iraq: Military aid to the Gulf States', Minute by Gillmore, 9 October 1980, FCO 8/3443.
149 Ibid.
150 Letter from Walker to the Secretary of State for Foreign and Commonwealth Affairs, 10 February 1981, FCO 8/3894.
151 Letter from Cambridge to the Secretary of State for Foreign and Commonwealth Affairs, 5 January 1980, DEFE 24/2679.
152 Letter from Roberts to the Secretary of State for Foreign and Commonwealth Affairs, 31 December 1980, FCO 8/3908.

War and peace, 1980 145

153 Telegram from the Foreign and Commonwealth Office to HM Yacht Britannia, 17 October 1980, FCO 8/3517.
154 Telegram from Abu Dhabi to the Foreign and Commonwealth Office, No. 342, 19 October 1980, FCO 8/3517.
155 'Arms sales to the UAE', Minute by Miers, 23 October 1980, FCO 8/3517.
156 'Defence sales to the UAE: Hawk/Alpha Jet', Minute by Passmore, 20 October 1980, FCO 8/3517.
157 Telegram from the Foreign and Commonwealth Office to Abu Dhabi, No. 235, 24 October 1980, FCO 8/3518.
158 Ibid.
159 Minute by Moberly, 17 December 1980, FCO 8/3518.
160 Letter from Omand to Whitmore, 10 December 1980, PREM 19/529.
161 Ibid.
162 Telegram from the Foreign and Commonwealth Office to Dubai, No. 74, 20 December 1980, FCO 8/3518.
163 Ibid.
164 Telegram from the Foreign and Commonwealth Office to Dubai, No. 75, 20 December 1980, FCO 8/3518.
165 Letter from Michael Alexander to Paul Lever, 22 December 1980, FCO 8/3518.
166 Ibid.
167 Ibid.
168 Telegram from the Foreign and Commonwealth Office to Dubai, No. 76, 22 December 1980, FCO 8/3518.
169 Letter from Thatcher to Zaid, 22 December 1980, FCO 8/3518.
170 Ibid.
171 Record of a call by the Secretary of State for Energy and Minister of State for Foreign and Commonwealth Affairs on Sheikh Khalifa bin Zaid, Crown Prince of Abu Dhabi and Deputy Supreme Commander of the UAE Armed Forces in Abu Dhabi on 6 January 1981, FCO 8/3812.
172 Ibid.
173 Letter from Hurd to Sheikh Khalifa bin Zaid, 27 January 1981, FCO 8/3850.
174 Ibid.
175 'Visit to the UAE – 6 January 1981', attached to a minute by Ellis, 9 January 1981, FCO 8/3812.

6 The empire strikes back? 1981

Tore Petersen claims that during the Thatcher years Britain sought to maintain, and even expand, British influence in the Gulf 'under the umbrella of the Carter Doctrine'.[1] While it is certainly the case that the Thatcher government paid renewed attention to the region, it was also wary of the increase in the US role implied by the Carter Doctrine and demonstrated a predilection for regional cooperation, especially among the states on the Arab side of the Gulf.

At the end of 1980, the Permanent Under-Secretary of State at the FCO, Sir Michael Palliser, asserted that President-elect Ronald Reagan would 'continue and probably intensify Mr Carter's policy of strengthening the American ability to intervene militarily in south west Arabia'.[2] He went on the state that 'I find it improbable, to say the least, that he [Reagan] would back away from Carter's plans for the Rapid Deployment Force (RDF), especially when so much of those plans is public knowledge'.[3] Palliser also expressed concern that 'the new Administration might talk themselves into believing that the only way to implement the RDF concept properly is to take the bull by the horns and seek to establish US forces in the Middle East in permanent bases'.[4] The Chief of Defence Staff, Admiral Sir Terence Lewin, had already warned that 'with few exceptions governments [in the Gulf] are reluctant to welcome them [US forces] overtly, even though they are privately reassured by [the US] presence'.[5] Palliser believed that the only way in which permanent US forces could be established in the Middle East without fatally undermining the friendly governments in the region, would be to achieve a 'comprehensive settlement on the Middle East problem, including the Palestinians'.[6] He concluded:

> In the absence of a settlement of the Middle East problem, and on our present reading of the threat, we see a strong case for trying to persuade the Americans not to seek such permanent bases. In our view, it would be politically destabilising in the region; it would expose the host governments to domestic regional and international pressures; and the West in general would be extremely vulnerable to Soviet (and non-aligned) propaganda – as Brezhnev[7] has recently reminded us. In our eyes the risk would be that these penalties would cancel out the benefits that might be expected from such a forward posture.[8]

In a similar vein, the FCO's Planning Staff, speculated that a locally based US force 'could increase the risk that the UK, and other Western countries, might be dragged into a conflict unwillingly, or at least without the kind of consultation which the NATO crisis management procedures provide within the NATO area'.[9] 'While we may support US objectives in the region', continued the Planning Staff, 'we cannot be certain that the Americans would always share our judgement on the action needed in any given crisis'.[10] The British government had already stationed a small force of two to three naval ships in the Gulf, styled the Armilla Patrol, to escort UK-registered shipping through Iran–Iraq war zone waters.[11] However, Assistant Under-Secretary of State at the FCO, P. H. Moberly, was insistent that 'any UK contribution to a rapid deployment force would be organised separately from and additional to the main US force'.[12] 'In other words', he continued, 'we aim to work alongside the Americans rather than be counted as an automatic part of a joint force under single command'.[13] The Minister of State at the FCO, Douglas Hurd, had already told the US Ambassador in London, Kingman Brewster, that

> it would be a mistake to push too hard for more forces in the Gulf. If we could show that Gulf states' cooperation was proceeding, there would not be the same need to position Western forces there. To do so would not necessarily increase our strength and would give the Gulf states political problems.[14]

Unsurprisingly, the British government supported moves towards greater Gulf cooperation.

One of the earliest concrete examples of regional collaboration was provided by the establishment in 1976 of the Gulf Organization for Industrial Consulting encompassing the six nations of the Gulf.[15] In May 1976, moreover, the Prime Minister of Kuwait and future Amir, Sheikh Jabir Al-Ahmad, had called for the 'establishment of a Gulf Union with the object of realizing cooperation in all economic, political, educational and informational fields'.[16] This effort was frustrated by the failure of Gulf foreign ministers to reach agreement on the formula for a security pact during a meeting in Muscat in December.[17]

James Worrall points out that 'The Iranian Revolution of 1979, and the rise to power of Saddam Hussein in Ba'athist Iraq that same year, transformed the regional security environment, giving fresh impetus to the work that had already been done towards regional cooperation'.[18] The Kuwaitis, in particular, sought to resurrect the idea of Gulf collaboration. Even before the outbreak of the Iran–Iraq War, the Kuwaiti Ambassador to the United Kingdom, Sheikh Saud, stated that his government 'saw the need for closer cooperation in security matters between the states in the region'.[19] Moreover, the Dubai Minister of Defence, Mohammed bin Rashid, asserted that a 'permanent organisation with proper communications would evolve' in the Gulf.[20]

Referring to regional cooperation in the Gulf, Bruce Maddy-Weitzman argues that the 'outbreak of the Iran–Iraq war in September 1980 gave Gulf leaders the final impetus to act on the idea'.[21] Equally, Pierre Razoux contends that 'The war served as a goad to convince the monarchs to put aside their rivalries in favor of their common interests'.[22] Indeed, following the outbreak of conflict between Iran and Iraq, the Deputy Ruler of Ras al Khaimah, Sheikh Rashid bin Saqr al Qasimi, told Douglas Hurd that Sheikh Zaid of Abu Dhabi was 'willing to improve his links with the other Gulf states'.[23] Against this background, the Foreign Ministers of Saudi Arabia, Oman, Kuwait, Bahrain, Qatar, and the UAE met in Riyah on 4 February 1981 and announced their agreement to establish an Arab Gulf Co-operation Council (GCC).[24] They also committed themselves to periodic meetings 'to reach the goals desired in all fields'.[25] Kristian Coates Ulrichsen has characterized the setting up of the GCC as 'an immediate and ad hoc reaction to the situation of profound uncertainty occasioned by the Iranian revolution and the outbreak of the Iran–Iraq war'.[26] He goes on to underline that the new body was 'neither a political nor military alliance and lacked an integrative supra-national decision-making institution for sharing sovereignty akin to the European Commission'.[27]

Despite the GCC's real limitations, the British government warmly welcomed its establishment. Douglas Hurd, for instance, described it as 'a very encouraging sign of closer cooperation among the traditional regimes of the peninsula'.[28] The Foreign Secretary, Lord Carrington, felt it was of sufficient importance to merit a message of support to Gulf Rulers from the Prime Minister on taking a step which Britain had been 'urging on them as a logical consequence of the ending of outside protection'.[29] Margaret Thatcher subsequently sent messages to all the members of the GCC in which she expressed her confidence that the new organization would play a 'valuable role' in confronting the dangers to which the Gulf region had been exposed.[30] The Prime Minister, however, subsequently found herself embroiled in controversy over comments she made in Washington on 28 February regarding a possible British contribution to the RDF. As *The Times* noted, 'Mrs Thatcher's insensitively phrased remarks in Washington about the need for a western military force in the Gulf have brought out the negative side of the always ambivalent Arab relationship with Britain'.[31] Moreover, the leader of the Opposition, Michael Foot, observed in the Commons on 2 March that 'On the Persian Gulf it would have been better, before making statements, if she had discovered what would have been the reaction to some of her statements in the places involved'.[32] The sagacity of Foot's intervention soon became apparent.

In response to Thatcher's comments, Crown Prince Fahd of Saudi Arabia pointedly stated that the Gulf States 'did not want anyone to participate in their protection' and that they could 'defend themselves if they got the right arms and technical expertise'.[33] An editorial in the Saudi newspaper *Al-Nadwa* reflected that there had been 'widespread angry reaction in the Gulf'.[34] The local media in Qatar also voiced 'strong criticisms' of Thatcher's remarks.[35] In a damage-limitation exercise, Britain's Ambassador in Doha, Colin Brant, impressed upon the Qatari Minister of Information 'how much the PM's remarks had clearly been taken out their real context, and unduly inflated'.[36]

Writing to John Nott (Secretary of State for Defence), Douglas Hurd was quick to underline that 'there is no question of our making offers of help to the Gulf States that they have not asked for. The RDF would not be used in the Gulf except with the consent of the Gulf States'.[37] Nott himself was able to tell Sheikh Khalifa during a visit to Qatar towards the end of March that Britain would 'never seek to interfere in any way with Qatar's own internal dispositions', but that if help was sought, it would be 'very ready to give the maximum assistance'.[38] Margaret Thatcher herself had already informed the Iraqi Foreign Minister, Dr Sa'adoun Hammadi, that the UK would only make a 'modest contribution' to the RDF, that there would be 'no question of bases', and that the force would 'not be deployed unless and until it had been invited'.[39] The Prime Minister had the opportunity to clarify her position on the Gulf in general, and the RDF in particular, during her tour of the region in April.

In its steering brief for the Prime Minister's visit, the FCO underlined that 'The Gulf is an area where British influence was once paramount but where an initiative of this kind is now necessary to maintain our position and in particular to counteract efforts which our competitors, especially the French, have been making at our expense to secure influence and large contracts'.[40] 'The principal aim of the visit', continued the FCO, 'should be to proclaim our determination to maintain a continuing and vigorous interest in the Gulf'.[41] In addition, the FCO emphasized the UK's need not only to 'demonstrate the importance we attach to our relations with Saudi Arabia and the Gulf States in the light of the Soviet invasion of Afghanistan and the Iran/Iraq war', but also to 'give a strong boost to our efforts to ensure a major share of contracts in the fields of defence sales, oil and gas development, civil engineering, medical and health co-operation'.[42] On the eve of Thatcher's departure, John Nott told her that

> The Gulf states appreciate that in a major emergency only the United States would have the clout to resist Soviet aggression and that we would be merely a small part of such a response. But in a way there is something to be said for us talking in terms of independent support simply because there is a feeling that we understand them better than the United States and are less likely to embarrass them with their own public opinion.[43]

In her memoirs, Thatcher recalled that 'I always regretted, even at the time, the decision of Ted Heath's Government not to reverse the Wilson Government's withdrawal of our forces and the severing of many of our responsibilities east of Suez. Repeatedly, events have demonstrated that the West cannot pursue a policy of total disengagement in this strategically vital area'.[44] Shortly before her visit, G. G. H. Walden, Principal Private Secretary to the Foreign Secretary, wrote to Thatcher's Assistant Private Secretary, Michael Alexander, emphasizing Lord Carrington's assumption that 'the Prime Minister would wish her visit to be seen as part of a fresh and more dynamic approach by HMG towards cooperation with the Gulf countries and the advancement of our strategic and material (eg commercial and defence sales) interests there'.[45] Before moving on to this objective, however, Thatcher had to smooth ruffled feathers regarding the putative RDF.

Even before her arrival in the Gulf, Thatcher emphasized with respect to the RDF that 'no one said it should be stationed in the Gulf; no one said it should go there without being requested'.[46] In the course of discussions with Prince Fahd, the Saudi Deputy Prime Minister, Thatcher downplayed the RDF, arguing that it was 'basically an aspect of contingency planning'.[47] She also assured Fahd that the proposed RDF would neither be stationed in the Gulf, nor was it intended for use only in the Gulf.[48] Similarly, she assured Sheikh Zaid of Abu Dhabi with respect to the RDF that 'The question was not one of imposing anything on anyone but of responding to sudden requests'.[49] Focussing on the 'great uncertainty' in the world, Thatcher told Sheikh Khalifah of Qatar that 'To create a force and to earmark (not station) the troops would be good contingency planning'.[50] In addition to reassuring nervous Gulf Rulers over the RDF, Thatcher set about promoting British commercial interests in the region. This was especially evident with respect to Qatar.

Initially a stop in Qatar had not been incorporated into the Prime Minister's itinerary. The FCO, however, made a powerful case for Qatar's inclusion. 'A visit by the Prime Minister in April would be an extremely important boost to our effort against determined French competition', the Foreign Secretary's Assistant Private Secretary, F. N. Richards, impressed upon Thatcher's Assistant Private Secretary, Michael Alexander.[51] The Head of the FCO's Middle East Department, H. D. A. C. Miers, also entered the debate, stressing that 'it would be prudent to assume that by April Qatar could be at least as deserving of Prime Ministerial intervention in favour of British interests as the UAE, which she is already committed to visiting'.[52] Richards subsequently gave Alexander details of possible contracts which included the development of Qatar's North-West Dome Gas Field (worth up to £2 billion); a new power station valued at £300 million, plus a further £300 million in associated contracts; as well as Qatar's air defence system. Richards concluded: 'These are all the sort of major projects on which our commercial competitors . . . are often able to bring extra-commercial pressures to bear, and where support from the Prime Minister at the right time and after due preparation could tilt the balance'.[53] FCO arguments proved persuasive and at the beginning of February the British Embassy in Doha was informed that Margaret Thatcher was willing to include Qatar in her itinerary on the grounds that by April 'the time may well then be ripe to give high-level political support to British firms bidding for important commercial and defence contracts'.[54] Sheikh Khalifah warmly welcomed the prospect of Margaret Thatcher's visit and made a point of thanking Her Majesty's Government for 'all the valuable assistance it has provided and is providing to our country in the fields of defence and security, by way of training and equipping our armed forces'.[55]

In the run-up to Thatcher's visit to the Gulf, there was an intense debate among British policy-makers over the correct approach to arms sales in the region. H. D. A. C. Miers insisted that Britain had to develop a 'political approach' which centred on a 'Government-wide effort and in particular intimate contact between FCO, Posts abroad and MoD/sales'.[56] Indeed, he lamented the lack of communication between these different bodies. He concluded:

> The sales effort has consequently been insufficiently political, broad-based and ambitious. While the French offer the Arabs participation in building a

whole generation of aircraft, marrying Pakistani and other technically qualified manpower with Saudi money and French design/manufacturing capability, we potter from Gulf State to Gulf State offering a single type, off the shelf, with no element of local manufacture/transfer of technology, and without imagination to find out, let alone offer, what the customers really want.[57]

Assistant Under-Secretary of State at the FCO, J. C. Moberly, was in full agreement, emphasizing 'the need for closer coordination between MoD (Sales), the FCO, other interested Departments in Whitehall and the manufacturers concerned'.[58] Moberly added that 'In considering the French performance against our own we must not lose sight of the advantage the French obtain by assiduously trying to create the impression in the Arab world that they are ahead of us in their support of and sympathy for Arab, particularly Palestinian, aspirations'.[59] On the eve of Thatcher's April 1981 visit to the Gulf, Britain's Ambassador to Qatar, Colin Brant, had ruminated: 'If the French have in fact given the Qataris a promise of a heavily subsidised price, then there will be little that we can do, I assume, beyond deploying further high-level political support to urge the Qataris to take Rapier as the best system going'.[60]

Writing to the British Ambassador to Saudi Arabia, Sir James Craig, with respect to defence sales to the Gulf, Miers stressed: 'For the future we need to think in more "strategic" terms. We need to emulate the French in some respects: offering, for example, a range of aircraft into the future and not just single types one at a time'.[61] Miers added: 'The Prime Minister has also been taking a personal interest, and tends to look to the FCO, as well as the MoD for action'.[62] British reluctance to supply offensive weapons such as aircraft and heavy tanks to the Gulf States also had gradually lifted following the Soviet of Afghanistan.[63] Margaret Thatcher herself had issued instructions to Whitehall Departments 'To continue to seek as a matter of high priority to increase the present level of overseas defence sales'.[64] The Prime Minister's visit to the Gulf in April afforded an opportunity to further this objective.

Writing to Sheikh Khalifah of Qatar in January 1981, Thatcher had underscored that 'We remain ready to co-operate with you as effectively as we can in the fields of defence and security, by training and equipping your armed forces'.[65] More specifically, during discussions with Khalifah on 25 April Thatcher emphasized that Britain was 'very anxious to supply Rapier to Qatar'.[66] She described it as a 'unique air defence system' and underlined that it had already been sold to the United States and to Switzerland.[67] She also stressed the growing competitiveness of British industry and improvements in delivery times. Emphasizing her 'personal interest' in the deal, she pledged that any substantial difficulties or complaints would be dealt with by her office.[68] As regards the North-West Dome, Thatcher expressed her wish to 'speak up for' BP which, she asserted, had a 'uniquely wide range of experience ranging from Alaska through the North Sea to Abu Dhabi'.[69] 'BP would not let the Qatar Government down', she declared.[70] Ambassador Brant was subsequently able to report that the Prime Minister's 'powerful advocacy of British expertise in offshore oil and gas development has given the United Kingdom a "head start" in the competition for the main consultancy in the North Field gas project'.[71] He also asserted that

> For the future, there can be no doubt that this visit raised the level of our game in Qatar by several notches, and put us ahead of the French once again. It also gave a powerful impetus to our attempts to capture a greater share of the business available here than we have hitherto manged to secure.[72]

During a tête-à-tête conversation with Thatcher following the main meeting on 25 April, Sheikh Khalifah stated that there would be 'no difficulty about the Rapier contract. It would certainly be given to Britain'.[73] The Qatari heir-apparent, Sheikh Hamad, gave separate assurance to the Prime Minister that Britain would secure the Rapier contract.[74] Nevertheless, H. D. A. C. Miers was quick to point out that the Prime Minister's advocacy of Rapier missiles seemed to have 'confirmed a sale that was coming our way anyway'.[75] Indeed, Sheikh Khalifah had already indicated to Defence Secretary John Nott, during the latter's visit to Qatar in March, that 'the way was open' for Britain to negotiate a Qatari purchase of Rapier.[76] On the formal signing of the Rapier contract in mid-June 1981, Ambassador Brant noted:

> I think the key to the campaign was the team-work which it involved, with BAe making their best efforts to secure the contract; Ahmed Mannai[77] giving valuable support as the "undeclared" agent of BAe; and the massive political support brought to bear on the project since last Summer.[78]

Brant also pointed out that external events, not least the outbreak of the Iran–Iraq War and the Israeli attack on the Iraqi Osirak reactor on 7 June 1981, had 'concentrated the Qataris' mind wonderfully'.[79]

The Chairman and Chief Executive of BAe, Admiral Sir Raymond Lygo, specifically wrote to John Nott and also the Minister of State at the Department of Trade and Industry, Norman Tebbit, expressing his appreciation for the governmental support the company had received with respect to Rapier.[80] Although the value of the order was £71.3 million, Ambassador Brant did express some disappointment that the Qataris only agreed to purchase one battery, whereas the original hope was that they would order three.[81]

In keeping with her strong support for Rapier, Thatcher was a firm proponent of the supply of Hawk aircraft to the UAE. At the end of 1980, she had written to Sheikh Zaid pledging Britain's readiness to 'co-operate with you in the defence and security fields by equipping and training your armed forces in ways which will make that co-operation most effective'.[82] She also criticized FCO officials and Britain's Mission in Abu Dhabi for being 'too casual' in the pursuit of a Hawk contract.[83] Taking matters into her own hands during her visit to Abu Dhabi the following year, Thatcher impressed upon Sheikh Zaid that 'It mattered to Britain that we should be able to supply this aircraft to the UAE. It mattered to the Government and to British industry. She put her personal authority behind the aircraft'.[84] During subsequent discussions with the Prime Minister of Abu Dhabi, Sheikh Khalifa bin Zaid, Thatcher reiterated these points, adding that the Hawk deal 'mattered greatly both to our industry and to our ability to support our friends'.[85] In response, Khalifa declared: 'he was very keen to maintain the traditional links in this field between the UAE and the United Kingdom. The UAE would therefore be very happy to purchase the Hawk aircraft'.[86] Reflecting the importance of Thatcher's intervention, Khalifa confessed: 'even if his Government had known nothing about the aircraft, they would have purchased it simply on the basis that it came with Prime Minister's recommendation'.[87] Writing in *The Guardian* on 23 April 1981, Martin Woollacott reported that 'Mrs Thatcher's tour of the Gulf States is turning into a highly personal arms sale drive which yesterday produced an on-the-spot commitment from the United Arab Emirates to buy British jet trainers'.[88]

In a letter to US President Ronald Reagan on her return to the UK, Thatcher remarked:

> I was glad to be told in Abu Dhabi that they would be ordering some of our training/strike aircraft. Our ability to make a contribution to the defence of the area in an emergency, even on the modest scale we have in mind, depends crucially on our being able to sell our defence equipment. This order was a great encouragement: we shall be following it up energetically throughout the area.[89]

Thatcher's second visit to the Gulf within a few months, which took her to Kuwait and Bahrain in September, gave her the opportunity to pursue this objective herself.

Thatcher's visit to Kuwait had been foreshadowed by that of the Lord Privy Seal, Sir Ian Gilmour, in February 1981. In its briefing material for Gilmour's trip, the FCO warned that 'the Kuwaitis like to show that their relationship towards us does not become favouritism, as it tends to in some of the other Gulf states with which our relations are more intimate'.[90] Despite rising from £40 million in 1974 to £261 million by 1980, the value of British exports to Kuwait still lagged behind those of Japan and the United States.[91] Indeed, on the eve of Gilmour's visit to Kuwait, figures demonstrated that Britain only held 13 per cent of OECD exports, compared with Japan's 24 per cent and the US's 20 per cent.[92] During talks with the Lord Privy Seal, the Amir of Kuwait, Sheikh Jabir Al-Ahmad, expressed regret that 'Britain had not tried harder to take its share of Kuwaiti contracts'.[93] In the report of his visit to Kuwait, Gilmour gloomily recorded that 'There is some residual affection for the UK but there has been a tendency to write us off since our withdrawal from the area and economic decline. This has been aggravated by the unwillingness of some British firms to tender for construction contracts in Kuwait'.[94] Gilmour also opined that the Kuwaitis were 'hard-headed businessmen and political factors will not greatly help us to secure orders either in the defence or civil field'.[95] In a similar vein, the FCO remarked in advance of a meeting at the end of June 1981 between the Chancellor of the Exchequer, Geoffrey Howe, and the Kuwaiti Finance Minister, Abdul Latif al Hamad, that 'Our relations with Kuwait remain cordial but the Kuwaitis make clear they are not prepared to favour us in commercial matters simply for old times sake'.[96] Moreover, the Permanent Under-Secretary of State at the FCO, Sir Michael Palliser, observed: 'In Kuwait contracts are not likely to be obtained for British firms by an appeal to sentiment. . . . The Kuwaitis are hard-headed customers, ostentatiously attentive to price, quality and speed of delivery'.[97] Despite these far from encouraging assessments, Margaret Thatcher, as she had done during her earlier visit to the Gulf, threw her weight behind British commercial activities, this time in Kuwait.[98]

On the eve of Thatcher's departure for the Gulf, the British Ambassador in Kuwait, S. J. G. Cambridge, stressed that 'Despite their [the Kuwaitis] ostentatious non-alignment they need real friends and support'.[99] He also recommended that 'the Prime Minister should be quite frank we are keen to sell, we are a natural partner for Kuwait in the West, and we are likely to be a more reliable supplier of defence material than either the U.S . . . or Mitterrand's France'.[100] In conclusion, he observed that 'there are no contracts, either defence or civil, which are likely to be clinched during the PM's visit. But there are plenty of worthwhile ones coming up in regard to which she should continue to argue the case for Britain'.[101] Thatcher needed little encouragement in doing this.

During her discussions with Crown Prince and Prime Minister of Kuwait, Sheikh Sa'ad al-Abdullah Al-Sabah, Thatcher warmly welcomed the formation of the GCC and expressed the hope that this grouping would have 'links outside'.[102] She proceeded to stress that

> Britain was glad to be able to help. We had loan service personnel in Kuwait[103] as in Oman.[104] We could supply equipment of the highest quality. Radar and the Jet engine had both been invented in Britain. Our electronic technology was the most advanced in the world. This could be of assistance to the Gulf countries in the establishment of an efficient communications system for rapid consultation on defence questions. Britain could also offer radar which was essential for early warning of attack. We could also offer the incomparable Rapier ground to air missile. If the United Kingdom had been tardy over the delivery of equipment in the past, this had been corrected in the past 2½ years. Suppliers of defence equipment were now delivering early in the UK. We therefore hoped to renew our business with Kuwait and to put forward acceptable tenders in this field where our products were pre-eminent.[105]

Sheikh Sa'ad responded to the Prime Minister's sales pitch by stating that 'it had long been Kuwait's policy to contact Britain as soon as specifications had been decided'.[106]

Thatcher made almost identical points during her talks with the Kuwaiti Minister of Defence, Sheikh Salim Al-Sabah.[107] Although the latter conceded that 'when a choice had to be made between equipments . . . whose performance was more or less the same, there was no doubt that the existence of a traditional relationship would help', he went on to point out that 'The difficulty was that sometimes the equipment being offered by one's friends was either not as good as that being offered by other countries or not as good as Kuwait needed'.[108] Thatcher's soothing words notwithstanding, Sheikh Salim proceeded to highlight missed delivery dates.[109] On the eve of Thatcher's visit to Kuwait, Salim had specifically told the Director of the UK's Military Assistance Office, Major General Ken Perkins, that with respect to the contract to supply Chieftain tanks 'The MoD were not showing the British virtue of promptness'.[110] In the report of his visit to Kuwait in early September, Perkins disclosed that 'I was made aware, politely, of Kuwait's dissatisfaction over the manner in which some defence contracts had been implemented and, while the Kuwaitis' own procedures may have contributed to the problem, they will undoubtedly need convincing that our performance in the future will be better'.[111]

Sir Michael Palliser, who accompanied Thatcher to Kuwait, reported that 'no holds were barred, whether in the political exchanges eg on Arab/Israel, or in the tone of complaints about the inadequacy of past performance by British business and industry'.[112] The question of Palestine, in particular, served to overshadow Thatcher's visit to Kuwait. 'I cannot help feeling', mused Ambassador Cambridge, 'that the unsatisfactory exchanges over this issue not only left less time for other more productive subjects, but probably discouraged the Kuwaitis from talking to us as frankly as I had hoped of their real worries'.[113] Thatcher's comments on Palestine during her press conference in Kuwait on 27 September also had the effect of undermining any goodwill that her visit had generated.

Earlier in the year, Thatcher had been invited to a dinner organized by Arab ambassadors in London. Despite initially agreeing to attend, she subsequently declined on discovering that the London representative of the Palestine Liberation Organization, Nabil Ramlawi, would be present. 'I cannot go', she minuted. 'I have been absolutely firm about British Ministers not meeting the PLO'.[114] Seeking to justify this stance while in Kuwait, Thatcher referred to the PLO's 'association with terrorism' and also statements by elements within the organization that 'their real objective is to drive Israel into the sea and wipe it off the face of the globe'.[115] In the immediate aftermath of Thatcher's remarks, Cambridge noted:

> I have read more virulent anti-British articles in the Kuwaiti newspapers during these last few days than at any time in my four years at this post. A paper today suggested that the Prime Minister deserved to be pelted with eggs and tomatoes when she was here. More ominously, and with signs of official direction, the media have been asserting that any increase in trade and cooperation between Kuwait and Britain now depends on our changing our attitude to the Palestinian cause.[116]

H. D. A. C. Miers, who accompanied the Prime Minister to Kuwait, expressed the hope that her visit would 'not be remembered more for the comments Mrs Thatcher made at her Press Conference on the PLO and the subsequent Press reaction than for anything else'.[117] Miers also contrasted Thatcher's comments with the more subtle approach of French President Giscard D'Estaing who during his trip to Kuwait in March 1980 had given 'the impression of movement by skilfully embracing a juggled formula on [Palestinian] self determination'.[118] 'It is a pity', added Miers, 'that we had to place on record so forcibly in the one Gulf state which has such an important Palestinian community'.[119] He concluded: 'I am afraid that I think the visit was only a qualified success'.[120] *The Times*, moreover, reported that 'Though Mrs Thatcher was welcomed with some warmth, it was not a wholly successful visit. The Prime Minister's call for increased political and economic ties with Britain was well received, but the Kuwaitis disapproved of some of her more critical remarks about the Palestine Liberation Organization'.[121]

Thatcher's time in Bahrain was altogether less controversial. In some respects, the ground had been prepared by a visit to London by the Bahraini Prime Minister, Sheikh Khalifa bin Sulman Al-Khalifa, a year earlier. During talks held on 16 September 1980, Thatcher had impressed upon her Bahraini counterpart that 'it was necessary to use the friendship between Bahrain and Britain for the greater stability of the Gulf – and the greater stability of the whole Western world'.[122] She added that there was a need to 'increase that friendship, to increase trade links and to keep in touch through personal contact'.[123]

Shortly before her departure for the Gulf, Sir Michael Palliser described the Bahrainis as 'extremely anglophile'.[124] Indeed, there was on the whole a greater meeting of minds during the Prime Minister's visit to Bahrain than the corresponding one to Kuwait. In the course of discussions with Thatcher, the Amir of Bahrain, Sheikh Isa bin Salman Al-Khalifah, declared that 'he wanted to see improved industrial and trading cooperation between Bahrain and the United Kingdom. The more contracts British firms won in Bahrain the easier it would be to maintain and deepen the special relationship between the United Kingdom and Bahrain'.[125] In response, Thatcher assured the Amir that she was 'sure' British firms would do all they could to win more contracts in Bahrain.[126]

During subsequent talks with Sheikh Khalifah bin Salman Al-Khalifah, Thatcher emphasized that Britain was 'keen to increase trade and ready to help over military matters', adding her hope that Bahrain would purchase British equipment such as Rapier and Hawk aircraft.[127] In reply, Sheikh Khalifa asserted that 'Bahrain preferred a British company even if slightly more expensive'.[128] Although stating that Bahrain's links with Britain were close 'whichever government was in power', he welcomed the 'recent greater interest in Bahrain shown by British foreign policy'.[129] Nevertheless, Sheikh Khalifa was quick to point out that that 'Although there were more British in the Gulf than ever before it was not possible to go back to the days when British troops were stationed there'.[130]

In the course of her final round of talks, the Bahraini Minister of Defence, Sheikh Hamad bin Isa Al-Khalifah, opined that 'British military equipment and British military technology were the best available'.[131] He also requested that Britain would assist in drawing up a regional air defence concept to which Thatcher responded with alacrity, the Director of the UK's Military Assistance Office, Major General Ken Perkins, being identified as the most suitable candidate for undertaking the task.[132]

Summing up Margaret Thatcher's visit to Bahrain, Britain's Chargé d'Affaires in Manama, M. J. Copson,[133] described it as 'immensely successful'.[134] He added: 'The extent of our withdrawal has in any case been much exaggerated. The ending of our special treaty relationship and military withdrawal were necessary but our diplomatic effort, trade relationships and a large British Community remained and have continued to flourish'.[135] However, Copson was forced to concede that even the Anglophile Bahrainis grumbled about high prices and poor delivery dates of British manufacturers and warned that Bahrain would go elsewhere if they remained 'as bad as they regrettably had been in recent years'.[136] Bahraini Prime Minister Sheikh Khalifah bin Salman, moreover, had informed Thatcher that one of Bahrain's two British-built Westland helicopters had had to be 'cannibalized' for lack of spares and that in consequence there had been a switch to the American aviation company, Sikorsky.[137] Earlier in the year, the inadequacies of British commerce had been highlighted with respect to the activities of car manufacturer, British Leyland (BL), in Qatar.

At the beginning of 1981, Ambassador Brant had been incredulous that BL had pressed ahead with arrangements for the launch of their Landtrain series of heavy goods vehicles in Doha without notifying the embassy first, let alone seeking its assistance. The Ambassador proceeded to depict the launch of Landtrain as the usual 'dismal story of BL incompetence, muddle and neglect', which included failure to co-ordinate publicity with local agents and an inability to supply essential spare parts.[138] 'My hearts sinks', admitted Brant, 'when I recall that BL are due to launch the Jaguar here at the forthcoming Doha Motor Show'.[139] He went on to contrast BL's performance with that of its principal rival, Toyota, concluding: 'I have only a small Commercial Staff: we could well devote our time to other ventures, if BL are going to let us down in this way'.[140]

Although Brant, in his valedictory despatch shortly before stepping down as Ambassador in mid-1981, had taken pleasure from the fact that Britain had been running 'neck and neck with the Japanese in the league table of imports into Qatar over the past year or so', he commented that 'with one or two notable exceptions, British industry sometimes seems cautious or slow to respond to the prospects here'.[141] This had been a consistent problem, Brant recalling that one of his predecessors, E. F. Henderson, had stated in May 1972: 'Our biggest weakness at present is that British industry still does not take Qatar seriously enough'.[142] Nearly ten years later, Brant pointed out that 'Our competitors especially the Germans, the Japanese and the French, can be expected to pull out all the stops to secure the major orders in this connection'.[143] Nevertheless, he emphasized that 'over the past 10 months, our position here has been greatly advanced and expanded, thanks to the Prime Minister's determination to demonstrate our concern for our interests in and with the Gulf States in striking fashion'.[144] *The Sunday Times* put it more bluntly, reporting in the wake of Thatcher's April 1981 visit: 'the British are willing to be as ruthless as the French in getting deeper into the arms business in the bottomless budgets of the Gulf'.[145]

Less encouraging news emerged in August regarding the construction of the Ras Laffan Power Station in Qatar which Thatcher had explicitly raised with the

Amir during her conversation with him on 25 April 1981.[146] In August, D. F. B. Edye of the British Embassy in Qatar reported that the contract had gone to the German firm Fichtner.[147] Edye lugubriously noted that

> this decision by the Amir would seem to represent a fairly major reverse for our commercial effort here and a chastening indication of the limited extent for which our influence and interests count in a matter of this sort. This conclusion would seem particularly valid given that the British firms received the maximum support possible through the Prime Minister's personal intervention on their behalf during her recent visit to Qatar.[148]

The only consolation, concluded Edye, was that the Amir had 'postponed an announcement of his decision until some three months after Mrs Thatcher's visit in the hope that this lapse of time would make his seeming disregard for her démarche and for British interests less apparent, and that memories might have become a bit blurred'.[149] Possibly bearing in mind this experience, Douglas Hurd intoned: 'Ministerial intervention is a tool which must be used sparingly if it is to remain effective'.[150] Although the new British Ambassador to Qatar, Stephen Day, in his annual review for 1981 reported that Britain was competing with the Japanese for the position of leading exporter to the Amirate, he was forced to concede that 'it is disappointing that our share of large orders slumped badly, especially in power generation and desalination'.[151]

British trade figures for Bahrain were equally disappointing. The new British Ambassador in Manama, W. R. Tomkys, recorded that in terms of exports, Britain had slipped from first to third place behind the Americans and Japanese, and that the value of British exports to Bahrain had remained flat in 1981, being about the same as the 1980 total of £115 million.[152] 'There have been several opportunities but all too often British firms have been pushed into second place', lamented Tomkys.[153] In a similar vein, the British Ambassador to the UAE, H. B. Walker, observed that

> The markets of both Dubai and Abu Dhabi have become horribly competitive. Such figures as are so far available show that in visible trade the United Kingdom's performance in 1981 is likely to be disappointing: our share of the market dropped by 2 per cent to 12.3 per cent in the first half of the year while our main competitors, Japan and the US, increased their shares.[154]

Although the value of British exports to Kuwait increased by 10 per cent in 1981 by comparison with the previous year's total, they remained the same in terms of volume.[155]

In keeping with previous occasions when Kuwait's vulnerability was exposed by external threats, the Iranian bombing of the Amirate's oil installations at Um al Aysh in September 1981 provided a fillip to Anglo–Kuwaiti relations. The Kuwaitis quickly turned to Britain for assistance, especially in the sphere of air defence. Ambassador Cambridge commented that the Ministry of Defence responded 'with alacrity, with the result that we are now about to add to the existing British service liaison team a nucleus of senior RAF officers who will advise the Kuwaitis on the purchase and installation of air defence equipment. The potential advantages for our defence sales are obvious'.[156] Ruminating on Anglo–Kuwaiti relations shortly before his departure from Kuwait in July 1982, however, Cambridge conceded that

> In the political field there is scarcely any evidence of a 'special relationship'. The ease and friendliness is still there at a personal level, but the Kuwaitis . . . have noted we are not the power in the world that we once were. They seldom show any disposition to consult us over their strategic or political worries.[157]

Injecting a dose of realism, Cambridge concluded: 'None of this should surprise us: Kuwait's rather assertive non-alignment, even the modified form which has emerged in this last year or so, requires them to keep a distance from us'.[158] Almost a year earlier, H. D. A. C. Miers had observed: 'Since our decision to withdraw from the Gulf . . . our built-in advantage has inevitably declined. And with a new generation of rulers emerging who will look to us less automatically than their fathers have done, we must expect to work hard for any successes'.[159] Even Anglo–Bahraini relations, which former Ambassador in Manama H. B. Walker described in November 1981 as possessing a 'special quality',[160] experienced identifiable modifications. This was highlighted by an attempted coup in Bahrain a month later.

On 13 December, Bahraini security authorities confirmed that a number of returnees from Iran had arrived in Bahrain with the intention of staging violent protests.[161] According to the Interior Ministry, the group's aims were to sabotage vital installations, spread terror among the local population, and attack senior government, police, and military officials.[162] The group was directed by the Shia Islamist organization, the Islamic Front for the Liberation of Bahrain led by Iraqi-born Hadi al-Modarresi.[163] Inspired by the Iranian Revolution, al-Modarresi and his elder brother, Mohammad Taqi, sought to export Islamic revolution to the Gulf.[164] Bahrain's Information Minister fulminated: 'Tehran denies it sponsored the plot, then it beams radio programmes over here telling people to rise up and how to make petrol bombs. Who are they trying to fool?'[165] On 19 December, the Bahrain authorities announced that the staff at their embassy in Tehran had been withdrawn and the Iranian Chargé d'Affaires had been asked to leave the Amirate.[166] Referring to the British head of the Bahrain Security Services, H. D. A. C. Miers remarked that 'The success in uncovering the plot was largely due to the efficient way Mr Henderson runs his organisation'.[167] Nevertheless, it was Saudi Arabia, rather than the United Kingdom as in former times, that provided Bahrain with the key external support in its moment of peril.[168]

On 14 December, the Saudi Cabinet condemned 'the criminal gang which had aimed to disturb the security of Bahrain and other areas of the Gulf'.[169] Towards the beginning of 1982, Miers commented that as a result of the attempted coup, Bahrain had 'reinforced its links with Saudi Arabia and signed a Security Cooperation

Agreement on 20 December. In the event of a serious threat to the Al Khalifa rule we believe the Saudis would resort to armed intervention'.[170] Similarly, Ambassador Tomkeys opined: 'I do not see revolutions succeeding in Bahrain so long as the Kingdom of Saudi Arabia is intact'.[171] 'The only danger', warned P. F. M. Wogan of the FCO's Middle East Department, 'is that Bahrain will snuggle so closely under Saudi Arabia's protection that it will lose its independence and liberal traditions'.[172]

While Saudi Arabia's role in the Gulf in general, and Bahrain in particular, was becoming more prominent, Britain's was adopting a more recognizably post-imperial aspect. When the Crown Prince and Prime Minister of Abu Dhabi, Sheikh Khalifa bin Zaid, requested in August 1981 that HMG bring its influence to bear on those states in the UAE which were not committed to 'total unity', Douglas Hurd retorted: 'it was not for us to tell the Rulers how to run their affairs'.[173] Responding to calls for Britain to raise with the Bahraini government the question of the alleged use of torture by Bahrain's Special Branch in the wake of the attempted coup, J. C. Moberly (Assistant Under-Secretary of State, FCO), advised: 'I believe we should be wary of seeming to arrogate to ourselves a role in all this which does not accord with the present relationship between the British Government and the fully independent Gulf States'.[174]

Far from the empire striking back in the Gulf under the guise of informal imperialism, British decision-makers sought to pursue a more identifiably modern relationship with the Gulf States. Despite the symbolism of Margaret Thatcher's two visits to the region in 1981, her approach to influencing the policy of the Gulf States, especially with respect to the procurement of arms, was very similar to that of other industrial powers, most notably the French. Indeed, the British relied upon ministerial visits and occasional prime ministerial intervention, coupled with emphasis on the appropriateness and technical superiority of British goods and services, to secure contracts. That Britain was not always successful in this approach was highlighted by the success of its industrial competitors in infiltrating Gulf markets and in some instances supplanting British commerce, a trend which Thatcher's Gulf sojourns did little, in the short term at any rate, to reverse. Although the Armilla Patrol, as the Ministry of Defence claimed, represented a 'clear demonstration of the UK's commitment to the security of the Gulf states and their economic interests',[175] its real purpose was to 'defend ships flying the Union Jack'.[176] In many ways, therefore, the patrol symbolized the transition of Britain's role from regional guarantor of security, to the more recognizably post-imperial one of preserving commercial interests against the background of regional instability.

Notes

1 Tore, T. Petersen, *Anglo–American Policy Toward the Persian Gulf, 1978–1985: Power, Influence and Restraint* (Brighton: Sussex Academic Press, 2015), p. 167.
2 Letter from Palliser to Sir Nicholas Henderson, 18 December 1980, FCO 8/3796.
3 Ibid.

4 Ibid.
5 Panagiotis Dimitrakis, 'The Soviet invasion of Afghanistan: International reactions, military intelligence and British diplomacy', *Middle Eastern Studies*, 48, 4 (2012), p. 527.
6 Letter from Palliser to Sir Nicholas Henderson, 18 December 1980, FCO 8/3796.
7 General Secretary of the Central Committee of the Communist Party of the Soviet Union, 1966–1982.
8 Letter from Palliser to Sir Nicholas Henderson, 18 December 1980, FCO 8/3796.
9 'An American rapid deployment force and the Soviet threat in SW Arabia', Planning Staff paper attached to a minute from C. L. G. Mallaby to P. H. Moberly, 4 March 1981, FCO 8/3796.
10 Ibid.
11 Jeffrey R. Macris, *The Politics and Security of the Gulf: Anglo–American Hegemony and the Shaping of a Region* (London and New York: Routledge, 2010), p. 220.
12 'American rapid deployment force', Minute by Moberly, 10 March 1981, FCO 8/3796.
13 Ibid.
14 Call by US Ambassador on Minister of State, Mr Hurd, 14 January 1981, FCO 8/3796.
15 James Worrall, *The International Institutions of the Middle East: The GCC, Arab League and Arab Maghreb Union* (London and New York: Routledge, 2017), p. 102.
16 J. E. Peterson, *Defending Arabia* (London and New York, 2017; first published in 1986), p. 218.
17 Ibid., p. 217, p. 218.
18 Worrall, *The International Institutions of the Middle East*, p. 103.
19 'Call by Kuwait Ambassador', Minute by J. C. Moberly, 24 January 1980, FCO 8/3525.
20 Telegram from Abu Dhabi to the Foreign and Commonwealth Office, No. 32, 24 January 1980, FCO 8/3454.
21 Bruce Maddy-Weitzman, *A Century of Arab Politics: From the Arab Revolt to the Arab Spring* (Lanham, MD: Rowman & Littlefield, 2016), p. 137.
22 Pierre Razoux, *The Iran–Iraq War* (Cambridge, MA: The Belknap Press, 2015), p. 111.
23 Call on Minister of State by Sheikh Khalid bin Saqr al Qasimi at the FCO, 6 November 1980, FCO 8/3445.
24 Telegram from the Foreign and Commonwealth Office, No. 66, 16 February 1981, FCO 8/3797. The GCC was for formally established on 25 May 1981.
25 Telegram from the Foreign and Commonwealth Office, No. 66, 16 February 1981, FCO 8/3797.
26 Kristian Coates Ulrichsen, 'The Gulf States and the Iran–Iraq War: Cooperation and confusion', in Nigel Ashton and Bryan Gibson (eds.), *The Iran–Iraq War: New International Perspectives* (London: Routledge, 2014), p. 114. See also Kristian Coates Ulrichsen, *Qatar and the Arab Spring* (London: Hurst and Company, 2014), pp. 21–2; Yoel Guzansky, 'Lines drawn in the sand: Territorial disputes and GCC unity', *Middle East Journal*, 70, 4 (2016), p. 545.
27 Ulrichsen, 'The Gulf States and the Iran–Iraq War', p. 114.
28 Letter from Hurd to Lord Chalfont, 23 February 1981, FCO 8/3909.
29 Letter from F. N. Richards to M. O'D. B. Alexander, 13 February 1981, FCO 8/3797.
30 Telegram from the Foreign and Commonwealth Office to Jedda, Muscat, and Dubai, No. 89, 16 February 1981, FCO 8/3797; Telegram from the Foreign and Commonwealth Office to Kuwait, Bahrain, and Doha, No. 66, 16 February 1981, FCO 8/3797; Telegram from the Foreign and Commonwealth Office to Abu Dhabi, No. 40, 16 February 1981, PREM 19/530.
31 Richard Owen, 'Keeping on terms with the Gulf', *Times*, 3 March 1981, http://find.galegroup.com/ttda/infomark.do?&source=gale&prodId=TTDA&userGroupName=unihull&tabID=T003&docPage=article&searchType=AdvancedSearchForm&

docId=CS201558115&type=multipage&contentSet=LTO&version=1.0 [accessed 8 December 2016].
32 'Consultations before use of rapid deployment force-Mrs Thatcher', *Times*, 3 March 1981, http://find.galegroup.com/ttda/infomark.do?&source=gale&prodId=TTDA&userGroupName=unihull&tabID=T003&docPage=article&searchType=AdvancedSearchForm&docId=CS117672035&type=multipage&contentSet=LTO&version=1.0 [accessed 8 December 2016].
33 Telegram from Jedda to the Foreign and Commonwealth Office, No. 155, 2 March 1981, FCO 8/3801.
34 'Gulf Force Urgent, Says Thatcher', *Daily Telegraph*, 2 March 1981, p. 1, *The Telegraph Historical Archive*, tinyurl.galegroup.com/tinyurl/4RsvD9 [accessed 27 February 2017].
35 Telegram from Doha to the Foreign and Commonwealth Office, No. 62, 3 March 1981, FCO 8/3801.
36 Telegram from Doha to the Foreign and Commonwealth Office, No. 69, 5 March 1981, FCO 8/4122.
37 Letter from Hurd to Nott, 19 March 1981, FCO 8/3802.
38 Telegram from Doha to the Foreign and Commonwealth Office, No. 84, 31 March 1981, FCO 8/3802.
39 Record of a discussion between the Prime Minister and the Foreign Minister of Iraq, Dr Sa'adoun Hammadi, at 10 Downing Street on 9 March 1981 at 17:00, PREM 19/497.
40 The Prime Minister's visit to Saudi Arabia and the Gulf: 19–25 April 1981, Brief by the Foreign and Commonwealth Office, CAB 133/514.
41 Ibid.
42 Ibid.
43 'Visit to the Middle East', Minute from Nott to Thatcher, MO 25/2/10/2, 2 April 1981, PREM 19/467.
44 Margaret Thatcher, *The Downing Street Years* (London: Harper Collins, 1993), p. 162.
45 Letter from Walden to Alexander, 11 March 1981, FCO 8/3819.
46 Richard Owen, 'Why Mrs Thatcher's change of mind pleased The Gulf', *Times*, 16 April 1981, http://find.galegroup.com/ttda/infomark.do?&source=gale&prodId=TTDA&userGroupName=unihull&tabID=T003&docPage=article&searchType=AdvancedSearchForm&docId=CS235112592&type=multipage&contentSet=LTO&version=1.0 [accessed 8 December 2016].
47 Record of a conversation between the Prime Minister and Prince Fahd, Deputy Prime Minister of Saudi Arabia, in Riyadh at 12.15 on 20 April 1981, PREM 19/757.
48 Ibid.
49 Record of a conversation between the Prime Minister and Sheikh Zaid bin Sultan, Ruler of Abu Dhabi, in Abu Dhabi on 22 April 1981 at 10.00 hours, PREM 19/757.
50 Record of a discussion between the Prime Minister and the Amir of Qatar, HH Sheikh Khalifah bin Hamad al Thani, in Qatar on 25 April 1981 at 10.00 hours, PREM 19/757.
51 Letter from F. N. Richards to M. O'D. B. Alexander, 12 January 1981, FCO 8/3818.
52 'Prime Minister's visit to the Arabian Peninsula', Minute by Miers, 20 January 1981, FCO 8/3818.
53 Letter from Richards to Alexander, 23 January 1981, FCO 8/3818.
54 Telegram from the Foreign and Commonwealth Office to Doha, No. 21, 5 February 1981, FCO 8/3818.
55 Translation of the letter of His Highness the Amir, Sheikh Khalifah bin Hamad al Thani, to H.E. the Prime Minister of the United Kingdom, the Right Honourable Margaret Thatcher MP, 7 February 1981, PREM 19/529.
56 'Hawk: Mr Hurd's visit to the Abu Dhabi', Minute by Miers, 27 January 1981, FCO 8/3850.

57 Ibid.
58 Minute by Moberly, 29 January 1981, FCO 8/3850.
59 Ibid.
60 Telegram from Doha to the Ministry of Defence, No. 210627Z, 21 April 1981, FCO 8/4113.
61 Letter from Miers to Craig, 5 February 1981, FCO 8/3850.
62 Ibid.
63 Letter from J. H. Turner (Middle East Department, FCO) to H. B. Walker, 9 February 1981, FCO 8/3902.
64 'Defence sales policy: Middle East', Note by the Defence Department, 9 February 1981, FCO 8/3850. Robin Renwick, leading diplomat during the Thatcher years, remarked in his memoirs that the Prime Minister saw it as her mission to 'arrest and reverse' British decline 'not only economically, but also in terms of our standing in the world' (Robin Renwick, *A Journey with Margaret Thatcher: Foreign Policy Under the Iron Lady* (London: Biteback Publishing, 2013), p. xvii).
65 Letter from Thatcher to Khalifah, 19 January 1981, FCO 8/4108. In his reply, Khalifah thanked Her Majesty's Government for all the 'valuable assistance' it had provided in the fields of defence and security by way of training and equipping Qatari armed forces (Translation of a letter from His Highness the Amir, Sheikh Khalifah bin Hamad Al-Thani, to the Prime Minister of the United Kingdom, the Right Honourable Margaret Thatcher (undated), FCO 8/4108).
66 Record of a discussion between the Prime Minister and the Amir of Qatar, HH Sheikh Khalifah bin Hamad al Thani, in Qatar on 25 April 1981 at 10.00 hours, PREM 19/757.
67 Ibid.
68 Ibid.
69 Ibid.
70 Ibid. Thatcher did not mention Shell Oil during her discussions with the Amir of Qatar because of the company's mishaps there which included an explosion at a natural gas liquids plant in 1977 and corrosion problems with a second such plant ('Shell's problems in Qatar', Brief by the Energy, Science and Space Department, 15 December 1982, FCO 8/4690).
71 Letter from Brant to Carrington, 29 June 1981, FCO 8/4106.
72 Letter from Brant to Carrington, 4 May 1981, FCO 8/3823.
73 Points from the Prime Minister's tête-à-tête conversation with Sheikh Khalifah of Qatar on 25 April 1981, PREM 19/757.
74 Ibid.
75 'Prime Minister's visit to the Gulf: Qatar', Minute by Miers, 14 May 1981, FCO 8/3824.
76 Telegram from Doha to the Foreign and Commonwealth Office, No. 84, 31 March 1981, FCO 8/3802.
77 Ahmed Mannai was founder and chairman of the Qatari company, the Mannai Corporation.
78 Letter from Brant to K. P. Jeffs (Ministry of Defence, 15 June 1981, FCO 8/4113.
79 Ibid.
80 Letter from Lygo to Nott, 18 June 1981, FCO 8/4113; Letter from Lygo to Tebbit, 18 June 1981, FCO 8/4113.
81 Letter from Brant to Jeffs, 15 June 1981, FCO 8/4113.
82 Telegram from the Foreign and Commonwealth Office to Abu Dhabi and Dubai, No. 75, 20 December 1981, FCO 8/3921.
83 Letter from Alexander to Paul Lever (Assistant Private Secretary to the Secretary of State for Foreign and Commonwealth Affairs), 22 December 1980, FCO 8/3921.
84 Record of a conversation between the Prime Minister and Sheikh Zaid bin Sultan, Ruler of Abu Dhabi, in Abu Dhabi on 22 April at 10.00 hours, PREM 19/757.

164 *The empire strikes back? 1981*

85 Summary record of a conversation between the Prime Minister and the Prime Minister of Abu Dhabi, Sheikh Khalifa, in Abu Dhabi on 22 April 1981 at 12.40 hours, PREM 19/757.
86 Ibid.
87 Ibid.
88 Martin Woollacott, 'Thatcher Gulf sales drive nets order for Hawk jet', *The Guardian*, 23 April 1981, https://search.proquest.com/docview/186239369?accountid=11528 [accessed 8 March 2017].
89 Letter from Thatcher to Reagan, 27 April 1981, PREM 19/757. Deputy Under-Secretary of State at the FCO, John Graham, informed the US Embassy in London that this passage in Thatcher's letter to the President was 'intended to make the point that our ability to make even a modest contribution to defence arrangements in the Persian Gulf, including perhaps particularly the provision of Loan Service Personnel, was dependent to a large extent on our ability to make defence sales in the area where we were traditional suppliers. We could not claim that the area was a reservation for us, but a massive US effort which had the effect of squeezing us out would make it very difficult for us to justify a continued effort; and if our Loan Service Personnel, for example, were withdrawn it would not be possible for other Western nations to replace them' ('Arms sales to the UAE', Minute by Graham, 1 May 1981, FCO 8/3922).
90 'Political background and UK/Kuwait relations', Foreign and Commonwealth Office brief, undated, FCO 8/3825.
91 Ibid.
92 Ibid.
93 Call by the Lord Privy Seal on his Highness Sheikh Jabir Al-Ahmad Al-Jabir Al-Sabah, the Amir of Kuwait, in Kuwait on Saturday, 7 February 1981 at 10.00 hours, FCO 8/3825. See also Telegram from Kuwait to the Foreign and Commonwealth Office, No. 115, 8 February 1981, FCO 8/3825.
94 Minute from Gilmour to the Secretary of State, 10 February 1981, FCO 8/3825.
95 Ibid.
96 'Kuwait: Political background', Note by the Foreign and Commonwealth Office, 23 June 1981, T 639/78.
97 Letter from Palliser to Sir Robert Armstrong, 24 August 1981, PREM 19/535.
98 Margaret Thatcher had previously visited Kuwait during her time as Secretary of State for Education and Science. The then British Ambassador to Kuwait, A. J. Wilton, reported: 'The Kuwaitis, for all their growing sophistication, are not really yet any more attuned to the notion of a woman Cabinet Minister than were Dr Johnson's contemporaries to the notion of a woman preaching a sermon; and they were astonished not only to see it done but to see it well done' (Letter from Wilton to the Secretary of State for Foreign and Commonwealth Affairs, 2 May 1973, FCO 8/1997).
99 Telegram from Kuwait to the Foreign and Commonwealth Office, No. 375, 20 September 1981, FCO 8/3836.
100 Ibid.
101 Ibid.
102 Record of a meeting between the Prime Minister and HH Sheikh Sa'ad Al-Abdullah Al-Sabah, Crown Prince and Prime Minister of Kuwait, at the Salaam Palace at 10.30 hours, PREM 19/535.
103 The Kuwait Liaison Team, established following an exchange of letters in 1963, consisted of 143 British servicemen who assisted with training Kuwaiti personnel and with the introduction into service of British military equipment. The KLT was described by the Ministry of Defence as 'one of our largest commitments to the Middle East' ('Prime Minister's visit to Bahrain and Kuwait, 25–28 September 1981: Defence relations', brief by the Ministry of Defence, 16 September 1981, FCO 8/3837).

104 During discussions with Douglas Hurd on 23 April 1981, the Omani Minister of State for Foreign Affairs, Qais Zawawi, raised concerns about the costs of Loan Service Personnel (Record of a conversation between the Minister of State for Foreign and Commonwealth Affairs and the Omani Minister of State for Foreign Affairs in Salalah, 23 April 1981, PREM 19/858). Margaret Thatcher herself intervened on the question of LSP, her Assistant Private Secretary, Michael Alexander, reporting that 'She wholly disagrees with the proposition that we should assess charges for Loan Service Personnel on a full cost basis. She believes that this approach does us very great harm. She considers that we are unnecessarily upsetting friendly countries by raising "trifling matters" such as this' (Letter from Alexander to Richards, 6 May 1981, PREM 19/858).
105 Record of a meeting between the Prime Minister and HH Sheikh Sa'ad Al-Abdullah Al-Sabah, Crown Prince and Prime Minister of Kuwait, at the Salaam Palace at 10.30 hours, PREM 19/535.
106 Ibid.
107 Record of a conversation between the Prime Minister and Sheikh Salim Al-Sabah, Minister of Defence of Kuwait on 27 September 1981 at 19.00 hours, PREM 19/535.
108 Ibid.
109 Ibid.
110 Meeting between Major General Ken Perkins and the Kuwait Minister of Defence, His Excellency Sheikh Salim Al-Sabah on Tuesday, 1 September 1981 at 10am, FCO 8/3941.
111 'Visit to Kuwait, 1–3 September by Director Military Assistance Office', Report by Perkins, 4 September 1981, DEFE 24/2679.
112 Telegram from Kuwait to the Foreign and Commonwealth Office, No. 399, 28 September 1981, PREM 19/535.
113 Letter from Cambridge to Carrington, 30 September 1981, FCO 8/3836.
114 Minute by Thatcher on a letter from Alexander to Richards, 15 June 1981, PREM 19/534.
115 Telegram from Kuwait to the Foreign and Commonwealth Office, No. 398, 28 September 1981, PREM 19/535. For Thatcher's attitudes towards the PLO, see Azriel Bermant, *Margaret Thatcher and the Middle East* (Cambridge: Cambridge University Press, 2016), p. 27.
116 Letter from Cambridge to Carrington, 30 September 1981, FCO 8/3836.
117 Letter from Miers to Cambridge, 29 October 1981, FCO 8/3836.
118 Ibid.
119 'Prime Minister's visit to Kuwait', Minute by Miers, 30 October 1981, FCO 8/3836.
120 Ibid.
121 David Hewson, 'Kuwait', *Times*, 15 October 1981, http://find.galegroup.com/ttda/infomark.do?&source=gale&prodId=TTDA&userGroupName=unihull&tabID=T003&docPage=article&searchType=AdvancedSearchForm&docId=CS285444431&type=multipage&contentSet=LTO&version=1.0 [accessed 8 December 2016].
122 Record of a conversation between the Prime Minister and the Prime Minister of Bahrain: Tuesday, 16 September 1980, PREM 19/3613.
123 Ibid.
124 Letter from Pallier to Armstrong, 24 August 1981, FCO 8/3835.
125 Note of a meeting held at the Rifa'a Palace at 9.35 on Saturday 26 September 1981, PREM 19/535.
126 Ibid.
127 Record of a meeting between the Prime Minister and Sheikh Khalifa bin Sulman Al-Khalifa, Prime Minister of Bahrain, at Government House on Saturday 26 September 1981 at 10.30 hours, PREM 19/535.
128 Ibid.

166 *The empire strikes back? 1981*

129 Ibid.
130 Ibid.
131 Summary of a conversation between the Prime Minister and Crown Prince Hamad, Minister of Defence in Bahrain, on 26 September 1981 at 15.30 hours, PREM 19/535.
132 Ibid.
133 The British Ambassador to Bahrain, D. G. Crawford, had died suddenly on the eve of Thatcher's visit to the Amirate, leaving Copson with the task of finalizing arrangements and accompanying the Prime Minister during her various engagements.
134 Letter from Copson to the Secretary of State for Foreign and Commonwealth Affairs, 30 September 1981, FCO 8/3836.
135 Ibid.
136 Ibid.
137 Record of a meeting between the Prime Minister and Sheikh Khalifa bin Sulman Al-Khalifa, Prime Minister of Bahrain, at Government House on Saturday 26 September 1981 at 10.30 hours, PREM 19/535.
138 Letter from Brant to O. H. Kemmis, 24 January 1981, FCO 8/4115.
139 Ibid.
140 Ibid.
141 Letter from Brant to the Secretary of State for Foreign and Commonwealth Affairs, 29 June 1981, FCO 8/4106.
142 Ibid.
143 Ibid.
144 Ibid.
145 Stephen Fay, 'We're all pals, Thatcher tells Gulf's rulers', *Sunday Times*, 26 April 1981, p. 8, *The Sunday Times Digital Archive*, http://find.galegroup.com/stha/infomark.do?&source=gale&prodId=STHA&userGroupName=unihull&tabID=T003&docPage=article&searchType=BasicSearchForm&docId=FP1800376451&type=multipage&contentSet=LTO&version=1.0 [accessed 28 February 2017].
146 Record of a discussion between the Prime Minister and the Amir of Qatar, HH Sheikh Khalifah bin Hamad al Thani, in Qatar on 25 April 1981 at 10.00 hours, PREM 19/757.
147 Letter from Edye to K. J. Passmore, 9 August 1981, FCO 8/4115.
148 Ibid.
149 Ibid.
150 Letter from Hurd to David Mudd, MP, 1 October 1981, FCO 8/4115.
151 Letter from Day to the Secretary of State for Foreign and Commonwealth Affairs, 2 January 1982, FCO 8/4682.
152 Letter from Tomkys to the Secretary of State for Foreign and Commonwealth Affairs, 13 February 1981, FCO 8/4332
153 Ibid.
154 Letter from Walker to the Secretary of State for Foreign and Commonwealth Affairs, 25 January 1982, FCO 8/4469.
155 Letter from Cambridge to the Secretary of State for Foreign and Commonwealth Affairs, 10 January 1982, FCO 8/4485.
156 Ibid.
157 Letter from Cambridge to the Secretary of State for Foreign and Commonwealth Affairs, 27 July 1982, FCO 8/4485.
158 Ibid.
159 'Valedictory despatch HMA Abu Dhabi', Minute by Miers, 19 May 1981, FCO 8/3910.
160 Letter from Walker to the Secretary of State for Foreign and Commonwealth Affairs, 19 November 1981, FCO 8/4469.

161 Telegram from Bahrain to the Foreign and Commonwealth Office, No. 221, 13 December 1981, FCO 8/3893.
162 Telegram from Bahrain to the Foreign and Commonwealth Office, No. 222, 14 December 1981, FCO 8/3893.
163 Hasan Tariq Alhasan, 'The role of Iran in the failed coup of 1981: The IFLB in Bahrain', *The Middle East Journal*, 65, 4 (2011), pp. 605–06.
164 Ibid., p. 606.
165 Robin Wright, *In the Name of God: The Khomeini Decade* (New York: Simon and Schuster Inc., 1989), p. 112. In the months leading up the coup attempt, Douglas Hurd had noted: 'There is no doubt that the shock-waves of the Iranian revolution have been felt in Bahrain, and that hostile broadcasts from Iran and the pronouncements of certain Iranian ayatollahs have occasionally made life difficult for the Bahraini authorities' (Letter from Hurd to Roland Moyle, MP, 24 September 1981, FCO 8/3893). Kylie Moore-Gilbert argues that 'The destabilising impact of the Iranian Revolution, together with the rise of political Shi'ism within Bahrain, provided the Al Khalifa with the conditions necessary to develop a sectarian-based model of divide and rule during the 1980s' (Kylie Moore-Gilbert, 'From protected state to protection racket: Contextualising divide and rule in Bahrain', *Journal of Arabian Studies*, 6, 2 (2016), pp. 174–5).
166 Letter from S. P. Collis to Passmore, 21 December 1981, FCO 8/3893.
167 'Attempted coup in Bahrain', Minute by Miers, 26 February 1982, FCO8/4332.
168 The restoration of Al-Khalifa authority against the background of the 'Arab spring' in early 2011 relied even more heavily on Saudi Arabia with some 1 500 Saudi-led GCC soldiers and police being sent to Bahrain in March to help quell unrest (Sean L. Yom and F. Gregory Gause III, 'Resilient royals: How Arab monarchies hang on', *Journal of Democracy*, 23, 4 (2012), p. 81). Referring to these events, Matthew Willis of the Royal United Services Institute has argued that 'The reality is that the most powerful force in Bahrain is Saudi Arabia, which holds Bahrain in a vise that it tightens and loosens at its discretion – a fact acknowledged by the most senior officials in the Bahraini government. The strength of this bilateral relationship is such that the UK, wielding only soft power, cannot hope to take precedence, even if heavyweights in the Bahraini government desired it to be so. Only if the crisis had risked destabilising the wider region or making the West's security presence on the island untenable – with the result that both British and American national security interests would be at stake – might it have been worth considering interposing between Saudi Arabia and Bahrain' (Matthew Willis, 'Britain in Bahrain in 2011', *RUSI Journal*, 157, 5 (2012), p. 68).
169 Telegram from Jedda to the Foreign and Commonwealth Office, No. 803, 15 December 1981, FCO 8/3893.
170 'Attempted coup in Bahrain', Minute by Miers, 26 February 1982, FCO8/4332.
171 Letter from Tomkeys to Lord Carrington, 4 February 1982, FCO 8/4332.
172 'Annual review and first impressions despatch from Bahrain', Minute by Wogan, 23 April 1982, FCO 8/4332.
173 Record of a meeting between Mr Hurd and Shaikh Khalifa bin Zaid, Crown Prince and Prime Minister of Abu Dhabi, in Hans Crescent, 5 August 1981, FCO 8/3923.
174 Minute by Moberly, 19 February 1982, FCO 8/4332.
175 'UK out of area activity', paper attached to R. T. Jackling's (Assistant Secretary, Ministry of Defence) minute, 16 September 1981, FCO 8/3848.
176 Macris, *The Politics and Security of the Gulf*, p. 220.

Conclusion
Imperialism after empire?

> [I]t is not a question of saying whether we thought what happened 10 years ago was right or wrong, it happened. There is no point in discussing it. We start from where we are now.
> – Margaret Thatcher, Press Conference, Kuwait, 27 September 1981[1]

While the decision in 1968 to withdraw from East of Suez might have coincided with the termination of Britain's status as a recognizably global power, it retained global interests, not least in the Gulf itself. Writing in 1981, the British Ambassador to Qatar, Colin Brant, remarked:

> One of our problems in presenting HM Government's policies is created by the constant reference by commentators and others . . . about Britain having 'left the Gulf' in 1971, as though HM Government had abandoned the area entirely. I suggest that such a description does less than justice to the work of our missions in the area, and the efforts of countless firms and commercial representatives who have worked to maintain their and the British connection with the Gulf States in the past decade. With the growing prosperity of this area, these efforts are now bearing valuable fruit.[2]

The British Ambassador to Oman, I. T. M. Lucas, was in full agreement, arguing that

> we 'withdrew' only in the sense that we removed our military presence from a number of these states, but the implication that we ceased to have any further interest in them is not borne out, I suggest, by the statistics of British expatriate communities in the Gulf or of commercial achievements over the past 10 years.[3]

Despite these positive assessments of Britain's continuing role in the Gulf following the East of Suez decision, there is considerable evidence that the British connection with the region after 1971 was subjected to a host of challenges. While Wm. Roger Louis' claim that 'by dismantling the system of protected states, the formal British presence disappeared, but invisible or informal influence remained',[4] has considerable merit, it was a diluted form of influence.[5]

As early as 1963, the British Ambassador to Kuwait, J. C. B. Richmond, asserted that 'In the 20th century outside forces cannot be kept out of an area where wealth is rapidly growing'.[6] Against the background of the Wilson government's decision to 'withdraw' from East of Suez, Britain's Political Resident in the Gulf, Sir Stewart Crawford, remarked in January 1968 that 'we shall have to meet competition from many powers now virtually unrepresented here'.[7] The prescience of this analysis was soon borne out as Britain's industrial rivals exploited the commercial opportunities in the Gulf States and eroded Britain's traditional dominance. At the end of 1969, Britain's Political Agent in Abu Dhabi, C. J. Treadwell, observed:

> salesmen from the United States, West Germany and Japan are making serious inroads on what was an exclusively British preserve. They are succeeding not because there is any dearth of good will in Abu Dhabi towards United Kingdom manufacturers. Politically our stock remains high and buyers generally would prefer, other things being equal, to buy British. But the sales methods of our competitors are sometimes more compelling. Their senior representatives seem generally more willing than our own to visit Abu Dhabi and seek out markets for their goods. We do not often hear complaints about delivery times, but there are several merchants who complain that other countries leave us standing when it comes to after-sales service.[8]

In 1974, the British Consul General in Dubai, Henry St. John Basil Armitage, aptly noted: 'the Gulf is no longer a British pearling ground'.[9] Four years later, the FCO's Middle East Department pointed out that although the people of the area retained a 'genuine trust' for British people and institutions, the 'historical relationship' with Britain would 'inevitably be eroded with time'.[10] In 1981, moreover, Ambassador Brant remarked:

> the Qataris are a shrewd bunch, who can always be relied on to make the best bargain they can for themselves and their projects. The Amir and his advisers maintain (sometimes truthfully) that they would prefer to buy from the UK. But the world is now their oyster, and the competition here is intense.[11]

A year earlier, Brant had asserted: 'The French, and other national manufacturers are also acutely aware of the openings for arms sales here: we have been warned!'[12] Referring to the Qataris, Brant also noted: 'They have ... decided to reap the political benefits which could be obtained from spreading the favours of their contracts more widely, and of acceding to official French importuning on behalf of their arms manufacturers'.[13]

The encroachment of other powers into the Gulf contrasted with the more-or-less exclusive British involvement in the region in earlier times, the Foreign Office declaring in 1936 that the Gulf States 'were a special preserve of HMG whose policy towards them rested on a kind of Monroe Doctrine'.[14] In 1981, the

Minister of State at the FCO, Douglas Hurd, mused: 'it is not surprising that, with the opening up of the Gulf to the rest of the world since 1971, others would have come in to seek their share of expanding and lucrative markets'.[15] Even in situations where close defence relations existed, this was no guarantee that these would translate into defence sales. For instance, despite the existence of a considerable number of British military personnel in the Kuwait Liaison Team (KLT), the British Ambassador in Kuwait, S. J. G. Cambridge, noted in 1981 that any attempt to create a link between Britain's willingness to support the KLT and the securing of defence contracts would be 'self-defeating'.[16] Elaborating on this point, Cambridge stressed that Kuwaiti Defence Minister, Sheikh Salim Al-Sabah, 'resented what he believed was an expectation on our side that Kuwait should buy British'.[17]

The Gulf States were also subjected to regional crosscurrents which the British were, for the most part, incapable of countering. This was amply demonstrated with respect to the use of the 'oil weapon' in 1973 and the Gulf States' tendency to follow the oil production and pricing policies of their larger neighbours. When Prime Minister Edward Heath tackled Sheikh Zaid about the use of the oil weapon in 1973, the Abu Dhabi Ruler admitted that 'it was impossible for one Arab State to take an independent line if the rest favoured such action'.[18] Responding a year earlier to British pressure for the UAE to improve relations with Iran, Sheikh Zaid informed Foreign Secretary Sir Alec Douglas-Home that 'the Union had to look to its own interests. It was most important that any move on their part to establish relations with Iran should not be opposed by the other Arab States'.[19] Referring in the mid-1970s to the growing influence of Egyptian and Palestinian advisers in the Gulf States, moreover, a Department of Trade mandarin lamented: 'Slowly but surely the position of the British in the Gulf is being eroded'.[20] More specifically, the Defence Attaché to the British Embassy in Abu Dhabi, Lt. Col. R. Jury, observed that the Emirate 'crawls with expatriate Egyptians, Jordanians and Sudanese officers; all of these have their own interests which, in many cases, do not coincide with either the UAE's or the UKs'.[21] The expansion in the number of Arab officers stemmed in turn from Zaid's 1973 decision to Arabize the Abu Dhabi Defence Force.[22]

While Britain's connection with the ruling families of the Gulf remained for the most part strong, there was a palpable erosion in the closeness of the relationship. Within a year of the Wilson government's 1968 announcement on the Gulf, Britain's Political Agent in Dubai, J. L. Bullard, remarked: 'the more sophisticated Rulers are already aware that the traditional friendship with Britain is only one of many possible alignments, and that in any case the next three years must bring about great changes'.[23] In 1980, Britain's representative in Abu Dhabi, D. A. Roberts, commented that whereas in the early days after British withdrawal the UK Ambassador continued to see Sheikh Zaid 'on a privileged basis and at very regular intervals', this practice had 'dropped away some time in the last five years or so'.[24] By contrast with the period of British imperial paramountcy in the Gulf, moreover, there was little or no scope for Britain to intervene in succession questions.[25] In response to Iranian pressure in 1972 for British cooperation in the deposition of the Abu Dhabi Ruler, the Head of the FCO's Middle East Department,

P. R. H. Wright, specifically stated: 'it would be extremely difficult and probably futile to attempt to replace Zaid with another member of his family'.[26] The British Ambassador in Tehran, Peter Ramsbotham, also informed the Iranian Minister of Foreign Affairs, Abbas Ali Khalatbari, that 'There was no question of our going along with any plans aimed at replacing Zaid'.[27] Indeed, in contradistinction to neo-colonial paradigms, there was a conscious attempt by British policy-makers to put its relations with the Gulf States on a recognizably post-imperial footing.

Speaking in Cairo in 1971, Sir Alec Douglas-Home defined British interest in the Middle East as 'that of a trading nation which has no interest in power politics or military bases and no wish to interfere in independent countries'.[28] While Britain's close involvement in counterinsurgency operations in Oman in the 1970s to some extent belied Douglas-Home's words, in the former Gulf Sheikhdoms there was a recognition that the withdrawal of formal British protection in 1971 did equate with a qualitative alteration in their relationship with Britain and that there could be no seamless transition to 'informal empire'. When the United Arab Emirates Ambassador in London, Mahdi Al-Tajir, attempted in 1973 to enlist British assistance in persuading Sheikh Rashid of Dubai to accept recent Cabinet changes in the UAE, P. R. H. Wright, replied: 'we must regard this as an internal matter on which it would be quite improper for us to advise'.[29] In a similar vein, E. F. Given, who held the position of Ambassador to Bahrain from 1975 to 1979, remarked: 'Throughout my tenure of this post I have been careful, by avoiding involvement in internal affairs, to show that I realise that our relations with Bahrain are very different from those which existed during my earlier service here'.[30] Equally, the British Ambassador to Qatar, E. F. Henderson, remarked:

> there are obvious dangers if our position were to become too open and too all-embracing. . . . They [the Qataris] have for a long time been very conscious of the dangers of appearing to be puppets of the British and with no British troops on Qatar soil to explain away, they have to a large extent been successful in avoiding these dangers.[31]

Reflecting the changed circumstances in which Britain was operating after 1971, the Assistant Head of the FCO's Middle East Department, T. J. Clark, mused with respect to the long-standing Qatar/Bahrain sea bed boundary dispute:

> we were, and still are, prepared to continue to take action with both sides in the hope of persuading them to settle their problems in an amicable fashion. But any attempt by us in today's circumstances to put pressure on one side alone could of course be construed as unjustified interference.[32]

Referring in 1978 to the former Trucial States, Assistant Under-Secretary at the FCO, M. S. Weir, observed: 'There was indeed something slightly unhealthy and unnatural about the old "special relationship" . . . and I think the new UAE generation are grateful to us for not trying to cling on to it beyond its time'.[33] Ambassador Brant, moreover, characterized the Queen's visit to the Gulf in early 1979 as 'the former Protecting and Protected States meeting on equal terms as sovereign powers'.[34] In the wake of the Iranian Revolution, Assistant Under-Secretary of State at the FCO, J. C. Moberly, counselled:

> The American experience with the Shah's regime suggests that little good is served by attempts, especially if inconsistent, to modify the internal regimes of other countries. If, for example, we were to seek to do so in the Gulf we should be in danger of being saddled with responsibility without the means to exercise it effectively.[35]

Towards the end of 1980, Douglas Hurd, declared that

> the relationship between the British government and the governments of the Gulf states is now one of equality and mutual respect – a mature relationship, in fact, and this is as it should be in the modern world. We have no intention of trying to turn the clock back, nor as it was once put, have we 'gone out of the door in order to come back through the window'.[36]

Writing on the eve of Margaret Thatcher's historic visit to the Gulf in April 1981, moreover, Britain's Ambassador to the United Arab Emirates, D. A. Roberts, observed: 'After independence in 1971 we went out of our way to avoid any appearance of seeking to preserve an imperial position in the area. We concentrated on maintaining and if possible improving our share in a growing commercial market'.[37]

The achievement of this objective, however, was impeded by the British economy's systemic problems in the 1970s, including a lack of competitiveness, poor delivery times, and, in some cases, a lack of entrepreneurship.[38] At the beginning of 1973, Ambassador Henderson remarked: 'whether we slide down from a peak or continue to mount a moderate slope to even better things will depend on the performance of British firms'.[39] The Ambassador added: 'The only thing to prevent British firms from striding in is, in too many cases, poor management and bad salesmanship'.[40] Shortly after this, P. R. H. Wright observed: 'We are fully conscious of the immense opportunities for trade in consumer goods which the rapidly increasing revenues in the Gulf States are producing and British industry's generally sluggish response'.[41] Summing up the deficiencies of British commerce, Sultan Qaboos of Oman told Margaret Thatcher in 1981 that

> People were inclined to think that the British were slow in commercial matters, and took a long time. The French on the other hand were very good at attracting people.... Britain must be prepared to react quickly, to deploy better publicity and propaganda, to improve delivery times, to offer good terms of credit, and in general to pay attention to the smaller points.[42]

As suggested by these comments, Britain lost any semblance of its former exclusive role in the Gulf in the years after 1971. The encroachment of Britain's commercial competitors into the region served to weaken any notion that formal British protection could be replaced by an informal imperial relationship between Britain and its former Gulf charges. Nevertheless, doubt can be cast on whether this was ever Britain's aim. Indeed, there was a strong determination after 1971 to respect the Gulf States' independence, in name and in reality, and to forge a new demonstrably post-imperial relationship. In the wake of the Iranian Revolution, the FCO's Middle East Department produced an important paper on British policy towards Arabia and the Gulf which firmly argued:

> To resume a tutelary or policing role, backed by a military intervention capacity, even if we shared this with our Western partners, would carry little appeal for our friends in the Arab world, embarrass or inhibit our broader relationship with the Third World and, as seen in Iran, would be unlikely to counter unrest arising from internal strains in any country. Moreover, heightened involvement might not even buy time for the present regimes in the area; it would exacerbate local nationalism and encourage immobilisme among the rulers.[43]

Equally, when Yusuf Alawi, Under-Secretary at the Omani Ministry of Foreign Affairs, bemoaned in November 1979 the loss of Britain's regional co-ordinating role, Ambassador Lucas commented: 'we certainly welcomed – and would do all we could to foster such co-ordination – but I did not imagine that anyone wished us to resume our former role in the area'.[44]

Despite the rejection of a return to the imperial past, Margaret Thatcher's visits to the Gulf in 1981, the first by a sitting British Prime Minister, served to reinforce ties between Britain and the Gulf States. While there was a keenness on the part of the Thatcher government to present this as a new departure in British policy,[45] the reality was that Britain had never lost interest in the Gulf, even in the aftermath of the 'withdrawal' decision in 1968. The region was too important, strategically and economically, to allow such a luxury. As the former British Ambassador to Bahrain, Robin Lamb, recalled in giving evidence to the Foreign Affairs Select Committee in 2013:

> We did not reduce our interest in the Gulf. Perhaps the appearance of people's interest declined, and there was a perception from Sheikh Zayed that it had done so. However, a great deal of attention never wavered because of the importance of the Gulf as a source of most of the oil in international trade and investment.[46]

Shortly before Britain's formal departure from the Gulf, the British Ambassador to Saudi Arabia, Willie Morris, told King Feisal that 'Although our relations with the Rulers were being modernised, and our military forces were being withdrawn, we would continue to be actively involved in the Gulf area'.[47] Margaret Thatcher's 1981 visits were perhaps significant mainly in terms of presentation and perception, serving as they did to underline Britain's continuing commitment to the region and allay Gulf fears regarding Britain's fidelity following the departure of British forces in 1971. Writing in 1981, Ambassador Roberts mused: 'Many believed that in 1971 we washed our hands of the UAE and retained only our commercial interest in obtaining contracts, for which of course others could compete just as well'.[48]

In emphasizing Britain's dedication to the Gulf during her tours of the region in 1981,[49] Thatcher was, in many ways, preaching to the converted. Reeling from the successive shocks of the Iranian Revolution, the Soviet invasion of Afghanistan,[50] and the Iran–Iraq War,[51] and conscious of the regional dangers of too close an association with the United States, the Gulf Rulers valued the continued support of Britain, particularly in the military field. The sale of Rapier missiles to Qatar and Hawk aircraft to the UAE should be seen in this context. In many ways, the Thatcher government's sales drive in the Gulf culminated in the September 1985 Al-Yamamah arms deal with Saudi Arabia, at the time the world's largest.[52]

In the aftermath of the Iraqi invasion of Kuwait in August 1990, Thatcher placed on record her wish that a Minister should travel to the Gulf to 'convey reassurance to the smaller states, explain the measures we are taking and offer to meet any particular needs'.[53] The Minister of State for Defence Procurement, Alan Clark, along with the Vice-Chief of the Defence Staff, Sir Richard Vincent, were subsequently despatched to the Gulf. On his return in mid-August, Clark informed Thatcher: 'I believe the mission was successful in attaining the objective that you set; that is to say of giving your personal regards to the Ruing Families, underlining UK support for them and pointing out the speed and effectiveness of our military response'.[54]

On the eve of her resignation as Prime Minister in November 1990, Margaret Thatcher assured the Amir of Kuwait: 'I know that my successor will continue to attach the highest importance to the relations between our countries. In particular I am sure that he will continue Britain's strong support for full implementation of United Nations Security Council Resolutions, and for the restoration of the legitimate government of Kuwait'.[55] Although America's leadership of the international coalition which ousted Iraqi forces from Kuwait in 1991, as well as its decision to retain US forces in the Gulf thereafter, reflected the growing dominance of the US in the region,[56] Britain did retain a significant role in Gulf States, especially in the fields of defence and security.[57] As the United Arab Emirates' Ambassador to the United Kingdom in the 1990s, Easa Al-Gurg, memorably observed: 'We had to recognise that although the British presence was officially no more, the British themselves were still very much with us'.[58]

Notes

1 Telegram from Kuwait to the Foreign and Commonwealth Office, No. 398, 28 September 1981, PREM 19/535.
2 Telegram from Doha to the Foreign and Commonwealth Office, No. 99, 15 April 1981, FCO 8/3802.
3 Letter from Lucas to H. D. A. C. Miers, 12 May 1981, FCO 8/3802.
4 Wm. Roger Louis, 'Britain and the Middle East after 1945', in L. Carl Brown (ed.), *Diplomacy in the Middle East: The International Relations of Regional and Outside*

Conclusion 175

Powers (London: I. B. Tauris, 2004), p. 48. In a similar vein, Uzi Rabi, surveying the post-1971 landscape, argues that 'In short, the practical content of the interchange between Britain and the Gulf in all fields exceeds anything that could have been predicted by previous generations' (Uzi Rabi, 'British possessions in the Persian Gulf and Southwest Arabia: The last abandoned in the Middle East', in Zach Levey and Elie Podeh (eds.), *Britain and the Middle East: From Imperial Power to Junior Partner* (Brighton: Sussex Academic Press, 2008), p. 276).

5 In May 1970, the Head of the FCO's Arabian Department, A. A. Acland, opined: 'It seems reasonable to assume that our influence will continue to decline rapidly as the visible signs of impending withdrawal accumulate. The Rulers will increasingly feel that they must sort out their own problems themselves and in their own way, so as to be prepared for the period after British withdrawal. This is as it must be; and is one of the purposes of withdrawal. But it means that they seek and take our advice less and less' ('The Union of Arab Emirates', Minute by A. A. Acland, 18 May 1970, FCO 8/1293).

6 Letter from Richmond to Stevens, No. 1059/63G, 3 February 1963, TNA, FO 371/168632/B 1052/9/G.

7 Cited in Shohei Sato, *Britain and the Formation of the Gulf States: Embers of Empire* (Manchester: Manchester University Press, 2016), pp. 131–2.

8 Letter from Treadwell to Crawford, 19 December 1969, cited in A. L. P. Burdett (ed.), *Records of the Emirates, 1966–1971: Volume 4: 1969* (Slough: Archive Editions, 2002), p. 12.

9 Letter from Armitage to P. M. S. Corley (Department of Trade), 10 October 1974, FCO 8/2361. See also Letter from A. T. Lamb to Corley, 10 August 1974, FCO 8/2198; Letter from D. J. McCarthy to D. F. Ballentyne (Trade Relations and Exports Department, FCO), 25 February 1974, FCO 8/2361.

10 Visit to the United Arab Emirates by the Minister of State for Foreign and Commonwealth Affairs, 10–12 March 1978: Briefs, p. 9, FCO 8/3142.

11 Letter from Brant to Lord Carrington, 4 May 1981, FCO 8/3823.

12 Letter from Brant to Carrington, 10 March 1980, FCO 8/3674.

13 Letter from Brant to P. H. Moberly, 11 November 1980, FCO 8/3674.

14 Glen Balfour-Paul, *The End of the Middle East: Britain's Relinquishment of Power in Her Last Three Arab Dependencies* (Cambridge: Cambridge University Press, 1994), p. 105.

15 Letter from Hurd to John Stanley MP, 23 February 1981, FCO 8/3909.

16 Letter from Cambridge to Miers, 17 June 1981, FCO 8/3941.

17 Ibid.

18 Summary record of discussions during the luncheon party given in honour of the President of the United Arab Emirates on 20 September 1973 at No. 10 Downing Street, PREM 15/1760.

19 Record of Secretary of State's conversation with Sheikh Zaid, President of the United Arab Emirates, Wednesday 13 September 1972, PREM 15/1086.

20 'Visit to Qatar, 28–31 March 1975', Minute by Dr R. Roberts (Head of International Technological Collaboration Unit in the Department of Trade), 2 April 1975, FCO 8/2528.

21 Letter from Jury to B. A. Major, 27 July 1978, FCO 8/3101.

22 Athol Yates, 'Western expatriates in the UAE armed forces, 1964–2015', *Journal of Arabian Studies*, 6, 2 (2016), p. 191.

23 'Dubai and the Northern Trucial States review of the year 1968', attached to Bullard's letter to Sir Stewart Crawford, 5 January 1969, cited in A. L. P. Burdett (ed.), *Records of the Emirates, 1966–1971: Volume 3: 1968* (Slough: Archive Editions, 2002), p. 21.

24 'British relations with the United Arab Emirates', Minute by H. D. A. C. Miers, 9 December 1980, FCO 8/3509.

25 'UAE annual review and the future for Dubai', Minute by K. J. Passmore, 17 February 1981, FCO 8/3908.

26 'Iran/UAE relations', Minute by Wright, 18 May 1972, FCO 8/1929.

176 *Conclusion*

27 Telegram from Tehran to the Foreign and Commonwealth Office, No. 478, 30 May 1972, FCO 8/1929.
28 Peter Mangold, *What the British Did: Two Centuries in the Middle East* (London: I. B. Tauris, 2016), p. 263.
29 Letter from Wright to D. J. McCarthy, 5 December 1973, FCO 8/2126.
30 Letter from Given to David Owen, 4 March 1979, FCO 8/3307. Ambassador Given had served as First Secretary and Head of Chancery in Bahrain from 1957 to 1960.
31 Letter from Henderson to the Secretary of State for Foreign and Commonwealth Affairs, 7 March 1972, FCO 8/1892.
32 Clark to D. G. Crawford, 9 January 1975, FCO 8/ 2527.
33 Minute by Weir, 24 April 1978, FCO 8/3140.
34 Letter from Brant to the Secretary of State for Foreign and Commonwealth Affairs, 29 June 1981, FCO 8/4106.
35 'Iran: Post-mortem', Minute by J. C. Moberly, 22 February 1979, FCO 8/3377.
36 Douglas Hurd, 'Britain and the Gulf', in *Arab Paper Number 5: Oil and Security in the Arab Gulf* (London: Arab Research Centre, 1980), p. 38.
37 'UAE attitudes to the United Kingdom', Memorandum attached to Roberts' letter to Miers, 1 March 1981, FCO 8/3820.
38 Christopher Davidson has noted that Abu Dhabi has purchased French military equipment 'owing to Sheikh Zayed bin Sultan al-Nahyan's initially poor experiences with British manufactures in the 1960s and 1970s compared to more straightforward transactions with French companies' (Christopher M. Davidson, *Abu Dhabi: Oil and Beyond* (London: Hurst and Company, 2009), p. 143). In his memoirs, moreover, former British Ambassador to Kuwait, Sir Archie Lamb, wrote: 'I remember two outstanding occasions when "experienced" businessmen put me in my place. I went to a Rover factory and explained the ever-increasing market for Landrovers opening generally but particularly in the Trucial States. I was told that the Rover Company was content with the level of its Landrover production and would not produce more. Rover lost the market to the Japanese Toyota Landcruiser. I went to Leicester to talk to some people in the wool trade and explained to them the demand for fine woollen cloth for the bisht (the Arab cloak) and other apparel in the Gulf. "Now lad", said he-who-knew-all, "I've been in this business for forty years and I've never sold wool to the Gulf". He refused to admit it was time he started. The motor industry let us down again by refusing to instal air-conditioning and cassette players as standard fittings in British cars for the Gulf, preferring to offer them as "optional extras" . . . . Again the Japanese provided what the market demanded' (Sir Archie Lamb, *A Long Way from Swansea: A Memoir* (Clunderwen: Starborn Books, 2003), pp. 76–7).
39 Letter from Henderson to Douglas-Home, 8 January 1973, FCO 8/2079.
40 Ibid.
41 'UK/Qatar trade', Minute by Wright, 6 March 1973, FCO 8/2085.
42 Record of a meeting between the Prime Minister and Sultan Qaboos of Oman in Salalah on 23 April 1981 at noon, PREM 19/757.
43 'UK policy towards Arabia and the Gulf in the wake of the Iran crisis', paper attached to letter from Sir Anthony Parsons to Sir John Wilton, 2 April 1979, FCO 8/3281.
44 Letter from Lucas to D. E. Tatham, 12 November 1979, FCO 8/3287.
45 'Visit to the Middle East', Minute from John Nott to Margaret Thatcher, 2 April 1981, PREM 19/467; Letter from Miers to Lucas, 29 May 1981, FCO 8/3802; Annex A: UK objectives, attached to a draft letter from the Permanent-Under Secretary, FCO, to Sir Robert Armstrong (undated), FCO 8/3834; Stephen Fay, 'Mrs Thatcher treads warily in the Gulf', *Times*, 20 April 1981, http://find.galegroup.com/ttda/infomark.do?&source=gale&prodId=TTDA&userGroupName=unihull&tabID=T003&docPage=article&searchType=AdvancedSearchForm&docId=CS18188436&type=multipage&contentSet=LTO&version=1.0 [accessed 10 December 2016]; James Wightman,

'Gulf "neglect" to end, says Thatcher', *Daily Telegraph*, 20 April 1981, p. 1, *The Telegraph Historical Archive*, tinyurl.galegroup.com/tinyurl/4Rtrk8 [accessed 27 February 2017].

46 'UK's relations with Saudi Arabia and Bahrain', Oral evidence taken before the Foreign Affairs Committee Tuesday, 22 January 2013, p. 20, https://publications.parliament.uk/pa/cm201213/cmselect/cmfaff/c917-i/c91701.pdf [accessed 29 August 2017].

47 Note by HM Ambassador Jedda of his conversation with King Faisal in Riyadh on 27 November 1971, cited in Richard Schofield (ed.), *Arabian Boundaries: New Documents, 1966–75: Volume 12, 1971* (Cambridge: Cambridge University Press, 2009), pp. 501–02.

48 'UAE attitudes to the United Kingdom', Memorandum attached to Roberts' letter to Miers, 1 March 1981, FCO 8/3820.

49 During her press conference in Kuwait on 27 September 1981, Thatcher remarked that 'We have in the Gulf a tremendous feeling of friendship for those countries and we know that that is reflected here. We therefore wish to be here more to demonstrate our support for the Gulf Cooperation Council, to have closer trading links, and in general to be even closer friends' (Telegram from Kuwait to the Foreign and Commonwealth Office, No. 398, 28 September 1981, PREM 19/535).

50 At the end of 1979, K. J. Passmore of the FCO's Middle East Department recorded: 'All these Gulf states will be highly alarmed at Russian intervention in Afghanistan and will fear for their own safety' ('Briefing on Afghanistan', Minute by Passmore, 31 December 1979, FCO 8/3291).

51 In his annual review for 1980, the British Ambassador to Iraq, S. L. Egerton, observed: 'An unnecessary war has been unleashed in a region still adjusting cautiously to the consequences of the Shah's downfall' (Letter from Egerton to Lord Carrington, 31 December 1980, FCO 8/4126).

52 Tore T. Petersen, *Anglo–American Policy Toward the Persian Gulf, 1978–1985: Power, Influence, and Restraint* (Brighton: Sussex Academic Press, 2015), p. 127.

53 Letter from Private Secretary to William Waldegrave, 14 August 1990, PREM 19/3076.

54 'Qatar – Bahrain – Abu Dhabi – Dubai Emirates', Minute from Clark to the Prime Minister, 19 August 1990, PREM 19/3076.

55 Letter from Thatcher to His Highness Sheikh Jabir Al Ahmad Al Sabah, 22 November 1990, PREM 19/3213.

56 Jeffrey R. Macris, *The Politics and Security of the Gulf: Anglo–American Hegemony and the Shaping of a Region* (London and New York: Routledge, 2010), p. 190.

57 See Zoe Holman, 'On the side of decency and democracy: The history of British-Bahraini relations and transnational contestation', in Ala'a Shehabi and Marc Owen (eds.), *Bahrain's Uprising: Resistance and Repression in the Gulf* (London: Zed Books, 2015), pp. 174–206; Clive Jones and John Stone, 'Britain and the Arabian Gulf: New perspectives on strategic influence', *International Relations*, 13, 1 (1997), pp. 1–24.

58 Rosemary Hollis, *Britain and the Middle East in the 9/11 Era* (London: The Royal Institute for International Affairs, 2010), p. 165. When asked in 1999 to reflect on how Britain's 'withdrawal' from the Gulf had affected the region, a long-standing British adviser to the Amir of Bahrain responded: 'British withdrawal? What withdrawal? We're still here!' (Holman, 'On the side of decency and democracy', p. 185).

Appendix 1
British Ambassadors to the Gulf States

Bahrain

CRAWFORD, David Gordon (1928–1981)

Joined Diplomatic Service, 1956; FO, 1956; Middle East Centre for Arab Studies, 1957–1959; Taiz, 1959; Bahrain, 1959–1962; FO, 1962–1964; First Secretary New York, 1964–1967; First Secretary and Head of Chancery, Amman, 1967–1969; Consul-General, Oman, 1969–1971; Head of Accommodation and Services Department, FCO, 1971–1974; Ambassador to Qatar, 1974–1978; Consul-General, Atlanta, 1978–1981; Ambassador to Bahrain, 1981.

GIVEN, Edward Ferguson (1919–2006)

Entered HM Foreign Service, 1946; served at Paris, Rangoon, Bahrain, Bordeaux, Office of Political Adviser to C-in-C Far East, Singapore, Moscow, Beirut; Ambassador to United Republic of Cameroon and Republic of Equatorial Guinea, 1972–1975, to Bahrain, 1975–1979.

LAMB, Robin David (b. 1948)

Joined FCO, 1971; language training, Middle East Centre for Arab Studies, 1974–1975; Second Secretary, Jedda, 1979–1982; First Secretary: Riyadh, 1985–1987; Head, Political Section, Cairo, 1993–1996; Counsellor and Deputy Head of Mission, Kuwait, 2001–2003; Ambassador, Bahrain, 2003–2006; Consul-General, Basra, April–Aug. 2006.

STIRLING, Sir Alexander John Dickson (1926–2014)

Entered Foreign Office, 1951; Lebanon, 1952; British Embassy, Cairo, 1952–1956 (Oriental Sec., 1955–1956); FO, 1956–1959; First Secretary, British Embassy, Baghdad, 1959–1962; First Secretary and Consul, Amman, 1962–1964; First Secretary, British Embassy, Santiago, 1965–1967; FO, 1967–1969; British Political Agent, Bahrain, 1969–1971, Ambassador, 1971–1972; Counsellor, Beirut, 1972–1975; Ambassador to Iraq, 1977–1980, to the Tunisian Republic, 1981–1984, to the Sudan, 1984–1986.

TESH, Robert Mathieson (1922–2002)

HM Foreign Service, 1947: New Delhi, 1948–1950; FO, 1950–1953 and 1957–1960; Delegation to NATO, Paris, 1953–1955; Beirut, 1955–1957; Bangkok, 1960–1964; Deputy High Commissioner, Ghana, 1965–1966; Lusaka, 1966; Consul-General British Interests Section, Canadian Embassy, Cairo, 1966–1967; Counsellor, British Embassy, Cairo, 1968; Head of Defence Department, FCO, 1970–1972; Ambassador to: Bahrain, 1972–1975; the Democratic Republic of Vietnam, 1976; the Socialist Republic of Vietnam, 1976–1978.

TOMKYS, Sir (William) Roger (b. 1937)

Entered Foreign Service, 1960; Middle East Centre for Arab Studies, 1960; 3rd Secretary, Amman, 1962; 2nd Secretary, FCO, 1964; 1st Secretary, Head of Chancery, Benghazi, 1967; Planning Staff, FCO, 1969; Head of Chancery, Athens, 1972; Counsellor, seconded to Cabinet Office, 1975; Head of Near East and North Africa Department, FCO, 1977–1980; Counsellor, Rome, 1980–81; Ambassador: to Bahrain, 1981–1984; to Syria, 1984–1986; Assistant Under-Secretary of State and Principal Finance Officer, FCO, 1987–1989; Deputy Under Secretary of State, FCO, 1989–1990; High Commissioner, Kenya, 1990–1992; Chairman, Arab–British Chamber of Commerce, 2004–2010.

WALKER, Sir Harold Berners (b. 1932)

Assistant Political Agent, Dubai, 1958; Foreign Office, 1960; Principal Instructor, Middle East Centre for Arab Studies, 1963; First Secretary, Cairo, 1964; Head of Chancery and Consul, Damascus, 1966; Foreign Office (later FCO), 1967; First Secretary (Commercial), Washington, 1970; Counsellor, Jedda, 1973; Deputy Head, Personnel Operations Department, FCO, 1975–1976, Head of Department, 1976–1978; Ambassador to Bahrain, 1979–1981, to United Arab Emirates, 1981–1986, to Ethiopia, 1986–1990, to Iraq, 1990–1991.

Kuwait

CAMBRIDGE, Sydney John Guy (1928–2014)

Entered HM Diplomatic Service, Sept. 1952; Oriental Secretary, British Embassy, Jedda, 1953–1956; Foreign Office, 1956–1960; First Secretary, UK Delegation to United Nations, at New York, 1960–1964; Head of Chancery, British Embassy, Djakarta, 1964–1966; FO, 1966–1970; Counsellor, British Embassy, Rome, 1970–1973; Head of Financial Relations Department, FCO, 1973–1975; Counsellor, British High Commission, Nicosia, 1975–1977; Ambassador: to Kuwait, 1977–1982; to Morocco, 1982–1984.

LAMB, Sir Albert Thomas, (Sir Archie) (b. 1921)

Embassy, Rome, 1947–1950; Consulate-General, Genoa, 1950; Embassy, Bucharest, 1950–1953; FO 1953–1955; Middle East Centre for Arabic

Studies, 1955–1957; Political Residency, Bahrain, 1957–1961; FO 1961–1965; Embassy, Kuwait, 1965; Political Agent in Abu Dhabi, 1965–1968; Inspector, 1968–1970, Senior Inspector, 1970–1973, Assistant Under-Secretary of State and Chief Inspector, FCO, 1973–1974; Ambassador to Kuwait, 1974–1977; Ambassador to Norway, 1978–1980.

WILTON, Sir (Arthur) John (1921–2011)

Entered HM Diplomatic Service, 1947; served Lebanon, Egypt, Gulf Sheikhdoms, Romania, and Yugoslavia; Director, Middle East Centre for Arabic Studies, 1960–1965; Deputy High Commissioner, Aden, 1966–1967; Ambassador to Kuwait, 1970–1974; Assistant Under-Secretary of State, FCO, 1974–1976; Ambassador to Saudi Arabia, 1976–1979.

Qatar

BRANT, Colin Trevor (1929–2015)

Middle East Centre Arab Studies, Lebanon, 1953–1954; Bahrain, 1954; Amman, 1954–1956; FO, 1956–1959; Stockholm, 1959–1961; Cairo, 1961–1964; FO, 1965–1967; Head of Chancery and Consul, Tunis, 1967–1968; Assistant Head, Oil Dept, FCO, 1969–1971; Counsellor (Commercial), Caracas, 1971–1973; Counsellor (Energy), Washington, 1973–1978; Ambassador to Qatar, 1978–1981; FCO Fellow, St Antony's College, Oxford, 1981–1982; Consul General, and Director Trade Promotion for South Africa, Johannesburg, 1982–1987.

CRAWFORD, David Gordon (1928–1981)

(see entry under Bahrain)

DAY, Stephen Peter (b. 1938)

Political Officer, Western Aden Protectorate, 1961, transferred to FO, 1965; Senior Political Officer, South Arabian Federation, 1964–1967; FO, 1967–1970; First Secretary, Office of C-in-C, Far East, Singapore, 1970–1971; First Secretary (Press), UK Mission to UN, NY, 1971–1975; FCO, 1976–1977; Counsellor, Beirut, 1977–1978; Consul-General, Edmonton, 1979–1981; Ambassador to Qatar, 1981–1984; Head of Middle East Department, FCO, 1984–1987; attached to Household of the Prince of Wales, 1986; Ambassador to Tunisia, 1987–1992; Senior British Trade Commissioner, Hong Kong, 1992–1993; Director, Council for Advancement of Arab–British Understanding, 1993–1994.

HENDERSON, Edward Firth (1917–1995)

Served in Arab Legion, 1945–1947; with Petroleum Concessions Ltd, in Arabian Gulf, 1948–1956; Foreign Service, 1956; served in Middle East posts and in the Foreign Office; Political Agent, Qatar, 1969–1971; Ambassador, Qatar, 1971–1974.

United Arab Emirates

McCARTHY, (Daniel) Donal John (1922–1997)

Foreign Office, 1946; Middle East Centre for Arab Studies, 1947–1948; 3rd and 2nd Sec., British Embassy, Jedda, 1948–1951; 2nd Sec., Political Division, British Middle East Office, 1951–1955; 1st Secretary, FO, 1955–1958; Assistant Political Agent, Kuwait, 1958–1960; British High Commissioner, Ottawa, 1960–1963; FO, 1963–1964; Counsellor, British High Commissioner, Aden, and Political Adviser to C-in-C Middle East, 1964–1967; Head of Aden Department, FO, 1967–1968, of Arabian Department, FCO, 1968–70; Imperial Defence College, 1970–1971; Minister (Economic and Social Affairs), UK Mission to UN, 1971–1973; Ambassador to United Arab Emirates, 1973–1977; FCO, 1978–1979.

ROBERTS, Sir David (Arthur) (1924–1987)

HM Foreign Service, Dec. 1947; served: Baghdad, 1948–1949; Tokyo, 1949–1951; FO, 1951–1953; Alexandria, 1953–1955; Khartoum, 1955–1958; FO, 1958–1960; Dakar, 1960–1961 (Chargé d'Affairs at Bamako and at Lomé during same period); FO, 1962–1963; Damascus, 1963–1966; Political Agent in the Trucial States, Dubai, 1966–1968; Head of Accommodation Department, FCO, 1968–1971; High Commissioner in Barbados, 1971–1973; Ambassador to Syria, 1973–1976; High Commissioner in Sierra Leone, 1976–1977; Ambassador to: the United Arab Emirates, 1977–1981; Lebanon, 1981–1983; Director-General, Middle East Association, 1983–1985.

TREADWELL, Charles James (1920–2010)

Sudan Political Service and Sudan Judiciary, 1945–1955; FO, 1955–1957; British High Commissioner, Lahore, 1957–1960; HM Embassy, Ankara, 1960–1962; HM Embassy, Jedda, 1963–1964; British Deputy High Commissioner for Eastern Nigeria, 1965–1966; Head of Joint Information Services Department, Foreign Office/Commonwealth Office, 1966–1968; British Political Agent, Abu Dhabi, 1968–1971; Ambassador, United Arab Emirates, 1971–1973; High Commissioner to Bahamas, 1973–1975; Ambassador to Oman, 1975–1979.

WALKER, Sir Harold Berners (b. 1932)

(see entry under Bahrain)

Appendix 2
Heads of the FCO's Arabian/Middle East Department

ACLAND, Sir Antony Arthur (b. 1930)

Joined Diplomatic Service, 1953; Middle East Centre for Arab Studies, 1954; Dubai, 1955; Kuwait, 1956; FO, 1958–1962; Assistant Private Secretary to Secretary of State, 1959–1962; UK Mission to UN, 1962–1966; Head of Chancery, UK Mission, Geneva, 1966–1968; FCO, 1968, Head of Arabian Department, 1970–1972; Principal Private Sec. to Foreign and Commonwealth Sec., 1972–1975; Ambassador to Luxembourg, 1975–1977, to Spain, 1977–1979; Deputy Under-Secretary of State, FCO, 1980–1982, Permanent Under-Secretary of State, FCO, and Head of Diplomatic Service, 1982–1986; Ambassador to Washington, 1986–1991.

LUCAS, Hon. Ivor Thomas Mark (1927–2018)

Entered Diplomatic Service, 1951; Middle East Centre for Arab Studies, Lebanon, 1952; 3rd, later 2nd Secretary, Bahrain, Sharjah and Dubai, 1952–1956; FO, 1956–1959; 1st Secretary, Karachi, 1959–1962; 1st Secretary and Head of Chancery, Tripoli, 1962–1966; FO, 1966–1968; Counsellor, Aden, 1968–1969 (Chargé d'Affaires, Aug. 1968–Feb. 1969); Deputy High Commissioner, Kaduna, Nigeria, 1969–1971; Counsellor, Copenhagen, 1972–1975; Head of Middle East Department, FCO, 1975–1979; Ambassador to Oman, 1979–1981, to Syria, 1982–1984.

MIERS, Sir Henry David Alastair Capel (b. 1937)

Private Secretary to Minister of State, FO, 1968; Paris, 1972; Counsellor, Tehran, 1977–1979; Head, Middle Eastern Department, FCO, 1980–1983; Ambassador to Lebanon, 1983–1985; Assistant Under-Secretary of State, FCO, 1986–1989; Ambassador to Greece, 1989–1993, to Netherlands, 1993–1996.

MUNRO, Sir Alan Gordon (b. 1935)

Middle East Centre for Arab Studies, 1958–1960; British Embassy, Beirut, 1960–1962; FO, 1963–1965; Head of Chancery, Benghazi, 1965–1966 and Tripoli, 1966–1968; FO, 1968–1973; Consul (Commercial), 1973–1974, Consul-Gen., 1974–1977, Rio de Janeiro; Head of East African Department, FCO,

1977–1978; Head of Middle East Department, FCO, 1979; Regional Marketing Director (Middle East), MoD, 1981–1983; Ambassador to Algeria, 1984–1987; Deputy Under-Secretary of State, Middle East/Africa, FCO, 1987–1989; Ambassador to Saudi Arabia, 1989–1993.

WRIGHT, Patrick Richard Henry (b. 1931)

Middle East Centre for Arab Studies, 1956–1957; Third Secretary, British Embassy, Beirut, 1958–1960; Private Secretary to Ambassador and later First Secretary, British Embassy, Washington, 1960–1965; Private Secretary to Permanent Under-Secretary, FO, 1965–1967; First Secretary and Head of Chancery, Cairo, 1967–1970; Deputy Political Resident, Bahrain, 1971–1972; Head of Middle East Department, FCO, 1972–1974; Private Secretary (Overseas Affairs) to Prime Minister, 1974–1977; Ambassador to: Luxembourg, 1977–1979, Syria, 1979–1981; Deputy Under-Secretary of State, FCO and Chairman, Joint Intelligence Committee, 1982–1984; Ambassador to Saudi Arabia, 1984–1986; Permanent Under-Secretary of State and Head of Diplomatic Service, 1986–1991.

WEIR, Sir Michael Scott (1925–2006)

Served RAF (Flt Lt), 1944–1947; subsequently HM Diplomatic Service; Foreign Office, 1950; Political Agent, Trucial States, 1952–1954; FO, 1954–1956; Consul, San Francisco, 1956–1958; 1st Secretary: Washington, 1958–1961; Cairo, 1961–1963; FO, 1963–1968; Counsellor, Head of Arabian Department, 1966; Deputy Political Resident, Persian Gulf, Bahrain, 1968–1971; Head of Chancery, UK Mission to UN, NY, 1971–73; Assistant Under-Secretary of State, FCO, 1974–1979; Ambassador, Cairo, 1979–1985.

Appendix 3
Secretaries of State for Foreign and Commonwealth Affairs

CALLAGHAN, (Leonard) James (1912–2005)

Parliamentary and Financial Secretary, Admiralty, 1950–1951; Opposition Spokesman: Transport, 1951–1953, Fuel and Power, 1953–1955, Colonial Affairs, 1956–1961; Shadow Chancellor, 1961–1964; Chancellor of the Exchequer, 1964–1967; Home Secretary, 1967–1970; Shadow Home Secretary, 1970–1971; Opposition Spokesman on Employment, 1971–1972; Shadow Foreign Secretary, 1972–1974; Secretary of State for Foreign and Commonwealth Affairs, 1974–1976; Minister of Overseas Development, 1975–1976; Prime Minister and First Lord of the Treasury, 1976–1979; Leader, Labour Party, 1976–1980; Leader of the Opposition, 1979–1980.

CARRINGTON, Peter Alexander Rupert, 6th Baron (1919–2018)

Parliamentary Secretary, Ministry of Defence, Oct. 1954–Nov. 1956; High Commissioner for the UK in Australia, Nov. 1956–Oct. 1959; First Lord of the Admiralty, 1959–1963; Minister without Portfolio and Leader of the House of Lords, 1963–1964; Leader of the Opposition, House of Lords, 1964–1970 and 1974–1979; Secretary of State: for Defence, 1970–1974; for Energy, 1974; for Foreign and Commonwealth Affairs, 1979–1982; Minister of Aviation Supply, 1971–1974. Chairman, Conservative Party Organisation, 1972–1974; Secretary-General, NATO, 1984–1988.

DOUGLAS-HOME, Sir Alexander (Alec) Frederick (1903–1995)

Parliamentary Private Secretary to the Prime Minister, 1937–1940; Joint Parliamentary Under-Secretary, Foreign Office, May–July 1945; Minister of State, Scottish Office, 1951–April 1955; Secretary of State for Commonwealth Relations, 1955–1960; Deputy Leader of the House of Lords, 1956–1957; Leader of the House of Lords, and Lord President of the Council, 1959–1960; Secretary of State for Foreign Affairs, 1960–1963; Prime Minister and First Lord of the Treasury, Oct. 1963–Oct. 1964; Leader of the Opposition, Oct. 1964–July 1965; Secretary of State for Foreign and Commonwealth Affairs, 1970–1974.

HURD, Douglas Richard (b. 1930)

HM Diplomatic Service, 1952–1966; served in: Peking, 1954–1956; UK Mission to UN, 1956–1960; Private Secretary to Permanent Under-Sec. of State, FO, 1960–1963; Rome, 1963–1966. Joined Conservative Research Department, 1966; Head of Foreign Affairs Section, 1968; Private Secretary to Leader of the Opposition, 1968–1970; Political Secretary to Prime Minister, 1970–1974. MP (C): Mid-Oxon, Feb. 1974–1983; Witney, 1983–1997. Opposition Spokesman on European Affairs, 1976–1979; Minister of State, FCO, 1979–1983; Minister of State, Home Office, 1983–1984; Secretary of State for Northern Ireland, 1984–1985, for Home Department, 1985–1989; Secretary of State for Foreign and Commonwealth Affairs, 1989–1995.

OWEN, David Anthony Llewellyn (b. 1938)

Principal Private Secretary to Minister of Defence, Administration, 1967; Parliamentary Under-Secretary of State for Defence, for Royal Navy, 1968–1970; Opposition Defence Spokesman, 1970–1972; Parliamentary Under-Secretary of State, DHSS, 1974; Minister of State: DHSS, 1974–1976; FCO, 1976–1977; Secretary of State for Foreign and Commonwealth Affairs, 1977–1979.

Appendix 4
British Prime Ministers

CALLAGHAN, (Leonard) James (1912–2005)

See under Secretaries of State for Foreign and Commonwealth Relations.

HEATH, Edward (Richard George) (1916–2005)

Lord Privy Seal, with Foreign Office responsibilities, 1960–1963; Secretary of State for Industry, Trade, Regional Development and President of the Board of Trade, Oct. 1963–Oct. 1964; Leader of the Conservative Party, 1965–1975; Leader of the Opposition, 1965–1970; Prime Minister and First Lord of the Treasury, 1970–1974; Leader of the Opposition, 1974–1975.

THATCHER, Margaret Hilda (1925–2013)

Secretary of State for Education and Science, 1970–1974; Leader of the Conservative Party, 1975–1990; Leader of the Opposition, 1975–1979; Prime Minister and First Lord of the Treasury, 1979–1990.

WILSON, (James) Harold (1916–1995)

Leader, Labour Party, 1963–1976; Leader of the Opposition, 1963–1964, 1970–1974; Prime Minister and First Lord of the Treasury, 1964–1970, 1974–1976.

Appendix 5
Gulf Rulers

Bahrain

HH Sheikh Isa bin Salman Al-Khalifah (1932–1999)

Eldest son of the late Ruler HH Sheikh Salman bin Hamid; appointed Heir Apparent, 1958; Amir of Bahrain, 1961–1999; decorations: KCMG, 1974.

Kuwait

HH Sheikh Jabir Al-Ahmad Al-Sabah (1926–2006)

Third son of Sheikh Ahmad Al-Jabir, Ruler of Kuwait, 1921–1950; representative of HH the Ruler with the Kuwait Oil Company and Aminoil, 1956–1959; Civil Service Commission and General Oil Affairs Office, 1959–1962; Ministry of Finance and Economy, 1962–1963; Minister of Finance and Industry, 1963–1965; Prime Minister, 1965–1977; named Heir Apparent, 1966; Amir of Kuwait, 1977–2006.

HH Sheikh Sabah Al-Salim Al-Sabah (1913–1977)

Son of Shaikh Salim (r. 1917–1921) and half-brother Shaikh Abdullah (r. 1950–1965); head of the Police Department until 1939–1959; head of the Health Department, 1959–1961; Minister of Foreign Affairs and Deputy Prime Minister, 1962; appointed Heir Apparent, 30 October 1962; Prime Minister, 1963–1965; Ruler of Kuwait, 1965–1977.

Qatar

HH Sheikh Khalifah bin Hamad Al-Thani (1934–2016)

Deputy Amir, 1960; Chairman, Qatar and Dubai Monetary Agency, 1966; Minister of Foreign Affairs and President of the Council of Ministers, 1971; Minister of Finance and Chairman of the Council for State Investment, 1972; Amir of Qatar, 1972–1995; deposed by his son, Sheikh Hamad bin Khalifah, 27 June 1995.

United Arab Emirates

HH Sheikh Rashid bin Said Al-Maktoum (1910–1990)

Ruler of Dubai, 1958–1990; Vice-President of the United Arab Emirates, 1971–1990; Prime Minister of the United Arab Emirates, 1979–1990.

HH Sheikh Zaid bin Sultan Al-Nahyan (1918[1]–2004)

Youngest brother of Sheikh Shakhbut, Ruler of Abu Dhabi, 1927–1966; Governor of Eastern Province, Abu Dhabi, until 1966; became Ruler of Abu Dhabi following the deposition of Sheikh Shakhbut in August 1966; President of the United Arab Emirates, 1971–2004.

Note

1 Sheikh Zaid's exact date of birth is unknown, although it is widely accepted that he was born in 1918 (*With United Strength: HH Shaikh Zayid Bin Sultan al Nahyan: The Leader and the Nation* (Abu Dhabi: Emirates Center for Strategic Studies and Research, 2005), p. 63).

Bibliography

Archival sources

The National Archives, Kew

Board of Trade

BT 241   Commercial Relations and Export Division: Registered Files

British Council

BW 180   Registered Files, Qatar

Cabinet Office

CAB 128   Cabinet Minutes
CAB 133   Cabinet Office: Commonwealth and International Conferences and Ministerial Visits to and from the UK: Minutes and Papers
CAB 134   Cabinet: Miscellaneous Committees: Minutes and Papers
CAB 148   Cabinet Defence and Oversea Policy Committees and Sub-committees: Minutes and Papers
CAB 186   Cabinet Office: Central Intelligence Machinery: Joint Intelligence Committee: Memoranda

Ministry of Defence

DEFE 24   Defence Secretariat Branches and their Predecessors: Registered Files
DEFE 69   Ministry of Defence (Navy): Registered Files and Branch Folders
DEFE 70   Ministry of Defence (Army): Registered Files and Branch Folders

Foreign Office/Foreign and Commonwealth Office

FCO 8   Arabian Department and Middle East Department: Registered Files
FCO 82   North America Department: Registered Files
FCO 93   Near East and North Africa Department: Registered Files
FO 371   Political Departments: General Correspondence

190 *Bibliography*

Prime Minister's Office

PREM 15	Correspondence and Papers, 1970–1974
PREM 16	Correspondence and Papers, 1974–1979
PREM 19	Correspondence and Papers, 1979–1997

Treasury

T 225	Treasury: Defence Policy and Materiel Division: Registered Files
T 317	Overseas Development Divisions and Successors
T 639	HM Treasury: Private Office of the Chancellor of the Exchequer: Geoffrey Howe's records

Churchill Archives Centre, Cambridge

British Diplomatic Oral History Programme

Hull History Centre, Hull

Papers of Sir Patrick Wall

Margaret Thatcher Foundation

Carter Library documents

Lyndon Baines Johnson Library, Austin

National Security File, Head of State Correspondence File

United States National Archives, College Park, Maryland

| RG 59 | Department of State Records: Subject-Numeric Files, 1970–1973; Electronic Telegrams, 1973, 1978, and 1979 |
| RG 273 | Records of the National Security Council: National Security Decision Memorandum |

Published primary documents

Aitchison, C. U., *Treaties and Engagements Relating to Arabia and the Persian Gulf* (Gerrards Cross: Archive Editions, 1987)

Ashton, S. R. and Wm. Roger Louis (eds.), *East of Suez and the Commonwealth: Parts 1 and II* (London: HMSO, 2004)

Burdett, A. L. P. (ed.), *Records of the Emirates, 1966–1971: Volume 1: 1966* (Slough: Archive Editions, 2002)

Burdett, A. L. P. (ed.), *Records of the Emirates, 1966–1971: Volume 2: 1967* (Slough: Archive Editions, 2002)

Burdett, A. L. P. (ed.), *Records of the Emirates, 1966–1971: Volume 3: 1968* (Slough: Archive Editions, 2002)
Burdett, A. L. P. (ed.), *Records of the Emirates, 1966–1971: Volume 4: 1969* (Slough: Archive Editions, 2002)
Burdett, A. L. P. (ed.), *Records of the Emirates, 1966–1971: Volume 5: 1970* (Slough: Archive Editions, 2002)
Burdett, A. L. P. (ed.), *Records of the Emirates, 1966–1971: Volume 6: 1971* (Slough: Archive Editions, 2002)
Burdett, A. L. P. (ed.), *Records of Qatar, 1961–1965: 1965* (Slough: Archive Editions, 1997)
Foreign Affairs Committee (House of Commons)
Foreign Office Annual Reports from Arabia, 1930–1960: Iraq, Jordan, Kuwait, Persian Gulf, Saudi Arabia, Yemen (London: Archive Editions, 1993)
Foreign Relations of the United States, 1969–76: Volume XXV: Arab-Israeli Crisis and War, 1973 (Washington, DC: United States Government Printing Office, 2011)
Foreign Relations of the United States, 1969–76: Volume XXXVI: Energy Crisis, 1969–74 (Washington, DC: United States Government Printing Office, 2011)
Foreign Relations of the United States, 1977–1980: Volume I: Foundations of Foreign Policy (Washington, DC: United States Government Printing Office, 2014)
Foreign Relations of the United States, 1977–80: Volume II, Human Rights and Humanitarian Affairs (Washington, DC: United States Government Printing Office, 2013)
Foreign Relations of the United States, 1977–80: Volume XVIII: Middle East Region; Arabian Peninsula (Washington, DC: United States Government Printing Office, 2015)
Hamilton, Keith and Patrick Salmon (eds.), *Documents on British Policy Overseas: Series III, Volume IV: The Year of Europe: America, Europe and the Energy Crisis, 1972–1974* (London and New York: Routledge, 2006)
Parliamentary Debates (Commons), 1970–1, Volume 812
Schofield, Richard (ed.), *Arabian Boundaries: New Documents, 1966–75: Volume 8, 1969* (Cambridge: Cambridge University Press, 2009)
Schofield, Richard (ed.), *Arabian Boundaries: New Documents, 1966–75: Volume 10, 1970* (Cambridge: Cambridge University Press, 2009)
Schofield, Richard (ed.), *Arabian Boundaries: New Documents, 1966–75: Volume 12, 1971* (Cambridge: Cambridge University Press, 2009)
Schofield, Richard (ed.), *Arabian Boundaries: New Documents, 1966–75: Volume 13, 1972* (Cambridge: Cambridge University Press, 2009)
Schofield, Richard (ed.), *Arabian Boundaries: New Documents, 1966–75: Volume 14, 1973* (Cambridge: Cambridge University Press, 2009)
Schofield, Richard (ed.), *Arabian Boundaries: New Documents, 1966–75: Volume 15, 1974* (Cambridge: Cambridge University Press, 2009)
Schofield, Richard (ed.), *Arabian Boundaries: New Documents, 1966–75: Volume 16, 1975* (Cambridge: Cambridge University Press, 2009)
Smith, Richard, Patrick Salmon, and Stephen Twigge (eds.), *Documents on British Policy Overseas: Series III, Volume VIII: The Invasion of Afghanistan and UK-Soviet Relations, 1979–82* (London and New York: Routledge, 2012)
Statement on the Defence Estimates 1966: Part I: The Defence Review (London: HMSO, 1966), Cmnd. 2901
Treaty of Friendship Between the United Kingdom of Great Britain and Northern Ireland and the State of Bahrain, 3 Sept. 1971 (London: HMSO, 1972), Cmnd. 4828

Treaty of Friendship Between the United Kingdom of Great Britain and Northern Ireland and the State of Qatar, 3 Sept. 1971 (London: HMSO, 1972), Cmnd. 4850

Newspapers

The Daily Telegraph
The Guardian
The Sunday Times
The Times

Autobiographies, memoirs, and diaries

Alam, Asadollah, *The Shah and I: The Confidential Diary of Iran's Royal Court, 1968–77* (London: I. B. Tauris, 2008)
Balfour-Paul, Glencairn, *Bagpipes in Babylon: A Lifetime in the Arab World and Beyond* (London and New York: I. B. Tauris, 2006)
Carrington, Lord, *Reflect on Things Past: The Memoirs of Lord Carrington* (London: Harper Collins, 1988)
Carter, Jimmy, *Keeping the Faith: Memoirs of a President* (London: Harper Collins, 1982)
Hawley, Donald, *Desert Wind and Tropic Storm: An Autobiography* (Wilby: Michael Russell, 2000)
Lamb, Sir Archie, *A Long Way from Swansea: A Memoir* (Clunderwen: Starborn Books, 2003)
Lucas, Ivor, *A Road to Damascus: Mainly Diplomatic Memoirs from the Middle East* (London: The Radcliffe Press, 1997)
Munro, Alan, *Keep the Flag Flying: A Diplomatic Memoir* (London: Gilgamesh Publishing, 2012)
Owen, David, *Time to Declare* (London: Penguin, 1992)
Parsons, Anthony, *The Pride and the Fall: Iran, 1974–1979* (London: Jonathan Cape, 1984)
Parsons, Anthony, *They Say the Lion: Britain's Legacy to the Arabs: A Personal Memoir* (London: Jonathan Cape, 1986)
Renwick, Robin, *A Journey with Margaret Thatcher: Foreign Policy Under the Iron Lady* (London: Biteback Publishing, 2013)
Sick, Gary, *All Fall Down: America's Tragic Encounter with Iran* (Lincoln, NE: iUniverse, 2001)
Thatcher, Margaret, *The Downing Street Years* (London: Harper Collins, 1993)

Books, articles, and chapters

Abir, Mordechai and Aryeh Yodfat, *In the Direction of the Persian Gulf: The Soviet Union and the Persian Gulf* (London: Frank Cass, 1977)
Acharya, Amitav, *U.S. Military Strategy in the Gulf: Origins and Evolution Under the Carter and Reagan Administrations* (Abingdon and New York: Routledge, 2013)
Alhasan, Hasan Tariq, 'The role of Iran in the failed coup of 1981: The IFLB in Bahrain', *The Middle East Journal*, 65, 4 (2011), pp. 603–17
Al-Nahyan, Khalid S. Z., *The Three Islands: Mapping the UAE-Iran Dispute* (London: Royal United Services Institute, 2013)

Alvandi, Roham, 'Muhammad Reza Pahlavi and the Bahrain question, 1968–1970', *British Journal of Middle Eastern Studies*, 37, 2 (2010), pp. 159–77

Alvandi, Roham, 'Nixon, Kissinger, and the Shah: The origins of Iranian primacy in the Persian Gulf', *Diplomatic History*, 36, 2 (2012), pp. 337–72

Alvandi, Roham, *Nixon, Kissinger, and the Shah: The United States and Iran in the Cold War* (Oxford and New York: Oxford University Press, 2014)

Ashton, Nigel John, *Eisenhower, Macmillan, and the Problem of Nasser: Anglo–American Relations and Arab Nationalism, 1955–59* (Basingstoke: Palgrave Macmillan, 1996)

Ashton, S. R., 'Introduction', in S. R. Ashton and Wm. Roger Louis (eds.), *East of Suez and the Commonwealth 1964–1971*, Part I (London: The Stationery Office, 2004)

Axworthy, Michael, *Revolutionary Iran: A History of the Islamic Republic* (London: Penguin, 2014)

Bacevich, Andrew J., *America's War for the Greater Middle East: A Military History* (New York: Random House, 2017)

Balfour-Paul, Glen, 'Britain's informal empire in the Middle East', in Judith M. Brown and Wm. Roger Louis (eds.), *The Oxford History of the Twentieth Century: Volume IV: The Twentieth Century* (Oxford: Oxford University Press, 1999)

Balfour-Paul, Glen, *The End of the Middle East: Britain's Relinquishment of Power in Her Last Three Arab Dependencies* (Cambridge: Cambridge University Press, 1994)

Bamberg, James, *British Petroleum and Global Oil, 1950–1975: The Challenge of Nationalism* (Cambridge: Cambridge University Press, 2000)

Barton, Gregory A., 'Informal empire: The case of Siam and the Middle East', in Alfred W. McCoy, Josep M. Fradera, and Stephen Jacobson (eds.), *Endless Empire: Spain's Retreat, Europe's Eclipse, America's Decline* (Madison, WI: University of Wisconsin Press, 2012)

Barton, Gregory A., *Informal Empire and the Rise of One World Culture* (Basingstoke: Palgrave Macmillan, 2014)

Beaugrand, Claire, 'Deconstructing minorities/majorities in parliamentary Gulf States (Kuwait and Bahrain)', *British Journal of Middle Eastern Studies*, 43, 2 (2016), pp. 234–49

Bermant, Azriel, *Margaret Thatcher and the Middle East* (Cambridge: Cambridge University Press, 2016)

Boyce, D. George, *Decolonisation and the British Empire, 1775–1997* (Basingstoke: Palgrave Macmillan, 1999)

Bradshaw, Tancred, 'The dead hand of the Treasury: The economic and social development of the Trucial States, 1948–60', *Middle Eastern Studies*, 50, 2 (2014), pp. 326–42

Burk, Kathleen and Alec Cairncross, *'Goodbye, Great Britain': The 1976 IMF Crisis* (New Haven and London: Yale University Press, 1992)

Butler, L. J., *Britain and Empire: Adjusting to a Post-Imperial World* (London and New York: I. B. Tauris, 2002),

Cain, P. J. and A. G. Hopkins, *British Imperialism, 1688–2000* (Harlow: Longman, 2002)

Cain, P. J. and A. G. Hopkins, *British Imperialism, 1688–2015*, 3rd edition (London and New York: Routledge, 2016)

Commins, David, *The Gulf States: A Modern History* (London and New York: I. B. Tauris, 2012)

Cross, Colin, *The Fall of the British Empire, 1918–1968* (London: Hodder & Stoughton, 1968)

Crystal, Jill, *Oil and Politics in the Gulf: Rulers and Merchants in Kuwait and Qatar* (Cambridge: Cambridge University Press, 1990)

Daigle, Craig, *The Limits of Détente: The United States, the Soviet Union, and the Arab-Israeli Conflict, 1969–1973* (New Haven and London: Yale University Press, 2012)

Daly, M. W., *The Last of the Great Proconsuls: The Biography of Sir William Luce* (San Diego: Nathan Berg, 2014)
Darwin, John, *Britain and Decolonisation: The Retreat from Empire in the Post War World* (Basingstoke: Palgrave Macmillan, 1988)
Darwin, John, 'British decolonization since 1945: A pattern or a puzzle?' *Journal of Imperial and Commonwealth History*, 12, 2 (1984), pp. 187–209
Darwin, John, 'Britain's withdrawal from East of Suez', in Carl Bridge (ed.), *Munich to Vietnam: Australia's Relations with Britain and the United States Since the 1930s* (Carlton, VIC: Melbourne University Press, 1991)
Darwin, John, 'Decolonization and the end of the British empire', in Robin W. Winks (ed.), *The Oxford History of the British Empire: Vol. V* (Oxford: Oxford University Press, 1999)
Darwin, John, 'Diplomacy and decolonization', in Kent Fedorowich and Martin Thomas (eds.), *International Diplomacy and Colonial Retreat* (London: Frank Cass, 2001)
Darwin, John, *The Empire Project: The Rise and Fall of the British World System, 1830–1970* (Cambridge: Cambridge University Press, 2009)
Darwin, John, *The End of the British Empire: The Historical Debate* (Oxford: Blackwell Publishing, 1991)
Darwin, John, 'Gallagher's empire', in Wm. Roger Louis (ed.), *Yet More Adventures with Britannia: Personalities, Politics and Culture in Britain* (London: I. B. Tauris, 2005)
Darwin, John, 'The geopolitics of decolonization', in Alfred W. McCoy, Josep M. Fradera, and Stephen Jacobson (eds.), *Endless Empire: Spain's Retreat, Europe's Eclipse, America's Decline* (Madison, WI: University of Wisconsin Press, 2012)
Darwin, John, 'Last days of empire', in Miguel Bandeira Jeronimo and Antonio Costa Pinto (eds.), *The Ends of European Colonial Empires: Cases and Comparisons* (Basingstoke: Palgrave Macmillan, 2015)
Darwin, John, 'An undeclared empire: The British in the Middle East, 1918–39', *Journal of Imperial and Commonwealth History*, 27, 2 (1999), pp. 159–76
Darwin, John, *Unfinished Empire: The Global Expansion of Britain* (London: Allen Lane, 2012)
Darwin, John 'Was there a fourth British Empire?', in Martin Lynn (ed.), *The British Empire in the 1950s: Retreat or Revival* (Basingstoke: Palgrave Macmillan, 2006)
Davidson, Christopher M., *Abu Dhabi: Oil and Beyond* (London: Hurst and Company, 2009)
Davidson, Christopher M., *Dubai: The Vulnerability of Success* (London: Hurst and Company, 2008)
Davidson, Christopher, *Shadow Wars: The Secret Struggle for the Middle East* (London: Oneworld, 2017)
Dimitrakis, Panagiotis, *The Secret War in Afghanistan: The Soviet Union, China, and the Role of Anglo–American Intelligence* (London: I. B. Tauris, 2013)
Dimitrakis, Panagiotis, 'The Soviet invasion of Afghanistan: International reactions, military intelligence and British diplomacy', *Middle Eastern Studies*, 48, 4 (2012), pp. 511–36
Donaldson, Frances, *The British Council: The First Fifty Years* (London: Jonathan Cape, 1984)
Doyle, Michael W., *Empires* (Ithaca: Cornell University Press, 1986)
El Mallakh, Ragaei, *Qatar: Development of an Oil Economy* (London: Croom Helm, 1979)
Fieldhouse, D. K., *Black Africa, 1945–1980: Economic Decolonization and Arrested Development* (London: Routledge, 2011)
Fieldhouse, D. K., *Unilever Overseas: The Anatomy of a Multinational, 1895–1965* (London: Croom Helm, 1978)

Friedman, Brandon, 'From union (ittihad) to united (muttahida): The United Arab Emirates, a success born of failure', *Middle Eastern Studies*, 53, 1 (2017), pp. 112–35

Fromherz, Allen J., *Qatar: A Modern History* (London and New York: I. B. Tauris, 2012)

Gallagher, John, *The Decline, Revival and Fall of the British Empire* (Cambridge: Cambridge University Press, 1982)

Gallagher, John and Ronald Robinson, 'The imperialism of free trade', *Economic History Review*, 6, 1 (1953), pp. 1–15

Gallagher, Julia, *Britain and Africa Under Blair: In Pursuit of the Good State* (Manchester: Manchester University Press, 2011)

Gause, F. Gregory, 'British and American policies in the Persian Gulf, 1968–1973', *Review of International Studies*, 11, 4 (1985), pp. 247–73

Gause, F. Gregory, *The International Relations of the Persian Gulf* (Cambridge: Cambridge University Press, 2010)

Go, Julian, *Patterns of Empire: The British and American Empires 1688 to the Present* (New York: Cambridge University Press, 2011)

Guzansky, Yoel, 'Lines drawn in the sand: Territorial disputes and GCC unity', *Middle East Journal*, 70, 4 (2016), pp. 543–59

Hahn, Peter L., *The United States, Great Britain, and Egypt, 1945–1956: Strategy and Diplomacy in the Early Cold War* (Chapel Hill and London: University of North Carolina Press, 1991)

Haight, G. Winthrop, 'Libyan nationalization of British Petroleum Company assets', *International Lawyer*, 6, 3 (1972), pp. 541–7

Halliday, Fred, *Arabia Without Sultans* (Harmondsworth: Penguin, 1979)

Hayman, Mark, 'Economic protectorate in Britain's informal empire: The Trucial Coast during the Second World War', *Journal of Imperial and Commonwealth History*, 46, 2 (2018), pp. 323–44

Heinlein, Frank, *British Government Policy and Decolonisation 1945–1963: Scrutinising the Official Mind* (London: Frank Cass, 2002)

Hollis, Rosemary, *Britain and the Middle East in the 9/11 Era* (London: The Royal Institute for International Affairs, 2010)

Holman, Zoe, 'On the side of decency and democracy: The history of British-Bahraini relations and transnational contestation', in Ala'a Shehabi and Marc Owen (eds.), *Bahrain's Uprising: Resistance and Repression in the Gulf* (London: Zed Books, 2015)

Howard, Rhoda, *Colonialism and Underdevelopment in Ghana* (London: Croom Helm, 1978)

Hurd, Douglas, 'Britain and the Gulf', in *Arab Paper Number 5: Oil and Security in the Arab Gulf* (London: Arab Research Centre, 1980), pp. 37–8

Hyam, Ronald, *Britain's Declining Empire: The Road to Decolonisation, 1918–1968* (Cambridge: Cambridge University Press, 2006)

Hynes, Catherine, *The Year That Never Was: Heath, the Nixon Administration and the Year of Europe* (Dublin: University College Dublin Press, 2009)

Jackson, Ashley, 'Empire and beyond: The pursuit of overseas national interests in the late twentieth century', *English Historical Review*, 123, 499 (2007), pp. 1350–66

Jackson, Ashley, 'Imperial defence in the post-imperial era', in Greg Kennedy (ed.), *Imperial Defence: The Old World Order, 1856–1956* (London and New York: Routledge, 2008)

Jarman, Robert L., *Sabah al-Salim al-Sabah: Amir of Kuwait, 1965–77: A Political Biography* (London: London Centre of Arab Studies, 2002)

Johnson, Rob, *The Iran-Iraq War* (Basingstoke: Palgrave Macmillan, 2010)

Johnson, Rob, 'Out of Arabia: British strategy and the fate of local forces in Aden, South Yemen, and Oman, 1967–76', *International History Review*, 39, 1 (2017), pp. 143–64

Jones, Clive and John Stone, 'Britain and the Arabian Gulf: New perspectives on strategic influence', *International Relations*, 13, 1 (1997), pp. 1–24

Joyce, Miriam, *Bahrain from the Twentieth Century to the Arab Spring* (New York: Palgrave Macmillan, 2012)

Joyce, Miriam, *Kuwait, 1945–1996: An Anglo–American Perspective* (London: Frank Cass, 1998)

Kelly, J. B., *Arabia, the Gulf and the West* (New York: Basic Books, 1991; first published 1980)

Kennedy, Dane, *The Imperial History Wars: Debating the British Empire* (London: Bloomsbury Academic, 2018)

Kennedy, Greg and Christopher Tuck, 'Introduction', in Greg Kennedy and Christopher Tuck (eds.), *British Propaganda and Wars of Empire: Influencing Friend and Foe, 1900–2010* (Farnham: Ashgate Publishing Limited, 2014)

Khalil, Osamah F., *America's Dream Palace: Middle East Expertise and the Rise of the National Security State* (Cambridge, MA: Harvard University Press, 2016)

Lienhardt, Peter, *Shaikhdoms of Eastern Arabia* (Basingstoke: Palgrave Macmillan, 2001)

Long, David E., 'The impact of the Iranian revolution on the Arabian Peninsula and the Gulf States', in John L. Esposito (ed.), *The Iranian Revolution: Its Global Impact* (Miami: University of Florida Press, 1990)

Louis, Wm. Roger, *The British Empire in the Middle East, 1945–1951: Arab Nationalism, the United States and Postwar Imperialism* (Oxford: Clarendon Press, 1984)

Louis, Wm. Roger, 'Britain and the Middle East after 1945', in L. Carl Brown (ed.), *Diplomacy in the Middle East: The International Relations of Regional and Outside Powers* (London: I. B. Tauris, 2004)

Louis, Wm. Roger, 'The British withdrawal from the Gulf, 1967–71', *Journal of Imperial and Commonwealth History*, 31, 1 (2003), pp. 83–108

Louis, Wm. Roger, 'The dissolution of the British Empire', in Judith M. Brown and Wm. Roger Louis (eds.), *The Oxford History of the Twentieth Century: Volume IV: The Twentieth Century* (Oxford: Oxford University Press, 1999)

Louis, Wm. Roger, 'Introduction', in Judith M. Brown and Wm. Roger Louis (eds.), *The Oxford History of the Twentieth Century: Volume IV: The Twentieth Century* (Oxford: Oxford University Press, 1999)

Louis, Wm. Roger, 'Suez and decolonization: Scrambling out of Africa and Asia', in Wm. Roger Louis (ed.), *Ends of British Imperialism: The Scramble for Empire, Suez and Decolonization* (London: I. B. Tauris, 2006)

Louis, Wm. Roger and Ronald Robinson, 'Empire preserv'd: How the Americans put anti-communism before anti-imperialism', in Prasenjit Duara (ed.), *Decolonization: Perspectives from Now and Then* (London: Routledge, 2004)

Louis, Wm. Roger and Ronald Robinson, 'The imperialism of decolonization', *Journal of Imperial and Commonwealth History*, 22, 3 (1994), pp. 462–511

Lynn, Martin, 'Introduction', in Martin Lynn (ed.), *The British Empire in the 1950s: Retreat or Revival* (Basingstoke: Palgrave Macmillan, 2006)

Macris, Jeffrey R., *The Politics and Security of the Gulf: Anglo–American Hegemony and the Shaping of a Region* (London and New York: Routledge, 2010)

Maddy-Weitzman, Bruce, *A Century of Arab Politics: From the Arab Revolt to the Arab Spring* (Lanham, MD: Rowman & Littlefield, 2016)

Maekawa, Ichiro, 'Neo-colonialism reconsidered: A case study of East Africa in the 1960s and 1970s', *Journal of Imperial and Commonwealth History*, 43, 2 (2015), pp. 317–41

Magdoff, Harry, 'Imperialism without colonies', in Roger Own and Bob Sutcliffe (eds.), *Studies in the Theory of Imperialism* (London: Longman, 1972)

Mangold, Peter, *What the British Did: Two Centuries in the Middle East* (London: I. B. Tauris, 2016)

Martell, Gordon, 'Decolonisation after Suez: Retreat or rationalisation?', *Australian Journal of Politics and History*, 46, 3 (2000), pp. 403–17

Martin, Vanessa, *Creating an Islamic State: Khomeini and the Making of a New Iran* (London and New York: I. B. Tauris, 2010)

Matthiesen, Toby, *The Other Saudis: Shiism, Dissent and Sectarianism* (New York: Cambridge University Press, 2015)

Mawby, Spencer, *British Policy in Aden and the Protectorates 1955–67: Last Outpost of a Middle East Empire* (London and New York: Routledge, 2005)

Mawby, Spencer, *The Transformation and Decline of the British Empire: Decolonisation After the First World War* (Basingstoke: Palgrave Macmillan, 2015)

McCourt, David M., 'What was Britain's "East of Suez role"? Reassessing the withdrawal, 1964–1968', *Diplomacy and Statecraft*, 20, 3 (2009), pp. 453–72

McGlinchey, Stephen, *US Arms Policies Towards the Shah's Iran* (London and New York: Routledge, 2014)

McGlinchey, Stephen and Andrew Moran, 'Beyond the blank cheque: Arming Iran during the Ford administration', *Diplomacy and Statecraft*, 27, 3 (2016), pp. 523–44

McGlinchey, Stephen and Robert W. Murray, 'Jimmy Carter and the sale of the AWACS to Iran in 1977', *Diplomacy and Statecraft*, 28, 2 (2017), pp. 254–76

McNamara, Robert, 'The Nasser factor: Anglo–Egyptian relations and the Yemen/Aden crisis 1962–65', *Middle Eastern Studies*, 53, 1 (2017), pp. 51–68

Miller, Rory, *Desert Kingdoms to Global Powers: The Rise of the Arab Gulf* (New Haven and London: Yale University Press, 2016)

Miller, Rory, 'The Euro-Arab Dialogue and the limits of European external intervention in the Middle East, 1974–77', *Middle Eastern Studies*, 50, 6 (2014), pp. 936–59

Miller, Rory, *Inglorious Disarray: Europe, Israel and the Palestinians Since 1967* (London: Hurst and Company, 2011)

Mintoff, Dom, *How Britain Rules Malta: A Brief Analysis of the Report of the Malta Constitutional Commission 1960* (Valletta: Union Press, undated)

Moore-Gilbert, Kylie 'From protected state to protection racket: Contextualising divide and rule in Bahrain', *Journal of Arabian Studies*, 6, 2 (2016), pp. 163–81

Morton, Michael Quentin, *Buraimi: The Struggle for Power, Influence and Oil in Arabia* (London and New York: I. B. Tauris, 2013)

Murphy, Philip, 'Britain as a global power in the twentieth century', in Andrew Thompson (ed.), *Britain's Experience of Empire in the Twentieth Century* (Oxford: Oxford University Press, 2011)

Murray, Donette, *US Foreign Policy and Iran: American-Iranian Relations Since the Islamic Revolution* (London and New York: Routledge, 2010)

Nkrumah, Kwame, *Neo-colonialism: The Last Stage of Imperialism* (London: Nelson, 1965)

Nwokeji, G. Ugo, 'African economies in the years of decolonization', in Toyin Falola (ed.), *Africa: Volume 4: The End of Colonial Rule: Nationalism and Decolonization* (Durham, NC: Carolina Academic Press, 2002)

Offlier, Ben, *US Foreign Policy and the Modernization of Iran: Kennedy, Johnson, Nixon, and the Shah* (Basingstoke: Palgrave Macmillan, 2015)

Onley, James, *The Arabian Frontier of the British Raj: Merchants, Rulers, and the Nineteenth-Century Gulf* (Oxford: Oxford University Press, 2007)

Orkaby, Asher, *Beyond the Arab Cold War: The International History of the Yemen Civil War, 1962–68* (New York: Oxford University Press, 2017)

Owtram, Francis, *A Modern History of Oman: Formation of the State Since 1920* (London: I. B. Tauris, 2004)

Palmer, Michael A., *Guardians of the Gulf: A History of America's Expanding Role in the Persian Gulf, 1833–1992* (New York: The Free Press, 1992)

Parsons, Timothy H., *The Second British Empire: In the Crucible of the Twentieth Century* (Lanham, MD: Rowman & Littlefield, 2014)

Paust, Jordan J. and Albert P. Blaustein, *The Arab Oil Weapon* (New York: Oceana Publications, 1977)

Peden, G. C., 'Suez and Britain's decline as a world power', *Historical Journal*, 55, 4 (2012), pp. 1073–96

Petersen, Tore T., *Anglo–American Policy Toward the Persian Gulf, 1978–1985: Power, Influence and Restraint* (Brighton: Sussex Academic Press, 2015)

Petersen, Tore T., 'Anglo–American relations over Aden and the United Arab Emirates, 1967–71', *Middle Eastern Studies*, 53, 1 (2017), pp. 98–111

Petersen, Tore T., *Richard Nixon, Great Britain and the Anglo–American Alignment in the Persian Gulf and Arabian Peninsula: Making Allies out of Clients* (Brighton and Portland: Sussex Academic Press, 2009)

Petersen, Tore T., 'Richard Nixon, Great Britain, and the Anglo–American strategy of turning the Persian Gulf into an allied lake', in Jeffrey R. Macris and Saul Kelly (eds.), *Imperial Crossroads: The Great Powers and the Persian Gulf* (Annapolis: Naval Institute Press, 2012)

Peterson, J. E., 'The age of imperialism and its impact on the Gulf', in J. E. Peterson (ed.), *The Emergence of the Gulf States* (London: Bloomsbury, 2016)

Peterson, J. E., *Defending Arabia* (London and New York: Routledge, 2017; first published in 1986)

Petrini, Francesco, 'The British government, the oil companies and the First Oil Crisis, 1970–3', in John Fisher, Effie G. H. Pedaliu, and Richard Smith (eds.), *The Foreign Office, Commerce and British Foreign Policy in the Twentieth Century* (Basingstoke: Palgrave Macmillan, 2017)

Petrini, Francesco, 'Eight squeezed sisters: The oil majors and the coming of the 1973 oil crisis', in Elisabetta Bini, Giuliano Garavini, and Frederico Romero (eds.), *Oil Shock: The 1973 Crisis and its Economic Legacy* (London and New York: I. B. Tauris, 2016)

Pham, P. L., *Ending 'East of Suez': The British Decision to Withdraw from Malaysia and Singapore, 1964–1968* (Oxford and New York: Oxford University Press, 2010)

Porter, Bernard, *British Imperial: What the Empire Wasn't* (London: I. B. Tauris, 2015)

Porter, Bernard, *The Lion's Share: A History of British Imperialism 1850 to the Present*, 5th edition (Harlow: Pearson, 2012)

Rabi, Uzi, 'Britain's "special position" in the Gulf: Its origins, dynamics and legacy', *Middle Eastern Studies*, 42, 3 (2006), pp. 351–64

Rabi, Uzi, 'British possessions in the Persian Gulf and Southwest Arabia: The last abandoned in the Middle East', in Zach Levey and Elie Podeh (eds.), *Britain and the Middle East: From Imperial Power to Junior Partner* (Brighton: Sussex Academic Press, 2008)

Rabi, Uzi, 'Oil politics and tribal rulers in Eastern Araba: The reign of Shakhbut (1928–1966)', *British Journal of Middle Eastern Studies*, 33, 1 (2006), pp. 37–50

Razak, Rowena Abdul, 'When guns are not enough: Britain's response to nationalism in Bahrain, 1958–63', *Journal of Arabian Studies*, 7, 1 (2017), pp. 63–80

Razoux, Pierre, *The Iran-Iraq War* (Cambridge, MA: The Belknap Press, 2015)

Robinson, Ronald, 'The excentric idea of imperialism, with or without empire', in Wolfgang J. Mommesen and Jürgen Osterhammel (eds.), *Imperialism and After: Continuities and Discontinuities* (London: Allen and Unwin, 1986)

Robinson, Ronald, 'Non-European foundations of European imperialism: Sketch for a theory of collaboration', in B. Sutcliffe and R. Owen (eds.), *Studies in the Theory of Imperialism* (London: Longman, 1972)

Romero, Juan, 'Decolonization in reverse: The Iranian oil crisis of 1951–53', *Middle Eastern Studies*, 51, 3 (2015), pp. 462–88

Rossiter, Ash, '"Screening the food from the flies": Britain, Kuwait, and the dilemma of protection, 1961–1971', *Diplomacy and Statecraft*, 28, 1 (2017), pp. 85–109

Rothermund, Dietmar, *The Routledge Companion to Decolonization* (London and New York: Routledge, 2006)

Sandbrook, Dominic, *Seasons in the Sun: The Battle for Britain, 1974–1979* (London: Allen Lane, 2012)

Sandbrook, Dominic, *State of Emergency: The Way We Were: Britain, 1970–1974* (London: Allen Lane, 2010)

Sato, Shohei, *Britain and the Formation of the Gulf States: Embers of Empire* (Manchester: Manchester University Press, 2016)

Schofield, Richard, 'The crystallisation of a complex territorial dispute: Britain and the Saudi-Abu Dhabi borderland, 1966–71', *Journal of Arabian Studies*, 1, 1 (2011), pp. 27–51

Sharifi-Yazdi, Farzad Cyrus, *Arab-Iranian Rivalry in the Persian Gulf: Territorial Disputes and the Balance of Power in the Middle East* (London: I. B. Tauris, 2015)

Smith, Richard, '"Paying our way in the world": The FCO, export promotion and Iran in the 1970s', in John Fisher, Effie G. H. Pedaliu, and Richard Smith (eds.), *The Foreign Office, Commerce and British Foreign Policy in the Twentieth Century* (Basingstoke: Palgrave Macmillan, 2017)

Smith, Simon C., 'Britain's decision to withdraw from the Persian Gulf: A pattern not a puzzle', *Journal of Imperial and Commonwealth History*, 44, 2, (2016), pp. 328–51

Smith, Simon C., *Britain's Revival and Fall in the Gulf: Kuwait, Bahrain, Qatar, and the Trucial States, 1950–1971* (London: Routledge, 2004)

Smith, Simon C., *Kuwait, 1950–1965: Britain, the al-Sabah, and Oil* (Oxford: Oxford University Press, 1999)

Spelling, Alex, '"Recrimination and reconciliation": Anglo–American relations and the Yom Kippur War', *Cold War History*, 13, 4 (2013), pp. 485–506

Stockwell, A. J., *Ending the British Empire: What Did They Think They Were Doing?* (Egham: Royal Holloway, University of London, 1999)

Stockwell, Sarah, 'Ends of empire', in Sarah Stockwell (ed.), *The British Empire: Themes and Perspectives* (Oxford: Blackwell Publishing, 2008)

Stockwell, Sarah, 'Exporting Britishness: Decolonization in Africa, the British state and its clients', in Miguel Bandeira Jeronimo and Antonio Costa Pinto (eds.), *The Ends of European Colonial Empires: Cases and Comparisons* (Basingstoke: Palgrave Macmillan, 2015)

Strong, Robert A., *Working in the World: Jimmy Carter and the Making of American Foreign Policy* (Baton Rouge: Louisiana State University Press, 2000)

Thomas, Martin, *Empires of Intelligence: Security Services and Colonial Disorder After 1914* (Berkeley: University of California Press, 2008)

Thomas, Martin, *Fight or Flight: Britain, France, and Their Roads from Empire* (Oxford: Oxford University Press, 2014)

Thomas, Martin and Andrew Thompson, 'Empire and globalisation: From "high imperialism" to decolonisation', *International History Review*, 36, 1 (2014), pp. 142–70

Turner, Michael J., *Britain's International Role, 1970–1991* (Basingstoke: Palgrave Macmillan, 2010)

Ulrichsen, Kristian Coates, 'The Gulf States and the Iran-Iraq war: Cooperation and confusion', in Nigel Ashton and Bryan Gibson (eds.), *The Iran-Iraq War: New International Perspectives* (London: Routledge, 2014)

Ulrichsen, Kristian Coates, *Insecure Gulf: The End of Certainty and the Transition to the Post-Oil Era* (London: Hurst and Company, 2011)

Ulrichsen, Kristian Coates, *Qatar and the Arab Spring* (London: Hurst and Company, 2014)

Vassiliev, Alexei, *King Faisal of Saudi Arabia: Personality, Faith and Times* (London: Saqi Books, 2012)

Von Bismarck, Helene, *British Policy in the Persian Gulf, 1961–1968: Conceptions of Informal Empire* (Basingstoke: Palgrave Macmillan, 2013)

Von Bismarck, Helene, '"A watershed in our relations with the Trucial States": Great Britain's policy to prevent the opening of an Arab League office in the Persian Gulf in 1965', *Middle Eastern Studies*, 47, 1 (2011), pp. 1–24

Walcott, Tom, 'The Trucial Oman Scouts 1955 to 1971: An overview', *Asian Affairs*, 37, 1 (2006), pp. 17–30

Wall, Patrick, 'The Persian Gulf – stay or quit?' in *Brassey's Annual: Defence and the Armed Forces 1971* (London: William Clowes & Sons Limited, 1971)

Watt, D. C., 'The decision to withdraw from the Gulf', *Political Quarterly*, 39, 3 (1968), pp. 310–21

White, Nicholas J., *British Business in Post-Colonial Malaysia, 1957–70: 'Neo-colonialism' or 'Disengagement'?* (London and New York: Routledge Curzon, 2004)

White, Nicholas J., *Decolonisation: The British Experience Since 1945* (London: Longman, 1999)

Willis, Matthew, 'Britain in Bahrain in 2011', *RUSI Journal*, 157, 5 (2012), pp. 62–71

Winks, Robin W., 'On decolonization and informal empire', *The American Historical Review*, 81, 3 (1976), pp. 540–56

With United Strength: HH Shaikh Zayid Bin Sultan al Nahyan: The Leader and the Nation (Abu Dhabi: Emirates Center for Strategic Studies and Research, 2005)

Woddis, Jack, *Introduction to Neo-Colonialism* (New York: International Publishers, 1967)

Worrall, James, 'Britain's last bastion in Arabia: The end of the Dhofar War, the Labour government and the withdrawal from RAF Salalah and Masirah, 1974–1977', in Tore T. Petersen (ed.), *Challenging Retrenchment: The United States, Great Britain and the Middle East, 1950–1980* (Trondheim: Tapir Academic Press, 2010)

Worrall, James, *The International Institutions of the Middle East: The GCC, Arab League and Arab Maghreb Union* (London and New York: Routledge, 2017)

Worrall, James, *Statebuilding and Counterinsurgency in Oman: Political, Military, and Diplomatic Relations at the End of Empire* (London: I. B. Tauris, 2014)

Wright, Robin, *In the Name of God: The Khomeini Decade* (New York: Simon and Schuster, 1989)

Wrigley, Chris, 'Now you see it, now you don't: Harold Wilson and Labour's foreign policy', in R. Coopey, S. Fielding, and N. Tiratsoo (eds.), *The Wilson Governments, 1964–1970* (London: Pinter, 1993)

Yaqub, Salim, *Imperfect Strangers: Americans, Arabs, and U.S.-Middle East Relations in the 1970s* (Ithaca and London: Cornell University Press, 2016)

Yates, Athol, 'Western expatriates in the UAE armed forces, 1964–2015', *Journal of Arabian Studies*, 6, 2 (2016), pp. 182–200

Yergin, Daniel, *The Prize: The Epic Quest for Oil, Money and Power* (London: Simon and Schuster, 1991)

Yom, Sean L. and F. Gregory Gause III, 'Resilient royals: How Arab monarchies hang on', *Journal of Democracy*, 23, 4 (2012), pp. 74–88

Zahlan, Rosemarie Said, 'The Gulf States and the Palestine problem, 1936–48', *Arab Studies Quarterly*, 3, 1 (1981), pp. 1–21

Zahlan, Rosemarie Said, *The Making of the Gulf States: Kuwait, Bahrain, Qatar, the United Arab Emirates and Oman* (Reading: Ithaca Press, 1998)

Zahlan, Rosemarie Said, *Palestine and the Gulf States: The Presence at the Table* (New York: Routledge, 2009)

Index

Abdul Aziz, Sheikh (Qatar) 38
Abdul Aziz Hussain 130–131
Abdullah, Sheikh (Qatar) 114, 133
Abdullah Salim, Sheikh (Kuwait) 9
Abu Dhabi: and Britain 40, 41, 83–84, 85, 89, 93, 98n139, 112, 131, 135, 136, 140, 153, 169; and Dubai 13, 110, 112, 113, 122n120, 158; and France 39, 65, 89, 112; and Pakistan 65, 75; and Saudi Arabia 84–85, 98n139
Abu Dhabi Defence Force 40, 41, 170
Abu Musa 30, 31, 32, 44n37
Acharya, Amitav 125
Acland, A. A. 13, 30, 31, 34, 41, 124, 175n5
Aden xi, 10, 11, 16
Afghanistan xii, 124, 125, 130, 139, 149, 151, 174, 177n50
Africa xi, 2, 3, 5, 7, 19n46; *see also* East Africa
Afshar, Amir Khosrow 42
Agnew, Spiro 48
Ahmed, Sheikh (Qatar) 12, 37
Al-Akri, Mohammed 114
Alam, Asadollah 44n37, 45n71, 49n167
Alexander, Michael 149, 150, 165n104
Al-Gurg, Easa 174
Allen, D. G. 128
Al-Tajir, Mahdi 111, 112–113, 126, 171
al-Takriti, General Hardan 42
Al-Thani 37, 133, 134
Alvandi, Roham 102
Amery, Julian 32
Anglo-American relations 50–51, 62–64, 70n154, 87, 137
Anglo-Iranian Oil Company 9
Anglo-Qatari Committee 77, 110
Anglo-Qatari Cooperation Agreement 77, 78, 110

Annenberg, Walter 28, 43n15, 51, 63
Aqueed Mohammed bin Said 136
Arabian American Oil Company 9
Arab-Israeli War (1973) 58–59
Arab League 11, 42, 57, 124
Arab nationalism 11, 58
Armilla Patrol 147, 160
Armitage, Henry St. John Basil 121n104, 169
Arthur, G. G. 169
Ashton, S. R. 4
Atiqi, Abdul Rahman 93

Bacevich, Andrew J. 102–103
Bahrain: and Australia 36; and Britain 9, 12, 23n126, 34–36, 41, 54–55, 80–82, 88–89, 116, 137, 156–157, 158, 159, 167n168, 171; disturbances in 34, 137; and France 36; and independence 5; and Iran 34, 45n71, 159, 167n165; and Japan 36, 80; and Parliament 79; and People's Bloc 80; and Qatar 171; and Saudi Arabia 13, 159–160, 167n168; and Shia minority 109, 114, 121n81, 137; and Treaty of Friendship 34; and United States 41, 80, 87–88, 137
Bahrain Defence Force 34, 122n137
Baker, Stephen 74
Balfour-Paul, Glen 1, 22n112
Balniel, Lord 52, 54, 54–55, 62
Bamberg, James 75–76
Barratt, F. R. 74
Bartholomew, Reginald 125
Barton, Gregory 6–7, 8
Bell, Jim 80, 109
Berry, Bill 80
Bismarck, Helene von 8, 11
Blair, Tony 15
Boyce, D. George 15

Boyle, R. H. M. 38
Bradshaw, Tancred 8
Brant, Colin 108, 110, 114, 115–116, 126, 127, 128, 132–133, 134, 135, 148, 151, 151–152, 157, 168, 169, 171–172, 180
Brewster, Kingman 147
Brezhnev, Leonid 63, 146
Briggs, Jack 186
British Aerospace 133, 138–139, 140, 152
British Council 80, 128–130
British Leyland 131, 157
British Petroleum 40, 48n150, 57, 94n31, 151
British Steel 74
Brown, George 26–27
Bullard, J. L. 170
Burk, Kathleen 79
Burrows, Bernard 10
Butler, L. J. 7

Cain, P. J. 7, 50
Cairncross, Alec 79
Callaghan, James 77, 79, 81, 90, 92, 184
Cambridge, S. J. G. 117, 128, 132, 136, 154, 155, 158–159, 170, 179
capitalism 3, 4
Carrick, R. J. 104
Carrington, Lord 184; and arms sales 125; and British Council 129; and the Gulf 13, 50–51; and Gulf Co-operation Council 148; and the Gulf States 134–135, 149; and Hawk aircraft 138–139; and Oman 33; and Rhodesian 132; and the Trucial States 30; and the United Arab Emirates 135
Carter, Jimmy 103, 104, 118n113, 124, 125, 140n9
Carter Doctrine 124–125, 146
Casey, William J. 62
Chieftain tanks 53, 90–91, 155
Clark, Alan 174
Clark, T. J. 83, 171
collaboration 1, 2, 5
Copson, M. J. 157, 166n133
Craig, James 115
Crawford, D. G. 33, 76, 77, 78, 79, 89, 96n78, 109, 166n133
Crawford, Sir Stewart 11–12, 22n117, 23n123, 27, 43n19, 168, 178
Cromer, Lord 58, 62, 63
Cross, Colin 14
Crossman, Richard 13–14
Curzon, Lord 8

Darwin, John 1, 4, 6, 14, 17
Davidson, Christopher 8, 10, 176n38
Davies, Roger P. 87
Day, Stephen 158, 180
Defence and Oversea Policy Committee 29, 33
Department of Trade 110
Dexter, M. R. W. 129
Dhofar rebellion 16, 33
Diego Garcia 125, 140n10
Douglas-Home, Sir Alec 184; and Abu Dhabi-Saudi Arabian relations 84, 85; and arms sales 39; and the Gulf 28, 31; and the Gulf States 30; and Jaguar aircraft 39; and Kuwait 61; and the Middle East 171; and oil 61; and Qatar 39; and Sheikh Khalifah (Qatar) 37, 55; and Sheikh Muhammad bin Mubarak 35; and Sheikh Zaid 84, 111, 170; and Sultan Qaboos 33
Dubai: and Abu Dhabi 13, 113; and Britain 86, 111; and United Arab Emirates 110, 111, 122n120

East Africa 7
East of Suez 13, 14, 15, 16, 17, 27, 30, 102, 125, 149, 168
Edye, D. F. B. 130, 158
Egerton, S. L. 61, 177n51
Egypt 6, 10, 32, 38, 53, 56, 58, 62, 63, 86, 88, 114, 115, 129, 136, 144n136, 170
Ellis, Sir Ronald 139, 140
Ennals, David 76, 77, 81, 93
Euro-Arab Dialogue 124
European Economic Community 59, 124
Ewbanks 90
Eyre, R. E. 131

Fahd bin Abdul Aziz, Prince 85, 98n139, 148
Feisal, King 41, 58, 85, 98n152, 128, 173
Fenn, Nicholas 58
Fieldhouse, D. K. 3, 5, 19n46
Foot, Michael 148
Ford, Gerald 103
Foreign and Commonwealth Office 27, 33, 35, 63, 75, 107, 109, 149
Foreign Office 10, 14, 26, 169
France: and Abu Dhabi 89, 112, 139; and Bahrain 36, 127; and the Gulf 126–127; and Palestine 131; and Qatar 38–39, 116, 126, 127, 133, 134, 169; and Sheikh Zaid 39, 138

204 *Index*

Franco-Qatari Commission 116
Fromherz, Alan 8

Gallagher, John 1
Gallagher, Julia 15
Gatch, John Newton 87
Gause, F. Gregory 108
GEC 77–78
Genscher, Hans-Dietrich 124
Ghana 2, 3
Gillmore, D. H. 126, 137
Gilmour, Ian 52, 139, 153
Giscard d'Estaing, Valéry 126, 127, 131, 138, 140, 155–156
Given, E. F. 81, 82, 87, 88, 88–89, 171, 178
Go, Julian 4
Godber, Joseph 31, 35
Gordon, R. D. 78
Gore-Booth, Sir Paul 27
Graham, Sir John 197, 164n89
Greenhill, Denis 54, 58
Gulf Co-operation Council 148, 177n49
Gulf Sheikhdoms 8–11; and British withdrawal 11–13

Hahn, Peter 6
Halliday, Fred 3–4
Hamad bin Isa, Sheikh (Bahrain) 54, 156
Hamad bin Jassim, Sheikh (Qatar) 114
Hamad bin Khalifah, Sheikh (Qatar) 89, 127, 130, 133, 135, 152
Hammadi, Dr Sa'adoun 149
Hannay, D. H. A. 107
Harris, A. D. 67n69, 73, 80
Haskell, D. K. 112
Hawley, D. F. 45n66
Hayman, Mark 8
Healey, Denis 12, 14
Heath, Edward 28, 186; and Jaguar aircraft 39; and oil 58, 59, 62; Sheikh Isa (Bahrain) 54; Sheikh Khalifah bin Hamad (Qatar) 36–37, 55, 57; and Sheikh Sabah al-Salim (Kuwait) 61; and Sheikh Zaid 83–84, 170; and United States 63
Heinlein, Frank 4
Henderson, E. F. 36, 37, 38, 39, 39–40, 55, 56, 57, 59–60, 65, 72, 73, 74, 74–75, 85, 129, 157, 171, 172, 179
Henderson, Ian 36, 80, 109, 137, 159
Hopkins, A. G. 7, 50
Hoveyda, Abbas 41

Howard, Rhoda 3
human rights 103, 118n13
Hunt, Sir John 59
Hunt, R. M. (Rex) 52–53, 105
Hurd, Douglas 128, 130–131, 134, 138, 139–140, 147, 148, 158, 160, 167n165, 170, 172, 185
Hussein, Abdulaziz 90
Hussein, Saddam 49n172, 136, 147
Hyam, Ronald 14
Hyundai Construction Company 88

imperialism of decolonization 4, 50
informal empire xii, 1, 2, 4, 5, 6, 7, 8, 14, 16, 42, 64, 117, 171
intelligence states 2
Iran 9; and American hostages 107; and Bahrain 34, 45n71; and Britain 107; and Gulf islands 31, 48n150; and Qom disturbances 103; and twin pillars 30, 102; and United Arab Emirates 40, 41, 48n149, 170; and United States 102–103
Iran-Iraq War 117, 134, 136–137, 139, 147, 147–148, 152, 174, 177n51
Iraq 9, 15, 32, 51–52, 53, 62, 79, 82, 83, 86, 90, 107, 108, 111, 113, 126, 128, 135, 136, 174
Isa, Sheikh (Bahrain) 43n16, 54, 87, 88, 156, 187
Islamic Front for the Liberation of Bahrain 159
Islamic Republic of Iran 106, 107, 109, 137
Israel 32, 57, 58–59, 60, 61, 62, 72, 114, 152, 155

Jabir Al-Ahmad, Sheikh (Kuwait) 60, 147, 153, 187
Jabir al-Ali, Sheikh (Kuwait) 130
Jackson, Ashley 15, 16
Jaguar aircraft 38–39, 91, 134
Japan 73–74, 78, 116, 153, 169, 176n38
Jassim bin Hamad, Sheikh (Qatar) 129
Jefferson, W. H. 129
Johnson, Lyndon Baines 26, 102
Johnson, Rob 16
Johnson, U. A. 50
Joint Intelligence Committee 9, 54, 56, 57
Judd, Frank 105, 112, 113

Kelly, J. B. 14
Kennedy, Dane 8

Index   205

Kennedy, Greg 15
Khalid, Sheikh (Sharjah) 17, 31, 32
Khalifa bin Zaid, Sheikh (Abu Dhabi) 136, 139, 153, 160
Khalifah bin Hamad, Sheikh (Qatar) 187–188: and Anglo-Qatari Cooperation Agreement 79; and Anwar Sadat 114–115; and Arab world 60, 57; and Britain 36, 39, 56, 76–77, 90, 109, 115, 115–116, 116, 150; and character 38, 96n78; and coup 38; and Edward Heath 36–37, 55, 58; and France 39, 55, 65, 73; and Iranian community 114; and Iranian revolution 115; and Jaguar aircraft 42; and James Callaghan 90; and Japan 74; and Margaret Thatcher 114–115, 116, 132, 150, 151–152; and oil 57, 60, 75; and OPEC 76; and the Shah 115; and steel 73; and UAE/Saudi Arabia dispute 85; and United States 73
Khalifah bin Salman Al-Khalifah, Sheikh (Bahrain) 12, 36, 55, 80, 81, 109, 131, 156
Khomeini, Ayatollah 106, 107, 108–109, 113, 114, 137
Kinchen, Richard 89
Kissinger, Henry 52, 62, 63, 103
Kobe Steel 74
Kuwait: and Arab world 61–62; and Britain 8, 9, 32, 51, 52–53, 61–62, 82, 83, 90–91, 97n120, 117, 132, 137, 153–154, 158–159, 170; and France 91; and Gulf co-operation 128, 147; and Gulf islands 32; and independence 9; and Iran 108; and Iran-Iraq War 136; and Iraq 9, 32, 52, 82, 90, 136, 174; and Japan 137, 153; and loan service personnel 154; and Margaret Thatcher 155–156, 164n98; and oil companies 75; and oil production 82; and oil weapon 60–61; and Palestine 60; and political assassinations 42; and the Shah 108; and Shia minority 109, 113, 121n81, 137; and Soviet Union 82, 96–97n114; and sterling balances 9; and United States 51, 96–97n114, 137, 153
Kuwait Liaison Team 52, 53, 91, 100–101n217, 164n103, 170
Kuwait Oil Company 9

Lamb, A. T. (Archie) 22n110, 83, 90–91, 92, 93, 97n120, 176n38
Lamb, Robin 173

Lennox, Lord N. Gordon 70n154
Lewin, Sir Terence 146
Libya 32, 40, 48n150
Lienhardt, Peter 8, 21–22n110
Lim Mah Hui 3
Louis, Wm. Roger 2, 4, 7, 50, 65, 168–169
Luard, Evan 84
Lucas, Ivor 82, 88, 90, 91, 105, 108, 111, 131, 143n92, 169, 173
Luce, Sir William 10, 11, 13, 21n104, 28–29, 31
Lygo, Sir Raymond 152
Lynn, Martin 6

MacArthur II, Douglas 102
McCarthy, D. J. 65, 83, 84, 85, 86, 92–93, 111, 181
McCluney, Ian 137
McCourt, David M. 15
McGlinchey, Stephen 102, 103
Macmillan, Harold 6
Macris, Jeffrey 16, 125
Maddy-Weitzman, Bruce 147
Maekawa, Ichiro 7
Maestrone, Frank E. 108, 113
Magdoff, Harry 3
Major, B. A. 112
Makins, Sir Roger 9
Malaysia 3
Mangold, Peter 114
Martell, Gordon 5
Marxism/Marxist 3, 4, 16, 34, 79
Mawby, Spencer 15
Meacher, Michael 78, 79
Meirs, H. D. A. C. 115, 126, 127, 131, 133, 136, 138, 150, 151, 152, 155–156, 159, 182
Miklos, Jack 103
Miller, Rory 10, 64–65
Mintoff, Dom 1
Mirage aircraft 38, 39, 89, 134
Moberly, J. C. 30–31, 127, 135, 136, 138, 151, 160, 172
Moberly, P. H. 125, 147
Mohamed bin Khalifah Al-Khalifah (Bahrain) 114
Mohammed bin Hamad Al-Thani, Sheikh (Qatar) 129–130
Mohammed bin Rashid, Sheikh 138
Moore-Gilbert, Kylie 167n165
Moran, Andrew 103
Morris, Willie 41, 98n139, 173

Muhammad bin Mubarak, Sheikh (Bahrain) 35, 87, 88, 127
Munro, Sir Alan 16, 104, 105, 109, 113, 117, 182
Murphy, Philip 15
Murray, Donette 104
Murray, Robert W. 103
Mussadiq, Muhammad 9

Nasser, Gamal Abdel 6, 10, 11, 64, 136
National Liberation Front 12
NATO 147
neo-colonialism 2, 3, 5, 7
Nixon, Richard 50, 51, 58, 59, 60–61, 102–103
Nixon Doctrine 102, 125
Nkrumah, Kwame 2–3
North Sea oil 59
Nott, John 148–149
Noyes, James 51, 66n13
Nwokeji, G. Ugo 3

Offiler, Ben 102
oil 9, 28, 29, 64; *see also* British Petroleum; Heath, Edward: and oil; Kuwait Oil Company; North Sea oil crisis (1973); oil weapon; OPEC Qatar National Petroleum Company; Qatar Petroleum Company; Shell
oil crisis (1973) 7
oil weapon 42, 51, 57, 58, 59, 60, 61, 62, 64, 72, 170
Oman: and Britain 16–17, 33, 51, 55, 125, 131, 154, 171; and British withdrawal 17; and Dhofar rebellion 16, 33, 171
Onley, James 8
OPEC 57, 59, 75–76
Orkaby, Asher 6
Osirak reactor 152
Otaiba, Mana Said 40, 135
Owen, David 104, 105, 105–106, 119n48, 143n92, 185

Pakistan 65, 75, 125, 151
Palestine/Palestinians xi, 52, 59, 60, 72, 86, 124, 125, 131, 147, 151, 155, 156, 170
Palestine Liberation Organization 155, 156
Palliser, Sir Michael 146, 154, 155, 156
Palmer, Michael 102
Parkinson, Cecil 131–132
Parramore, P. J. 110
Parsons, Anthony 118n29; and Abu Dhabi 85; and Anglo-American talks 32–33, 113, 120n56; and Arab-Israeli conflict 62; and Arab world 59, 62; and Bahrain 12; and Iran 103–104; and Kuwait 53; 53–54; and Qatar 38; the Shah 104, 105, 106, 109, 120n56; and the United Arab Emirates 113
Parsons, Timothy 6
Passmore, K. J. 77, 125, 126–127, 138
Peden, P. G. 14
Pelly, C. J. 8–9
People's Bloc 80
Perkins, Major-General K. 133, 135–136, 138, 155, 156
Petersen, Tore 16, 50, 58, 64, 103, 146
Peterson, J. E. 16, 102
Petrini, Francesco 59
Pham, P. L. 14
Porter, Bernard 4–5, 7
Pridham, B. R. 89
Puma helicopters 39

Qaboos, Sultan (Oman) 16, 33, 45n66, 55, 85, 172
Qatar: and Arab world 59–60, 64, 76; and Bahrain 128, 171; and Britain 8, 37, 38–39, 41, 55, 73–75, 76–78, 79, 89–90, 109–110, 115–116, 130, 132–134, 135, 148–149, 151–152, 157–158, 163n165, 169, 171; and British Council 128–130; and France 38–39, 55–57, 73, 74, 76, 90, 110, 116, 127, 133, 134, 152, 169; and independence 5, 37; and Iranian revolution 108, 114, 135; and Japan 74, 76, 89, 110, 158; and loan service personnel 74–75; and Margaret Thatcher 149, 150; and oil 36, 57, 64, 75; and Pakistan 75; and Saudi Arabia 57, 59, 75; and the Shah 108, 122n127; and Shia minority 113–114; and sterling balances 9; and Treaty of Friendship 37; and United Arab Emirates 128
Qatar National Petroleum Company 57, 94n34
Qatar Petroleum Company 57
Qatar Security Forces 38
Qom disturbances 103

Rabi, Uzi 175n4
Raftery, P. A. 89
Ramlawi, Nabil 155
Rapid Deployment Force 146, 147
Rapier missiles 89, 133–134, 135, 136, 151, 152, 154, 156, 174

Ras al Khaimah 12, 30, 31, 32, 44n37, 111, 137, 148
Rashid, Sheikh (Dubai) 188: and Britain 86, 112, 171; and British withdrawal 12, 22n121; and Shah of Iran 106; and Sheikh Zaid (Abu Dhabi) 13, 40, 110–111; and unification with Abu Dhabi 13; and United Arab Emirates 110–112, 171
Rashid bin Saqr al Qasimi, Sheikh (Ras al Khaimah) 148
Razak, Rowena Abdul 8
Razoux, Pierre 102, 147–148
Reagan, Ronald 146, 153
Renwick, R. W. 89, 163n64
Riad, Mahmoud 42
Richards, F. N. 150
Richardson, Elliot 51
Richardson, Gordon 83
Richmond, J. C. B. 169
Roberts, D. A. 95n57, 111, 112, 113, 116, 130, 131, 135, 136, 138, 170, 172, 174, 181
Roberts, Goronwy 11, 12, 17
Robinson, Ronald 1, 2, 50
Romero, Juan 2
Rothermund, Dietmar 6
Royal Navy 29, 30

Sa'ad al-Abdullah, Sheikh (Kuwait) 90, 91, 91–92, 154
Sabah al-Ahmad, Sheikh (Kuwait) 31–32, 61, 87
Sabah al-Salim, Sheikh (Kuwait) 9, 61, 187
Sadat, Anwar 58
Said bin Taimur, Sultan (Oman) 33, 45n66
Salim Al-Sabah, Sheikh, (Kuwait) 130, 136, 154, 170
Saqqaf, Omar 84
Saqr, Sheikh (Ras al Khaimah) 12, 31, 32, 111
Saqr, Sheikh (Sharjah) 11, 32
Sato, Shohei 1–2, 5, 8, 17, 71
Saudi Arabia: and Abu Dhabi 84–85; and Al-Yammah 174; and Arab nationalism 58; and Bahrain 13, 159–160, 167n168; and Britain 62, 85, 98n139, 125, 149; and Grand Mosque, seizure of 115; and Gulf co-operation 128, 148; and Gulf islands 31; and Iran 30; and Kuwait 32; and oil 9, 57, 75; and Qatar 14, 59; and Sheikh Zaid 41–42, 85; and Shiites 115; and Trucial States 13; and twin pillars 30, 102, 107; and the UAE 85, 128; and the West 50
SAVAK 113
Sayyid Fahr 131
Schlesinger, James R. xi, 62, 63
Second World War 2, 3, 7, 8, 10
Shah of Iran: and Bahrain 45n71, 80; and Britain 48–49n167, 104, 105–106, 107, 109; and character 103; and fall 106, 107, 143n92; and Gulf Islands 30, 31; and Islam 103; and Sheikh Zaid 40; and the United Arab Emirates 48n149, 48n167; and the United States 102–103, 104–105, 172
Shakhbut, Sheikh (Abu Dhabi) 11, 21–22n110, 22n112
Sharjah 11, 30, 31, 32, 86
Shell 57, 75, 94n31, 163n70
Shore, Peter 77, 81, 93
Sick, Gary 104–105
Sisco, Joseph 33, 51
Smith, Richard 72
Sonnenfeldt, Helmut 64
South Arabia 10, 11–12, 13, 22n117
Soviet Union 41, 82, 96n114, 102, 107, 124, 125, 128, 130, 139, 146, 149, 151, 174
Spain, S. W. 72
sterling 27, 53, 79, 116
sterling area 10
sterling balances 9
sterling devaluation 26
Stevens, Sir Roger 10
Stewart, Michael 13, 27
Stirling, A. J. D. 34–35, 41, 178
Stockwell, A. J. 5
Stockwell, Sarah 5
Strang, Sir William 9
Strong, Robert 103
Suez crisis 6, 14, 15, 16, 26
Sulman bin Da'ij Al-Khalifah, Sheikh (Bahrain) 25
Suwaidi, Ahmad 40, 48n149, 48n167, 83
Syria 53, 58, 62

Tajir, Mahdi *see* Al-Tajir, Mahdi
Tatham, D. E. 106–107, 125, 132
Taylor Woodrow 78
Tehran agreement (1971) 46n102
Tesh, Robert 35, 36, 41, 53–54, 79–81, 179
Thatcher, Margaret 186; and Afghanistan 139; and Bahrain 156–157; and Carter Doctrine 146; and defence sales 125, 138–139, 151, 152–153, 154, 156,

157, 164n89, 174; and France 139; and Gulf co-operation 148, 154, 177n149; and Gulf visits (1981) 160, 173, 173–174; and Iran 115; and Kuwait 153–156, 164n98, 174; and Loan Service Personnel 154, 165n104; and Palestine 155–156; and Qatar 150, 151, 157–158; and Rapid Deployment Force 148, 149, 149–150; and Ronald Reagan 153; and Sheikh Khalifah bin Hamad, (Qatar) 114–115, 115, 132–133, 150, 151, 152; Sheikh Khalifah bin Salman Al-Khalifah, (Bahrain) 116; and Sheikh Zaid, (Abu Dhabi) 138, 139, 152; and Soviet Union 139; and Sultan Qaboos 172; withdrawal East of Suez 149
Thomas, Martin 2, 5, 5–6
Thompson, Andrew 5
Thomson, George 27–28
Tindale, G. A. 129
Tomkys, W. R. 158
Treadwell, C. J. 39–40, 41, 42, 83, 84, 110–111, 169, 181
Treasury 26, 30, 86
Trucial Oman Scouts 22n112, 30
Trucial States 8, 13, 30, 31, 40, 86, 171, 176n38
Trucial States Development Office 29
Tuck, Kennedy 15
Tunbs 30, 31, 32, 44n37
Turner, Michael 15–16
Twinam, Joseph 136
twin pillars 30, 102, 125

UK/UAE Committee 77, 95n57
Ulrichsen, Kristian Coates 108, 148
United Arab Emirates: and Afghanistan 130; and Arab world 40, 42; and armed forces 111, 112; and Britain 65, 84, 92–93, 111–112, 116, 131, 135, 136, 138, 140, 153, 160, 171, 174; and British Military Advisory Team 186; creation of 13; and France 135; and independence 5; and Iran 42, 48n149; and Libya 60; and Palestine 86; and Saudi Arabia 128; and Soviet Union 41
United States: and Arab-Israeli conflict 62; and Bahrain 41; and British role in the Gulf 32–33, 50–51, 137, 147, 164n89; and Diego Garcia 125, 140n10; and the Gulf 125, 137, 174; and Iran 102–103; and Israel 62; and Kuwait 51, 96–97n114, 153; and the Shah 102–103, 172; and twin pillars 30–31,

103; *see also* Anglo-American relations; Carter doctrine; Nixon Doctrine

Vance, Cyrus 115
Vaughan, Gerald 132
Vietnam War 66n13, 102
Vincent, Sir Richard 174
Vosper Thorneycroft 92

Walker, H. B. 85, 114, 116, 122n137, 127, 128, 137, 158, 159, 179
Walker, Patrick Gordon 14
Wall, Patrick 28, 43n16
Walsh, John 51
Watt, D. C. 14
Weir, M. S. 13, 171
Westmacott, P. J. 106
White, Nicholas 4, 7
Willis, Matthew 167n168
Wilson, Harold 14, 26, 72, 85, 111, 149, 169, 170, 186
Wilton, A. J. 32, 42, 49n172, 52, 53, 60–61, 62, 82–83, 164n98, 180
Winks, Robin 1
Woddis, Jack 3
Wogan, P. F. M. 160
Woollacott, Martin 153
Worrall, James 16–17, 147
Wrampelmeir, Brooks 57
Wright, J. O. 64
Wright, P. R. H. 35, 38, 39, 42, 44n33, 52, 53, 54, 57, 61, 72–73, 85, 171, 172, 183

Yaqub, Salim 103
Young, J. R. 56

Zahlan, Rosemarie Said 60
Zaid, Sheikh (Abu Dhabi) 188: and Abu Musa 31; and Arab world 42, 170; and Britain 11, 12, 31, 39–40, 41–42, 65, 83–84, 84–85, 89, 112, 135, 136, 138, 170–171; and Edward Heath 83–84, 170; and Feisal, King (Saudi Arabia) 128; and France 39, 138; and Giscard d'Estaing 138; and Gulf co-operation 13, 148; and Gulf islands 40; and Harold Wilson 72; and Iran 40, 170; and Mahdi Al-Tajir 113; and Margaret Thatcher 138–139, 139, 150, 152; and oil weapon 170; and Saudi Arabia 85, 98–99n152, 128; and Sheikh Khalifah (Qatar) 85; and Sheikh Rashid (Dubai) 13, 40, 110–111, 112; and Sheikh Shakhbut 11, 22n110; and Soviet Union 40; and unification with Dubai 13

CW01263369

ぶたりのアトリエ

松坂たけし　羽佐間 凌

ボートのりば

■画家紹介

つかさ　おさむ
司　修

　群馬県前橋市に生まれる。1960年ごろから油絵の個展を十数回ひらく。1964年，主体美術協会の創立に参加。以後，絵画・版画・絵本・装丁とはば広く活躍中。松谷みよ子とのコンビでは，長編連作〈直樹とゆう子の物語〉5編のさし絵，絵本「まちんと」（1984年，ボローニャ国際児童図書展グラフィック賞推奨。1989年，ライプチヒ国際図書デザイン展・美しい子どもの本展金賞），「ぼうさまになったからす」など数々の名作を生みだす。80年代から小説も執筆し，代表作に「犬（影について・その一）」（1993年，第20回川端康成文学賞）がある。

■著者紹介

まつたに　　　こ
松谷みよ子

　東京に生まれる。1951年，「貝になった子供」で第1回児童文学者協会新人賞を受賞。以来，「龍の子太郎」（1960年，第1回講談社児童文学新人賞）。1962年，国際アンデルセン賞優良賞），「ちいさいモモちゃん」（1964年，第2回野間児童文芸賞），「モモちゃんとアカネちゃん」（1975年，第5回赤い鳥文学賞），「アカネちゃんのなみだの海」（1992年，第30回野間児童文芸賞），「あの世からの火」（1994年，第43回小学館文学賞）など，受賞多数。民話の研究に情熱をそそぎ，松谷みよ子民話研究室を主宰，「現代民話考」など民話関係の著作も多い。

1 列車は花浦についた……………………6

2 歩くいすと、ふしぎな家……………15

3 おほりばたに出るものは……………24

4 見えなくなったゆう子………………33

5 ゆう子といす…………………………41

6 りつ子…………………………………50

7 ふたりのイーダ………………………58

8 おそうじ、おそうじ…………………67

9 それは、むかしの話なのだ…………80

10 赤んぼうは、しっている……………90

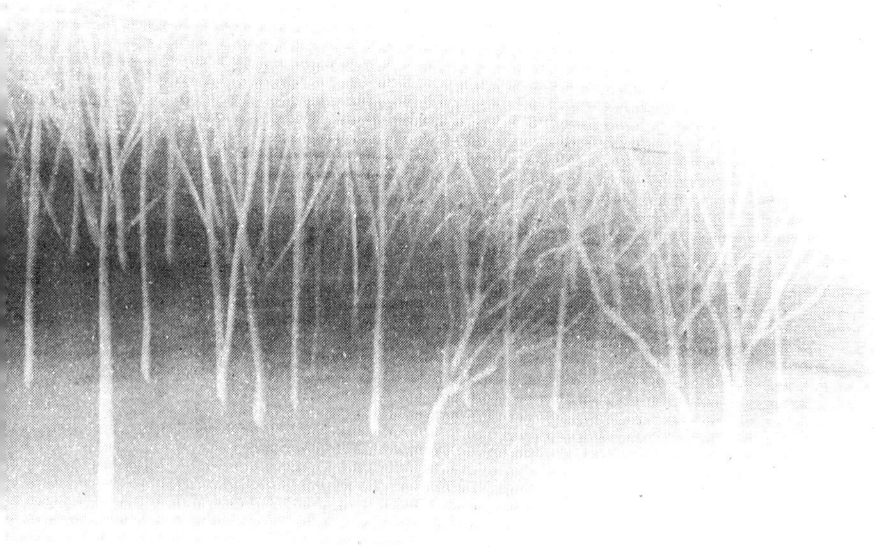

11 このいすはだれが——……101

12 おかしなカレンダー——……112

13 協力者……122

14 数字の意味はわかった……131

15 りつ子、ふしぎな家へいく……141

16 とうろう流し……154

17 生まれかわり……167

18 ほんとうのことをはなしたとき……178

19 これですべてが——……187

20 りつ子からの手紙……197

あとがき……208

1 列車は花浦についた

チャイムが鳴って、車内アナウンスがひびいたとき、直樹はやれやれとほっとした。

——あと五分後に、花浦に到着いたします。お出口は進行方向左側、停車時間は二分です。——

なにしろ新幹線にのって、東京から新大阪まで三時間十分、新大阪でのりかえて、花浦まで五時間、合計、八時間十分の旅だ。持ってきたまんが雑誌は、すみからすみまで読んでしまったし、アイスクリームは二度もなめた。直樹は早くおりたくて、うずうずしていた。ゆう子ならいい、おかあさんにおはなしして、おはなししてとおねだりし、ぼくも指あそびをさんざんやらされた。二さい十一か月のちびだから、まわりはまだゆるしてくれる。でも直樹はもう四年生だった。いくら汽車の旅でたいくつしても、座席でボール投げをするわけにはいかない。

「直樹ちゃん、荷物をおろしてね。ひとりでおろせる？　だいじょうぶ？　ゆうちゃん、ゆうちゃ

ん、おきるのよ、もうついたのよ。」

おかあさんはいそがしい。　あんまりうれしくて、はしゃいだものだから、くたびれにはなしかける。ゆう子はぐっすりね

ていた。あんまりうれしくて、はしゃいだものだから、くたびれたのだ。すとんとねてしまった。直

樹は座席の上に立って、白とグレーのかばんを一つずつおろしながら、座席の背にもたれているゆう

子を見おろした。こうしてみると、まだほんとうに小さい。足をなげ出してえんこしてねているとこ

ろは、おもちゃのくまみたいだ。　生まれてからまだいっぺんもきったことのない長いかみの毛が、色

白のゆう子の顔を、やさしくふちどっていた。

「ゆうちゃん、ゆう子、おきるのよ。」

ゆう子は長いまつげをふせて、まだねむっている。　おかあさんはたまりかねたのか、

「イーダちゃん」

と、ちょっときつくいった。　そうしたらどうだろう、ゆう子のやつ、ぱっと目をさました。そして、

しばらくふしぎそうにあたりを見まわしていたが、座席に立った直樹が、にやにやして見おろしてい

るのに気がつくと、

「イーダ。」

7

と、にくたらしい顔をしてみせた。直樹はおかしくてわらってしまった。イーダ、というのは直樹が教えたのだけど、ゆう子はすっかり気に入ったらしく、なにかいうと、イーダ、という。そして、イーダちゃん、というと、ああい、なんてへんじをするのである。

「やれやれ、おきるととたんにイーダ、ですか。こまった人ね。さあ、おんりよ。おくつをはいてね。おじいさんと、おばあさんがまっていますよ。」

直樹はうでに力をこめて、二つのスーツケースをおろした。グレーは、直樹とゆう子とふたりぶんの荷物だ。白のは、おかあさんの荷物だ。本がはいっているから、ずしりと重い。

「おかあさん、うんと長く九州にいっているの？」

直樹はわざと、なんでもなさそうな声できいた。

「なるべく早く帰ってくるわ。でもね、お仕事だから……、わかっているでしょ？」

「うん、わかってるよ。」

直樹は、むねのへんが重くるしい気がした。おかあさんの仕事は、直樹が生まれない前からあって、おかあさんというものはみんな仕事をしているものだと、ずっと思っていた。あれは直樹が五つぐらいのときだったろうか、おかあさんは直樹をつれて、長野へ取材にいくことになっていた。りんごのなる村にいるおばさんのところへ直樹をあずけるつもりだった。

8

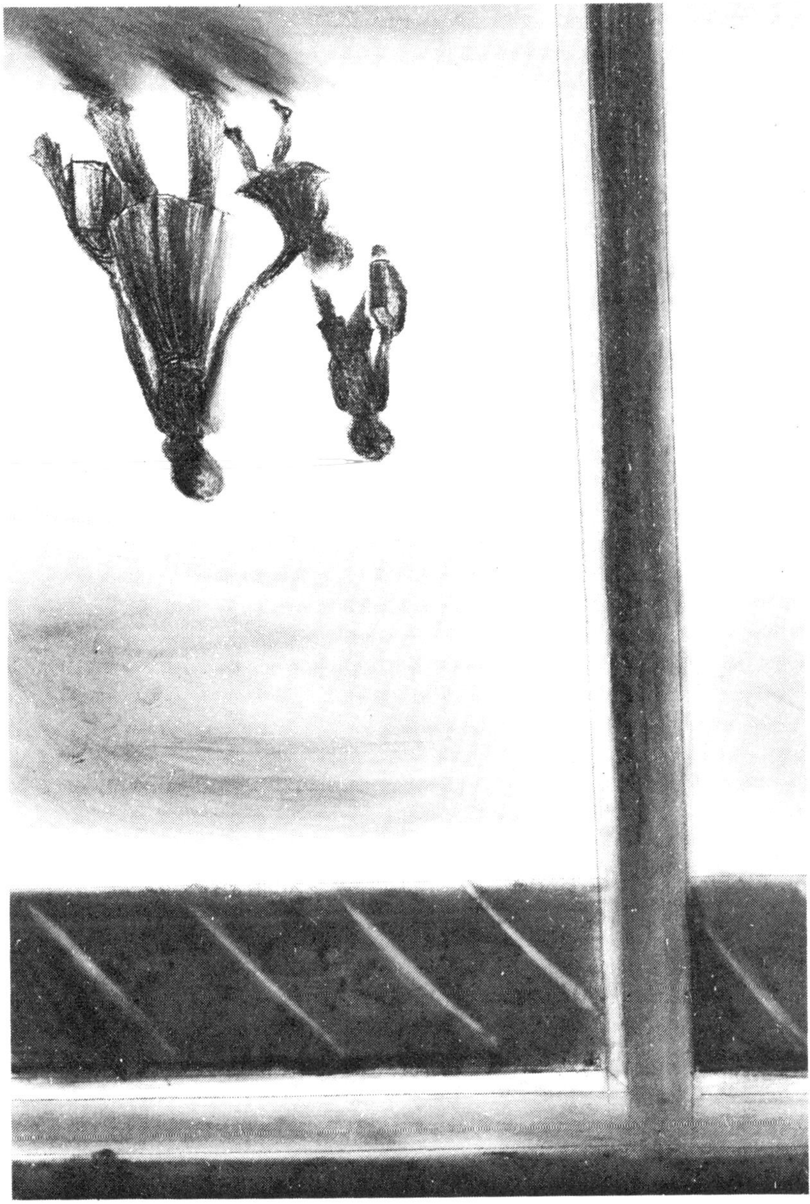

ところがその朝、おかあさんが直樹の手をにぎったら熱かった。これは熱がある、と思ってはかったら、すこしあった。すぐに薬を飲ませ、さておかあさんは考えたそうである。つれていくべきか、おいていくべきか……。しかし一汽車おくらせて、おかあさんは直樹をつれて出た。汽車の中で頭をひやしながら長野へつくと、すぐ医者にとびこんだ。そしてつぎの日から直樹をおばさんの手にあずけて、仕事に出てしまった。直樹はおとなしくねていたそうである。そして、おかあさんの顔が、ちっと見たいよ、などといって、おばさんをふびんがらせたそうである。

なにしろそういうおかあさんだから、直樹は、るす番だの、ほっておかれるのにはなれていた。このんどおかあさんが直樹とゆう子をつれて、はるばる花浦までやってきたのも、仕事のためなんだ。九州へ仕事でいくときまったとき、おかあさんはすぐこういった。

「ねえ、こうしましょうよ。直樹とゆう子は花浦のおじいさんのおうちにまっているの。おかあさんはそのあいだ九州へちょっといってくるからね。花浦までいけば九州はすぐだしさ、ちょうど直樹は夏休みだし、いいじゃない?」

もちろん直樹は賛成した。おじいさんたちの住んでいる花浦がどんなところか、とても楽しみだし、新幹線にのるのもいい。ただ、ゆう子のおもりをしなくちゃならないことを考えると、やれやれだった。その気持ちを見ぬいたように、おかあさんは、

10

「ゆう子をたのむわよ。」

と、直樹に念をおした。

「おじいさんも、おばあさんも、もうお年ですからね、わかった？」

「わかったよっ、さあ、おりようよ。」

グレーのスーツケースをさげて出口へ出ると、おかあさんは白のスーツケースをさげ、ゆう子の手をひいてあとにつづいた。汽車は花浦のプラットホームにすべりこんでいった。

おじいさんの家は、花浦の駅から、車で二十分ばかりはいったところにあった。むすめと孫がいっぺんにやってきたので、むかえにきたおじいさんは、車の中でも目を細めっぱなしだった。

「それで、あんた、いつ九州へたつんじゃ。ゆっくりしてからでいいのじゃろう。」

「いいえ、とんでもない。今夜の夜行でたたせてもらいます。もうしわけないけど、直樹とゆう子、おねがいします。」

「そりゃ、いそがしいんじゃな。」

おじいさんも、おどろいたようだった。まったく、いくらおじいさんの家だからといって、子どもをあずけるのに、一晩もいっしょにいないで、さっさと出発する。そういう人もあんまりないだろう。

11

「それで、九州には何日ぐらいおるんじゃ。」

「そうねえ、四日か……五日、もしかしたらもうすこし長いかな、早いかな。」

おかあさんは首をかしげた。

「なにしろね、取材って仕事でしょ。予定がたたないんです、ほんとのとこ……。でも、なるべく早く帰ります。」

「そうじゃなあ、直樹はまあいいが、ゆう子ちゃんがどうかな。なんといってもまだ三つだからな。」

おかあさん、おかあさんいうやろ。」

「ゆう子、二ちゅだもん。」

ゆう子がかわりにへんじをした。

「はっはっは、そうかそうか、これから三つになるんだったな、えらい、えらい。」

おじいさんが感心した。するとゆう子は、もっとかしこいところをみせるつもりでもないだろうが、とんでもないことをいった。

「おじいちゃん、おじいちゃんのかんかんには、どうして毛がないんでしょう。」

「いやあ、こりゃまいったのう、こりゃまいった。」

みんな大わらいになった。きょとんとしていたゆう子は、じぶんがわらわれたと思ったのか、べそ

12

をかきそうになって、

「わらっちゃだめ、わらっちゃだめ。」

と、なみだをためて抗議した。おとなは大わ
らいしそうになって口をおさえ、

「はい、わらいません、わらいません。」

と、あわててへんじをする。大にぎやかだっ
た。気がつくと車はいつのまにか繁華街をぬ
け、住宅地をぬけ、山の手へさしかかってい
た。

花浦にはむかし、殿さまが住んでいたの
だそうだ。山城と、居城と二つあって、山城
のほうは早くとりこわされ、居城は、そっく
り東京へはこんだとかで、そのあとが庭園に
なっている。遊ぶところはたくさんあるか
ら、直樹もゆう子も、たいくつすることなん
ぞありゃあせんよと、おじいさんは保証し

13

た。

「しかし、一晩もとまらんで今夜たつというたら、かあさんががっかりするぞ。」

おじいさんがいったとおり、家につくとおばあさんは気がぬけたように、

「やれまあ、やれまあ、いそがしいことじゃ。」

と、そればかりくりかえした。

「帰りにまたよりますから、そのときは一晩ぐらい、とまります。」

おかあさんはけろっとしている。

「まあまあ、それではともかく、お茶をいれて。あんたまあ、こえたな。」

それからながながと、おとなの話がはじまった。おとなの話はほんとににいやだ。なんでおもしろいのかわからない話を、さもおもしろそうに、けらけらわらったり、そうかと思うと、ひそひそ声になったりして、いつまでも、いつまでもつづく。そのあいだには、それ、ゆう子がわらったとか、ゆう子がないたとかで大さわぎだ。ぼくのことなんか、いたっていなくたっていいみたいだ。直樹はそう思ってむくれていた。ようし、あしたっからはゆう子が、ぼくのこしにくっついてくるにきまっている。とすると、きょう、それも、あと数時間の自由だぞ、直樹はそっとおじいさんの家をぬけ出した。

14

2 歩くいすと、ふしぎな家

　直樹がおじいさんの家をぬけ出したとき、もう夕ぐれだというのに、風はぴたりとやんで、とろりとした暑さが、町におりていた。この空気はすきとおったゼリーが、そのまんまじっと熱くなったみたいだな。ぼくはその中を歩いていくんだ。直樹は、そんなおかしなことを考えながら、道をすかして見た。さて、どっちへいこう……。

　「どちらにいこうかな、てんじんさまのいうとおり……。左だ、よし。」

　このやり方は、おかあさんのくせだった。ケーキをたべるときだって、シュークリームがいいか、チーズケーキがいいかまようと、いつもおかあさんはこうやってきめる。どこへでもさっさととんでいってしまう仕事のやり方を見ていると、そんなことにまようのがおかしいみたいだった。でもあん

がい、仕事のとちゅうでこまったことがおこったとき、どちらにしようかな……てんじんさまのいう

とおり、なんて、指をうごかしてきめているのかもしれない。

ずうっと、白い土べいのつづく町らしい。へいがおわるとおほりに出た。見おろすといちめんの藻だっ

た。細いくきに、うす緑のやなぎのようなやさしい葉をつけた藻が、水面をおおいつくすほど、もつ

れあい、からまりあいながらただよっている。そのななめ上から、まっかなあめ玉のように光った夕

日が、いまにもしずもうとしながら、かっとさしこんでいた。すると藻におおわれた水面は、わずか

なすきまからもその光にこたえてきらめき、おほりぜんたいがまるで、光と影で織られたうす緑の織

物のようにかがやいていた。

直樹はおほりのそばに、どのくらい立っていたのかおぼえていない。ふっと気がついたとき、直樹

は足もとを、だれかがコトリ、コトリ、と通りすぎる音をきいた。それと同時にひくいつぶやきがき

こえた。

「イナイ、イナイ、ナイ……イナイ。」

声はひくく、しわがれているのに、足もとからきこえる。直樹は、ぎょっとして足もとをすかして

見た。いすだった。小さな……そう、ゆう子がちょこんとすわったらちょうどいいくらいの、よりか

16

かりのついたまるい、木のいすだった。そのいすが、コトリ、コトリと、ほりばたの白い道を、足を

ひきずるように、歩いていく……。直樹はぼうぜんとした。そんなことが、あるはずがない。いすが

歩くなんて……。けれど、それはゆめではなかった。

「イナイ、イナイ、ドコニモ……イナイ……」

ひくい、しわがれた声でそうつぶやきながら、いすは歩いていく。かっとてりつける、あめ玉のよ

うに赤い夕日の道を、歩いていく……。人っ子ひとり通らない、しんとしたおほりばたを歩いてい

く……。直樹はこおりついたように、木のいすを目で追いながら立ちすくんでいた。いすは、ひどく

年をとった小人の老人のように、コトリ、コトリと、遠ざかり、ふっと消えた。

「………」

直樹は、口をあけて、なにかいおうとしたけれど、声が出なかった。直樹はふらふらと歩きだし

た。しかし、一足、一足が、ひどく重く、からだが前にすこしも進まない。

──ゼリーだ。空気が、ゼリーになっているんだ。だから前へ進むのがつらいんだ。──

直樹は、重い、とろりとした空気を、かきわけるように、一足、一足、進みながら、心の中でくり

かえしていた。日がかげった。光と影のつづれ織りのようにきらめいていたおほりは、きゅうにしっ

とりとした、あわい緑にぼかされて、ねむたそうにさえ見えた。直樹はのろのろと歩き、いすが消え

17

たあたりで立ちどまって、

「ああ……。」

といった。おほりばたにところどころ植えられている、木のしげみでうっかり見おとしていたが、右へおれる道がある。いすはそこをまがったのだろうか、直樹はその道をすかして、もういちど、あっといった。左手のうっそうとした木立で、うす暗くかげった道を、あのいすが、小さく、コトッ、コトッ、と歩いていくのが見えたような気がしたからだった。しかし、もういちど目をこらして見たとき、いすのすがたはなかった。

直樹は歩いた。ゆめの中を、のろのろと歩くようなもどかしさを感じながら、いすがいたように思われる木立のあたりまで、走るように歩いた。

そこにも道があった。細く、くねって、うめの老木の林のおくへ消えている。

「よし、このおくだな。」

そろそろと進むと、なんのことはない。また、城下町らしい土べいの道へ出た。いすは影もかたちもなく、それどころか、かごをさげたおばさんたちが、二、三人のんびりと立ち話をしていた。直樹はくちびるをへの字にまげ、むやみやたらに横町をまがり、気がつくともとの通りに出たりしながら、とつぜん、山にまぢかい雑木林の前に出た。

18

──どこかで見たことのあるような林だ。──

直樹は、しばらくその前に立って考えていた。細い道はあったが、ほとんど人が通ったようすはない。しかし、いすが、あのふしぎないすが帰っていくとしたら、ここしかない。直樹には、そう思えた。

直樹は思いきって、うす暗い林のおくへはいっていった。

と、ふいに、ぱっかりと林はおわり、直樹はあれはてた門の前に出た。門といっても、ただ太い丸

太を焼いて二本立てただけの、ひどく素朴なものだった。のびるにまかせたかいづかの生け垣が、家のまわりをとりかこんでいた。そのあたりにはもう家はなく、花浦の山城があったという城山のくぼみに、ひっそりとだかれた一けん家だった。

その家に、人の住んでいるけはいはなかった。それは、かいづかの生け垣を見ればすぐわかった。長い年月のあいだ、手を入れたり、かりこまれたとのないかいづかの木は、悪魔から息をはきかけられたとでもいうように、ねじくれたうでを空につき立てていた。それはまるで、地獄ののろいのほのおが燃えくるうありさまにも見えた。そして、あれはてた土地にかならずはえるかなむぐらが、くさりのように、またあるところではあみのように、おおいかぶさり、まつわりついていた。

直樹は、しばらく門の前で考えていた。とびらというものがないのだから、はいっていくことはわけなかったが、人のけはいのない、しんとした垣根の中へふみこむことがこわかった。けれども、そのままひきかえすのもくやしい。直樹はおそるおそる門から中へふみこんだ。こまかいじゃりがしきつめられていたらしい細い道が、いまは雑草におおわれながらゆるやかにカーブしている。その道にそって、左側にもかいづかが植えられ、右手の垣根のかいづかと両側からぶきみな枝をアーチのようにさしのべていた。

「あ……。」

20

直樹はぎくりとした。なあんだ、びっくりさせるなよ。つきあたりにひらけた小さなあき地に植え

られたあじさいのしげみの間からじいっと直樹を見つめるように立っているのは、大理石まがいの、

白っぽい男の子の像だった。ああわかった。いつかおかあさんと東京の山手線にのったとき、なんと

かという駅のプラットホームのはずれに立っていた……えぇと、しょうべん小僧っていったかな、か

わいい男の子がおしっこしているすがたの人形だった。おしっこが噴水になって、きらきら光りなが

ら小さな池へ水をはねとばしていた。それではこのへんに、池があるはずだぞ。

直樹は草の間に顔をつっこんだ。あった、れんがをたたんだ四角な池が、からからにひからび、く

ずれかけている。そのまわりに、まつばぼたんが、赤や黄やぼたん色のあざやかな花を、ぞっくりさ

かせていた。池のふちには、四角い台がある。しょうべん小僧はそこにすえられ、この家にまだ人が

住み、子どもたちがかけまわっていたころには、いきおいよくおしっこの噴水をきらきらととばして

いたのだろう。いつ、どんなときに、この小僧は台からころげおちたのだろうか、だれひとりおこし

てやる人もなかったのだろうか、こわれた足をふんばって、小僧はやっぱり、見ればわらわないでは

いられないあどけない顔と、すがたでおしっこをしている。

直樹は足を草の間からひきぬくと、またこまかいじゃり道を二足、三足進んだ。

左手にカーブしたとき、

21

「ほう。」

直樹は目をまるくした。いままでちらちら見えてはいたのだが、ちょうどベールをぬぎすてたよう
に、くちかけた小さな洋風の家がぽっかりとあらわれたからだった。このあたりには、どういうわけ
か、こういう感じの洋館がところどころに見かけられた。列車のまどから見ていても、どういうわけ
か、あらわれては消えて直樹を感心させ
した海べに、古いし、大きくもないけれどしっかりした洋館が、瀬戸内海に面
た。いま東京によく建てられているモルタルづくりの洋館より、木造ながら、この家ははるかにしっ
かりと、家らしかった。そんな洋館が、この古びた城下町にあるなんて……。

ほのかな夕やみが、気がつかないほどうっすりと、あたりにただよいはじめていた。玄関の左手
は、これものびるにまかせた、きょうちくとうの木が、赤い花をつけていた。その向こうは庭になっ
ていた。もとしばふだったらしいのに、ほりかえして畑にしたあとがあり、ふりかえれば垣根にちか
く、ふじだながななめにかたむいて、あやうく立っていた。そこにも夕やみは、ただよいはじめてい
た。いや、気のせいか、くちかけた洋館のまわりには、とりわけこい夕やみがただよっているよう
で、直樹はまた、ためらった。けれどもどうしてもこのまま帰りたくはない。直樹はあたりに気をく
ばりながら、玄関のドアをそっとあけてみた。玄関にはれんががしきつめられ、家の中はもう暗くてはっきりしない。ただ
ドアはすぐひらいた。

ひらきかけたドアからはいる外の光に、玄関におかれたたなの上の古いつぼがほのかにうかんだ。外国のお酒でもはいっていたようなつぼだった。直樹はつぼに目を向けてぎょっとした。大輪のひまわりらしい花が何本か、黒く焼けた紙のようにかれはててささっている。だらりと首をおとした花も、しおれてぶらさがった葉も、カサカサといまにもくずれてくずれていない。直樹はそっとつぼに手をふれようとした。そのとたん、バサバサと音をたてて、黒い花は灰のように散った。それっきり、あたりはやっぱり、しんとしていた。直樹はあとしざりをすると、ぱっと表へとび出した。ふりかえりもせず、門から外へ走り出た。

しかし、直樹はしらなかった。直樹がとび出したあと、暗くなってきた家のすみから、コトリ、コトリと、木のいすが出てきて、じっと直樹を見おくっていたのを——小さないすは、じっと身うごきもせず、長いあいだ立っていた。夕やみがこくおりたころ、ようやく、いすは家の中へ足をひきずりながらはいっていった。

「イナイ、イナイ、ドコニモ、イナイ……。」

いすのつぶやく声は、いすにしかききとれぬほど、ひくかった。

23

3 おほりばたに出るものは

直樹は、はあはあいって立ちどまった。さわりもしないのにくずれた黒い花のいくひらかが、まだ手にこびりついているようで、直樹は手をこすりあわせた。すると声がきこえた。

「どっちにまがろうかな、かみさまのいうとおり、てんじんさまのいうとおり。」

うたうような声だった。おとなが、小さい子の手をひいて、うたうようにいっている声だ。おかあさんだ。直樹はほうっと力がぬけて、

「おかあさん。」

とどなった。

「ここだよ、ぼく、ここ。」

24

「なあんだ、こんなとこにいたの。もっと遠くで、まい子になっているんじゃないかと思って、これからさがしにいくとこだったのよ。」

のんびりと、そんなことをいいながら、おかあさんがゆう子の手をひいて、すぐそこの道から出てきた。山ぎわの雑木林と、板べいの間の細い道だった。

「こんなところって……。」

直樹はあたりを見まわした。あれ、さっきとちがうぞ、そうか、さっきとちがう道をきたんだ。雑木林に、二つの道がついていたんだ。

「ここ、どこなの。」

「いやあね、ほら、この道をはいればおじいさんのおうちのうら口よ。」

「なあんだ、そうか、ちかいんだね。」

「あんまり歩いて、帰り道がわからなくなったんでしょう。」

おかあさんはわらった。

「どこへいったの。殿さまのおやしきのあとへいった？」

「うん、おほりのとこは通ったけど。」

「ああ、あのおほりの向こうがそうよ。いまはもうおやしきはなくて、ぼたん園と、お庭があるだけ

25

だけどね。」

おかあさんは、大きく息をすいこんで空を見あげた。

「いいわねえ、空気がきれいで……。」

ゆう子は、じいっと直樹を見ていたが、たどたどしくいった。

「おにいちゃん、どこいってたの。」

「いいとこさ。」

直樹は、へんじをしたついでに、こぶしをつくって、こつんとゆう子の頭をたたいた。ちょっとさわっただけなのに、ゆう子はみるみる口をまげ、うえーんとなきだした。

「直樹、なにするの。かまうんじゃありません。ゆう子ちゃんも、なかないの。よしよし、どこいたかったの。」

ちぇっ、直樹は、道におちていた石をけとばした。女の子はこれだからいやになる。男の子だったら、あのふしぎな家と、ふしぎな歩くいすがなにものかを探検しに、つれていってやるんだけどな。

だけど、これはいい考えだぞ、ゆう子をつれてあした、あのへんてこな家へもういちどいってみよう。

「さあ、おうちにはいりましょ、ごはんですよ。」

おかあさんは、なきやんだゆう子の手をひいて、歩きだした。

26

「もも、あるもん、ねえ。」

「そうよ、もも、あるわねえ。」

「もも、ピンクだもん、ねえ。」

「そうね。」

おかあさんのへんじが、すこしあぶなくなる。ももをピンクというべきか、考えているんだ、きっと。

「あのね、おかあさんは、ピンクとあお、どっちすき?」

ゆう子がはねながらきいている。

「そうね、青。」

「ゆうちゃんはね、どっちともすき。」

もう、おじいさんの家の、うら口の木戸だった。

夕ごはんには「おばあさん風ピロシキ」が出た。おばあさん風のピロシキという名の、ごじまん料理で、小麦粉で焼いたうす焼きに、あまい油みそをぬりつけ、そこにあまからくいりつけた牛肉と、細くきってさらしたねぎをのせて、くるっとまいてかじるのだ。

「うわあ、わたし、おかあさんのつくったピロシキにあこがれていたのよ。」

27

おかあさんがよろこんだ。この家へついたらそのとたんに、おかあさんは小さい子になってしまっ

たみたいだった。おばあさんも小さい子にいうように、

「ほれ、これをおあがり、こっちがおいしいよ。」

と、せわをやく。ゆう子はおさかながすきなので、はしでおさしみをつまみあげては、口にはこび、

直樹は、両方ともぱくついた。

「夏はこれがええ。」

おじいさんは、おとうふのひややっこを口にはこんでいる。直樹は、さっきからききたくて、うず

うずしていたことを、きいてみた。

「あのねえ、このへんに、おばけとか、そういうの出る?」

「おばけ?」

おじいさんはびっくりしたようにいって、それから、あっはっはあと、天じょうをあおいでわらっ

た。

「そうじゃなあ、おばけ、おばけと……うむ、お城のおほりにかっぱが住んでいるぞう。むかしは夜

になるときれいな女にばけて人をだましたり、すもうをしかけたり、いたずらばかりしておったとい

うことじゃ。」

28

「ああ、あのおほりだね、ぼく、さっき通っ
たよ。」

直樹は、きみょうな気持ちになった。それ
じゃ、あの、ふしぎな歩くいすは、かっぱな
んだろうか。そんな、ばかな……いまごろ、
かっぱが出るなんて……。

「そのかっぱ、どんなかっぱ。」

「どんなかっぱといってもなあ、はて、どんな
んかなあ。そうそう、あるとき、日ぐれどき
のことだったが、さむらいがお城からさがっ
て、おほりばたにきかかると、いきなり声が
かけられた。——おさむらいさま、おねがい
があります。ちょっとこの子をだいていてく
ださいませ、すぐまいりますから——。そこ
でさむらいがふりかえってみると、まあ、な

んともいえんきれいな女の人が、赤んぼうをだいて立っていたそうじゃ。きれいな女の人のたのみだ

からなあ、いやとはいえん。さむらいは、よしよし、だいていてやろうというてな、赤んぼうをうけ

とった。女の人はよろこんで、すぐまいりますというてどこかへ走っていってしまった。ところがそ

れっきり、いつになっても帰ってこない。さむらいはこまって、うろうろ、うろうろしていたが、そ

のうち、へんだな、と思ったんじゃな。赤んぼうがいつのまにか、ふわっとした、羽のようなはだざ

わりにかわっている。そこでとっくりと赤んぼうをながめたが、やっぱり赤んぼうは赤んぼうだ。と

ころがそのさむらい、はっと気がついた。うん、こりゃかもだ、かものはだざわりだ。さてはいまの

女の人はかっぱにちがいない。さむらいは、その赤んぼうをだいたまま、うちまでかけだした。かけ

てかけてわが家にとびこんで、さてあかりの下で赤んぼうを見ると、それは、やっぱりかもじゃっ

た。さむらいの家では、その晩、かもじるをはらいっぱいくうたそうじゃ。」

「まあ、ずいぶんせつなかっぱねえ。」

おかあさんが感心した。

「さむらいはすっかりとくいになってな、人はかっぱにばかされるが、わしはかっぱからかもをとり

あげたぞといって、じまんしとった。ところがそれからしばらくしたある夜のこと、さむらいがおほ

りばたを歩いていると、また出たんだな、女の人が。」

30

「赤んぼうをだいてたの？」

「うむ。——どうぞその子を、すこしのあいだ、だいていてくださいませ——。よしよし、さむらいはおかしいのをこらえてだいてやると、女の人は走っていってしもうた。そのうちにまた赤んぼうの手ざわりが、おかしくなってきたんじゃな、ふわふわと羽のような——。それっとばかりさむらいはかけだした。ほくほくして、家へとびこむと、大声で、かもじるの用意をいたせ、とどなった。ところがあかりの下でよくよく見たら、それは死んだねこだったとさ。」

みんな大わらいし、ゆう子までが、

「ねこ、ねこ、ニャーン。」

といってはねた。

「そのかっぱね、あと、なににばけた。」

直樹はまたきいた。

「そうさなあ、ほかになににばけたかなあ。」

おじいさんは首をひねった。

「たとえばさ、あのう、ほら、たんすとか、つくえとか、いすにばけたりは、しなかった？」

「はっはっはあ、かっぱがつくえに？ いやあ、そいつはきかんのう。」

31

おじいさんは大わらいし、おかあさんは、へんな顔をして、直樹を見た。直樹は真剣だった。

「それじゃあね、そういう……つくえとかさ、そういう、おばけは、出ない？　ここに。」

「出ないのう、そういう、ハイカラなやつは……。」

「でも、ぼく……。」

直樹は、そういいかけて、口ごもった。小さな木のいすが、コトリ、コトリとおほりばたを歩いて

いったなんて、だれにいったって、ほんとうにしてもらえっこない……。

するとおかあさんが、たしなめるようにいった。

「この町におばけが出るなんて、そればっかりいうなんて、失礼ですよ、直樹ちゃ

ん。」

するとおばあさんが、とりなすようにいった。

「殿さんのお墓所にでもいかれたのじゃろ、まあ、あそこには古いお墓が、ずらあっと、あるもんな

あ。おばけが出るかと、ききたくもなるじゃろ。」

ちがう、ちがう、直樹はそういいたかったが、もうなにもいわなかった。そろそろ、おかあさんが

九州へいく夜行列車の時間だった。

32

4　見えなくなったゆう子

つぎの日は雨だった。

「まあ、これでは阿蘇は見えんじゃろ。せっかく九州を横断しようというのに、つまらんのう、おかあさんも。」

おばあさんが空を見あげてなげいた。

「だいじょうぶだよ。おかあさんが阿蘇へいく日になったら、きっと晴れちゃうよ。うちのおかあさんて、そういうふうにできている人なんだ。」

直樹がなぐさめた。そして心の中で、それどころじゃないや、こっちが外へ出れないで、じりじりしてるのに、と思っていた。

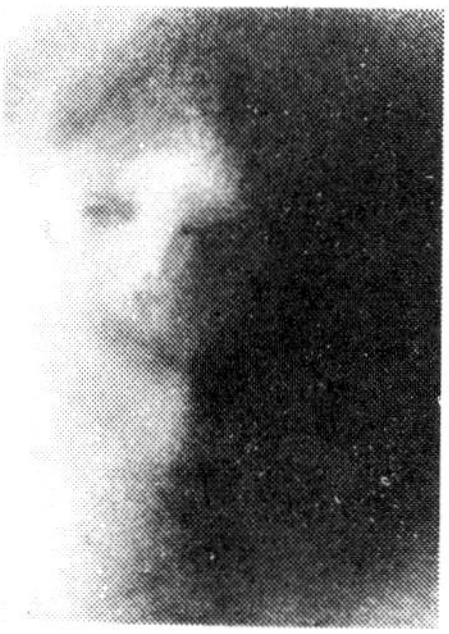

ゆう子は、おかあさんがいなくても、けろりとしていた。いつもおいていかれるのでなれているの
だ。なきだしたのは、お昼寝のときだった。

「ばぶ、ばぶ、イーダちゃんのばぶよう。」

ねむくてねむくて、じれながらゆう子はなき、おばあさんはおろおろして、

「ばぶって、なんじゃろうねえ。ゆう子ちゃんや、ばぶってなあに。え？　教えておくれ。」

と、なんべんもきいて、ゆう子をおこらせた。

「ばぶよう、ばぶよう、イーダちゃんのよう。」

わあわあなくゆう子をもてあまして、おばあさんは、いじわるクイズという本に熱中している直樹
のところへとんできた。

「ばぶ？　ああ、毛布のことだ。」

そこでおばあさんはあせだくになって、しまいこんであった毛布をひっぱり出し、ゆう子に、

「はい、ばぶちゃんですよ。」

と、わたしたが、ゆう子はかんかんになって、

「ちゃうよう、ばぶ、ちゃうー。」

と、まっかになってなきつづけ、おまけに、イーダ、といったものでおばあさんは、

34

「まあ、どうしたらええじゃろ。」

と、なさけながった。

「だいじょうぶ、すぐねちゃうよ。前はね、ばぶがないとぜったいねなくて、どこへいくんでも、ばぶをしょってったんだよ。でもこのごろはそうでもないの、ときどき思い出していうけどね。」

ゆう子はもうなきやみかけていた。そして目をこすり、小さなあくびを一つすると、ころりと横になって、あっというまにねてしまった。

「まあまあ、ようようねてくれたわ。それじゃねえ直樹ちゃん、ちょっとおるす番していておくれ。

おばあさん、買い物をしてくるけえ。」

「はあい。」

「あんたもお昼寝、しんさいよ。」

「はあい。」

ゆう子のおなかに、湯上がりタオルをふわりとかけ、ついでに直樹のまくらとタオルの上がけをわたすと、おばあさんはいそいで出ていった。おじいさんは図書館の仕事をしているので、とっくに出かけていたから家の中はきゅうにひっそりとした。

直樹はごろりと横になって空をながめた。いいぞ、もうじき雨があがりそうだ。そうしたらすぐ、探検に出かけよう。そのとき、ゆう子がねていた

35

らおいてくし、おきてたらつれていこう。ひとりより、ゆう子みたいなちびでもいたほうが心づよいからね。そして、きょうこそ、あの家の中へはいってやろう。そうして……。

目を大きくあけて考えていたはずだったのに、直樹はいつのまにかねてしまったらしかった。気がついたとき、となりにころりとねていたはずのゆう子のすがたがない。直樹は目をこすってすわりなおし、ぼんやりした頭をはっきりさせようとした。おばあさんが帰ってきて、ふたりでどこかへいったのだろうか、きっとそうだ……。

電話のベルがけたたましく鳴った。直樹はとびおきると、どたどたと走って、玄関のわきにおいてある受話器をはずした。

「ああもしもし、直樹ちゃん？　おばあさんじゃけどね、ちょっともう一けん、用事ができてまわるから、もうすこしまっとってね、ええかい？」

「うん、だいじょうぶ。」

「じゃあすぐ帰るからね、すまんねえ。」

カチャリと電話はきれた。直樹はのろのろと、受話器をおいた。おばあさんとゆう子は、いっしょじゃない。じゃ、ゆう子はどこだろう。茶の間かな。

茶の間にも、おじいさんの書斎にも、ゆう子はいなかった。手入れのよくゆきとどいた小さな庭に

36

も、うらにもゆう子はいなかった。直樹はじぶんでも、ひざが、がくがくするのがわかった。

「ゆう子ー、ゆう子ー、ゆう子ー。」

サンダルをつっかけて、直樹は表にとび出した。右をながめ、左をながめまわした。

「ゆうちゃん、ゆう子ー、イーダー。」

白い土べいのつづくしずかな町には、きのうとおなじように人影もなかった。いくら耳をすまして

みても、ゆう子のへんじはきこえてこない。

——もし、おほりにおちたら——。

直樹は顔色をかえていた。走って走って、おほりばたに出た。そこで、二、三人の子がせみ取りの

あみをかついでやってくるのにあった。気がつくと、雨はすっかり晴れていた。

「三つぐらいの女の子にあいませんでしたか。かみの毛が長くて、色の白い……。」

その子たちは顔を見あわせ、

「しらん。」

「あわんかった。」

と、口々にいい、よそものの直樹をめずらしそうにながめた。

「ありがとう。」

37

直樹は礼をいってかけだした。ゆう子、どこへいったんだ。東京の家にいても、だまってどこかへ

いってしまうなんてこと、いっぺんもなかった。いや、そうじゃない、いっぺんだけあった。おかあさ

んが旅行へいっていない日、ひとりで、じぶんのせいより高いかさを持ち、小さな手さげをさげ、ま

だほんとによちよちなのに、表へ出ていってしまって大さわぎしたっけ。あのときは家からすこしは

なれた、小さな雑木林の入り口で遊んでいるのを、やっと見つけたんだ。あのとき、おうちへ帰ろう

ね、っていったら、ちゃうよ、おうち、ここ、といって、雑木林の中を指さして、どうしても帰るっ

ていわないんでこまったっけ……。

直樹はじりじりしながらもういちど、

「イーダー、ゆう子ー」

とさけんだ。へんじはなくて、目の前の家からかいづかの垣根ごしに、ちらりと人がのぞくのが見え

た。このへんはほんとうに、かいづかの垣根や、木が多い。でもここの垣根はちゃんとかりこまれて

いる……。のろのろと直樹は歩きだして、あっと思った。そうだ、家のちかくの、雑木林、秋になれ

ばあかがね色になるけど、あのときは夏で、うっそうとしげっていた。手入れしていない、のびるに

なにかがぱっとひらめいたのに、消えてしまった。それがとって

もたいせつなことなのに、いったい、なんだったろう……。

とつぜん、直樹は立ちどまった。

38

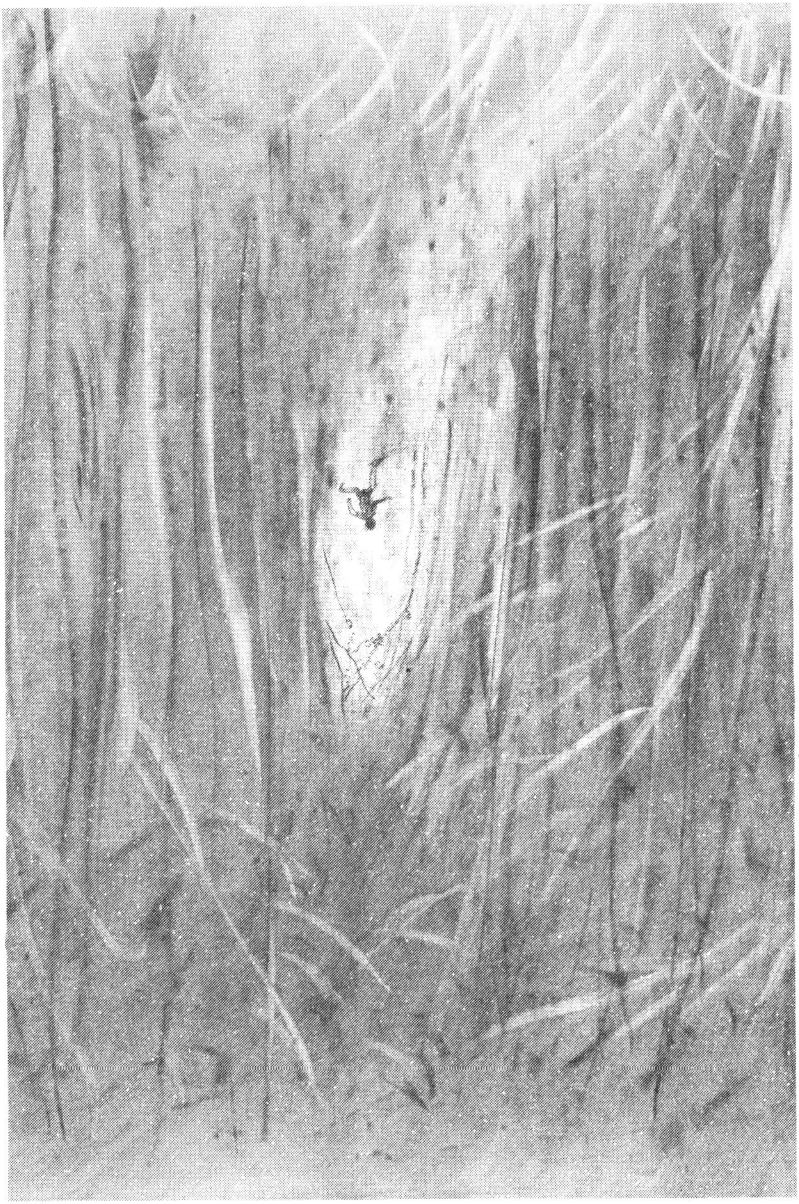

まかせたあの林と、あのふしぎな家のまわりをとりまくかいづかや、しいや、その入り口にある雑木林……そうなんだ。あれはてた感じがどこかにてていると、さっきちらりと思ったんだ。あそこらへんにゆう子はいるにちがいない。

直樹はかけだした。そうだ、なぜ早く気がつかなかったろう。おじいさんの家のうらから出れば、あのふしぎな家はじきなんだ。表からかけだしたから直樹はおほりのほうへきてしまったけれど、ゆう子はうらから出たのかもしれない。

あのふしぎな家に、ゆう子がたったひとりでいるかもしれないということで、直樹は青くなっていた。あせもふこうとせず、かけだしながら、でも直樹はどなっていた。

「ゆう子、ゆう子ったらあ、おうい。」

40

5　ゆう子といす

　まだ日ざしは強いのに、雑木林の中は、ひんやりしていた。せみがシャンシャン鳴いていたが、直樹には、空のはてで鳴いているように遠かった。林の間の道をぬけると、あの、きみのわるい家だった。

　垣根のかいづかの木は、やっぱり地獄ののろいがかかっている、とでもいうように、ねじくれた枝々を天につき立てていた。　直樹はしんとした門の中へ、足をふみこんだ。ジャリッ、ジャリッ、足もとで、じゃりが鳴った。

　「あい、おうどんでしゅ、たべてくだしゃい。」

　ふいに、やわらかな、あどけないひとりごとがきこえた。　いた。ゆう子の声だ。直樹はぺったりとすわりこみたいほど、ほっとした。すぐにかけだしていこうとして、まてよ、と思った。ゆう子のや

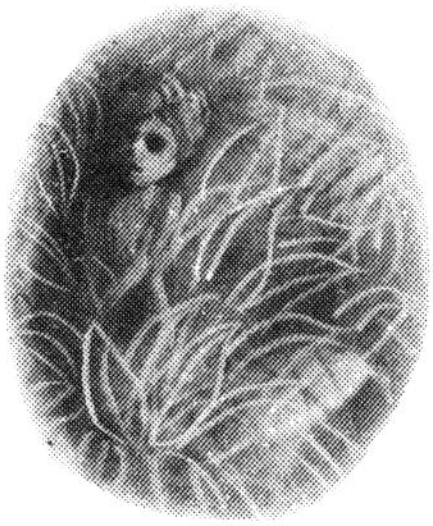

つ、なにをしているのだろう……。直樹はひときわどっしりと立って目かくしの役をはたしているか

いづかのかげに身をよせると、そっと庭をのぞいてみた。

ゆう子は、きょうちくとうの下にしゃがんでいた。花びらをひろっては、なにかに入れているらし

い。だれも住んでいないこの家の庭に、たったひとりでいるこわさなど、ゆう子は、てんで、感じて

もいないようだった。あ、こっちを向いた。手に持っているのは、まわりが黒く、中が朱ぬりのおわ

んだった。そこへ、きょうちくとうの花びらを入れ、

「あい、おうどんでしゅ。どうぞ。」

といって、見えないだれかと、おままごとしている。そして、もうひとつのおわんをとりあげると、

小さな手をいそがしくうごかして、あらうまねをした。ちょっと手を上にあげて、指さきをひねるま

ねは、きっとあそこに、水道があるつもりなんだろう。

「おうどんでしゅ、はやくたべてくなさあい。」

ゆう子がまたいっている。ようし、出ていってびっくりさせてやろう。からだをおこしかけて、直

樹はあっといった。

「はああい。」

すんだ声をひびかせて、ゆう子がいきなり立ち上がり、パタパタと家の中へかけこんだからだっ

42

た。それは、じぶんの家で、母親によばれた子どものしぐさだった。

「あいつ……ちょうしいいぞ。」

まだ二さいと十一か月のゆう子は、こわさとか、きみわるさとかは、感じないものなのだろうか。ゆう子が中にいると思っても、直樹にはやっぱり、この見しらぬ家に、さかさかはいっていくのはためらわれる。

家の中から、ゆう子の、はじけるようなわらい声がきこえた。——じゃあ、だれか、住んでいるのかな。そして、ゆう子となかよくなって、いっしょに遊んでくれているのかな。たしかにひとりじゃない。東京の家でだって、めったにきかないはしゃいだ声だった。だいたいゆう子は、昼間は家にいないんだ。おかあさんが仕事をしているおかあさんだったから、直樹もそうだったが、ゆう子も一さいになると保育園の赤ちゃんべやにあずけられて大きくなった。だからなお、昼間ゆっくり、ゆう子と遊ぶ時間がない。また、わらい声がした。しかたがない。直樹はまっすぐせなかをのばすと、玄関の前へ立って、

「ごめんください。」

といった。

「…………」

43

へんじはなかった。おくのほうで、足音と、いすをひきずるような音と、おかしそうなゆう子の声が、またきこえた。直樹はあたりを見まわした。やっぱり、人は住んでいないんだ。まどのガラスがなんまいかわれていたし、廊下の白いかべも、どさりと一か所おちていた。天じょうには、くもが糸をはっていた。しかし、きみょうなことに、床だけはほこりっぽくなかった。ぴかぴかとはいえないにしても、だれかがどうにかしているように見えた。

「……わからないなあ。」

直樹は首をひねり、どなった。

「ゆう子、ゆう子。イーダー。」

ようやく、

「はあい。」

というへんじがかえってきた。それと同時に、あぶないですよう、はいし、はいしというさけび声がして、うまにまたがるように、木のいすにまたがったゆう子が、おくからからだをゆすりゆすり、とびだしてきた。はいし、はいし、ゆう子はいすをカタカタとゆすりあげ、いすは生きもののようにゆう子をのせて、はねていた。ゆう子がはねまわっているのか、いすがゆう子をのせて、はねまわって

44

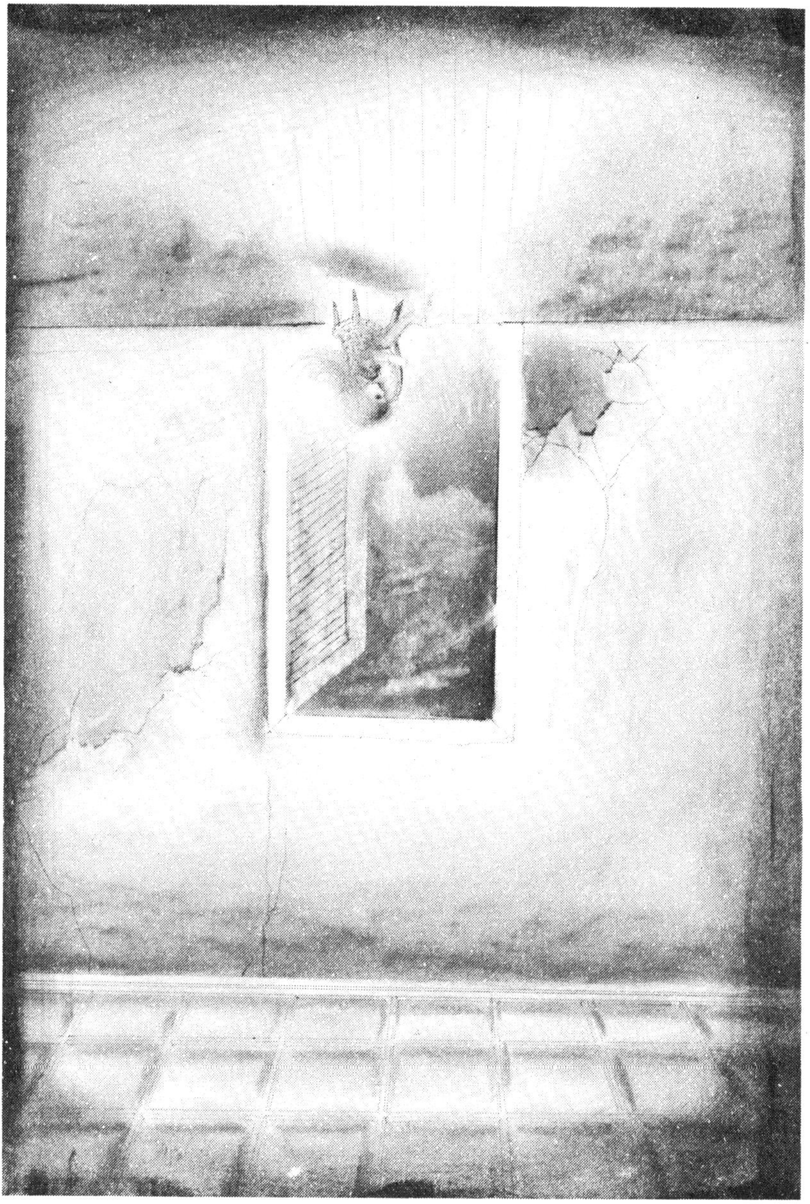

いるのか、とにかくいすとゆう子は、どんなうまとその乗り手よりも、ぴったりと息があっていた。

「ゆう子、あぶない。」

直樹はどなった。しかし、ほっぺたをまっかにさせたゆう子には、そんな直樹の声はきこえないらしい。目の前でくるりとユーターンすると、はいしはいしと、家の中へかけこんでいく。

「ゆう子、イーダー。」

はいし、はいし、床をふみ鳴らし、くっくとわらいながら、ゆう子はまた、おくのへやからいすにのってきた。ぴたりととまると、ふしぎそうに直樹をながめ、

「だあれですかあ。」

といった。

「ゆう子、なにいってるんだ。おにいちゃんじゃないか、さあ、早くおうちへ帰ろう。」

それでもゆう子は、大きく目を見はって、ふしぎそうに直樹を見ているだけだった。それからやっ

と、

「どうぞ、おあがりくなさい。」

といって、おじぎをした。

「ゆう子、ふざけるときかないぞ。さあ、いすからおりなさい。」

46

「いやっ。」

ゆう子はしっかりいすにつかまり、そのままくっく、くっくとわらいながら、足をばたばたさせた。

「おんま、はいし、はいし。」

あっというまもなく、ゆう子をのせたいすは、ドアから外へ一とびにとびおりていた。そしてほんとうのうまよりも、かるがるとはねあがり、きょうちくとうの木の横から、しばふのおもかげが残っている庭へととびこむと、輪をかいてかけめぐった。

「いすだ……歩くいすだ……。」

直樹はぼうぜんとそれを見ていた。いまここにいるじぶんがほんとうなのか、ゆめを見ているのか、もうわからなかった。

「ゆう子、おりなさい。けがしたらどうするんだよっ。」

そのとたん、いすは草の根にひっかかって、ゆう子はほうり出され、のびほうだいのびたしばふの上にころがった。

「ほらごらん、にいちゃんが、あぶないって、いっているだろっ。」

しかしゆう子は、かけよってくる直樹には見向きもせず、ころがったいすをかかえると、

「いい子、いい子、ないちゃだめ。」

47

と、いすがまるでいぬかねこか、小さな友だちででもあるように、やさしくなぐさめた。いすは、コトリともいわなかった。

「ゆう子、だまっておうちを出てきちゃだめだろ。さあ、おばあさんのうちへ帰ろう、ふたりともいなくなっていたら、おばあさん、心配してるぞ。」

ゆう子はふり向いた。色白の顔がまっかに上気して、目がきらきら光っている。ゆう子は、まるで見たこともない男の子を見るように、にくたらしそうに直樹を見ると、

「あっち、いきなちゃい、イーダ。」

と、顔をくちゃくちゃにしてみせた。

「おうちへ帰るんだよ、ゆう子。」

直樹はにいさんらしく、威厳を見せて、もういちど、いってきかせた。けれどゆう子には、水の中でものをいっているように、直樹のいうことがすこしもわからないようだ。きょとんとして、

「おうち？　おうちだもん。イーダちゃんのおうち、ここだもん。」

といった。

「なにいっているんだ、ゆう子は。」

直樹はきつい声になった。直樹だって、つかれていた。暑い日ざしの中を、どのくらい走りまわっ

48

たかしれやしない。それなのにゆう子のやつ、ひとりでのうのうと、まるでじぶんのうちのように、

この、ふしぎな家をわがもの顔に遊んでいる……それにこのいすだ、直樹は足を上げると、いすを思い

きり、けっとばした。

「なんだ、こんないす、こわしちゃうぞ。」

歩くいすだ、けっとばしたらとびかかってくるかもしれない。直樹はそう思って、すぐ身がまえた

が、いすは、歩いたり、ゆう子をのせてかけまわったことはわすれたように、ごろりとたおれている

だけだった。かわりにゆう子がわっとなきだした。なみだをふりとばし、なきじゃくりながら直樹に

とびついて、めちゃくちゃに直樹をぶった。

「イーダちゃんのおいすよう、イーダちゃんのを、あーん、あーん。」

「ごめんごめん、さあ、おうちへ帰ろう。」

直樹はしゃがんで、ゆう子へせなかを向けた。ゆう子はなきじゃくりながら、それでもすなおに直

樹のせなかへおぶさった。あせだらけで、ずっしり重い。つかれたのか、顔をせなかにもたせてき

た。

直樹はふっとかなしくなった。いつのまにかもう、夕ぐれてきていた。直樹はゆっくりと玄関へ

まわると、ドアをしめ、じゃりをふんで門を出た。おかあさんは、なにをしているのだろう。はじめ

てきたこの町で、なにか、わからないことがおこっているというのに……。

49

6 りつ子

その晩、直樹はねつかれなかった。花浦のおじいさんの家へきてからおこった、ふしぎな家と、歩くいすと、ゆう子との三つがからみあって、いくらねようと思ってもねつかれない。直樹はかやの中で、バタン、バタンとねがえりをうっては、ため息をついた。

「どうしたの、ねつかれんの。」

となりのへやから、おばあさんの声がした。直樹はあわてて、息をひそめた。おばあさんはしばらくようすをうかがっているようだった。直樹はうんむにゃむにゃと、いかにもよくねているような声を出してみせた。それに安心したのだろう。おばあさんはまたまくらに頭をつけたようだった。

――そうだ、あした、ゆう子のやつが昼寝をしたらすぐ、あの家へいってみよう。そして、あのい

50

すとちゃんと話をつけてやろう。そしてあの家がなんなのか、なぜいすのくせに、カタカタ歩きまわ

るのか、きいてやろう。そうしないとこれからさき、なにがおこるかしれやしない。ただ、あそこで

ゆう子が遊ぶ、それだけならいいけれど……直樹はそこまで考えると、ようやくねむけがおそってき

た。となりを見るとゆう子は、手も足もなげ出して、ぐっすりねむっていた。いったい、こういうう

びは、なにを考えているんだろう。この小さな頭の中で、なにを考え、なにを思っているんだろう。

直樹はあくびをして、タオルの上がけをひっぱりあげ、まくらをうらがえしにして、つめたいところ

へほおをおしあてた。ねむけがおそってきて、直樹はすとんと、深いねむりにおちこんでいった。

「うみいくの、うみいくのよ、おふねにのるんだもんねえ。」

うたうように、ゆう子の声が、くりかえし、くりかえし、ひびいてくる。ゆう子のやつ、なにいっ

ているんだろう……どこかでそう思いながらねむたくて、直樹はねがえりをうった。

「おにいちゃん、おっきしなさい。おふねいくのよ、おじいちゃんとおばあちゃんとおにいちゃんと

イーダちゃんといくのよう。」

ゆう子にどんとからだの上にのられて、直樹はようやくほんとうに目がさめた。顔をあらっている

とおばあさんが、まちかねたようにいった。

51

「直樹ちゃん、きょうはねえ、みんなで宮島へいきましょう。おじいさんがお休みとれたので、つれていってあげますって。」

「こまったなあ、ぼく、なんだか頭がいたくって。」

直樹はいった。ほんとうは頭なんかすこしもいたくなかった。ただ、みんなで宮島へいくときいて、とたんにチャンスだ、とひらめいたのだ。宮島がどういう島かしらないけれど、あのふしぎな家を探検するほどのスリルがあると思えなかった。おばあさんは、たちまち心配そうに手をのばし、直樹のひたいに手をあてた。

「熱はないようじゃけどねえ。そういえば直樹ちゃん、きのう、ねぐるしそうにしておったねえ。」

おばあさんはどうしましょうというように、おじいさんを見た。

「そうじゃなあ、宮島にはきれいなお宮もあるし、しかもおるし、船でいくのはいいぞう、頭がちょっとくらい、いたいのはがまんして、いくといいんじゃがのう。」

直樹は首をふった。

「でもぼく、わるいけど、おるす番しているよ。」

「そんなら、わたしも残ろうかねえ。」

「だっておまえは、庵主さんにあう用があるのじゃろ、またなかなかいけんぞ。」

52

「そうねえ。」

おばあさんは首をひねる。

「宮島の尼寺の庵主さんにねえ、ちょっと用があるもんでねえ。」

おばあさんはこまったように直樹を見た。

「だいじょうぶだよ、ぼくひとりで、ちゃんとるす番してるよ。きのうみたいに、どこかへいったりしないよ。」

直樹はそうやくそくした。

「そんならそうしよう。せっかく、みんなでいこうと思ったのに、ざんねんじゃけど、しかたない。

じゃ直樹ちゃん、あと、たのむな。」

おじいさんは男だからさっぱりとそうきめて、ごはんがすむと、三人は出かけた。直樹は、仮病をほんとうらしくするために、あまりごはんもたべず、なんとなくごろごろしていた。おばあさんはそれを見ると、また心配になったらしく、くどくどいったが、直樹はへいきだからといって、おばあさんを玄関からおし出した。

「さあ、いよいよ、探検だぞ。」

直樹はしんとしずまりかえった家で、口に出していってみた。ところが、いざ出かけようというと

53

きになって、とんでもないじゃまがはいった。ガラリと玄関の戸があいて、

「直樹さん、いるう？」

と、心やすくいいながら、ひとりのむすめさんが上がりこんできたのだ。むすめさんはぼうしをか

ぶった直樹を見ると、ちょっと首をかしげて、

「あなた、直樹さん？」

とたずねた。

「はい、そうです。」

「頭いたいんでしょう、ねていなくていいの？」

直樹はじろじろとそのむすめさんをながめた。すきとおるように色が白く、すんなりと長く毛をた

らしているのがよくにあう。でもどういうんだろう、頭がいたいんでしょ、なんて、どこできいたんだ。

むすめさんは直樹の心を見ぬいたように、にこっとわらった。

「わたしね、りつ子っていうの、おたくのおばあちゃまにたのまれて、おるす番にきたのよ。もし熱

でも出るといけないから、そばにいてやってくれって。でも直樹ちゃん、だいじょうぶそうね。ぴん

ぴんしているもの。ぼうしかぶって、どこへいくところだったの。」

「どこもさ。」

54

直樹はがっかりして、ぼうしをほうり出した。ちぇっ、せっかくえた自由を、こんなかたちでうし
なうなんてさ……。りつ子はガサガサと紙のふくろからアイスクリームをとり出していた。じぶんも
なめながら、一つを直樹にわたして、またにこっとした。
「おなかはだいじょうぶなんでしょ。もしいたいんならだめよ。わたしがなめるから。」
「いたくない。だいじょうぶだよ。」

直樹はあわてて手を出した。わりにはなせそうだぞ、このおねえさん。だけど直樹は、おとなにな

んかなにもいうまいと心にきめていた。おとなになんて、こんなたいせつなこと、はなせるもんか、

子どもにだって……。東京の友だちの顔がうかんだ。くやしいなあ、東京の友だちがいたら、いっ

しょに探検できるのに。ゆう子じゃしょうがありゃしない。まるで赤んぼなんだもの。

直樹は、アイスクリームがとけかかるのにも気がつかず、のろのろとなめながら考えこんでいた。

りつ子はそれを見ると、やっぱりすこしはぐあいがわるいんだな、と思ったらしく、直樹をそっとし

ておいて、そこらをかたづけたり、直樹のために、お昼をつくってくれたりした。

「ぼく、だいじょうぶです。ひとりでもちゃんとおるす番できるよ。」

直樹がくりかえしそういうので、りつ子は、お昼のサンドイッチをおぜんの上にのせると、

「じゃあね。」

といって、にこっとわらった。

「じゃあね。」

直樹もわらった。そんなりつ子のわらい顔を見ていると直樹は、ねえ、おねえさん、いっしょにへ

んな家へいってみようよ、といいたくて、うずうずしてきた。でも直樹はぐっとこらえて、りつ子の

出ていくのを見おくった。

56

——さあ、こんどこそ、ひとりになれた。

直樹はサンドイッチをつめこむと、玄関の戸や、ざしきの戸をすっかりしめた。そして、うら口から、そっと外へ出た。

おじいさんの家は、むかしお城があったというお城山の、山ぎわにあったが、そこはまだ雑木林が残っていて、その林にそって左におれ、つきあたって右におれると、あの家だった。山ふところにいだかれているような家だし、雑木林のおくになっているし、そのうえ、かいづかの生け垣にびっしりととりかこまれているから、このおくに家があるなんてだれも気がつかないのだろうか。この林の中の道も、あの家の人が住まなくなってからは、通る人もないのか、落ち葉にうもれていた。せみがシャンシャン鳴いていたが、木が多いこのしずかな山ぎわの町では、ここまでせみ取りにくる子もいないのだろう。空の青さをきりとってちりばめたように、ほたるぐさがさき、きんみずひきや、ぎんみずひきもつんつんと細くさいていたが、花をつむ子もいない。いったい、何年前に、この家の人たちは出ていったのだろう。そのとき、この雑木林は、きょうのように夏のすがたただったのだろうか。それとも、あかがね色の葉をおとしていたのだろうか。きょうの直樹はすこしおちついた気持ちで、あのいすの住む家へ、まっすぐに門をくぐってはいっていった。

57

7　ふたりのイーダ

きのうけっとばしたあのいすは、あのまま庭にころがっているだろうか、それとも、直樹たちが立

ちさったあと、ひとりでカタカタと、家の中へはいっていっただろうか、直樹が昨夜からたしかめた

いと思っていることの一つはそれだった。もし、あの小さな木のいすがうごくことができるなら……。

直樹のゆめや、見まちがいでないのなら……木のいすはあそこにないはずだった。

直樹は、こいもも色の花をつけているきょうちくとうのかげをまわった。右手のかどは、応接間に

なっているらしく、細長い、古風なまどに、色ガラスをはめこんだステンドグラス風の開き戸がつい

ている。いすは、ちょうどそのまどの下にたおれていなくてはならないはずだった。

いすは、やっぱりなかった。のびほうだいのびたしばと、あいまにのびてきた雑草が、ふみしだか

れている。ゆう子やいすや直樹がふんだあとだった。しかし、いすのすがたはない。やっぱりそうだった。いすはひとりでおき上がり、あの足をひきずるような歩き方で、この家にはいっていったのだろう。直樹は石をたたんだベランダに上がると、家の中をのぞいた。カーテンがさがっているのでよくわからないが、そこは、食堂のようにも見えた。

「やっぱり、玄関からはいらなくちゃ、だめなのかなあ。」

直樹は口の中でいいながら、そろそろと家にそって、そのまま進んだ。つぎは和室らしく、ガラス戸の向こうにしょうじがしまっていた。直樹はそのまま家にそって右へまがった。この家はがけぎわに地形を利用して建てられたらしく、西から北へかけて、がけが自然のかこいになっていた。かきの木が二本立っていて、そのかげをまわって直樹は、ほう、と、うれしげな声をあげた。がけの中腹にパイプがさしこんであり、自然のいずみがわき出している。下にうけるところがあるのをみると、そ
の水を使っていたらしい。水は石をたたんでつくったためからあふれ、ちょろちょろとみぞをつくって流れていく。直樹は両手にうけて口をつけてみた。歯にしみるつめたさだった。ゴクゴク飲んだ。

「ふうう。」

口をふくと、生きかえったような気がした。

「この家、いいなあ、ほんとにいいよ。きれいにして、ぼく、住みたいや。」

59

東京の、せせっこましい団地の生活が、味気なく思い出された。たったいっぺんだけねこを飼ったけど、どんなにそのことで、かたみがせまかったことか——。この家をすっかりきれいにして、子どもの家にしたい。木のぼりしたっておこられない、さか立ちしたってもんくをいわれない。そんな家にしたいなあ。

直樹は気をとりなおして、もういちど右へまがった。ふろ場があって、つぎが台所口だった。ガラスのはまった板戸のところに、古びたこんろが一つ、よせてあった。直樹はめずらしげに、こんろをながめた。ずうっと前、こんなこんろが家にあって、おかあさんが炭をおこしていた。しかし、それは、小さいときの思い出だった。まるめた新聞紙にマッチをすって火をつけると、こんろからは、めらめらと赤いほのおとこいけむりがいきおいよくふき上がり、おかあさんはその上に、黒い炭をのせたっけ。でも、ゆう子が生まれるころ、団地にはいってから、こんろはどこかへいってしまった。いまではおさかなを焼くのもガスの上にあみをのせて焼く。いやそうじゃない。このごろは、なんとかいう器械で焼くんだっけ。直樹が男の子のくせにどうしてこんなことをおぼえているかというと、このあいだお客さんがきたときに、おかあさんが手まね身ぶりもおかしく、こんろで炭をおこすまねをして、わらっていたからだった。

「いまはさらあらい機まで出てきているでしょう。なんだか、あんまりべんりになりすぎて、つぎは

60

どうなるのか、こわいみたいね。」

お客さんがそういったら、おかあさんが、

「そうよ、もういっぺん、こんろで火をおこして、焼きたてのさんまなんてたべたいわ。」

そんな話をしていたのだ。直樹はそのときあざやかに、うす暗くなったうら口へこんろを出して、バタバタあおいでいるおかあさんのすがたを思い出した。あれはいくつのときだったろう。直樹はそれがひどくさびしくみえて、わすれられないでいたのだ。

そのこんろが、なんで台所の口をふさぐように、じゃまっけな場所においてあるのだろう。直樹は、こんろに手をかけて、持ち上げようとした。そのとたん、こんろはくずれて、音もなくくだけ、うら口のガラス戸がゆらりとあいた。そうか、うら口の戸をおさえるためにおいてあったのか。

直樹は、ぶるっと身ぶるいした。でもきょうは、こんなことでは、けっしてひきかえすまいと、決心してきたのだ。あいたうら口から、家の中は暗く見えた。直樹は口をむすんで、せまっている城山のがけと、家のうらの間を通りぬけた。サイダーのびんが二、三本ころがっていたり、まきがわずかばかり積んである、細いところから、かいづかの木のうらをぬけていくと、ひろがるだけひろがったあじさいのしげみがあり、そこをすりぬけると、しょうべん小僧の噴水の横だった。もうそろそろ、三時かな、いそがなくっちゃ。

61

直樹は、ドアの取っ手に手をかけて、ひらいた。

「ごめんください。」

直樹は、口の中でつぶやいた。だまってはいるのもためらわれ、かといって、しんとした家に向かって、声を出すのもこわかった。じぶんの声しかひびかないのだから……。ところが、口の中でつぶやいただけなのに、家のおくで、うごくけはいがした。コトッ、コトッ、コトッ、ひきずるような、規則正しい音がちかづいてくる。木のいすだった。

「マッテイタ。」

木のいすは、ひくい声でつぶやいた。

「アガリナサイ。」

コトッ、コトッ、コトッ、木のいすは、くるりと向こうを向くと、家の中へはいっていく。思いがけない出むかえ方をされて、直樹はいささかあわてていた。直樹がいすと話をつけなくちゃ、と思っていたように、いすのほうでも、そう考えているらしい。そうでなかったら、まっていたよ、などといわないだろう。直樹はおへそのあたりに、うんと力を入れると、運動ぐつをぬぎすてて、いすのあとについておくへはいっていった。

外は暑いのに、家の中は、ひんやりとしていた。長いあいだ、とじこめられていた空気はかびくさ

62

く、ガラス戸のカーテンごしにさしこんでくる日の光で、へやの中は、うす暗かった。

食堂らしいへやにはいると、直樹はそうきいた。いすがへんじをしないので、

「戸をあけてもいいだろ？」

「じゃあ、あけるよ。」

とことわって、カーテンをひらいた。もとは黒い布だが日に焼けて、茶色に変色したカーテンは、

さっとひらくと、ベリベリとさけておち、直樹の手にまとわりついた。直樹は顔をしかめた。ガラス戸のかぎもさびついていた。力をこめてまわしてもまわらない。しかたがないのでおちたカーテン地をひろって、かぎにまきつけ、全身の力をかけたら、ようやくかぎはうごいた。

ガラス戸をあけると、さわやかな風がふきこんできた。いすはじっと立っていた。直樹はふりかえって、いすをながめた。いままでこれほどゆっくりいすをながめたこととはなかった。いましげしげとながめて見ると、このいすは小さいくせに、ひどく手のかかったいすだった。

ちょうどいいくらいだから、ひどく小さく、愛らしいものだったが、どうしてどうして、大きさはゆう子にうっているようなものではなかった。せなかのよりかかりに、なにかわからない彫刻がしてあり、それがどうかすると、人の顔めいた影になる。それがなお歩くいすを、あやしい生きものらしくさせていた。だれがつくったのかしらないけれど、このたった一つのいすを、心をこめてつくりあげた人がいるにちがいない。このへやには、ほかにもいすが四つとテーブルと食器戸だながあったが、ほかのいすはとりたてて、すばらしいいすでもない、ごくふつうのものだった。

「ワタシハウレシイノダヨ。」
いすがはなしはじめた。
「チイサナイーダガ、マタカエッテキタノダカラ。」

64

直樹はへんな顔をして、いすを見た。

「それ、どういうこと。」

「イーダダヨ。キノウモ、マタキノウモ、イーダヲ、ワタシハマッテイタ。ソレナノニオマエハ、カエッテキタイーダヲツレテイッタ。ダガ、ワタシニハワカッテイル。イーダハマタジキニクル。」

「なにをいっているのか、ぼくには、ちっともわからない。」

　直樹はいらいらしていった。

「いっておくけどね、イーダ、つまりゆう子のことだけどね、ぼくの妹なんだ。ぼくたちは東京から、ほんのすこしのあいだ、この花浦にきているだけなんだ。おかあさんが帰ってきたら、ぼくたちはすぐ東京へ帰るんだよ。」

「オカアサンダト？」

　いすは、ふしぎそうにいった。

「イーダノオカアサンハ、シンダ。イーダハオジイサント、コノイエニスンデイタンダ。」

「ねえ、きみ、きみはなにか、勘ちがいをしているんじゃないの。きみのイーダちゃんは、べつの子だ、うちのゆう子じゃない。ちがうんだよ。」

「イイヤ、チガワナイ。アノコガ、ワタシノマッテイタ、イーダダ。アノコハ、タダイマアトイッ

65

テ、コノウチヘカエッテキタンダヨ。オマエサンノヨウニ、ドアヲアケタリ、カンガエタリ、ウチノ
マワリヲ、ドロボウネコミタイニ、カギマワッタリシナイ。コンニチハナンテイウモノカ。タダイマ
ア、トイッテカエッテキタンダ。ソシテイツモアソンデイタキノオワンヲサッサトダシテキテ、イツ
モアソンデイルヨウニ、オママゴトヲシタノダ。キョウチクトウノ、モモイロノハナビラヲオワンニ
イレテ、ハイ、オウドンデス、ドウゾ、トイッテ、オンナジサ、キノウトオンナジョウニ、アソンデ
イタサ。ヨソノコジャナイ、ウチノコナンダヨ。」

「ちがう、ちがうちがう。」
直樹はどなった。もう、なんといってこのばかげたいすをやっつけたらいいのか、直樹はいよう
がなくて、なきたいくらいだった。

「いいかい、それならだよ。どうしてぼくが帰ろうっていったのさ。ぼくはゆう子の
おにいちゃんだぞ。ゆう子はぼくの妹なんだ。生まれたときから、そうなんだ。」
いすは、コトリ、コトリと歩きだした。

「イーダニ、オニイチャンガイルトハ、ハジメテキイタ。ソレナラ、オマエサンモ、ココノウチノコ
ダ。」

8 おそうじ、おそうじ

いくらはなしても、いくらいいあっても、どうしても、おたがいのいっていることが一つにならないことがある。直樹はいすをまたけとばしたくなった。でも、もうけとばすのはやめようと思った。

けとばすなんて、いいことじゃない。しかし、いったいどうしたらこのいすに、直樹とゆう子がこの家と、なんのかんけいもないのだと、わからせることができるのだろう。答えはかんたんだった。

帰ってしまえばいいのだ。もう何日かすれば、おかあさんが帰ってくる。そして直樹たちは列車にのって、東京へ帰る。いすはなにもしらないで、この家の中を歩きまわっているのだろう。ここまで考えたとき、ふいに直樹は、むねがしめつけられるようにいたんだ。いすの、「ナイ、イナイ、イナイ……。」という、孤独なつぶやきが、耳の底によみがえった。いすは、だれかをさがしもとめてい

るのだ。そしてゆう子を、だれかと、まちがえているのだ。いったい、どうしたらいいのだろう。

「イーダハ、クル、ココヘクル。」

とつぜん、いすがいった。どんなことがあっても、くるにきまっている、そういう自信にみちた声をきくと、直樹はまたはらがたってきた。そして、思いついたことを口にした。

「イーダちゃんて子はね、外国人じゃないのかい？　ここだって、ふつうの日本人の家みたいじゃないし……こんろなんてあったり、ちょっとへんだけどさ。」

いすは気分をわるくしたようだった。

「イーダヲ、オマエサンガイモウトダトイウナラ、ナンデ、ガイコクジンダナドト、カンガエルノカネ。イーダハニホンジンサ、キマッテイルジャナイカ。」

「だって、イーダって外国の名まえだよ。ぼく、アンデルセンの童話で読んだ。イーダちゃんの花という話だ。」

「ソレソレ、ソレダ。」

いすはくっくとわらった。

「オマエサン、ナンデモシッテルクセニ、ソウイウコトヲイウ。オカアサンガマダ、オゲンキノコロダ。マダチッチャナイーダニ、ソノ、アンデルセントカイウヒトノ、『イーダチャンノハナ』トイウ

68

エホンヲ、ヨクミセテイタ。イーダチャンハソノホンガスキデナ、ジブンノコトヲ、シマイニハ、イー
ダ、イーダ、トイウヨウニナッタ。ソレデ、イーダトミンナガイウヨウニナッタンダ。ソウダロ？」

「ちがうよ。うちのイーダは、イーダといって、へんな顔をするからなんだ。それはぼくが教えたん
だけどね。いっぺんやったら、もうぜったいにおぼえちゃうんだから、かなわないよ。」

「ソウダ、イーダハカシコイ。」

いすはあいづちをうった。

「一ツノトキダ。ヒトリデオサジヲモッテ、ゴハンヲタベルト、チャント、オワンヤゴハンノチャワ
ンヲカサネテ、ゴチソウサマノオジギヲシタモンダ。ソレカラ、チャワンヲモッテヨチヨチアルイ
テ、ナガシニホウリコンダ。」

「そうだそうだ。おてつだいしてくれるのはうれしいけど、おちゃわんがわれちゃううって、おかあ
さん、こまっていた。」

「ソウダ、ソウダ。」

あいづちをうたれて、直樹はあれっと思った。そんなばかな……いつのまにか直樹といすは、おん
なじ子のことをはなすように、はなしあっている。そんなばかなこと。すこしおちついて考えよう。
こんがらかって、なにがなんだかわからなくなってきた。

69

直樹は立ち上がって、ゆっくりと家の中を歩きだした。食器戸だなには、花もようのスープざら

や、コーヒーセットや、コーヒーポットがならべてあった。たなの上には、古ぼけたおかしなはこが

あった。布をはったアーチ形のまどがあって、ダイヤルがついている。ラジオらしい。

「そうだ、テレビがないぞ。」

直樹はひとりごとをいった。テレビがこの家にないとすると、ここの人たちがいなくなったのは、

テレビというものが世の中にあらわれる以前なんだろうか。もちろん、いまだって、テレビのない家

はある。

だけど——。

ラジオの横には、古い本立てがあって、なんさつかの本が立っていた。その横の柱に、日めくりが

ついていた。毎日はがすようになっているよみだ。6という数字だけが読めた。

直樹は食堂から台所へ出た。なんというさびしい台所だろう。まっ白な電気冷蔵庫もないし、トー

スターも、ガスレンジもない。布のふくろからはまめがすこし、こぼれているだけだ。かごの中には

かさかさにひからびて木のかけらのようになったやさいがころがっている。しかし、人が住んでいた

しょうこには、たなには、なべややかんがおいてあったし、ながしの木のおけには、ちゃわんが二つ

と、はしが二ぜん、からからにかわいてころがっていた。一つはおとなの、それも男の人のものらし

70

く、一つは赤いぬりの、ちょうどゆう子が使っているような、愛らしいはしだったし、ちゃわんにもいぬのもようがついていて、小さな女の子のものらしかった。

「ここにだれが住んでいたの。その人たち、どこへいったの。」

直樹はいすにきいた。

「オジイサントイーダサ、キマッテイルジャナイカ。ドコヘイッタカッテ。ソレハワカラナイ。デモイインダ、イーダハカエッテキタ、カエッテキタンダ。」

「おじいさんは、帰ってこないんだろ？」

「アア、デモ、モウカエッテクルヨ。イーダガカエッテキタンダカラ。」

「そのおじいさんとイーダは、いつまでここ

ナ、イーダノカラダヲオボエテイル。ソレナノニ、アノコハイナイ……。ワタシハキノウ、ハジメ

テ、ソトヘデテミタ。ソシテ、オマエサンニアッタ。シカシ、イーダハ、イナカッタ。」

いすはだまりこみ、とつぜん、

「モウイル。イーダハカエッテキタ。モウジキ、ココヘカエッテクル。」

と、うれしげにつぶやいた。

「こやしない。きみのまっているイーダと、ぼくの妹はちがうんだ。」

いすは直樹のことばをきいていなかった。じっと、遠い物音をきいているようだった。

「アノコガカエッテクル。ホラ、ジャリヲフンデ……チイサナアシオトダ。ヤッテクル……。」

「やめろよ。」

直樹は立ち上がった。そんな、おびきよせるようなまねは……といいかけて、はっとした。ゆう子

の声だった。

「おかえりなしゃあい、ただいまあ。」

パタパタとかけこんでくる。ゆう子、いったいどうしたんだ。

「イーダダ、ワタシノイーダダ。」

いすはそういいすてると、とびこんできたイーダをひざでうけとめた。ということは、ゆう子がか

73

けこむなり、いすにちょこんとこしかけたということなのだが。

「イーダ、ドコヘイッテキタンダネ。」

いすがやさしい声できいた。

「いったの、うみ、いったの、おふね、いったのよ。」

ゆう子は、足をぱたぱたさせながらいった。

「オジイチャンハ？」

「あのね、さよなら、あんころもち、またきなこ。」

そしていきなり、床の上にすとんとおしりをおとすと、小さないすを持ち上げ、じぶんはねころん
で足と手でゆらゆらとゆすりはじめた。それはちょうど、たかいたかいをしてやっているようだった。

「おふね、おふね、ゆれるじょう。」

ゆう子はきゃっきゃっとわらった。

いすはうれしそうにゆすられながらきいた。

「ソウカ、サヨナラシタノ。ジャア、スグクルネ。」

ゆう子はもういすにへんじをする気はないらしく、いすをおろしていきなりとび上がると、両手を
にぎりこぶしにして、しっかりあわせ、ふりながらうたいだした。

74

「ギッチョー、ギッチョー、こめつけ、こめつけ。ギッチョー、ギッチョー、こめつけ、こめつけ。」

そうしては、またはじけるようにわらう。それはいままで直樹が見たこともない、きいたこともない遊びだった。

「おせんべやけたかな、おせんべやけたかな。」

一つやりはじめると、おもしろくてたまらないのか、のばした左のてのひらの上に、右のてのひらをのせ、ゆっくりひっくりかえしながらゆう子はうたっていた。ひとしきり遊ぶと、ゆう子は食堂の向こうにあるへやにさっさとはいって、おしいれから小さな毛布をひっぱり出してきた。

「ばぶ、ばぶ。」

そういいながら、毛布をひろげると、ごろりとその上にねころんだ。ふちどりの布をやさしくなでながら、うたうように、

「うみ、いったもん、ねえ。おふね、のったもん、ねえ。しかちゃん、いたもんね……。」

「イーダハ、コノモウフヲ、バブ、バブトイッテ、コレガナケレバネナイノダ。」いすはいった。

「ゆう子だってそうさ、いつもそうなんだ。」むっとして直樹はいいかえした。しかし、ゆう子はなぜ、となりのへやから、じぶんのものでも

75

持ってくるように、毛布をとってきたのだろう。それにあの遊び、いつ、どこで、おせんべ焼けたか

な、とか、ギッチョーギッチョこめつけこめつけなどという遊びをおぼえたのだろう。おまけにゆ

う子は、ここにいるときは、直樹のほうなど見向きもしない。きょうも、へやのすみにいるのに、に

いちゃんともいわず、とびついてもこなかった。まるで直樹が見えないように、通りこしてほかのも

のを見ていた。

「ワカッタロウ、イーダハココノコナンダヨ。ソシテ、オマエサンガモシ、ドウシテモコノコノニイ

サンダトイウナラ、オマエサンモコノウチノコサ。」

「ふうむ、このうちの子か……。」

直樹は口をへの字にむすんでうなった。

「わかった。」

直樹はいきなりどなった。ある考えがうかんだのだ。そうだ、ここをぼくたちの、ひみつの家にし

よう。花浦にいるあいだのひみつの家だ。いいぞう——。しかし、直樹の声があまり大きかったので、

いすはびっくりしてとび上がり、毛布の上でころげていたゆう子まで、はねおきた。

「おにいちゃん、いたのう。」

ゆう子はゆめからさめたように、直樹をながめて、のんびりといった。

76

「イーダも、ぼくもこのうちの子さ。だからこのへんを、ちっときれいにしようや。これじゃきたなくて、ぬき足、さし足で歩かなくっちゃならない。まるでばけものやしきだぜ。」

「おばけ、おばけ。」

ゆう子はすぐよろこんだ。まったく、こうなんでもよろこばれては、はりあいがないくらいだった。

「おばけ、いるじょう。」

ゆう子はへっぴりごしになって、あたりを指さした。いすはおおいに不服そうだった。

「ワタシハ、イツダッテ、チャントヤッテキタンダ。イツ、イーダヤオジイサンガカエッテキテモイイヨウニ、キレイニシテオイタ。」

ぶつぶつとそういった。

「わかってる、わかってる。きみの努力はみとめるよ。まわりより、床はとてもきれいだ。でもさ、きょうはぼくがもっときれいにしてあげるよ。」

直樹はゆう子をだいて、その下の毛布をとった。

「ほらごらん、ばっちいだろ。ここにはね、ほこりおばけや、くもの巣おばけや、いろんなおばけがいるんだ。ね、イーダちゃん、おばけたいじしようよ。」

「うんうん。」

77

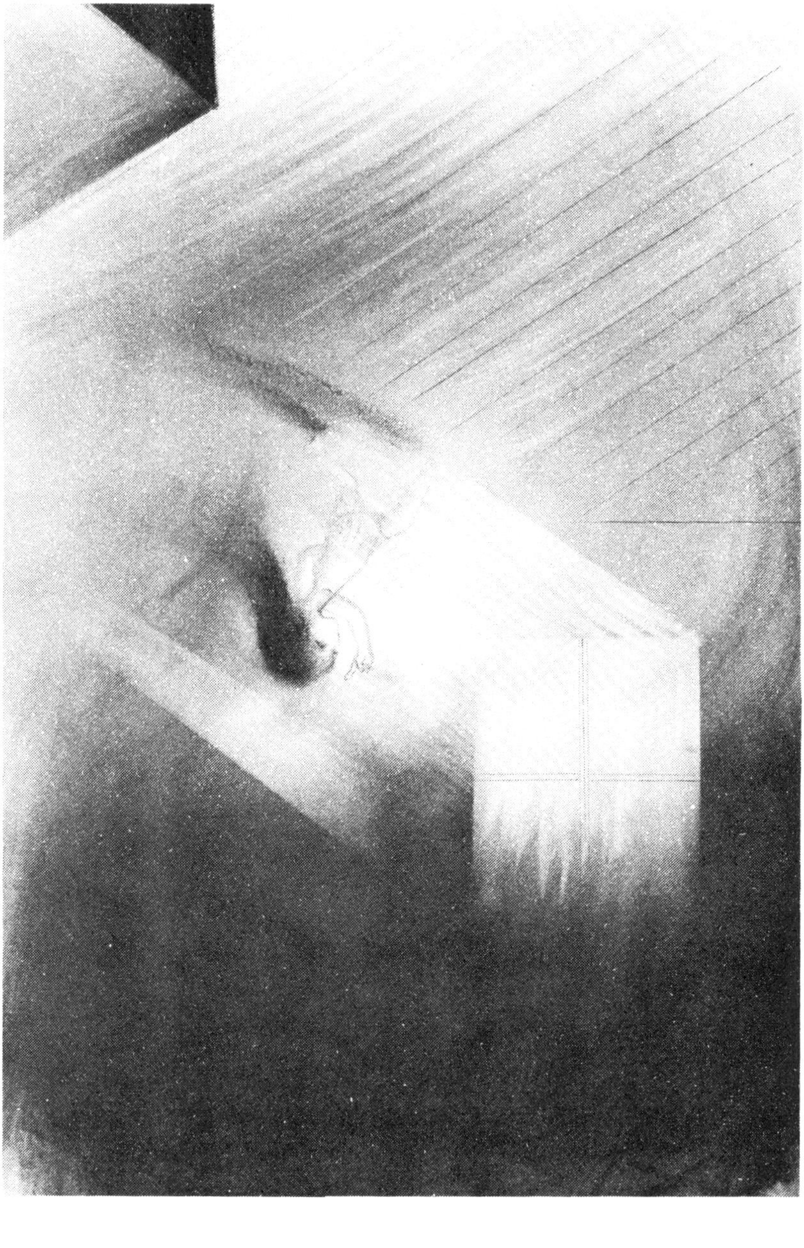

ゆう子ははねまわり、指を一本立て、

「くものしゅおばけ、いっちゃええ。」

とどなった。

　直樹は台所からほうきをさがしてきた。電気そうじ機をさがしたが、そんなものはありっこなかった。いや、ほうきにしてからが、まずほこりだらけだった。そのあやしげなほうきではき出すと、つぎはぞうきんがけだった。どこをさがしても、ぞうきんらしいものはない。

「えい、いいや。」

　直樹はシャツをぬいで、ランニング一まいになっていたが、いせいよく、そのランニングをぬぎすてた。それから、うらのわき水からバケツに水をくんで、ランニングをつっこんで、そこらをふいた。まあ、おっそろしいほこりで、ランニングはみるみる、ねずみ色になったが、食堂はずいぶんとさっぱりした。

　直樹はコップに水を入れ、きょうちくとうの枝をおって、テーブルの上においた。とたんにこの家ぜんたいが生きかえったようになった。

　いすは、こうふんして、ゴトゴト歩きまわり、ゆう子はおわんに水をくんできて、おままごとに熱中した。こうして、そうじがすっかりすむころには、もう夏の日も、おちかかっていた。

79

9 それは、むかしの話なのだ

直樹のおじいさんとおばあさんは、手わけをしてそこらをさがしていた。宮島からようやく家へたどりついてみれば、うちはからっぽで直樹はいない。まあ、どこかへ遊びにいったんやろか、といっているまに、ちょろっとゆう子のすがたまで見えなくなってしまった。直樹といっしょなら、そう心配しないのだが、ゆう子ひとりでどこへいったのだろうと、おばあさんはあわてた。そして、さっそくふろをたきにかかっているおじいさんをせきたてて、ふたりは表に出たのだった。

しかしふたりとも、家のうら手にあたる雑木林のほうには気がつかなかった。ふだんでもそちらのほうは山へつきあたるだけだと思っていたし、だれも通らない道には草がはえていて歩きにくかった。そこでふたりはおほりやお殿さまのお墓のあるあたりや、公園・史料館などくまなくさがしまわった。

り、いないので青くなって、もしや家にもどっているのではと、帰ってきたところだった。

帰ってみると、ゆう子も直樹もざしきにひっくりかえっていたが、おきあがる元気もないほど、くたびれているらしい。

「まあ、ふたりとももどっとるわな、まあよかった。おじいさん、ゆう子も直樹も、もどっとりますよ。」

「そうか、やれやれ、心配したぞ。まあふたりともどこへいっとったんじゃ。」

おじいさんとおばあさんは、ふたりのそばへぺったりとすわって、やれやれと肩で息をしたが、またひめいをあげた。

「まあ、このふたりのきたないこと、まるで大そうじでもしてきたようじゃ。いったい、あんたがた、なにしとったんじゃね。」

おばあさんは、あきれはてたという表情である。

「つかれたよう、おなかすいたよう。」

直樹がいう。

「ちゅかれたよう、おなかすいたあ。」

と、べそをかく。おばあさんはこういわれるとよわくて、

「はいはい、それじゃごはんにまずしてと。」

81

と、台所へ立った。おじいさんもふろをたきつけにかかって、

「ゆう子、おじいさんとはいろうな。きょうは、頭あらうのじゃぞ」

と、ふろ場から声をかけた。ゆう子にとって、かみあらいくらいきらいなものはない。

「あした、かんかんあらうのよう。きょうは、おぺちょだけよう。あしたよう、かんかんはあしたよう。」

「あれ、あんなこというて。ほれ、ゆう子ちゃん、きのうの夜な、あしたかんかんあらいますって、やくそくしたじゃろ？　きょうがそのあしたですよ。」

おばあさんがゆう子にいった。

「ちゃうよう、あしたあらうって、いったでしょう。きょうじゃないもん。」

ゆう子はなきながら抗議する。あしたといったのだからあしたで、けっしてきょうではないという

のである。おばあさんも直樹も、へとへとだったけれど、ゆう子のきみょうなりくつにはおなかをか

かえてわらった。そして直樹ははっとした。そうだ、いすの考え方もそうなんだ……。

「わらっちゃだめ、わらっちゃだめ。」

ゆう子はじぶんがわらわれることには、がまんできない。なきながら抗議をつづけ、さいごに、お

とくいのイーダを連発した。

82

「まあまあ、女の子がそんなお顔をすると、おさるさんになるが。」

「ちゃうよ、ちゃうよ。おさるさん、ちゃうもん、どうぶつえんだもん。」

あんあんあん、ゆう子のふんがいは、なかなかおさまらなかった。

こうやっていると、ゆう子はいつもとちっともかわらないゆう子だった。みんなでにぎやかにごはんをたべながら、直樹はなんべんもゆう子をながめた。おちゃわんをかかえてたべているゆう子を見ると、ゆう子のやつ、大きくなったな、と思う。もっと小さいときゆう子は、直樹のことをにいにいちゃんといっていた。ここえんと、えんとしなちゃい、といって、小さないすにすわらされ、おままごとの相手をさせられた。直樹がかまってやらないと、にいにいちゃん、たいへんよ、たいへんよ、どうちょう、とさわぎたててじぶんのところへよびよせた。あれはたしかゆう子が二つになる前だった。あのとき、たいへんよたいへんよといったら、ねこのミーまでいっしょにかけつけたんだ。目をまんまるくしてかけつけた。だからよくおぼえている。ミーはあれからすぐ死んだ。自動車にひかれて犬猫病院で死んだんだ。直樹はそれをしっていたけれど、ゆう子にはだれも教えなかった。ゆう子はだから、ずいぶん長いあいだ、ミーは、ミーは、といって、うちの中をさがして歩いた。ミーは小さくて、古いオルガンのペダルがついているあなから中へもぐりこんだりした。それをおぼえていて

83

ゆう子は、オルガンの下をのぞきこみ、ミーをよんだ。そして、ミー、ない、ない、といいながら家じゅうを歩きまわったっけ……とつぜん直樹は顔をしかめた。あのいすの、イナイ、イナイ……というう声がまた耳の底でよみがえった。あのいすがさがしつづけているイーダは死んだのかもしれない。

もしゆう子が死んだとしたら……そこまで考えて、

「いけない。」

直樹はうめいて、目をつぶった。そんなこと、いったいなんで考えたんだ。

気がつくと、おじいさんとおばあさんが、心配そうに直樹をのぞきこんでいた。

「頭がいたいの？　やっぱりぐあいがわるいようじゃねえ。」

「早くねたほうがええな。」

直樹はうなずいた。そして首をはげしくふって、頭からへんなことを追い出そうとした。なにを考えても、どうしても、あのいすのことへ頭がいってしまう。いったい、どうしたらいいんだろう。

「さあ、おふとんしいたからね、いつでもねなさいよ。」

おばあさんは、いつのまに席を立ったのか、もどってくると直樹にいった。直樹ははしをおいた。そうだ、ひとりになって、よく考えよう、それにはねたほうがいい。つかれて、ほんとうにめまいもしていた。直樹はおとなしく立ち上がると、となりのへやにはいって、ねまきに着かえ、ふとんにころがった。

84

まず、考えなくちゃいけないことは……、直樹はがんがんする頭を、おちつかせようとしながら、一つ、と指をおった。あのいすはゆう子とおんなじなんだ。ゆう子もそうだけど、あしたっていった、あしたなんだ。きのうっていったらきのうなんだ。ゆう子は一月前に動物園にいったのに、きのうのう、いったもんねえ、動物園に、いったもんねえと、大まじめでいう。いすもそうだ。きのうそのおじいさんと、イーダという子がいなくなったというが、それがいつのきのうか、はっきりさせることがたいせつなのだ。そして、できるならその子をさがし出さなくっちゃ……まてよ、直樹はきょとんとした。その子がもし見つかったとしても、その子はもう大きいんだ。そうだ、それをいすにわからせれば、ゆう子をじぶんのうちの子だ、なんていえないはずだ。なあんだ、かんたんじゃないか……。どうしてこんなことに気がつかなかったんだろう。直樹はふとんの中でにやっとわらった。

ねむけがおそってきた。

直樹が目をさましたとき、へやはまっ暗だった。ただ一すじ、となりのへやのあかりが細くもれていた。それといっしょに、ききなれない声もまじってぼそぼそとはなし声ももれてきた。この声が耳について、直樹は目をさましたのだった。

——あれだけの人が死んだんじゃもの、見わたすかぎりの焼け野原に、人だまがとんでのう、そのころは、ちょうちんもいらん、懐中電燈もいらん、人だまのあかりで夜道が見ゆる、そういったもんですがな。

85

——骨がなあ、ごろごろしとりましたもん、燐も燃えましょうよ。青い火だそうですの、燐の燃ゆ
るのは。

——わしは人だまを見たが、ちょうど昼間見る電気の光のようじゃったの。ぼうっとだいだい色をし
て、ふわふわ、とんでいったがのう。おおかた、下からは燐の青い火がめらめらと燃え、上には人だ
まがとびこうておったろうよ。それはほんとうじゃ。

——海へも流されておりましょうなあ。

——海へもよけい、流されておりましょう。かぞえきらんほど、流されておりましょう……七つの
川があなた、死人でうずまりましたもの。

声がとぎれて、茶をすする音がした。

——死なれたあと、たたみをとおして、床板に、コールタールがしみたように人形がついておりま
したと。それがひとりやふたりでなし……一つの寺に何十人ですわ。庵主さんがわすれられんという
とられました。

——男か女か、それもわからん。焼けこげて火もともさんへやに、ぼうっとならんですわっとるあ
りさまは、ゆうれいのように見えたといいます。

——宮島は、神の島じゃというて、人は焼かれんしきたりですもの。かというて、本土の焼き場は

86

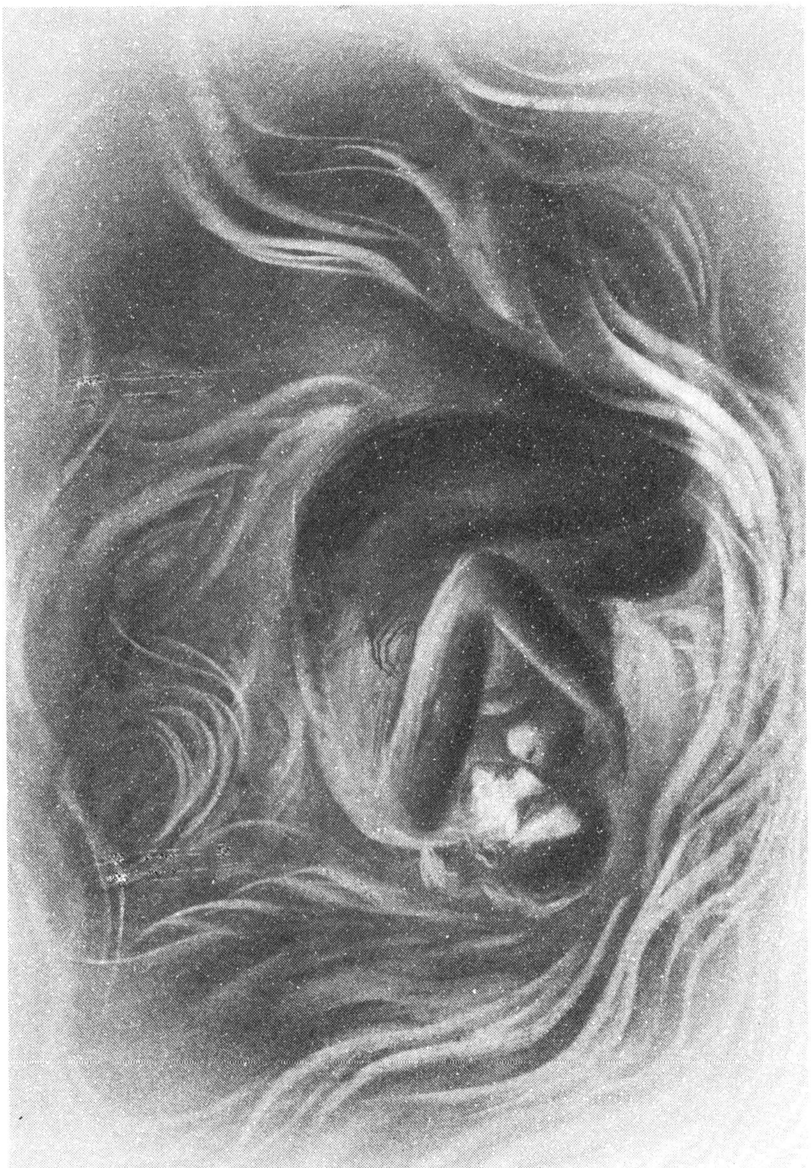

いっぱいじゃ。死なれた人をただ積んであったそうですのう。

——どうして運んでこられたですか。

——やさい船の船底に積んで、その上にふたをしてきましたと。そのあいだに死ぬる人も多かった

といいますよ……。

直樹は、じぶんでも気がつかないうちに、ふらふらと立ち上がっていた。ふすまをあけていた。

「それ、いつのこと。」

おじいさんも、おばあさんも、お客さんもぎょっとしたように直樹を見た。おばあさんがすぐ気を

とりなおし、立って直樹をだきかかえるようにした。

「ゆめ見たんか、え、直樹ちゃん。まだ夜よ、はようねたから、目がさめたのじゃね、さ、ねておいで。」

「ねぼけたのう。」

おじいさんがいって、はっはっとわらった。

けれど直樹は、うごかなかった。

「いまの話、いつのこと?」

「ああ、いまの話きいたんか、やれ、こまったのう。」

おばあさんは、はっとしたように、直樹をもっとしっかりだいた。

88

「あれはな、むかしむかしのことなの、いまの話ではないの。ええかい、むかしのこと、な。」

こっくりして、直樹はおばあさんにつれられて、またねどこにはいった。

それをしおに、お客さんは立ち上がって、あいさつしたようだった。おじいさんは立って送った

が、おばあさんはいそがしく、直樹のえりや、わきの下あたりに手をあてた。

「まあ、ひどいあせかいとるのう。」

「ねえ、むかしって、どのくらい、むかしのこと。」

「ううんと、ううんとよ。いつかねえ、おとなになったらきかせてあげるから、さあ、もうわすれてねなさいや。」

おばあさんは玄関から帰ってきたおじいさんに、かわいたタオルと、ねまきをたのんだ。そして直樹のからだをかわいたタオルでこすり、あらいたてのゆかたに着かえさせた。

「さあ、気持ちよくなったじゃろ。」

「うん。」

のりのにおいがして、ぴんとかわいたあらいたてのゆかたは気持ちよかった。直樹は安心して目をつぶった。いまのはむかしの話だったんだ。もしかしたら、おさむらいさんのいたころの、話だったのかもしれない……。

89

10 赤んぼうは、しっている

直樹が朝の勉強をやっているとき、郵便屋さんが一通の絵はがきをほうりこんでいった。おかあさんからだった。

——前の日はきりがひどくて、火口へは出られないし、やまなみラインもぜんぜん見えなかったというのに、わたしののぼった日は、一年のうちでもかぞえるほどのよい天気でした。

そんなことが書いてあった。

「ね、ぼくがいったとおりでしょう。おかあさんて、こういうふうに、なんでもうまくいっちゃう人なんだ。」

直樹はけむりをふきあげている阿蘇の火口の絵はがきをながめながらいった。

90

「ほんとにまあ、のんきな子じゃ。みんな元気ですかとはそれでもお義理に書いてあるけど、いつ帰

るとも書いてないじゃないの。」

おばあさんは、あきれたようにいった。

「それじゃ、ぼくたち、もうすこし、ここにいるんだね。」

直樹はうれしそうにいった。いすのことを考えると、ちゅうとはんぱなまま帰りたくない。

「おにいちゃん、おんもいこうよ、おんもいこうよ。」

ゆう子はさっきからまちくたびれていた。

「あれっ、ゆう子ちゃんがこんなもの、書きましたよ。」

おばあさんがすっとんきょうな声をあげ、直樹は、ああっとさけんだ。

「ぼくの原稿用紙じゃないか。ゆう子、なにしたんだよっ。」

直樹が学校から作文の宿題のためにもらってきた原稿用紙の、ます目の一つ一つに、ゆう子は字と

もなんともわからぬものを、えんぴつでびっしりとうめていた。

「なんでおにいちゃんのもの、いたずらするんだよっ。」

わっとゆう子はなきだした。おばあさんのむねに顔をおしつけて、なきながらいうのである。

「ゆう子ちゃん、じじかいたんだもん。おはなし、かいたんだもん。おにいちゃん、おこっちゃだ

91

め。おこっちゃだめ。」

「よしよし、ゆう子ちゃんは、勉強したんだもんねえ。おにいちゃん、おこらんといてねえ。それでもほれ、ゆう子はごめんなさいしなさい。ごめんねって、ゆう子ちゃんや。」

ゆう子はしゃくりあげながら立ち上がり、両手を頭の上にのせ、ひざをひょいとまげながら、

「ごめんねっ。」

といった。そのかっこうがまるでおさるのようだったから、かんかんにおこっているはずの直樹もついふきだした。おじいさんとおばあさんはもちろんのこと、ころげてわらった。

「わらっちゃだめ、わらっちゃだめ。」

なきながら抗議しているのは、ゆう子ひとりである。直樹はうっかりわらったくやしまぎれに、べええをしてみせた。

「まあ、このごめんねはなんじゃろね。」

「ぼくが教えたんだ。テレビのまんがでね、そういうの、やったんだよ。そしたらいっぺんでおぼえちゃった。」

「しょうのないにいちゃんじゃこと。イーダだの、おさるさん式ごめんねだの教えて。なあ、ゆう子ちゃんや。」

92

ゆう子はこっくり、こっくりしていた。

「しかしなあ、これはたいへんなことじゃぞ。」

おじいさんが、ゆう子の書いた原稿用紙を取りあげた。

「三つにもならん子が、ひとりでなにを考えながらこれを書いたのじゃろうか。人間いうもんはな、赤んぼうのときに、いちばんなにもかもしっとるんやとわしは思う。大きゅうなるにつれて、世の中の俗事が一つ一つ頭にはいるかわり、たいせつなことを、一つ一つ、わすれていくのじゃと、わしは思うな。」

「そういうもんですかなあ。」

そういいいおばあさんは、お茶をいれた。

直樹は首をかしげた。

「だって、赤んぼうは赤んぼうでしょ、なにもしらないとぼく思うな。」

「外から見たところはそうじゃ。けどな、人間のいのちというもんは、ひょこっと出てくるもんじゃない。生まれた子は、おとうさん・おかあさんの血やら性質やら、つまり、遺伝いうものをうけとるじゃろ？」

直樹は首をかしげた。このへんになると直樹にはもうわからなくなってくる。

93

「しかしじゃな、そのおとうさん・おかあさんにしてからが、それぞれの両親の遺伝いうもんをしょってこの世に出てきた。いうてみれば、ただないたり、手をふったり足ばたばたさせていよる赤んぼうは、人間が生きてきた、気も遠くなるような時間の重みを、一身にせおうて生まれてきたといえるんじゃ。」

おじいさんはおばあさんの出したげんまい茶を入れた分厚なちゃわんを両手でかかえ、こうばしいにおいをたのしみながら、あとをつづけた。

「いのちの流れというもんがあるようにわしは思う。そこにぽっかりういたあわのようなものが、人それぞれ、生きとるということじゃ。死ねばその流れに帰っていく。あわで

94

あることは、水ということや。じぶんでもしらん長い時の流れの一部や。」

直樹はため息をついた。わからないや……けれど、赤んぼうの時代にいちばんちかいゆう子が、いちばんなにかをおぼえているのかもしれないということだけが、ひどく直樹の心に残った。

そうだ、ゆう子なら、なにもかもしっているのだ。あのふしぎな家のひみつも……ゆう子がゆう子なのかどうかということも……。

「おにいちゃん、おんも、いこうよう。」

ゆう子がせきたてた。

「おぼうしかぶって、いくの。」

「よし、いこう。」

直樹は、はずみをつけて立ち上がった。

「そうじゃ、わしももういかんならん。バスにのりおくれるわい。」

おじいさんも、あわてて立ち上がった。

「そうじゃ、そこまでいっしょにいこうな。これ、ゆう子にぼうしかぶせてやれよ。」

「はいはい。」

おばあさんは、原稿用紙をていねいにたたんだ。

95

「これ、たいせつにしておこうねえ。ゆう子ちゃんが、いっしょうけんめい、書いたのじゃものねえ。」

「おぼうし、かぶるの、おんもいくの、さよなら、あんころもち、またきなこ。」

ゆう子がはねながら手をふった。

「あれまあ、ゆう子ちゃんは、いいことしっとるねえ、どこでおぼえたのじゃろ。」

「わからないんだよ。きのうから、とつぜんいいだしたんだ。」

「生まれる前の記憶かな。はっはっはっ。」

ネクタイをしめながらおじいさんがわらった。直樹はおじいさんをながめた。おじいさんまで、な

にもかもしっているようなことをいう……。

「あんころもち、たべようねえ。おいしいものねえ。」

おばあさんが、ゆう子のかみの毛をゴムひもでまとめ、ぼうしをかぶせながらいった。

「あんころもち、たべられないよう。」

ゆう子はふしぎそうにいう。

「たべられるのよ、あんころもちは。おいしいのよ。」

「へええ、たべられるのう、へええ。」

ゆう子がひどく感心したようにいったので、またみんなおかしがった。生まれる前のこと、しって

96

いるなら、あんころもちくらいしっていそうなのに、やっぱりなにもしらないんだ。直樹はくすりと

わらって玄関へ出た。さおと、虫かごを取ると、

「さあ、いくぞ、ゆう子。」

「うん、いこう。」

「こらこら、まてまて。」

おじいさんがくつをはきはきいう。

「おじいちゃん、いくよ。ゆう子ちゃん、さきいくもん。」

ゆう子ははねながらとんでいく。ミーンミンミンミン、オシーツクツクオシーツクツク、きょうも

また晴れだった。白い土べいにそった道をおじいさんとゆう子と三人で歩いていきながら、直樹はさ

おをふった。ようし、きょうはせみを二十ぴきぐらい取ってやろう。おばあさんに、きのう、東京の

子はせみをよう取れんのじゃねえ、などといわれてしまったしかえしをしなくっちゃ……。

けれど、直樹のその決心はたいして長つづきしなかった。駅にいくおじいさんにわかれて、おほり

にかかっている石のめがね橋をわたって、もと、殿さまが住んでいたというおやしきあとにはいった

とき、直樹は木かげにすわって本を読んでいるりつ子に、ばったりあってしまったからだった。

「あら、直樹ちゃん、せみ取り?」

97

「うん。」

「この小さい人が、イーダちゃん。」

「あれ、おねえさん、イーダちゃんなんてよくしってるね。」

「おたくのおばあちゃまにきいたのよ。いっぺんきいたらわすれられない名まえですもの。イーダちゃん、こんにちは。」

「こんにちは。」

イーダはすこしはにかんで、直樹のうしろにかくれるようにしながらこたえた。

「ここ、たくさん木があって、いいでしょう。あら、あらあら。」

りつ子が立ち上がったので、直樹はつられてそっちを見た。男の子たちが五、六人、さおで一本の木をたたいている。

「なにしてるの、あんたたち。」

「かしの実取るんだい。」

「かしの実は、まだまださきよ、秋になってからよ。さおでたたいたりしちゃだめ。」

りつ子がきりりとした声でいったので、男の子たちは、口々にあくたいをつきながら、わっ、と散った。

「かしの実だって、ちゃんと大きくなって、下へおちるころじゃなけりゃ、取ってほしくないってい

98

「うわ、ね、そうでしょ。」

直樹はあいまいにうなずいた。東京育ちの直樹は、かしの実がいつ取りごろなのかしらなかった。

「このお城山には、どんぐりやしいの実が多いのよ。おしりがふくらんでいるのをさがしてねえ、かじるのよ。生のくりみたいよ」

「そんなの、おいしい？」

「そうねえ、わたしの小さいころは、よくたべたわ。しいの実をね、水をふりかけながらフライパンでいると、なおおいしいの。こうばしくて……。それはそうと直樹ちゃん、史料館見た？」

「史料館ってなあに」

「ここのお殿さまが使ってたものとか、いろんなものがあるの。まだならちょっと見ましょうよ」

「ふうん」

直樹はさおを見た。

「せみなんてさ、そのあとで取ればいいわ」

「でも、ぼく、お金持ってないよ」

「おねえさんが持ってるわ。刀やかぶとや、よろいなんかあるわよ」

「お金持ってるの。刀やかぶとや、よろいなんかあるわよ」

りつ子にせきたてられて、直樹もその気になった。とくべつ、うんとおもしろくはないにしても、つまらなくはないかもしれない……。

100

11 このいすはだれが——

　史料館は殿さまの居城だった……といってもおやしきのようなものらしいのだが、そのあとの広い敷地のかたすみに建っていた。前にはお庭がひろがっていたが、そのうちの一か所は、畑のように整然と、ぼたんが植えられていた。

　「ぼたん畑よ、春になると、そりゃあきれい。向こうの細道、ぼたんがさいた。さいたもさいた、みごとにさいた、おてんとさまにさしあげた、ってわらべ歌があるの。ほんとうに両手で持って、おてんとさまにさしあげたいような花よ。」

　「ふうん、おねえさん、むかしのことがすき？」

　「どうして。」

101

「だってぼくに、よろいや、かぶとがあるから見なさいなんていうし……。」

「だって、ここまできて見ないなんて、つまらないじゃないの。」

「そうかなあ。」

直樹は、せみ取りのほうがいいような気もした。

「そうそう、そのさおね、虫かごも、事務所の人にあずかってもらいましょうよ。すみませーん。」

史料館には、めったにくる人もないのだろう。受付にはだれもいなかった。りつ子の声で年とった男の人があわてて出てくると、さおや虫かごをうけとり、きっぷを売ってくれた。おとなが二十円、子どもは十円、ゆう子はただだ。

「ね、アイスクリーム買うより安いでしょ？」

りつ子がいたずらっぽくいった。アイスクリームのほうがいいやといおうとしたけど、直樹はやめた。だって、このおねえさんとはまだ知り合いになったばかりだった。それなのにお金出してもらっちゃわるいや、と、直樹は考えた。そのうえ、アイスクリームのほうがいいやなんて、あくたれをいったら、おねえさん、きっとかなしがるにちがいない。

むかし、土蔵だったのをそのままいかして使ってあるという史料館は、夏だというのに、ひんやりとして、うす暗かった。さっきのおじいさんがきて、しんせつに、電気をつけてくれた。

102

「あ、ほんとだ、よろいがある、かぶともあるね。」

直樹がはずんだ声を出したので、りつ子はうれしそうだった。刀もあった。つめたい氷のような刀身をすっとそらせて、刀かけにかかっている。つぼや置物・かけじく・手紙などは直樹にはさっぱり興味がなかった。それよりも黒ぬり金まき絵の、なに姫さまだかのおけしょう道具というのがおもしろかった。かみしもや、うちかけもあった。

はなやかにぬいとりしたうちかけをゆう子に、

「ほら、おべべよ、きれいでしょう。」

そういってりつ子は指さしたが、ゆう子は、

「おべべ、ちゃうでしょう。」

と、口をとんがらしてもんくをいった。ゆう子にはあんまり大きすぎて、おべべという気がしなかったのかもしれない。がんどうというのもあった。鉄でつくった携帯用のあかりだ。

「いまの懐中電燈だね。」

直樹はガラスのケースにおでこをおしつけてながめた。ずいぶん重そうだった。なにかあるとむかしはこれをふりまわしたのだから、ずいぶんたいへんなことだったろう。あんどんもあったし、殿さまが使ったという火ばちとか、書見台というようなものもあった。こういうのはテレビの時代劇によ

103

く出てくるから、本物を見るのはおもしろい。

そのうちに、だんだん時代の新しいものが出てきた。殿さまが日露戦争にいったときの軍服なんかが出てきて、直樹をびっくりさせた。しかし、そのつぎにつくられている一コーナーを見たとき、直樹はくぎづけになったように立ちすくんでしまった。それは、ごく古めかしい洋家具であった。木ぼりの洋風の戸だなと、つくえといすが、古びたじゅうたんの上にならべられ、ロープをはって、中にはいれないようにしてあった。

「どうしたの。」

りつ子がよってきた。直樹が息づまるような顔でいすを見つめているのに気がついたからだった。

「このいすをつくったのは、だれ。」

直樹はきいた。

「さあ、どこかに書いてあるんじゃない？」

りつ子は心もとなさそうにいって、そこらをながめた。しかしそこには、旧藩主邸におかれた家具で、とういかたがこられたときにもおすわりになったいすである、というような説明文が書かれているにすぎなかった。

直樹は、立ったりしゃがんだりしながら、うす暗い中におかれている、いすのよりかかりにほられ

104

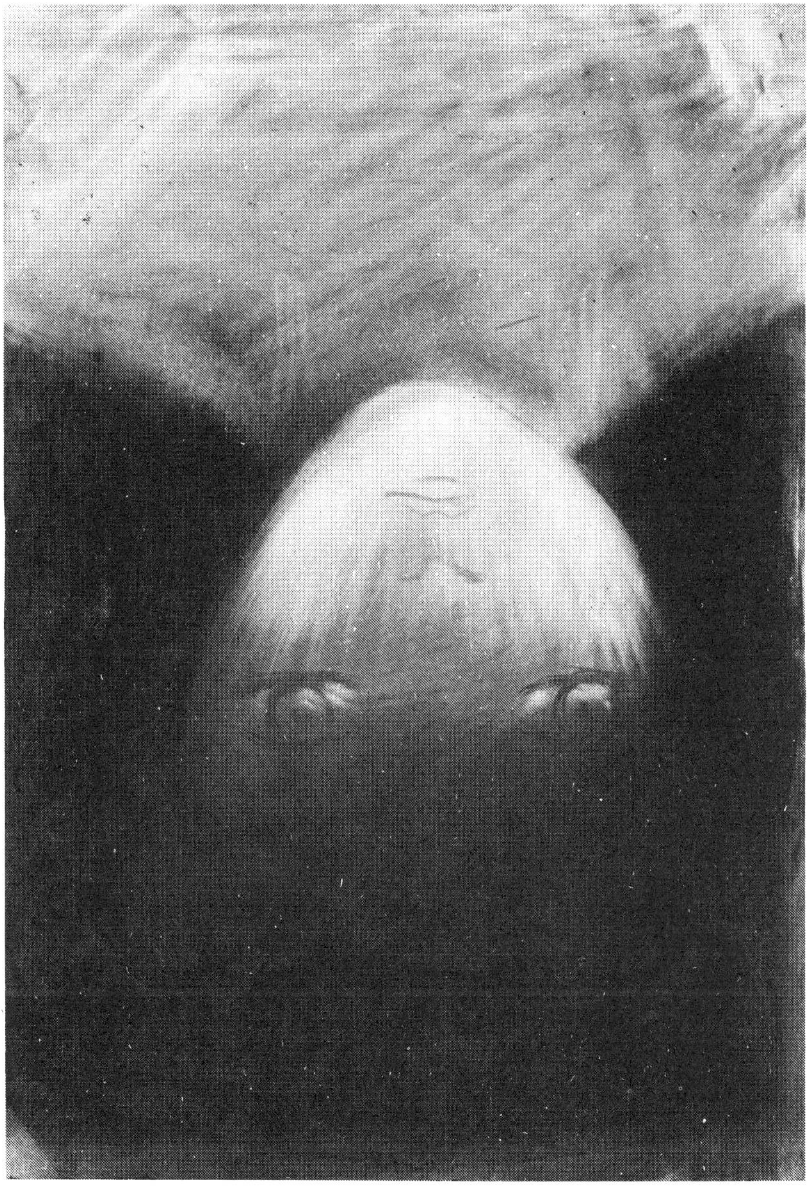

てあるもようを見ようとした。おなじだった。なんともわからないきみょうな形の組み合わせがほってある。

「たしかにおなじ人がつくったいすだ。」

直樹はこうふんして、ひとりごとをいった。

「それ、なんのこと。これとおなじいすを直樹ちゃん、どこかで見たの。」

「うん。」

直樹はうなずいた。

「これほった人、おねえさん、しらない？」

「さあ、しらないわねえ。でも考えてみるとへんよね、いすは残っているのに、つくった人の名がわからないなんて……。でも、家具なんて、そんなものかもしれないけど……。」

直樹はいますぐ、あの小さないすにあいたかった。きみのなかまがいるよと教えてやりたかった。いったいあの小さいいすは、ここの殿さまのところにいたのだろうか。それがたった一つだけ、なにかわけがあって、あの家にいるのだろうか。それとも、あのいすをつくった人が、あのふしぎな家に住んでいた人なんだろうか。直樹はいすに、そのことをきいてみたかった。いすはなんというだろう……。

106

いつまでも直樹が立ちどまったまま、なにかを考えこんでいるので、りつ子はわらいだした。

「もう出ましょうよ。」

そういって、そっと直樹の肩をおした。ゆめからさめたように、直樹は史料館を出た。夏の日ざし

が、はっとするほどまぶしかった。

「どうもありがと、おねえさん。」

直樹がいうと、ゆう子もまねをして、

「どうもありがとう。」

といって、はずかしそうにまた直樹のかげにかくれた。

「ぼく、いくね。」

直樹は、せいいっぱい、へんにならないよう、気をつかってことばをいったつもりなのに、りつ子

はまた、高い声でわらった。

「おかしな直樹ちゃん、せみ取りはどうしたのよ。」

「あ、そうだっけ、せみ取るんだった。」

「おかしなおにいちゃんね。」

りつ子はくっくとわらうと、かわいくてたまらないというように、ゆう子をだきあげた。

107

「直樹ちゃんは古いものなんかきらいみたいだったのに、ずいぶん、いっしょうけんめい見ていたじゃないの。いすなんて、つくった人の名まえまでしりたがって……おねえさん、びっくりしちゃったわ。家具なんてすきなの？」

「うん……すきっていうんでもないけど、あのせなかんとこにほってあるの、ちょっとおもしろそうだったから。」

「わたしもね、木ぼりってすき。このブローチもわたしがほったのよ。そうだ、これ、イーダちゃんにあげましょうね。くまちゃんのブローチ。」

りつ子はゆう子をおろすと、むねのブローチを取って、ゆう子のむねにつけてやった。親ぐまと子ぐまが二ひき、ちょこんとすわっている、とてもかわいいブローチだった。

「ありなとう。」

ゆう子はうれしくてぴょんぴょんはねた。なにしろ、ゆう子がいちばんすきなのは、くまちゃんなんだから。

「ぼく、さおをかえしてもらってくるね。」

直樹はかけだして、受付からせみ取りのさおと、虫かごをかえしてもらった。

「じゃあね。」

108

「じゃあね。」

手をふりあうと、ゆう子がはねながら、

「さよなら、あんころもち、またきなこ。」

とどなった。りつ子の顔がぱっとかがやいた。

「イーダちゃん、よくそのもんくしってるのね。おねえさんも小さいとき、そういったのよ。」

かけよって、もういっぺんだきしめると、こんどこそという顔で、

「じゃあね。」

と、手をふり、くるっとりつ子は向こうを向いて歩きだした。

「じゃあね。」

直樹も元気よくいうと、ゆう子の手をひいて歩きだした。そうだ、まっすぐにこのまま、あのふしぎな家へいってみよう。しかし、そううまくはいかなかった。ゆう子はすこし歩くとしゃがんで、

「おみず、ぱんぱん。」

といった。おなかがすいたらしい。

「ちぇっ、なにかしようと思うとこれだからな。おにいちゃん、おんぶしないよ。おうちへ帰ったら

ごはんだからね、あんよするの。」

109

ゆう子は、しゃがんだまま足をさすっている。おかあさんだったらこういうとき、けっしておんぶしない。すましてあたりのけしきを見ている。すると、ゆう子もだまって立ち上がって歩きはじめる。

でも直樹だとゆう子はあまくみてるんだ。直樹のほうも、ついおぶってしまうのだ。直樹はあきらめて、ゆう子をおぶうと、おばあさんの家のほうへ歩きはじめた。いいんだ、ゆう子はいないほうがい い。そうだ、ゆう子が昼寝をしたら、そのすきにぬけ出そう。大いそぎでいすとはなしてもどってこよう。

家へはいると、おばあさんはおそうめんをつめたくしてまっていてくれた。それを見ると、直樹もきゅうにおなかがすいて、

「ああ、暑かった。」

といって、ぺたんとすわった。

「おお、おお、暑かったじゃろ、さあ手をあらっておいで。」

「おばあさん、このへんにね、いすをつくる人、住んでいないかい。」

とつぜん直樹がへんなことをいったので、おばあさんは目をまるくした。

「さあ、きかんけど、そんな人は。」

「おばあさんは、この町に古いんでしょう?」

110

「そうねえ、古いいうても、まだ十年、いや十四、五年かねえ、そんなとこじゃねえ。」

「ふうん、そうかああ。」

「なんでそんなときくの。」

「なんでもないけどさ。」

ゆう子はとっくに手をあらってきていた。

「おてて、あらったよ、とりであらったよ。」

と、大じまんである。とりでというのは、ひとりでということだった。

「さあ、直樹ちゃんもあらってきなさいよ。」

「はあい。」

直樹は立ち上がった。やっぱり、あのいすに、直接きくしかないようだった。

111

12　おかしなカレンダー

「きみさ、だれにつくってもらったの。」

直樹は玄関の入り口にこしをかけて、いすにきいていた。いすはひどくこまって、考えこんでいた。

「ソンナコト、オボエテイナイ。」

いすは、はらをたてたようにいった。

「キガツイタラ、ワタシハコノイエニイタンダ。ソシテ、チイサナイーダハ、ハイハイシテイタ。」

「じゃあ、どこかのお店から買ってきたのだろうか。」

「チガウ、ソレハチガウ。」

いすはまた、考えこんだ。

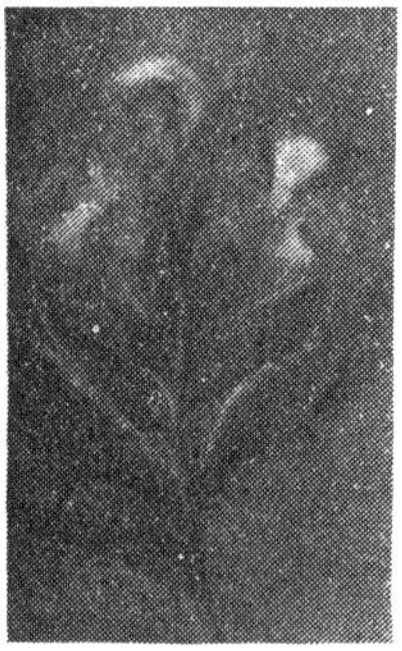

112

「オジイサンダトオモウヨ。オジイサンハ、ワタシヲキレイデコスッテ、ツヤヲダシテイタソウダ。オジイサンハ、ヨクイッテイタ。オマエダケガ、ホントウノ、ワシノ、サクヒンダ……タシカニ、ソンナコトヲイッテイタ……。コッチノヘヤデ、オジイサンハ、コツコツトナニカ、ツクッテイタナ、ソウダ……。」

一つ、一つ、いすはゆっくりと思い出してくるようだった。

「そうか、やっぱりおじいさんは、いすつくりをしていたんだね。よし、そのへやをあけてみよう。」

直樹は立ち上がると、いままでいっぺんもあけたことのない、玄関をはいって右手のへやのドアをあけた。ぷうんとかびくさいにおいがしたが、そこが仕事べやであるのは、直樹にもはっきりわかった。下絵というのだろうか、すみでえがいたいすや家具のでき上がり図のようなものもあったし、さまざまの彫刻刀やのこぎりや、かんなや、塗料がきちんとおかれてあった。いすの材料にするらしい丸太や、板もたてかけられていた。外国の本もあって、それにはさまざまなつくえやいすの絵があった。

「おじいさんのつくったいす、きみにそっくりな、ただし、おとな用のだけど……を、お城あとの史料館で見たんだよ。でも殿さまのいすをつくっていたとしたら、ずいぶんむかしの人なんだろ。そこんとこがわからない。」

113

直樹は首をかしげた。直樹には、このへんまでくると、どうしていいのかわからなくなる。けれど
も、小さな直樹にもわかるのは、その仕事場にただよう、きびしさのようなものだった。きっと、た
だのいすつくりのおじいさんじゃなかったんだ、直樹はそっとドアをとじた。名人のような人だった
んだ……だから、このイーダのいすにも、たましいがはいったのだ。きっとおじいさんは、赤んぼう
のために、心をこめてあのいすを組み立てたり、ほったり、みがいたりしたにちがいない……。

直樹はいいはじめた。いすは、だまされないぞというように、きいているのか、いないのか、わか
らない態度をしていた。

「あのねえ、気をわるくしちゃ、いけないよ。ぼく、思うんだけどねえ。」

「おじいさんとイーダちゃんがいなくなったのは、どういうわけか、わけはわからないけどだよ、と
にかく、ずうっと前のことだと思う。いろんなことを考えて、そうとしか思えないんだ。それでだ
よ、もしそうなら、イーダちゃんがこの家へ帰ってきたにしても、ずいぶん大きい……ほんとのこと
いうと、おばさんになっていると思うよ、ね、わかるだろ。」

「オジイサント、イーダガイナクナッタノハ、キノウナンダ。」

いすは、おこったようにいった。

「キノウデナケレバ、キノウノキノウナンダ。」

114

「こまったなあ。」

直樹はため息をついた。いったいどうしたら、このいすのまちがいを、ちゃんといってきかせてやれるだろう……。

「ねえ、きみのイーダちゃんは、門からはいったとこにある、お池で遊んだかい。」

直樹は話をかえてみた。

「アア、アソンダ。」

いすはうれしそうに、からだをゆすった。

「オトコノコガ、オシッコスルノガフンスイニニナルイケダロ。フンスイヲミテ、キャッキャットイッテ、ヨロコンデイタ。アノマワリニハホレ、アジサイガアルダロウ。ハナガサイタトキニハ、ソレハキレイダ、ムラサキヤアオノハナガサイテ……。」

あじさいも、草にうもれていまははっきりしなかった。けれど直樹は、あおむらさきの大きなまるいあじさいと、しょうべん小僧の噴水と、そこで遊ぶ小さなイーダのすがたが目にうかぶように思われた。

「イーダガ一ツハンノトキ、イーダノオカアサンガシンダ。シヌトキ、イーダノヤワラカイカミノケヲサスッテ、ナミダヲナガシテイタ。イーダノカミノケハ、ソノトキノマンマノビテ、フサフサト、

115

コシノヘンマデノビテ、スコシクセッケダカラ、ナオ、カワイインダ。イマモカワイイイダロ？」

いすは、イーダのことなら、いつまでもはなしたいらしかった。しかし直樹は、きょうはもうひとつ、どうしてもしらべたいものがあった。

「おくの食堂の日めくりね、ほら、カレンダーさ。あれ見せてくれる？　あれを見れば、それがいつのことか、わかるかもしれない。」

いすは、

「イイダロウ。」

といって、コトリと立つと……というのはおかしい。いすはいすで、立つことはできないのだから……でも、まるでそんなふうに見えたし、小さなからだだから、しゃがれた声を出すところは、小人そっくりだった。いすはカタッ、カタッと足をひきずって家の中へはいり、直樹はあとにつづいてはいっていった。

カレンダーは、食器だなの横の柱についていた。おとなにはちょうどいい高さだろうけれど、直樹にはすこし高かった。

「ちょっときみの上にのるぜ、いいだろ。」

いすがべつに反対もしなかったので、直樹はいすの上に足をのせ、日めくりに目をよせた。すっか

116

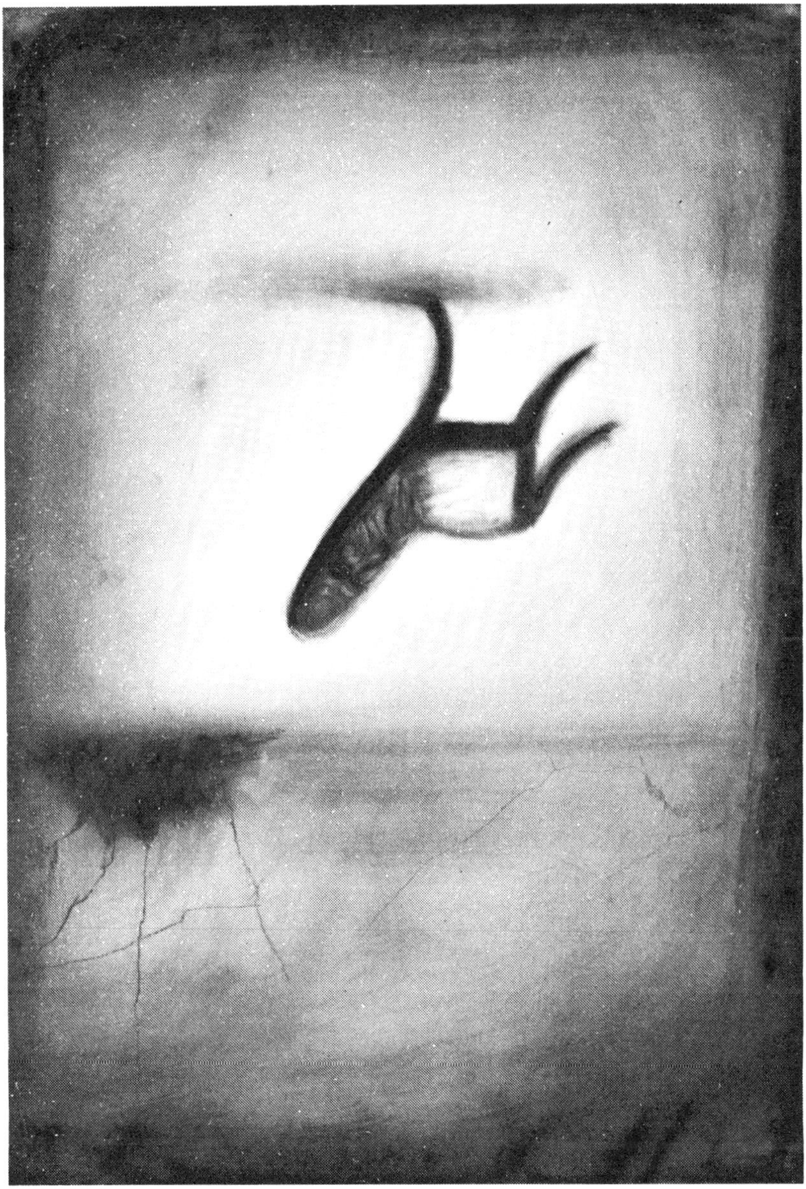

変色して、茶色になっている紙には、まず大きく、6という字が見えた。下に月曜日とはいっている。それから直樹には読めないむずかしい字が、いくつか小さくならんでいた。ふうん、直樹は日めくりがついているボール紙に目をうつした。ほうおうとでもいうのだろうか、きれいな鳥が二羽、日の丸をまん中にして舞っている絵がかすかに見え、日の丸のま下に、横に数字がならんでいる。年号だな、直樹はかすれかかっている数字に目をこらした。そして、

「なんだって。」

と、思わず大声をあげた。

「ねえ、きみ、いすくんてば、いまは何年だっけ？」

「シラナイ。」

いすはおこったようにいった。そうだった、このいすには、きのうとあしたしかないんだっけ。

「いまは……千九百……ええと、とにかく二十世紀だよね。それがこのこよみは二十七世紀だ。ええと、二六〇五年、って書いてあるよ。いったいこれ、どうなっちゃってんだろ。」

直樹はいすからとびおりた。この家だけ二十七世紀の世界に住んでいるんだろうか。そんなばかなこと……二十七世紀は宇宙時代だ。コンピューター時代だ。あんなおんぼろなこんろなんてあるはずがないし、だいいち、この家にはテレビだってないじゃないか。殿さまのいすをつくったおじいさん

118

と二十七世紀、いったい、どこでどう、つながっちゃっているんだろ……。

「ぼく、すこし、考えごとしなくっちゃ。——帰るね。」

直樹はぶっきらぼうにいった。それから思いついて、もういっぺん、失礼ともいわないでいすの上にのっかると、カレンダーをはずした。ほこりがぱっとたった。日めくりのカレンダーだから小さい。

「どうして持っていこうかな。」

このままで持っていけば、おばあさんにあやしまれるにきまっていた。直樹は半そでシャツをぬぐと、その中へくるくるとカレンダーをしまいこんだ。ランニング一まいだけど、夏だからまあいいだろう。

「じゃあ、またくるよ。」

「イーダヲヨコシテクレ、イーダヲカエシテクレ。イーダハココノウチノコダ。」

いすはぶつぶつといった。

「だってさ、イーダがたとえばイーダだとしてもだよ、こんなとこ、住めるわけないだろ。ごはんだって、だれがたべさせるんだ。それに、きみのイーダは、いたとしても、もうおばさんなの！」

直樹はむしゃくしゃしていたので、ぽんぽんいった。

119

いすにはそれが、ひどくこたえたようだった。いすはもうなにもいわないで、かべのほうを向いて、じっとうごこうともしなかった。それはちょうど、ねこがすねると、かべのほうを向いてすわっているのににていた。

「またくるからさ、ね？」

直樹はいすがひどくいじらしくなって、そういうと、家を出た。長いあいだ人が通らなかった雑木林の間の道には、雑草がはえていた。その間をひろって歩きながら、直樹はポケットに手をつっこみ、なにかをときほぐそうとして、いっしょうけんめいだった。

雑木林をぬけておじいさんの家のうら口へはいるところまできたとき、

「あ、おにいちゃん、きたよ。」

という、ゆう子のはずんだ声がした。

「まあほんと、よかったわね。」

その声はりつ子だった。りつ子はゆう子と手をつないで、いまおじいさんの家を出てきたところらしい。

「いくの、あっち、いくの。」

ゆう子は直樹の出てきた雑木林のほうへ、りつ子の手をひっぱった。直樹はあわてた。

120

「だめ、あっちはだめ、なにもないよ。」

「そうよ、林だけよ。それにほら、道があんなにわるいでしょ？　せみしかいないの、あら、直樹ちゃんはせみ取りじゃなかったの。」

直樹はあいまいに口をうごかした。直樹をすくってくれたのはゆう子だった。ゆう子はふんぜんとしていったのである。

「あっち、ゆう子ちゃんのおうちだもん、いくの、おうち、いくのよう。」

「まああ、東京のおうちへ帰りたいのねえ。」

りつ子は、勘ちがいしたらしく、ゆう子をやさしくなだめた。

「そうだ、ぶらんこのりにいきましょうよ、どう？」

「うん、ぶなんこ、いくの。」

ゆう子はたちまち、ぶらんこにだまされて、りつ子の手をひくほうへ歩きだした。

「直樹ちゃん、いっしょにいきましょうよ。」

「ぼく……。」

「いすをね、つくった人が、わかったのよ。」

121

13 協力者

りつ子はゆう子と直樹を、お宮へつれていった。

が、古びたお宮で、さくの中にはしかが三頭ほど、もぐもぐと口をうごかしていた。ゆう子は宮島で、しかを見たのを思い出したのだろう、

「しかちゃん、しかちゃん。」

といって、はねた。

しかを飼ってあるさくのおくには、池があって、ここにもふじだなやら植えこみがあり、池にはこいがゆらゆらとおよいでいた。さすが殿さまが住んでいたあたりだけあって、このへんには、しずかでいいところがたくさんあると直樹は感心した。ぶらんこもある。

なんの神さまがおまつりしてあるのかわからない

122

やくそくなので、四人のりのぶらんこをゆらしながら、りつ子ははなしはじめた。

「あれからね、わたし、図書館へいってね、この町の歴史を書いた厚い本をかりたのよ。そうした

ら、史料館に出ているいろんな写真があってね、あのいすの写真も出ていたわ。宗方進吉郎作、って

書いてあったわ。むずかしい名まえね。」

「むなかたしんきちろう……おねえさん、しってる？　きいたことある？」

りつ子はわらった。

「しってっこないでしょ、そんな人。なんでもその人はね、ここの殿さまのおめがねにかなって、イ

ギリスへね、いすつくりの技術を勉強にいったらしいの。そうして帰ってきてからは、殿さまのいす

や、家具をつくっていたらしいのよ。」

「それでその人、まだ生きているの。」

「どうかしら、とにかく、もうよっぽどのお年でしょう。」

りつ子は首をかしげた。

「その人のことは、それしか書いてないんですもの、わからないけどね。」

「でも、イギリスへ勉強にいったっていうんなら、徳川時代じゃないでしょう。」

「そうね、明治になってからだわね。その人、もしかしたら、東京にいっているかもしれないわ。殿

123

さま……っていうとおかしいけど、つまり、ここの殿さまの子孫ね。そのかたたちも東京よ。けさ遊んだところね、あそこにもと住んでいたのだけど、おやしきごとそっくり東京へひっこしていったんですって。」

「じゃあ、そのときかな？　そのとき、いっしょに……もしかしたらそうかも……。」

直樹は立ち上がった。とつぜんなのでぶらんこはぐらりとゆれ、ごきげんでうたっていたゆう子は、おびえて、ぼうにしがみついた。

「おにいちゃんは、もう。」

口をとがらしておこっている。　直樹はあわててすわり、ぐいと足に力を入れてぶらんこにはずみをつけた。

――しかし、それはおかしい。もし、殿さま、いや殿さまの子孫にしてもだ。いっしょに東京へいくとしたら、それならちゃんと荷物をまとめて、かたづけて出ていくはずだ。あんなふうに、消えてしまうみたいに、いなくなるだろうか……。

「どうしたのよ、直樹ちゃん。いったいなにを考えているの。あなたすこしへんよ。はなしてくれない、おねえさんに。」

目を上げると、りつ子はひどく真剣に、直樹を見つめていた。その顔を見ると直樹は、むらむら

124

と、なにもかもはなしたくなくなってきた。そうしたらどんなにさっぱりするだろう……。でも直樹は、いえなかった。いすが歩いているんだ。そして、そのいすと話をしている……そんなことを、まじめにきいてくれるおとながいるだろうか。

「いまは二十七世紀でしょう？」

直樹はべつのことをきいた。

「そうよ。」

「二六〇五年じゃないよね。うぅん、つまり、ことしがそうだって意味じゃないんだけど、とにかく、二十七世紀ではない……。」

「もちろんじゃないの。」

りつ子はおかしそうにわらった。

「そうだよねえ。ああ、ぼく、なにがなんだかわからない……。」

「それ、どこに書いてあったの。それともだれかが、いま、二十七世紀だっていったの。」

「うぅん、だれもいわないけどね。もしだよ、カレンダーにそういう数字がはいっていたとしたら？そう思うより、しかたがないでしょ？」

「そうねえ。」

125

りつ子はぶらんこをゆすった。

「そうねえ……たとえば、電話番号って
こともあるでしょ？　ほら、カレンダーによく、お店の名
や、電話番号がはいっているじゃない。」

「だって……ちがうと思うな。」

りつ子はわらいだした。

「いやあねえ、見もしないで、なにもいえないわ。せめてそのカレンダーがここにあれば、そうした
らなにか、いっしょに考えてあげられるけどさ。」

「ふうん、カレンダーかあ。」

直樹はもじもじして、ひざに目をおとした。半そでシャツの間から、きたないボール紙のかたはし
がのぞいている。

「ははあ、ひざの上があやしい。ね、直樹ちゃん、人間おたがい、信頼がたいせつよね。信頼あると
ころに協力ありだわ。あなたがわたしを信頼してくれれば、おねえさん、協力をおしまないんだ
けどな。」

「わかったよ。」

直樹は、にやっとわらって、カレンダーを取り出した。

126

「これなんだ。あのね、ある家にね、このカレンダーがかかっていたとするでしょう。」

「うんうん。」

「ここで、ぷっつりと、とぎれていたとしたら、この日に、なにか意味があると思わない？　このカレンダーは、毎日一まいずつめくるカレンダーなんだもの。」

「ふんふん、いい線いってるじゃないの。」

「ひやかしちゃだめだよ。それでぼく、わからなくなったんだ。ね、これは電話の番号なんかじゃなくて、年のこといってると思うんだ。でもいまは二十世紀でしょ。だからわからないんだよ。」

「なあるほど、ね。」

りつ子は、カレンダーを取りあげ、顔をしかめた。

「ああきたない、ひどいもんね。ま、いいわ。おねえさんがかならず、このこよみがいつのかしらべてあげる。だからこれ、ちょっとかしてよ。」

直樹はすこしためらったが、

「ん、いいや。」

と、元気よくいった。

「そのかわり、だれにもひみつだよ。」

「ようし、ゆびきりかんきり、うそついたらはり千本のむ」。

ふたりが小指をからみあわせ、はずみをつけてふっているのを見ると、ゆう子は、

「ゆう子ちゃんもするの、するの」。

といって、小指を出してきた。そうだ、ゆう子にだって、このひみつは守ってもらわなくっちゃ。い

ちばん、なにもかもしっているのは、この、ゆう子かもしれないのだ。

三人は小指をからみあわせ、もういちど大きくふった。

「ゆびきりかんきり、うそついたら、はり千本、のむ」。

ゆっさゆっさと、そのさわぎでぶらんこはゆれ、直樹もりつ子もゆう子も、きゃあきゃあさわいだ。

「じゃあ、きっとたしかめてあげる。まかせといて」。

りつ子が、ぽんとむねをたたいた。

「おねえさん、いま、夏休み？」

ふいに思いがけないことをいわれて、りつ子はびっくりしたように目を見はった。

「いいえ、どうして」。

「じゃ、学校いっているんじゃないの？」

「ええ、学校じゃないわ」。

128

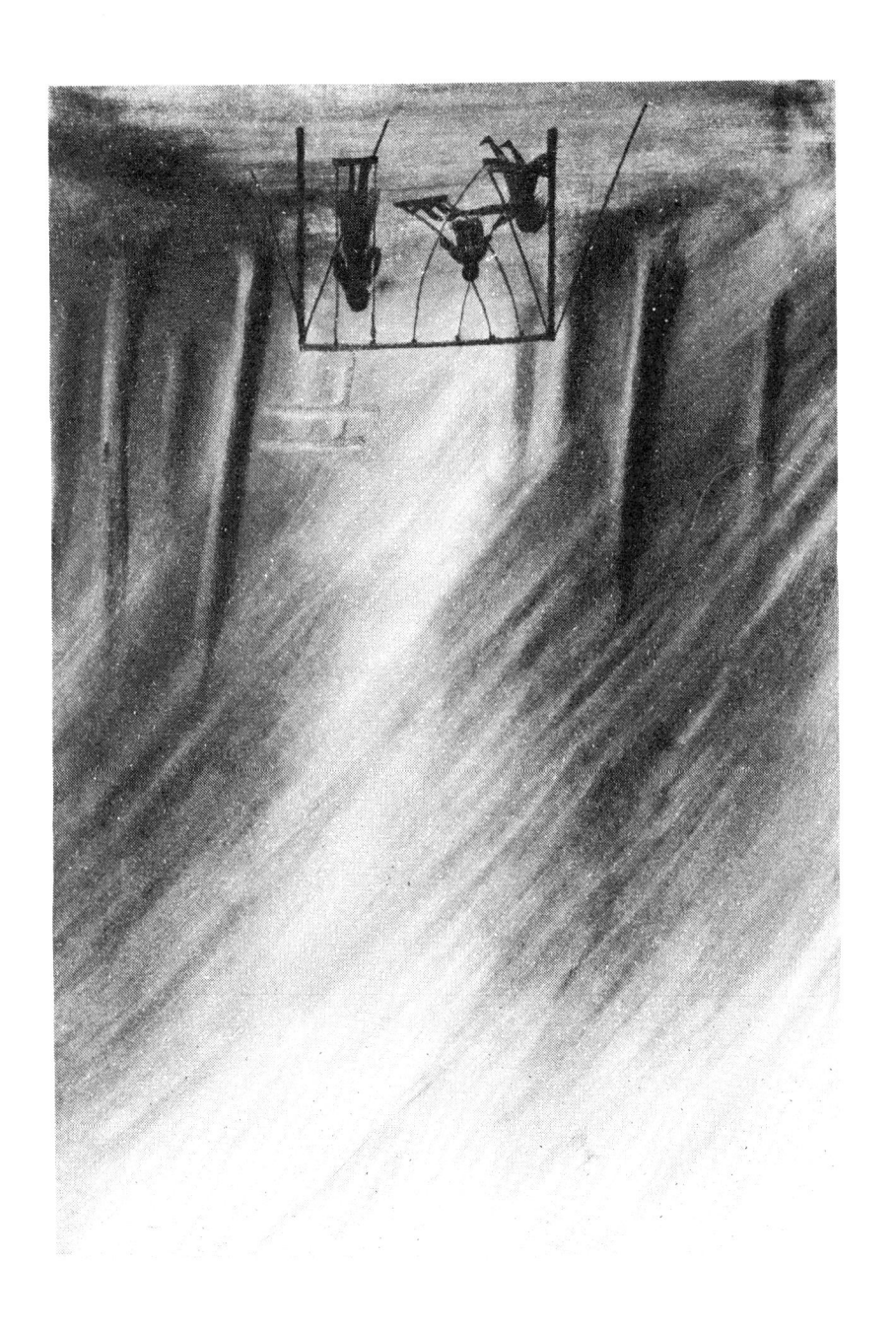

「じゃあ、おつとめ、いってないの？」

ふいにりつ子の顔が、暗くかげった。直樹ははっとした。

「ごめんなさい、へんなこと、きいちゃって……だってほら、おとなって、みんないそがしがってる
のにさ、こんなふうに遊んだり、ぼくのこと心配してくれるからさ。」

「おねえさんね、なまけんぼうなのよ。」

りつ子は、もとのあかるさをとりもどしていった。

「食っちゃあ寝、食っちゃあ寝のねえ子さんなの。じゃあね、ゆう子ちゃん、さよなら、あんころも
ち、またきなこ。」

「さよなら、あんころもち、またきなこ。」

ゆう子は、手をふって、くっくとわらった。直樹も手をふった。あのおねえさん、なんてたよりに
なるんだろう。大すきだ。直樹はゆう子の手をひいて歩きだしながら、ふりかえった。ちょうどりつ
子もふりかえったところだった。直樹はよごれたシャツをふり、りつ子はぼろぼろのカレンダーをさ
しあげてみせた。このとき直樹には花浦の町が、もう何年も住みついているように、したしく感じら
れたのだった。

130

14 数字の意味はわかった

つぎの日、直樹はなんとなくおちつかなかったが、りつ子が朝早くからくるはずもないので、勉強にとりかかった。

「えらいな、直樹ちゃんは、よう勉強しよる。」

おじいさんが出かけるしたくしながら、声をかけた。

「おじいさん、きょうも会議?」

「ああ、きのうのつづきでな、県庁へいかんならん。」

「その会議、おじいさんがいっぱい集まるの?」

「おじいさんが集まるかって? いや、これはこまったのう、はっはっはっ。」

131

おじいさんは大わらいした。

「そうだよ、おじいさんも、中にはおるのう。」

「それじゃねえ、こういう人のこと、しらないかきいてみて。」

直樹はノートのかたすみにえんぴつで大きく、

宗方進吉郎

と書いた。へたくそだが、できるだけ、わかりよく書いた。

「ほほう、この人はどういう人じゃね？」

「あのね、いすなんかつくる人なの、史料館でその人のつくったいす、見たんだ。」

「ほう、いつのまにやら直樹は、えらい勉強しとるな。よしよし、きいてやろう。おおかたしっとる

人もおるじゃろう。」

おじいさんはかばんを持った。

「きのうは出がけになにやら生命について演説しとったもんで、バスにのりおくれてしもた。きょう

ははよういかんならん。では、いってきます。」

「いっていらっしゃあい。」

直樹とゆう子は、玄関へ送っていって、盛大にさけんだ。いつも、おじいさんとおばあさんだけの

132

さびしいくらしなので、それがおじいさんにはひどくうれしいらしい。おばあさんも、いつまでもお

かあさんが帰ってこないといいみたいに、はりきっている。

「ゆうちゃんや、ちょっとおんもへお使いにいきましょう。」

といって、たいした用でなくても、すぐにゆう子の手をひいて出たがった。東京の孫ですのや、なん

て立ち話をするのがうれしいらしい。いいぞいいぞと直樹は思った。りつ子ねえさんがきたとき、お

ばあさんはいないほうが、安心してしゃべれる。なにしろ、ひみつなんだもの。

おんもへいくなら、いつでもゆう子はオーケーだった。すぐ手をひかれて、とんで出た。

「昼までにもどるから、直樹ちゃん、まっとってね。」

「はあい。」

直樹は元気のよいへんじをした。そうするともう、おちついて勉強なぞしていられなかった。直樹

はなんべんも玄関から外へ出て、右をながめ、左をながめ、あるときは土べいにそって百メートルほ

ど歩いてみたりした。

「おねえさん、こないのかなあ。あの殿さまのおやしきのあとへいってみようかなあ。おねえさん、

あそこでまっているのかもしれない。」

口に出して、そんなことをつぶやいてみたりした。すると、どうしてもそうだという気がした。そ

133

こで直樹はぼうしをかぶり、外へ出ようとしたとき、

「ごめんください。」

という、ばかにしとやかな声がした。りつ子だった。

「あ、おねえさんだ。まちくたびれて、ぼく、いこうかと思ったんだよ。」

直樹がいうと、りつ子は、しいっというように口に手をあてた。

「おばあちゃまは？」

「いまね、いないの、お使い。」

首をちょっといたずらっぽくすくめて、りつ子は上がってきた。おばあさんがいると思って、よそ

ゆきの声を出してきたんだなと、直樹はおかしかった。

しかし、テーブルの前へすわったとき、りつ子の顔はひきしまって見えた。

「ねえ、わかった？　どうだった？」

りつ子は、直樹の顔を、というより目を見て、ふかくうなずいた。

「わかったわ、直樹ちゃん。でもね、一つおねがいがあるの。」

「おねがい？　なあに、そのおねがいって。」

「これはね、直樹ちゃんがひとりで考えないほうがいいことだと思うの。だからおねえさんに、きか

134

せてほしいの。」

「だって……。」

「きっと、ひみつなんだろうと思うわ。だからかたくやくそくするわ、だれにもいわないって。で

も、わたしにだけは教えて。」

直樹はため息をついた。

「けっしてわらわないって、やくそくする？」

「ええ、するわ。」

りつ子は、そのときもわらい顔もせず、まじめにいった。その顔には、きびしさがあった。

「わかった、じゃあみんなははなすよ。でもその前に、そのカレンダーのこと、教えてよ。」

「これはね、こういうことなの。」

かごの中から、ふろしきにつつんだカレンダーを取り出すと、りつ子はあたりのようすに気をく

ばった。うん、これならだいじょうぶだ、直樹は心の中でそう思った。

「ここね、字がうすくなっているけど、二六〇五年とある前の字、読める？」

直樹は首をひねった。日に焼け、変色しているので、よくわからない。

「ええと、げん、っていう字かな、元でしょう。」

135

直樹は指で書いてみせた。

「そう、こっちはね、ほら糸へんでしょ。それから、こう書いて……。」

りつ子はやっぱり指で、紀という字を書いてみせた。

「きげん、と読むの。つまり、紀元二六〇五年ということ。わかった？」

「わからない。」

直樹はしょうじきにいった。

「わたしたちにはわからないけど、お年よりにはひどくかんたんなことなの。つまり、戦争中の日本は、西暦を使わないで、日本ができた年からかぞえて、こういうよび方をしていたわけ。」

「ふうん、ぼく、はじめてきいた。じゃあ、西洋の国より、日本のほうが古いってこと？」

「それはね、はっきりそうとはいえないようよ。いつを日本の国のはじめと考えるか、ということだって、しっかりきまっていないし、いまは、ぜんぜん使っていないのよ。」

「そうか、それでわかった。それじゃ、紀元二六〇五年は、つまり何年なの。」

「西暦で一九四五年のことなの、昭和でいえば二十年。」

「その何月かの六日なんだね。」

「何月はね、すぐわかったわ。」

136

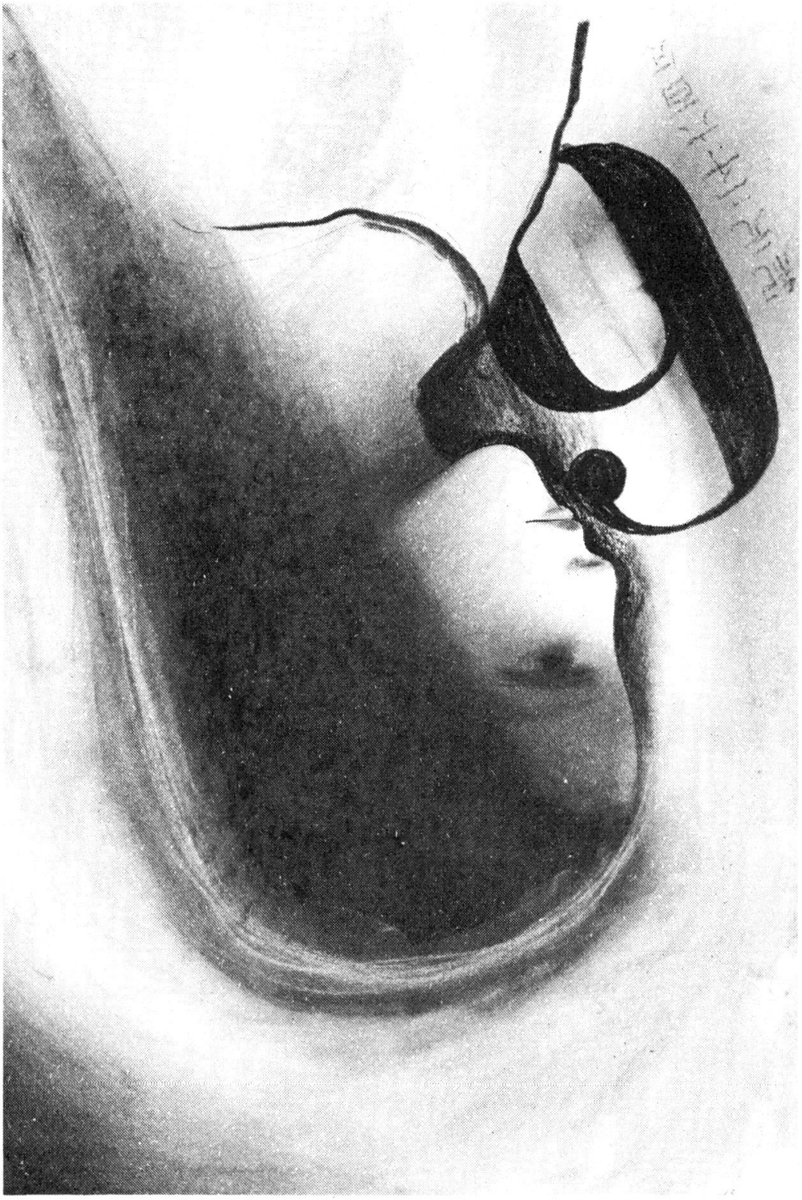

りつ子はそのあとをめくっていった。すると31という数字のあとに、9月という紙が一まい出て、

つぎをめくると1とあった。

「わかった、八月六日だ。」

「そう一九四五年、八月六日。」

直樹は感心した。

「よくわかったね、やっぱりおねえさん、えらいや。あっ、それじゃきょうとおなじだ。きょう八月

六日だもんね。」

りつ子は、のんきに感心している直樹をじっと見つめた。かなしい、さびしい目だった。しかし直

樹はそれに気がつかなかった。

「さあ、こんどは直樹ちゃんの番よ、はなしてくれるわね。」

「うん、はなすよ。」

直樹はつっかえたり、さきへいきすぎてまた前へもどったりしながら、ふしぎな家でめぐりあった

できごとをはなした。

そのあいだりつ子は、ひざに手をおいて、またたきもせずきいていた。見たところ、なにごともそ

の顔にはあらわれていなかったが、りつ子が直樹の心配していたように、いいかげんな気持ちや、お

もしろ半分でなく、心からこの話をきいているのだということはよくわかった。

ききおわると、りつ子は長いあいだだまっていた。

やがて、

「わたしを、その家へつれていってくれなくちゃいけないわ。」

といった。直樹はうなずいた。そのとき、外からゆう子のはりあげる歌声がひびいてきた。りつ子はすばやくカレンダーをふろしきにつつみ、かごの中へおしこむと立って玄関のほうへいった。同時に戸があいた。

「お帰りなさい。ゆう子ちゃん、こんにちは。おばあちゃま、おじゃましています。」

おばあさんはりつ子を見ると、うれしそうに、

「まあまあ、ようこられた。このあいだはまあ、えらいごむりおねがいして。それから孫たちがおせわになっております。」

と、あいさつをした。

「あの、おばあちゃま、これすこしですけど、母がひとつめしあがってくださいって……。岡山から送ってまいりましたの。」

りつ子はかごからももを出した。

139

「まあ、それはそれは……。みごとなももですのう。さ、こちらへ、お茶でもいれましょう。」

おばあさんは台所へ立った。そのすきに直樹はささやいた。

「二時ごろ、ゆう子がお昼寝するんだ。そのころ、史料館のとこへいく。」

「わかったわ。」

おばあさんはなにもしらず、

「まあ、毎日暑いことじゃ。さあ、ひえた麦茶をいかがですか。」

そういいながら、コップを運んできた。

「コーヒーのむの、のむの。」

「はいはい、牛乳入れてねえ。」

ゆう子はつめたい麦茶に、牛乳を入れて、コーヒー気どりで飲むのがすきだった。

140

15 りつ子、ふしぎな家へいく

直樹が史料館の前まで走ってくると、りつ子はもうきていて、白い手を高くあげて合図した。まわりに緑が多いので、白い手も、白い服も、緑にそまって見える。

「ごめんね。ゆう子のやつ、ぼくが出かけるのかぎつけたみたいにね、なかなかねないんだ。ぼくがちょっとでもへやを出そうになると、おんもいくの、ってはねおきるだろ、こまっちゃった。」

「子どもって、みんなそうらしいわね。わたしも三つぐらいのときは、おかあさんのおしりにくっついて、お手あらいにまでついてきたがったって、うちのおかあさん、わらうのよ。」

「あ、うちのねこもそうだよ。ぼくがおふろへはいっていると、ドアの外で、入れてくれ、入れてくれって、ニャーニャー鳴くの。ドアをあけるとね、ねこって、ぬれるのきらいでしょう、それなの

141

に、中まではいってきて、湯船に前あしかけてね、ニャーニャーっていうんだよ。」

「まあ、じゃああたしはねこににてるんだわ。」

ふたりはくすくすわらいながら歩いていたが、ふっとりつ子が立ちどまった。

「こっちのほうなの？　直樹ちゃんのおばあちゃまの家のほうへいく道じゃない。」

「うん、そのへんな家はね、じつをいうと、うちのすぐうらなんだ。」

「へえ、ちっともしらなかった。」

りつ子は、目をくりくりさせた。

「でもね、見つかるとうるさいだろ？　だから、遠まわりしていこうよ。べつの道からもいけるんだ。その両方とも、入り口に雑木林があるから、そのおくに家があるなんて、だれも気がつかないらしい。」

「わあすごい、ひみつの家ね。」

「東京だったらさ、そんなこと、ぜったいにないと思うよ。どんなすみっこにだって、あいているところがあったら、わあっておしよせてくると思うよ。なにしろ家がたりないからね。」

「直樹ちゃんたら。」

りつ子はくすくすわらった。直樹はきょとんとした。

142

「ぼく、へんなこと、いった？」

「そうじゃないけど、だって、おとなみたいな口、きくんですもの。」

しかし、白い土べいにそった道をいくまがりかして、雑木林の細い道にはいったころから、りつ子はあまり口をきかなくなった。一つ一つの木からもなにかをきき出そうというようにはいっていたし、ときにはふっと、遠いところへつれていかれたような表情がうかんだりした。

かいづかの、あれはてた生け垣と門までできたとき、りつ子は大きな息をした。そして、ここね、というように直樹をふりかえると、つかつかと中へはいっていった。しかし、りつ子はすぐ足をとめた。草の間から顔を出しているしょうべん小僧を見つけたのだった。からからにかわいた池のふちには、きょうもまつばぼたんが、赤や、黄や、こいもも色の花をせいいっぱいというようにひらいていた。

「あ、ばらだ、このあいだまでさいていなかったのに。」

クリーム色に、うすくべにをぼかしたばらが一輪、草の間からすっとからだをのばして、ふくよかな花をつけている。

りつ子はまだ、しょうべん小僧に、目をあてたままだった。

「わたしね、これ、見たような気がするの、このへんのけしきを、そっくりね。ほら、よく、はじめてなのにいっぺんきたことがあるって感じすることがあるでしょ。ゆめの中でこんな家きたみたい。」

143

りつ子は、とつぜんほほえんだ。

「おかしいわね、そんなこといったりして。さあ、いきましょうよ。」

一列にならんだかいづかのなみ木にそって、ゆるくカーブしているじゃり道をぬけると、直樹はさきに立って玄関のドアをあけた。

「はいりますよう。」

そういうと、りつ子を手まねきして、中へはいっていった。

「きれいになっているじゃないの、あ、そうか、あなたたちがおそうじしたんだっていったわね。」

りつ子はあちらこちらをながめながら、食堂へ通った。小さないすは、むっつりとして、身うごきもしなかった。

「まあ、ほんと、史料館のいすそっくりね。」

りつ子は、おどろいたようにいった。そしてそこにしゃがむと、しげしげといすを見つめ、それからあいさつした。

「こんにちは、わたし、りつ子です。」

しかしいすは、カタッともいわなかった。まったく、そのようすは、そこにある食堂のいすとなにひとつかわらなかった。直樹はいすにいった。

144

「きみ、なにかしゃべれよ。うごいてくれよ。そうでないとぼく、おねえさんにうそいったことになっちゃうじゃないか。」

しかし、いすは、がんこにおしだまったままだった。

直樹はよわりはてて、りつ子をちらりと見た。いまにもりつ子が、おなかをかかえてわらいだすか、さもなければ、あきれた人ね、まるで、小さい子みたいに、いすを相手にお人形さんごっこを

やっていたわけね。そういう目つきをするだろうと思ったのである。しかし、りつ子は、わらいだしもせず、直樹をばかにしたようなそぶりも見せなかった。ただ、しずかに立ち上がって、あたりを見まわした。そして、柱に残るあとを見て、

「ここに、カレンダーがかかっていたのね。」

とつぶやいた。それから、ゆっくりと視線を移して、食器だなの上にある本立てから絵本を一さつひきぬいた。

「まあ、めずらしいこと、外国の絵本よ。」

外側は変色していたが、ひらいてみると、中はわりあいにきれいだった。

「おねえさん、なんの絵本かわかる？」

「ええとね、これは、アンデルセンの、イーダちゃんの花っていうお話じゃない？」

「ああ、それだ。このうちのイーダちゃんがね、その本がとてもすきだったんだって。それで、イーダってよばれるようになったんだって。」

直樹はいすを見た。こういう話が出たのだから、いすだって、ひとことぐらい、なにかいいそうに思えたのだ。しかし、それでもいすはだまりこんでいた。直樹はいすをかかえて、へやのかたすみに持っていった。

146

「きみ、いすくん、どうして口をきかないのさ。あのおねえさんとは、口をききたくないっていうのかい。あのおねえさんは、心配ないんだ。へんなおとなでなんかないんだよ。口きいてくれよ。」

それでもいすはカタリともいわなかった。ふくれっつらをして、直樹が顔を上げたとき、りつ子はちょうど、絵本をとじるところだった。

「イーダちゃんは、まき子って名まえだったらしいわ。」

「どうして。」

りつ子はなにもいわず、とじた絵本をふたたびひらいて、さいごの、見開きの余白を見せた。すみ黒々と、おさない字で、

　　むなかた　まきこ

と書かれてある。

「ほんとだ、このうちのイーダちゃんは、まき子っていうんだ。」

直樹はさけんだ。とつぜん、いすがガタリとうごいた。しわがれた声がひびいた。

「チガウ。」

「あっ、口をきいた、口をきいたよ。いすが——。」

直樹はこうふんしてさけんだ。

147

「ねえ、そのあといってよ。きみのイーダは、ほんとうの名まえはなんていったの。」

けれどもいすは、また貝のように口をとじ、なにひとつ、いおうともしなかった。

「きっと、いすにとっては、イーダという名まえしか、その子の名まえはないのよ。ちがう名でよばれたくないのだと思うわ。」

りつ子が、しずかにいった。

ふいに、パタパタという足音がしたので、直樹とりつ子ははっとして、玄関のほうを見た。

ゆう子だった。

「ただいまあ。」

大きな声でどなりながら、パタパタと食堂へかけこむと、うれしそうにわらった。

「ゆう子、お昼寝からもうおきたのか、早いなあ。」

直樹はやれやれというように、おとなのいすにこしをおろした。きょうこそゆっくりと、おねえさんとこの家について研究しようと思ったのに。

「ゆう子、おべんきょうだもん。」

ゆう子は食堂のおくの六畳にはいって、さっさと、クレヨンのはこを出してきた。こわきにかかえてきた絵かき帳を床にひろげて、クレヨンをよって取ると、

148

「おかあさんだもん、これ、ゆう子ちゃん。おにいちゃん……。」

と、ひとりごとをいいいい、ぐるぐる、ただわけもわからない丸だの線をかいている。

「ぼくね、ほんとにときどき、へんな気持ちになるんだ。だってゆう子のやつ、まるでじぶんの家みたいに、なんでもあるところがわかっているんだよ。いまだって、クレヨンをさっと出してきたでしょう。ゆう子のやつ、そのイーダちゃんて子の、生まれかわりかな。それでイーダ、っていうのかな。」

「生まれかわりって、あるらしいわね。」

りつ子がいった。

「日本だけじゃなくて、外国にもよ。わたし、きいたことがあるわ。」

「やだなあ、そんなこと考えると、へんな気がする。」

「もし、生まれかわりだとすれば、このいすくんのいっていることは、正しいといえるかもしれないわ。」

どこまでも、りつ子がまじめなので、直樹は、だんだん、気分がおかしくなってきた。

「おじいさんのへやへいってみようよ。」

直樹はさそった。

149

おじいさんのへやでも、りつ子のしらべ方は綿密だった。インキがうすくなって、よく読めない紙きれを見つけて、じいっと見ていたし、そのうちのいくまいかは、手さげかごに入れた。しかし、そのようすはいかにも……なんといっていいのか直樹にはうまくいえなかったが、神さまの前でうごいているように真剣だったので、直樹は、ひとことも、むだ口をたたく気になれなかった。

「おにいちゃん。」

いつのまにかゆう子がきていた。

「おんも、いくの、きょうはいいおてんきでしゅね。」

「あれっ、いいお天気ですね、なんて、だれにならったんだ。」

「おんも、いっていらっしゃいな。」

りつ子がいった。

「わたし、このへやをしめて、食堂をかたづけて出るわ。だれも住んでいなくても、どなたかのおうちですものね、ちゃんとして出なくちゃ。」

「はあい。」

やっぱりおねえさんはおとなだ。直樹はゆう子と庭へ出た。

「ゆう子、かくれんぼしよう。」

150

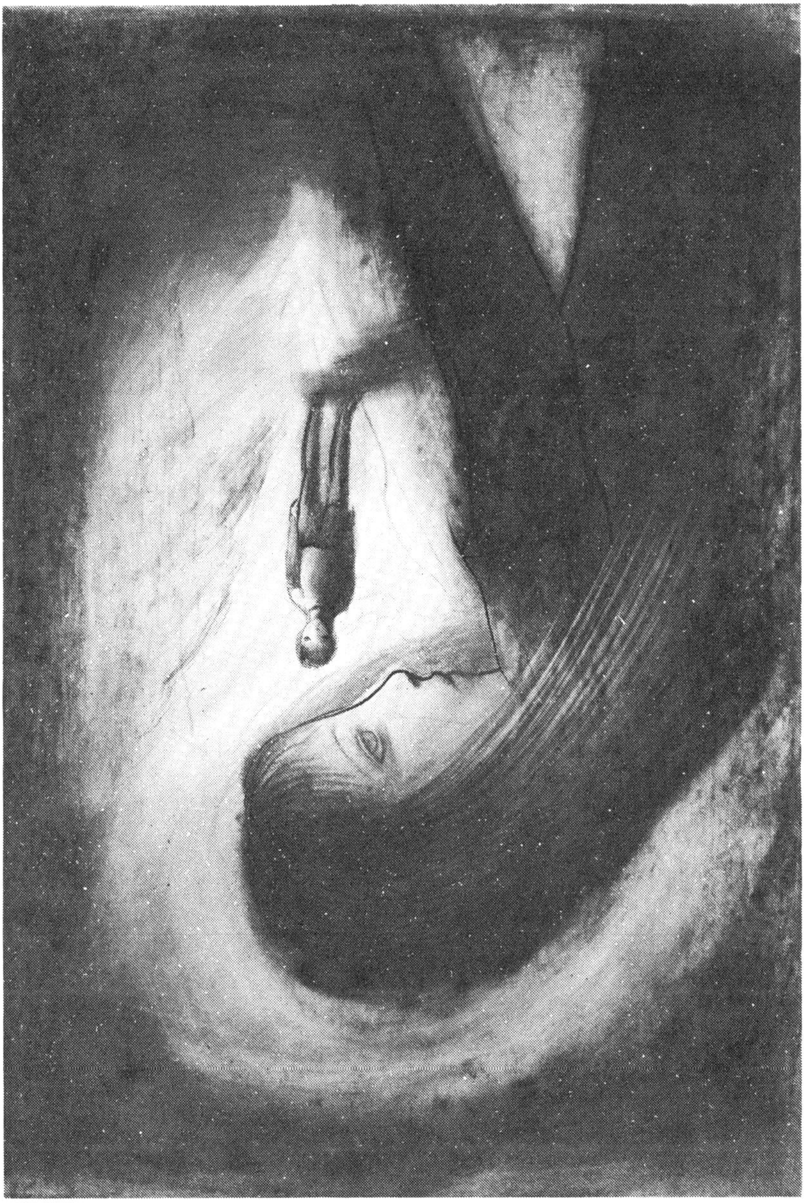

「うん、うん。」

「じゃんけんでおにきめだぞ。」

「うん、じゃんけんだもんね。」

ゆう子は手をふった。

「じゃんけんぽん。」

ゆう子は手をぱっとひろげて出し、直樹がぐうを出したので、直樹の負けになった。

「ようし、ゆう子、かくれるんだ。おにいちゃんがさがすからね。」

「ああい。」

パタパタとゆう子が走っていく。直樹は目をつぶって数をかぞえた。

「もういいかあい。」

あたりはしんとしている。サラサラという風が木の葉をゆする音がしている。シャンシャンとせみの声もした。この家で、このまんまくらせたらいいのにな、直樹は手をはなした。ようし、いくぞう。

ゆう子は、しょうべん小僧のうしろにしゃがんでいた。見つからない前から、けらけらわらいだし、とび出してくるのだからわけはない。つぎは直樹がかくれる番だった。そのとき、りつ子が出てきた。

152

「なにかあったの？」

直樹は思わずきいた。それほど、りつ子の顔は青ざめて、目がきらきら光っていた。

「ううん、なにもよ。」

りつ子はこたえた。なんだか、うわの空のようだった。

「でもね、きっと、わかるわ。直樹ちゃん、きっとわたし、なにもかも、はっきりさせてみせるわ。」

りつ子はそういうと、じっと立っていたが、はっとしたようにうでどけいを見た。

「たいへん、いそがなくっちゃ。」

「どこかへいくの。」

「とうろう流しよ。そうだわ、直樹ちゃん、いまからいきましょう、いっしょに。いいわ、直樹ちゃん、家へ帰ってて、わたし、着かえたら、すぐむかえにいくから。」

りつ子は、あわただしくいうと、手をふって、走りだした。なにかよくわからないが、おもしろそうだった。よし、いこう。

「さあ、とにかく早くおばあさんのおうちへ帰ろう。」

直樹はゆう子の手をひっぱった。

153

16　とうろう流し

りつ子は、ゆかたをきちんと着ていた。白地に紺の大きなちょうがとんでいるゆかたは、りつ子によくにあった。列車にのっていくのだときいて直樹はびっくりした。

「ぼく、花浦のとうろう流しかと思ったよ。」

りつ子は、白いほおにほほえみをうかべて、ゆっくり首をふった。列車のいすにすわったりつ子のひざには、ふろしきにつつんだなにかかさばるものがおかれてあった。その上には色とりどりのダリアの花たばがあった。

「ねえ、それ、なあに。ふろしきにつつんだやつ。」

直樹はきいた。

154

「これ？　とうろう。」

「見せて。」

「だめ、あとで流すとき見られるわ。」

「けち。」

りつ子はけちといわれても、やっぱりふろしきをとこうとはせず、ただほほえみをうかべただけだった。

「ねえ、どこまでいくの。」

「広島よ。」

「ふうん。広島にとうろう流しがあるの？」

「そうよ、きょうは八月六日だから……。」

「八月六日？　八月……六日？」

直樹は、あっと思った。あのカレンダーの日も八月六日だった。八月六日という日に、いったいなにがあったのだろうか。

「直樹ちゃん、原子爆弾のこと、しっているでしょう？　この前の戦争のとき、その原子爆弾がはじめて、日本の、広島におとされたのよ。」

155

そういえば、そんな話を、いつか、どこかできいたことがある。そうだ、いつだか思い出せないけど……。

「いまから、二十何年前になるのかしら……一九四五年、八月六日の朝、広島はよく晴れていたそうよ。サイジョウノテンキ、ヒロシマ、サイジョウノテンキ、ヒロシマ、ってね、ようすを見にきたアメリカの偵察機が、あとからくる飛行機にモールス信号をうったの。それをうけとった原爆搭載機『エノラ゠ゲイ』はね、まっすぐに広島へとんでくると、一発の原子爆弾をおとして、さっとにげ出したのよ。」

直樹は、りつ子の顔を見つめたまま、じっときいていた。

「原子爆弾は、パラシュートにつけられて、ゆっくりおちてくると、広島の上空五百メートルのところで、炸裂したの。そのいっしゅん、ぴかっと、すさまじい光がほとばしって、ドーンという音があとにつづいたというわ。それからはねえ、まるで地獄だったというわ。女の人のかみの毛はみんなか立ち、だれの顔ももうわからないように火ぶくれて、ひどい人は顔の皮がぺろりとはげてねえ、あごのところにぶらさがって、ふらふらゆれていたんですって。手の皮がべろりとむけて、まるで、手が四本あるようになっている人もいたって……。二十万人という人が、死んだのよ、たった一発の爆弾で……。」

156

直樹のおびえた顔を見て、りつ子ははっとしたように、話をやめた。

「それじゃあ、それじゃ、あのふしぎな家のおじいさんとイーダは、その日……。」

「でしょうねえ、そうとしか考えられないの。日めくりが八月六日でおわっている。そして、家の中はそのまんま……。おそらく六日の朝、なにか用事があって、おじいさんは広島へイーダちゃんをつれて出かけたんでしょう。そして原爆にあったのだと思うわ。」

「それじゃ、いすつくりのおじいさんも、イーダも死んだの？」

直樹は、のどになにかがひっかかったように、むねのあたりが苦しくなった。

「そうとは、はっきりいえないわ。ぜんぶの人が死んだのではないから……。でもね、生きているとすれば、あの家へ帰ってくると思うの、だから……。」

「死んだのかもしれないよね。」

直樹はなみだがこみあげてくるのをこらえた。死んだのかもしれないとは、何回か考えてみたけれど、小さなイーダの死が、ほとんど決定的になったいま、まちつづけていたいすのことを思うと、どうしていいかわからなくなる。直樹はまどに顔をよせた。消えてはあらわれ消えてはあらわれる海が、ぼうっとなみだにかすんで見えた。

列車は広島へついた。駅の外へ出ると、りつ子は、

157

「このへんも、みんな、見わたすかぎりの焼け野原だったそうよ。いまはうそのように、新しい町が
できているけれどね。」

そういいながら、駅前から赤い色のバスにのりこんだ。しばらくして平和公園についた。もう人々
でいっぱいだった。みごとな噴水が緑や赤や青の光にいろどられながら、空へ空へとほとばしり、は
げしいしぶきを上げておちていく。

「この噴水はね、いのりのいずみというの。そのとき原爆をうけた人たちは、みんな、水、水をとい
いながら死んでいったんですって。わたしの知っている人の話をきくとね、どこもかしこも死んだ人
がごろごろして、その灰色のかたまりからまっかに焼けた兵隊さんが水をくれええといって、よろ
よろと立ち上がったんですって。それがもう、仁王さんの像のようで、むちゅうでにげたって……。
なかには、ほりょになったアメリカ兵もいて、両手をうしろ手にくくられてころがったまま、水、水と
いっていたそうよ。でもねえ、水を飲ませるとすぐに息をひきとるからといって、それほどほしがっ
た水をそのとき飲ませなかったのですって。水もなかったのでしょうけれど……。
夜空にきららかにしぶきを上げている噴水は、その人たちへのたむけの水だという。けれど、死ん
でいったその人たちの、のどのかわきは、けっしていやされることはないだろう。
「ごめんなさい、直樹ちゃん。まだ小さいのに、こんな話をきかせてしまって。こわかった？　ほら、

158

わたしたちの前にあるのが資料館よ。そのときのようすや、いろいろな品物がここにはいっているの。こんなもんじゃない、あのひどさは、こんなもんじゃないって、しっている人は思うらしいけど、いつか直樹ちゃんにも見てほしいわ。」

「きょうはだめなの？」

「夜だからね。」

りつ子は直樹の背に手をまわして、その建物の下を通りぬけた。一階がなくて、すぐ二階からはじまっているような建物の、コンクリートの太い柱の下をくぐりぬけていくと、正面の夜空に、どきりとするほどあざやかに廃墟がうき上がっていた。外国の寺院のようにまるい屋根は鉄骨だけとなり、かべはおち、いたましいすがたなのに、オレンジ色の照明をあてられたすがたには、廃墟だけがもつかなしいような美しさがただよっていた。

「あのあたりが、原爆がおちた中心地なの。世界ではじめておとされた原子爆弾が、どんなに悲惨なものかをつたえるために、そのまま残されているのよ。」

人々の群れは流れるように、原爆ドームへの道を進んでいた。石畳の両側はしばふで、点々とずくまっているのは、はとの群れだった。しだいにこくなっていくやみに、庭園燈のあかりが青くさし、線香の白いけむりがただよっていく。読経の声が、木立のおくから流れて、人々のかなしみをそ

159

そっていた。

「石段よ、のぼるのよ。」

りつ子の声がした。直樹はわれにかえって、石段を七、八段のぼると、そこに慰霊碑があった。古代の墓か、家なのか、そうしたすがたを思わせる、ふしぎなかたちの碑がえがく弓なりのシルエットの中に、ドームがくっきりとはめこまれうかんで見える。人々はその前に花をそなえ、線香をそなえ、かしらをたれていのった。下におさめられた墓石のような碑には、

安らかにねむってください

あやまちはくりかえしませぬから

160

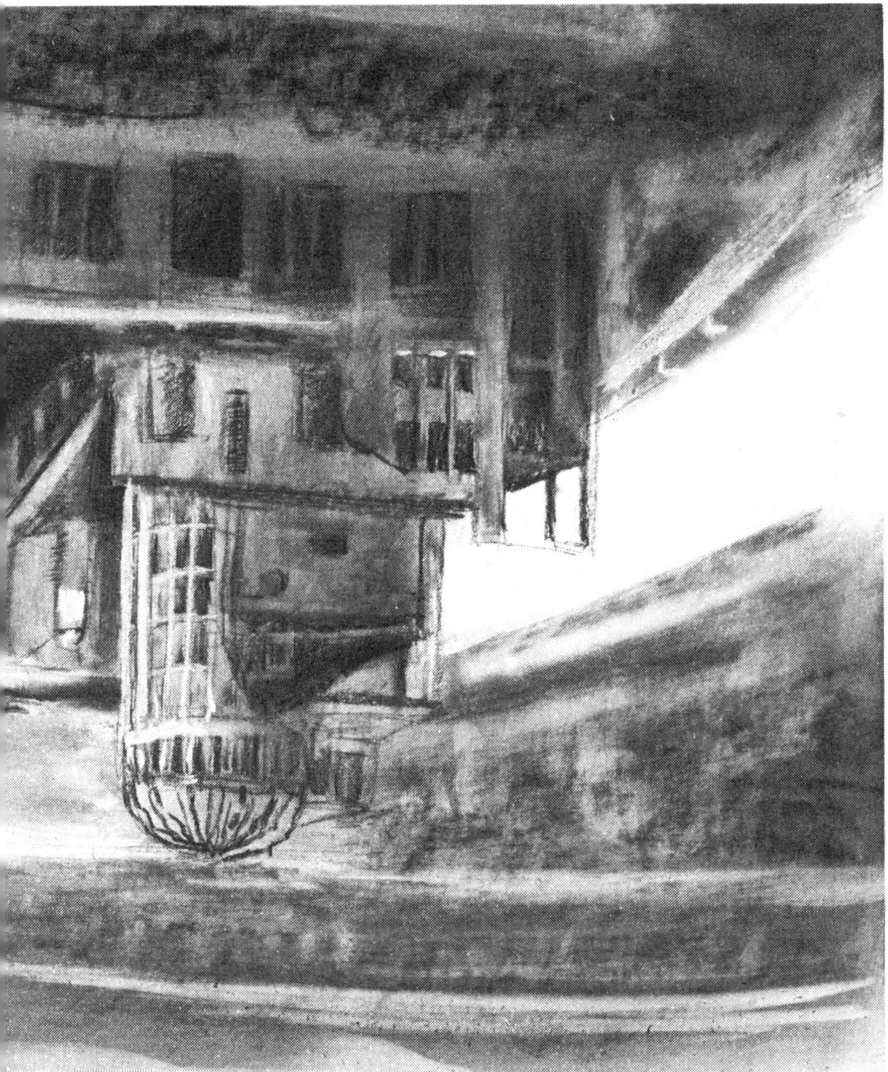

とほってあるという。

直樹は、りつ子の横にならんで手をあわせた。

（いすつくりのおじいさん、あなたのいすは、おじいさんやイーダちゃんを、まって、まって、まちつづけています。）

直樹は、そこまで心の中でつぶやいたが、あと、どうつづけていいのか、わからなかった。しかしそれだけで、なにもかもわかってくれるだろうと思った。

たえまなく、ボーン、ボーン、という鐘の音が鳴りひびいていた。平和をいのる鐘の音だった。ゆかたがけの人々は、まだあかりのはいっていないとうろうをむねにいだき、慰霊碑からドームのほうへ、平和の鐘のあるお堂のほうへ、しずかに流れていく。りつ子も直樹もその中にまじって、慰霊碑をかこむ四角い石でたたんだ池の横を、まっすぐにドームのほうへ進んだ。

「平和の火よ。」

りつ子が教えた。池の中につくられた石の台に、平和の火はあかあかと燃えていた。こい夜空とめらめらとなびく赤いほのおは水にうつり、ほのおにてらされた人々の流れるような群れもまた、水にうつり、ゆらめく。しずかだった。これほど人が集まっているのに、しずかだった。

「あ、かいづか。」

162

直樹は小さくさけんだ。

池の両わきにどっしりとならぶ木は、美しくかりこまれたかいづかだった。しかし、ふしぎな家の

まわりに、くるったように枝をさしのべているかいづかの木と、なんというちがいだろうか。あの家

のまわりをかこむむかいづかが、地獄ののろいのほのおならば、ここに立つかいづかは、しずかないの

りのほのおを空に向かって燃えたたせているようだった。

人々の流れは、やがて木立の間に立つ原爆の子の像の横へおれて、平和の鐘のほうへ流れていく。

「たくさんの子どもが死んだの。そのときはきずひとつうけなかったのに、何年も何年もしてから、

放射能による白血病が出て、死んでいった子がたくさんいるの。原爆がおちたとき、おかあさんのお

なかにいた子どもでさえ、原爆のために、白血病になって、死んでいったの。これは、そういう子の

ための像なのよ。子どもたちの力でつくられた像なのよ。」

りつ子の声は、ひくく、つぶやくようだった。直樹はなにもこたえなかった。だまってきき、だ

まって、白い塔をあおぎ、その上に立つ愛らしい少女のすがたを心にきざんだ。

鐘は鳴りつづいていた。人の流れははす池にかこまれた鐘つき堂の前でたゆたっている。ひとり、

ひとり、平和のねがいをこめて、つき鳴らしているのだ。手をあわせ、やがてしずかにとうろうに火

を入れる。ちらちらとゆらめくとうろうをささげた人々の群れは、木立のおくへ進んでいく。それは

からだがひきしまるほど、かなしいいのりにみちたすがただった。

いつのまにか、りつ子と直樹の番がきていた。りつ子はとうろうを直樹のうでにあずけると、白い

手をのべて、つなをしっかりにぎり、力いっぱいひいた。

ボーンンンンン。

もういちどどつく。

ボーンンンンンン。

りつ子はしずかに手をあわせていのると、直樹からとうろうをうけとった。直樹もつなをにぎっ

た。ぶらさがるように力を入れてぐいとひいた。

ボーンンンンンン。

りつ子は、とうろうに火を入れていた。字が書いてあるのが見えた。

ボーンンンンンン。

りつ子はそででとうろうをかこい、直樹をふり向くと、

「おわった？　いきましょう。」

といった。

火はちらちらと木の間をぬい、土手へ出た。そこに川があった。あのとき、いく万の人のしかばね

164

を海へ流しさった川があった。人々は川へ石段をおりていく。手になにも持たずのぼってくるのは、すでにとうろうを流しおえた人々だった。カタカタと石段をふむげたの音にまじって、ききとれぬほどかすかに、ヒタヒタと、川は波をよせている。一つ、また一つ、とうろうはたゆたったり、くるりとまわったりしながら、光を川の面にうつして流れていく。りつ子もそっと水の面へとうろうをおいた。そして、もういちど、手をあわせた。直樹はそのとき、あざやかにしるされた字を読みとった。

わたしは、こんなに
おおきくなりました。

「さあ、いきましょう。」

りつ子の声に、直樹はあわてて石段をのぼった。土手の上から川面を見ると、いく百ともしれぬとうろうは、まっかに川面をうずめ、光をうつしてまたたきながら、しずかによりそい流れていく。水の面にうつる原爆ドームの影をちらちらとくずしながら流れていく。父を思い、母を思い、おさなくして死んでいったわが子へのいのりをのせて、とうろうの火は海へ流されていく。

「広島には、七本の川があるの。その川へ、原爆で死んだ人たちへのいのりをこめて、八月六日の夜、とうろうが流されるのよ。」

直樹は、はっと思い出した。

——海へも流されておりましょうなあ。

——海へもよけい、流されておりましょう。 かぞえきらんほど、流されておりましょう……七つの川が死人でうまったと……。

いつか、夜ねむってから、ふっと目がさめてきいた話は、原爆の話だったのだ。広島じゅうが焼け野原になって、人だまがとび、おに火が燃えて、ちょうちんもいらないといわれたほど、それほど人が死んだのだ……。

けれど、流されていくとうろうの火はきれいだった。死んで何年もたてば、そんなにたくさんの人が、何十万の人がいっぺんに殺されたというおそろしい思い出も、きれいになるものなのだろうか。

すると、りつ子がつぶやいた。

「こうして、火がともって、海へ流されていくときはいいの。でもね、ま夜中、上げ潮になるとね、半分こわれたり、もちろん、火も消えたとうろうのかたまりが、海からまた潮にのって、帰ってくるのですって。もうだれもいないしんとしたま夜中の海べや、川に、こわれたとうろうが帰ってくる……。

わたしはそれをきいたとき、それがほんとうだと思ったの。たくさんの、海に流されていった人たちのたましいは、けっして、休まることはないのよ。どんなことがあってもゆるせないのよ。その思いが、潮にのってうちかえされてくるのよ……。」

166

17 生まれかわり

一九四五年八月六日という日が、それほどおそろしい日だということを、直樹はなにもしらなかったのだ。きけばきくほど、いすつくりのおじいさんと、小さなイーダは、原爆のために死んだとしか思われない。だとしたら、ゆう子は、ふしぎな家に住んでいたイーダの生まれかわりではないだろうか。だからこそゆう子は、あの家へ、ごめんくださいというかわりに、ただいまあ、といってかけこむのではないだろうか。まるでじぶんのものでも取り出すように、さっさとおもちゃや毛布をひっぱり出すのではないだろうか。

帰りの列車の中で、直樹が考えたのはこのことだった。りつ子にその話をすると、りつ子は、うんとうなずいた。

167

「そういうことだって、あるかもしれないわ。わたし、よくおぼえていないけど、たしかにそういう話、きいたことあるの。」

りつ子はいった。

「ぼく、おじいさんにきいてみる。おじいさん、いろんなことしってるもの。」

直樹はやくそくした。りつ子は直樹を、おじいさんの家へ送りとどけると、おじいさんが、ぜひ中へはいるように、お茶を飲んでいくようにというすすめをふりきって、いそいで帰っていった。

「どうじゃったね。とうろう流し、きれいだったじゃろ。」

おじいさんがいった。

「うん、きれいだったけど……あれだけの人が死んだと思ったら、こわかった。」

「そうやなあ、広島の七つの川が、死人でうずまったいうもんなあ。わしらもあのまま、広島に住んどったらえらいことじゃった。」

「えっ、それじゃ、おじいさんたちも、あの町に住んでいたの。」

「そうじゃ、それもまあ、原爆のおちた中心地のすぐそばに、本屋さんをひらいとったのよ。それが、どうも仕事がうまくいかん。それで、可部いう町へうつってのう、そこで本屋さんをしておったが、その後花浦の図書館へこんかという話があったもんで、本屋はやめて、こっちへうつってきたん

168

じゃ。まあ、あのまま広島におったら、一家ぜんめつ、おかあさんも女学生のときに死んでおったのう。」

直樹はぞうっとした。そんなことがあったのか、原爆といっても、まだどこかで人ごとのように思っていたのに、もしかしたら、おかあさんもあっていたのかもしれないのか……。

「もうひとつ、おかあさんは、いのちびろいしとるんじゃ。あの日まで、おかあさんは毎日毎日、広島へいっとってなあ。」

「なにをしに。」

「軍の工場へ、徴用されていっとったんじゃな。それが、あの日にかぎって、材料がない。それまで、日曜も休まんと仕事に出ておったのが、その日だけ、ふいっと休みになった。」

「それでたすかったの。」

「そうじゃ、おなじ女学校の生徒でも、ほかの工場へいっとったもんは、みな死んだ。生と死は、紙一重じゃった……。」

「おかあさんがもし、死んだら、ぼく、この世に生まれてなかったんだね。」

「そういうことになるのう。」

直樹は、ため息をついた。

「ねえ、おじいさん、人間って、生まれかわる?」

169

「なんじゃと、生まれかわるかって、とっぴょうしもないこといいだす子じゃな。ま、そういうこともあるらしいのう。」

「それ、どんなふうに。」

「いろいろあるが、日本には、こんなんがある。ええと、あれはたしか和歌山あたりの話だったと思うが、そこに、赤尾長者という長者がおってな、長いこと子どもがおらなんだが、とうとう玉のような男の子がさずかった。長者はよろこんで、いのちながかれとねごうて、亀千代と名をつけたそうな。そして、毎日毎日亀千代の目方をはかってよろこんでおった。ところがある日、はかりのひもが切れてのう、亀千代は庭へおち、打ちどころがわるかったかして、死んでしもうた。」

直樹は首をかしげた。

「はかりのひもが切れるって、どういうこと。はかりにひもがついているの。」

「はっはっは、むかしだもの、いまのようにぽんとのればいいというはかりではなくて、さおばかりというはかりを使うておったのさ。さおのかたはしに重しの分銅をつけてな、かたほうにかごでもつけて、赤んぼうを入れてはかったのじゃろ。」

「そうか、それでひもが切れたのか。」

「長者はなげきかなしんで、死んだ子のてのひらに、赤尾長者の一子亀千代と書いて、お墓にうめたと。」

170

「そうしたら。」

「そうしたら、つぎの年じゃったか、何年かたってからか、ともかくあるときのこと、わかい夫婦が赤子をせおうて、長者のやしきへたずねてきた。赤尾長者さまいうたらここか、そうや、それならいうて、負うていた子のてのひらをひらいて、長者に見せたそうな。そこにはまぎれもない長者の字で、赤尾長者の一子亀千代と、すみ黒々と書いてあったというぞ。」

「へええ。」

「赤尾長者はないてその子をだきしめて、この子は亀千代の生まれかわりや、どうぞこの子をくれというたが、その夫婦はくれるといわん。ただこうして生まれかわった子のてのひらの字は、水であろうても消えん、砂でこすっても消えん、その子が生まれかわる前のもとの家の、墓の土つけてあらえば消えるということやから、わざわざたずねてきたのやいうてな、墓の土もろうて帰っていったそうじゃ。」

「ふうん……。」
直樹は目をまるくして、ため息をついた。

「それ、ほんとうのこと。」

「さあてなあ、ま、いいつたえやからな。だが、これににた話は日本にたくさんあるし、外国にもあ

171

る。」

「それどういうの。はなしてよ。」

「さあて、どの本に書いてあったかな、七、八年前に読んだのじゃが。」

おじいさんは本だなを見わたした。

「あれは借りた本じゃったかなあ、これは実話として記録されておった話じゃ。なんでもアメリカで生まれたある少女が、じぶんはこういう家に住んどって、家にはこうこう、こういう家族がおって、ということを、いっしょうけんめいいうのだと。ところが、両親にはなにをいっているのやら、さっぱりわからん。ところがあるとき、親類のだれかがその話をきいておどろいた。というのは、その少女の何代か前のおばあさんが、アムステルダムの古い家に住んでいて、その親類のものは、その家にいったことがあるのだが、少女の話とぴったりあうというのだよ。なにしろ間取りとか、どういうところに石段があるとか、ぜんぶことこまかにいうのだそうだ。

そこでとうとうアムステルダムへだれかがしらべにいったそうだ。古い家なので、そっくり残っていたそうだが、その子のいうたこととぴったり符合したそうじゃ。」

「それでは、その子は、そのおばあさんの、生まれかわりだったの？」

「生まれかわりといえるか、そこがそれ、わからんところだが、つまり、ある記憶が遺伝子に鮮明に

172

残るということなのだろうな。ということは生まれかわりといえるかもしれん。現代はだな、あまりにも教えこまれることが多く、刺激が強い。だからそういう、人間の、ふしぎな力、テレパシーというものは、うしなわれつつあるんだな。原始的な時代には、そういうことはたくさんあったのではないかな。」

「ふうう。」

直樹はうなった。

「そのアムステルダムって、どこ。アメリカ？」

「いいや、オランダの首都じゃ。」

「オランダと、アメリカみたいにはなれていても、そういうことがおこるんだね。」

「うむ、アメリカは、移民の国じゃ。だからその少女の両親か、祖父母がおそらくアメリカへ移民したのじゃろうな。」

「ふうう。」

直樹はまたうなった。そんなこと、あるのかなあ。

「で、その少女っていくつだったの。」

「たしか三さいぐらいだったと思う。おそらく三さいをこえたら、そういう記憶は俗事の中へうずも

173

「それだ、それかもしれないぞ。」

直樹はこうふんして立ち上がった。そうかもしれない……。

あの小さないすにこしかけていたイーダという子の、生まれかわりかもしれない……。ゆう子は生まれかわりかもしれない。じぶんのおもちゃや毛布をひっぱり出すように、あの家でおもちゃや毛布をひっぱり出して、遊んでいるのだ。

あの家にはいるときは、こんにちはともいわないで、ただいまあといってはいっていくのだ。じぶん

直樹がこうふんして、へやの中をぐるぐる歩きまわるのを、おじいさんはあきれたように見ていた。直樹はようやくそれに気がついて、すわりなおした。

「ところで、直樹ちゃんにたのまれた、ええと、ほれほれ、宗方進吉郎という人のことだがね。ほとんどの人がしらんかったなあ。たったひとり、ああ、それは、外国へまで、いすだのなんだのをつくる勉強にいった人やが、なんでも東京へいかれたのやないか、もうはや、生きとられまい。生きとられれば九十何さいにもなられるじゃろ。そういうておられたな。なんでもむすめさんがひとりおりおって、牧子さんいうたそうな。その人はその牧子さんと友だちだったそうなが、牧子さんもどうなったか、なにぶん、おさな友だちのことでわからんということやった。」

174

「どうもありがとう、おじいさん。」

「だが、直樹ちゃんは、なんでその人のことをしりたいんじゃ。」

「なんでってね、史料館でちょっと見たから……。」

「ほう、えらいもんじゃなあ、いまの子は。」

おじいさんは、えらく感心したようだった。

直樹はあわてて、

「おやすみなさあい。」

といって、ざしきのふすまをあけ、かやにはいった。ふとんにころりと横になってはっとした。

「あっ、そうか。」

むなかたまきこという、おさない字が目にうかんだ。まき子はおじいさんのむすめだったのか……。

その声で、ゆう子のそばにそいねしていたおばあさんが、おきあがった。

「ああ、ゆう子ちゃんをねかしとるうちに、なにやらしらん、こっちがうとうとしてしもた。あれ、直樹ちゃん、もどったの、おじいさんも帰っておられるのやねえ。」

「うん、ぼくが帰ったときには、うちにいたよ。」

「まあまあ、お茶もあげんと。それで直樹ちゃん、夕ごはんは。」

175

「りつ子ねえさんが、ごちそうしてくれた。」

「まあまあ、すまんこと。」

おばあさんが出ていくと、直樹はもういっぺん、ふとんからはい出した。そして、茶の間からそっと持ってきた、小さな懐中電燈をつけて、ゆう子のてのひらにあてた。もちろん、むっちりと太ったゆう子のてのひらのどこにも、なにも書いてあるはずはない。足のうらをてらしてみた。そこにも、

なんのしるしもなかった。直樹はぱたりとふとんにたおれると、懐中電燈のまるいあかりを、かやの天じょうにあててうごかした。ゆらゆらと、まるい光の輪が、思いがけないしみをうかびあがらせてゆれる。わすれられていたなにかに、こうして光があてられているのかもしれない……。直樹はそう思うと、なおねむれなかった。

直樹がようやくとろとろしかけたとき、電話のベルが鳴るのがきこえた。おばあさんが出て、ふたことみことはなしている。やがて、そっとふすまがあいた。

「直樹ちゃんや、あすの夕がた、おかあさんがもどるそうな。」

おばあさんの声だった。直樹は、

「ほんとう。」

と、ねぼけた声を出した。

「ごめんごめん、ねとったところおこしてしもたな。」

おばあさんは、そっとふすまをしめた。

直樹は、ひき入れられるようなねむけのなかで、さあたいへんだ、もう日がないぞ、と思っていた。

そうだ、日がもうなくなる。あしたはいすのところへいいにいかなくてはいけない……。

177

18　ほんとうのことをはなしたとき

つぎの朝、ごはんがすむと直樹は、
「ねえ、おにぎりつくってよ。ゆう子をつれて遊びにいって、どこかでおにぎりたべてくるの。いいでしょう？」
と、おばあさんにいった。
「そりゃいいけど、おかあさんが午後にはつくというのに、なにも弁当持っていかんでもええじゃろ。」
おばあさんは、ふしぎそうにいった。
「おべんとたべたら、じき帰ってくるよ。だってそうしたいんだもの。」

「そうかそうか、そんならいっといで、ちょうどごはんもあまっとるし。」

おばあさんは、うめぼしのはいっている三角のおにぎりをむすび、ごま塩をふりかけ、つやつやしたのりをまいてくれた。いやそのうえに、ももまで手さげに入れてくれた。そのうえ、つめたい麦茶のはいったまほうびんも用意してくれたし、ドロップまでくれた。

「そんなら、気いつけていっといで。けど、どこへいくの。」

「ひみつ、ひみつ。」

直樹はふざけていった。

「まあまあ、ひみつなの。でもまあこのへんには、遊ぶところがたんとあってええわ。じゃ、はよう お帰り。」

「さよなら、あんころもち、またきなこ。」

ゆう子が手をふりふりどなり、直樹も、重たいバスケットをふって、

「いってまいりまあす。」

とさけんだ。肩にはまほうびんをかけ、そのうえ、水彩絵の具の道具も持ったので、おおげさな荷物だった。しかし、おかあさんが帰れば、もう東京へ帰らなくてはならないことは、目に見えていた。

直樹はあのふしぎな家で、きょうこそゆっくり遊ぼうと思った。もしゆう子があのいすのさがしてい

179

るイーダの生まれかわりなら、この花浦にいるあいだに、たっぷりとゆう子といすを遊ばせてやりたかった。

「まてよ、それより、あのいすを東京の家へ持っていこう。そのほうがいいかもしれない。」

あのいすが、たったひとりでこの家にとり残されることを思うと、直樹はむねがいたかった。

「そうだ、いすになにもかもはなして、いっしょに東京へいこうっていってみよう。小さないすだから、かついでいけばいい。」

直樹は立ちどまった。りつ子にこのことをはなしてみたかった。でも、きっとりつ子もあの家へくるにちがいない。

門をはいって玄関のドアをあけると、ゆう子はすぐに庭へいすを持ち出して、おままごとをはじめた。朝のすずしい風がきょうちくとうの花をゆらし、遊んでいるゆう子の手もとへ花びらをいくつもおとした。そのたびにゆう子は、はねあがり、声をたててよろこんだ。

直樹は食堂のいすを持ち出し、こしかけると写生にとりかかった。一つ一つを紙にうつしていくと、家のかたちも、しょうべん小僧の愛らしいすがたも、かいづかも、なにもかもが、もういちど直樹に声をかけてくるようだった。

「ごはんでしゅよう。きてくなさあい。」

180

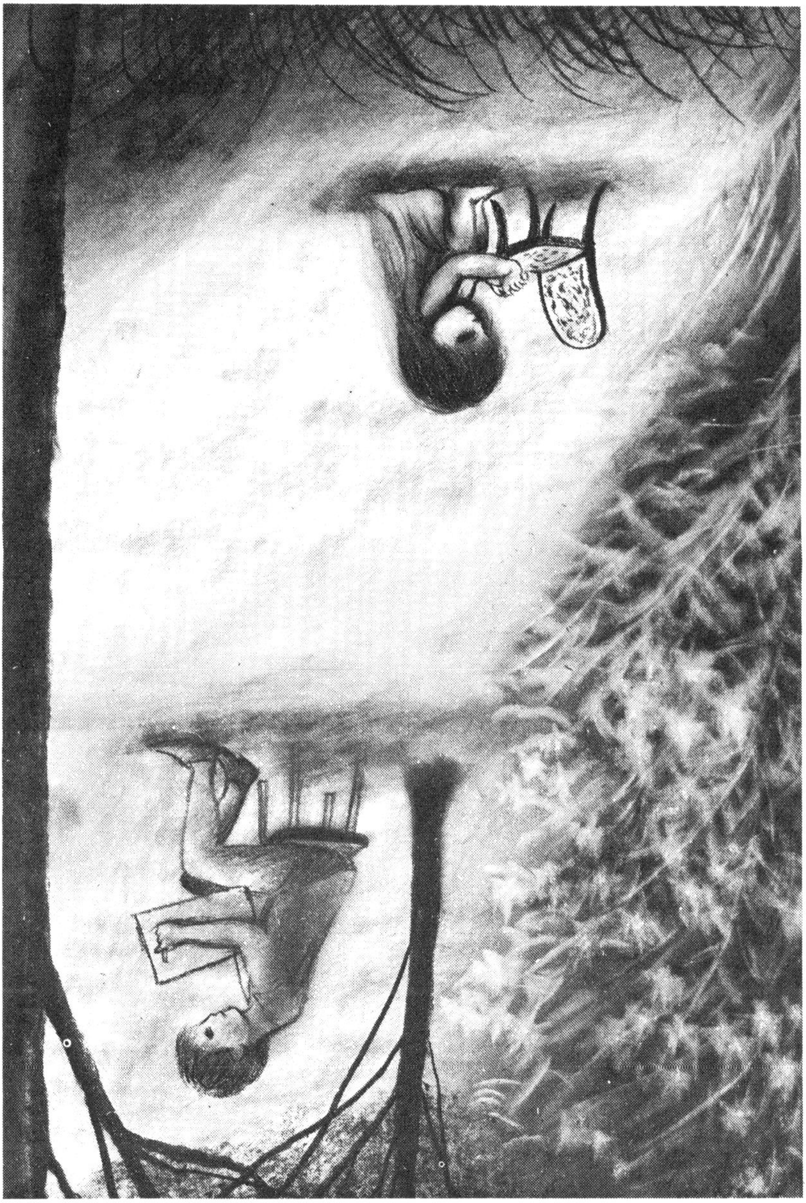

ゆう子が声をはりあげている。いすがお客さまになっているのか、しきりにはなしかけている。木のしげみごしに日の光のふりこぼれる庭にいると、直樹はゆう子ばかりでなく、かつてじぶんもこの家に住んでいたのではなかろうかと思えてくるのだった。

うらの清水から水をくんできて絵の具をとかし、色をつけるころには、日はかなり高くのぼっていた。

「おにいちゃん、おにぎり。」

ゆう子はおなかをすかせていた。

「よし、これでおわりだから、まっていろよ。」

木にかげをつけると、直樹は立ち上がった。

「さあごはんにしよう。どうする？　ゆう子、お庭でたべるかい。」

「うん、うん。」

ゆう子ははねた。

「まっといで、ももひやしたの、持ってくるからね。」

うらの水うけにひやしておいたももを取ってきて、直樹はおにぎりをひろげた。口に入れると、のりとごはんと、ごま塩のこうばしさがひろがって、ほっぺたがおちそうだった。ゆう子はよっぽどお

182

なかがすいていたのか、みるみる二つたいらげた。つめたくひえたももにもかぶりつき、麦茶も飲む

と、直樹はバスケットにすっかりしまった。さきへ、さきへ、のばしたい気持ちが、直樹にあった。

しかし、時間がない……りつ子はこなかった。こなくてもいおうと直樹は思っていた。

「ねえ、いすくん、よく思い出してほしいんだ。おじいさんとイーダがいった日ね、いいお天気だっ

たかい？」

「ウン。」

いすはあいまいなへんじをした。

「そのとき、おじいさん、どこへいくっていっていた。」

「オボエテイナイ。」

「広島へいくって、いわなかったかい。」

「ヒロシマ……。」

いすはおどろいたようにいった。

「ソウダ、ソウイッテイタ……。」

「そうか、やっぱりそうか。で、その日、朝早くいったの。」

「ウン、ソウダトオモウ。」

183

「その日、おじいさんたちが出てから、ぴかっと光ったり、ドーンという音がしなかったかい。」

いすは、しばらくだまっていた。

「ソウダ。」

と、ぽつりといった。

「アノトキ、イケニタッテイルニンギョウガ、シタニオチタンダ。キットソウダ、ヒカッタヨ。タシ

カニ、クロイカーテンシテイタノニヒカッタ。ソシテ、ガラスガバリバリットワレタ。アトデドーン

トイッタトキダ、ズイブンアトデ。」

「すぐじゃなかったの。」

「アア、スコシシテ、ズイブンシテ。」

そこのところがどうもおかしかった。ぴかっと光ってから、そんなに長いあいだかかって、ドーン

というだろうか。でもこのいすがこれだけくわしくおぼえているというのは、たいしたことだった。

「あのねえ、おちついてきいておくれよ。おじいさんとイーダは、原子爆弾にあって、死んだらしい

んだ。」

いすはそれをきくと、とび上がった。

「シンダ？　ソンナコトハナイ。ココニイーダハイルジャナイカ。」

184

「だからいったろ？　これはぼくの妹だって……。ねえ、おじいさんとイーダが出かけた日は、一九四五年の八月六日の朝なんだ。広島へ八時十五分に爆弾がおち、二十万の人が死んだ。もし生きているとすれば、おじいさんかイーダは、とっくに帰ってきていると思うよ。」

「ソンナコトハナイ、ソンナコトハナイ。」

いすは歩きだした。カタッ、カタッ、足をひきずりながら歩きまわった。

「ソンナコトハナイ、ソンナコトハナイ……。」

ふいにいすは、こちらに向きなおった。

「ヨシ、ソノコガ、ワタシノイーダダトイウショウコヲミセヨウ。」

「しょうこだって？」

「ソウダ、セナカヲ……。ヨウフクヲメクッテ、セナカヲミセテクレ。三ツ、キレイニナランダホクロガアルハズダ。」

直樹はいっしゅんおびえたようにいすを見た。直樹のしっているかぎりでは、ゆう子にそうしたほくろがあるとは思えなかった。しかし、それは記憶ちがいだろうか。ほくろはあるのだろうか。直樹はこわかった。あってもこわく、なくてもこわかった。

「ハヤクミルンダ。ソレトモ、ミラレナイノカ？　ソウダ、ミラレナインダロウ。」

185

直樹はゆう子をよんだ。

「向こうを向いてごらん、ほら、むしむしがついているから取ってあげるね。」

直樹はそういうと、ゆう子のみじかいワンピースをひき上げ、パンツを下におしさげて、小さな

なかをむき出しにした。

「やあよう。」

ゆう子がからだをねじり、ワンピースは下へおちた。やわらかなゆう子のせなかに、ほくろはな

かった……。

「見たろう。」

直樹はいすのほうを見ないでいった。そしてゆっくり、ゆう子のパンツを上げ、ぽんとおしりをた

たいた。

「はい、いいよ、いっても。」

ゆう子が、じぶんの遊んでいた場所へかけもどると、直樹ははじめて、いすをふりかえった。いす

はこきざみにふるえていた。そして、とつぜん、カタカタとくずれ、よろめいたかと思うとばったり

とたおれた。足も、背も、すべてがばらばらになって、そこに散った。

186

19 これですべてが――

直樹はどんなふうにして家に帰りついたのか、おぼえていなかった。いっしゅんのうちに、カタカタとくずれたいすを見たとき、恐怖が直樹をつかまえた。直樹はむちゅうでバスケットをつかみ、ゆう子のところへとんでいって、いちもくさんにふしぎな家を走り出たのだった。

おじいさんの家のうら口をあけたとき、はなやかなわらい声がした。

「あっ、おかあさんだ。」

直樹に手をひきずられて、べそをかきながら走ってきたゆう子は、たちまち元気をとりもどすと、家の中へかけこんだ。

「おかあさん。」

直樹もバスケットをほうり出してかけこんだ。

「まあまあ、どこへいっていたのよ。まあ、太ったじゃないの、まあ黒くなって、ゆう子も直樹も。」

そういうおかあさんこそ、まっ黒だった。あいかわらずのんきそうな声を出してひざにのったゆう子の重さをはかっているようだった。直樹はほっとして、ぺたりとそこにすわった。

「直樹ちゃん、なんや青いように見えるが、どこぞぐあいわるいの。」

おばあさんが声をかけた。

「ううん、なんでもない。」

直樹は首をふった。

「どうれどうれ、こっちへきてごらん。はあ、だいじょうぶよ、熱はないし、まあ、黒くなって……。」

おかあさんののんきそうな声をきき、あたたかな手がひたいにさわったとき、直樹はきゅうにわっとなきだした。おかあさんが帰ってきて、ほっとしたのもあった。また、るすのあいだに直樹が、これだけさまざまのできごとにめぐりあったというのに、黒くなった、黒くなったとしかいってくれないおかあさんの、のんきさがくやしくもあった。そして、くずれたいすへの、どうにもならないすまなさもあった。直樹はじぶんでもどうにもならない、じれったさとかなしさに、どうにもならないすまおいおいと声をあげ

188

てなきつづけた。

とつぜんのことに、おかあさんとおばあさんはとほうにくれ、直樹にことばをかけたり、なぐさめたりしたが、直樹はなかなかなきやまなかった。

「つかれとるんじゃ。あんたのおらんあいだ、よくゆう子ちゃんのめんどうみたものな。」

おばあさんがいった。

「よしよし、直ぼう、よくやったから、つかれたのね。さ、ちっとねなさい。ゆう子、ゆう子もお昼寝よ。」

おかあさんは、つめたいタオルで直樹の顔や手をふいてくれ、まくらをあてがってくれた。しゃくりあげているうちに、直樹はいつのまにかぐっすりねむってしまっていた。

直樹が目をさましたのは、もう夕ぐれだった。ごはんのしたくをする音が、ひびいてきた。ゴトゴトとなべがにえる音、ぷうんとなすのにもののにおいがする。トントントントントン、あれはきっと、きゅうりをきざんでいるんだ。直樹は、みちたりた気持ちでぼんやりと手も足ものばしていた。顔の皮もつっぱっていたけれど、はげしくきずついたずきいてないて、目がはれぼったかったし、口に、油ぐすりをぬり、包帯をあてたような安らかさもあった。

茶の間からおじいさんの声と、おかあさんの声がきこえてきた。するとおばあさんの台所からいっているらしい大声がした。

189

「まあ、そんなにいそがんかて、いいじゃろに、なにも今晩の夜行でいかんかて──」。

直樹はとびおきた。茶の間をのぞきこんだ。

「おかあさん、今夜帰るって、ほんとう？」

おかあさんはびっくりしたように、直樹を見上げた。ひざにはもうちゃんと、ゆう子がこしかけている。

「そうなのよ、今夜の寝台が取れたからね、あしたの特急も、あさっても、もう満員なの。急行じゃ

どうしても時間が長いでしょう？」

「そんなこといったって。」

直樹はまたなき声になった。

「ぼく、　用事残ってんだ。」

おとなたちは思わずわらいだし、　直樹はますますふんがいした。

「おかあさんなんて、　いつだって、子どものつごう、ぜんぜん考えてくれないんだ。」

「なにいってるんです。おかあさんはいそがしいの。子どものつごうより仕事のつごうがさきですよ。」

おかあさんは、こわい顔をした。　直樹は台所へかけこんだ。

「おばあさん、りつ子ねえさん、こなかった？」

「さあねえ、きょうはみえんかったようよ。」

190

「そう……。」

直樹は、すぐに考えをきめた。

「ねえ、おばあさん、りつ子ねえさんの家、教えてよ。すぐいかないとまにあわないんだ。」

「まあ、いそがしいことじゃ。もう暗いからおじいさんについていってもらわんと。」

「だいじょうぶだよ、まだあかるいもの。ねえ、早く。」

おばあさんにかいてもらった地図を持って直樹はとび出した。おほりからもっとにぎやかな町より

の細い坂道のとちゅうにある家だった。ようやくさがしあてたとき、直樹がっかりした。家の中

は、まっ暗で、人っ子ひとり、いるけはいはなかった。

ベルをおしても、ごめんくださいとどなっても、だれも出てこない。直樹はどうしても、東京へ帰る前に、りつ子にあい

おろした。さて、どうしたらいいのだろう……。直樹は力なく門の前にこしを

たかった。いすのことをはなしたかった。

玄関の石段で、直樹のおしりがつめたくなってきた。直樹はしょんぼり立ち上がった。しかたがな

い、あえないなら、手紙を書いて、おばあさんにたのんでいこう。直樹はとぼとぼと、りつ子の家を

ふりかえり、ふりかえりしながらおばあさんの家にもどった。

「おらんかったって？」

おばあさんは、直樹からるすだったときくと、あきれたようにいった。

「おかあさんもおらんの？　おとうさんも。まあ、めずらし。一家そろってるすにするとはのう。」

「だからさ、ぼく、手紙書くから、わたしてね。」

「はいはい、ほなら、封筒あげましょ。」

直樹は、ごはんもそこそこにして、つくえの前にすわると、ノートをひろげた。

192

りつ子ねえさん、ぼくは今夜、きゅうに東京へ帰ることになりました。おねえさんのうちへいってみたのですが、るすなので、手紙をおばあさんにたのむことにしました。

ぼくはいすに、わるいことをしました。きみのイーダは、げんばくで死んだというしょうこを見せるといいました。そうしたらいすは、うそだ、といって、ゆう子がイーダだというしょうこを見せるといいました。そのしょうこというのは、せなかに三つ、オリオン星座のようにならんだほくろがあるというのです。ぼくはゆう子のせなかを見ました。ほくろはありませんでした。いすはそれを見たとたん、カタカタとくずれて、ばらばらになってたおれました。

ぼくはゆう子が、いすのまちつづけていたイーダちゃんの生まれかわりではないかと、思いはじめていました。だからいすを、東京のぼくのうちへ、つれていこうと思っていました。でも、それをいわないうちに、いすは死んでしまいました。とてもかなしい気持ちです。

りつ子ねえさんへ

直樹

もうひとつ、わすれていました。まき子というのは、進吉郎おじいさんのむすめだそうです。

193

イーダのおかあさんだと思います。これは、うちのおじいさんが、きいてきてくれた話です。

書きおわると、直樹はほっとして、ノートをちぎり、封筒に入れた。りつ子ねえさんへと書いて封をした。

「おばあさん、これ、あげてね。」

「はいはい、よろしくいうとくからねえ。ほんとに、りっちゃんには、ようしてもらってよかったねえ。やさしい、いい子や……。」

おかあさんの声がした。

「直樹ちゃん、早くしたくなさいよ。わすれもの、ないわね。」

おかあさんは、スーツケースをひろげて、大いそがしだった。

「ゆう子ちゃん、またおいでねえ。さよならしても、おばあちゃんを、わすれんといてねえ。」

おばあさんは、なんべんもゆう子をだいていい、おじいさんは、たばこばかりふかしていた。

「さよなら、あんころもち、またきなこ。」

ゆう子ははしゃいで、はねた。

「ああら、あんた、いつそれいうようになったの。」

194

おかあさんがはずんだ声を出した。

「それがおかしいんだ、こっちへきてから、きゅうにいいだしたんだよ。ギッチョー、ギッチョーとか

ね、ゆう子、ギッチョーギッチョーやってごらん。」

直樹にいわれて、ゆう子はてれくさそうに立った。そして小さなにぎりこぶしをつくると、両手を

向かいあわせてすっとのばし、

「ギッチョー、ギッチョー、こめつけ、こめつけ。」

と、米をつくまねをした。

「ははあ、やっと教育の成果があらわれたんだわ。へええ。」

おかあさんが、感心したようにいった。

「じつはね、ハンガリーから帰られた羽川先生がね、日本の子どもに日本のわらべ歌をというので、

ゆう子の保育園にきて教えてくださっているの。赤ちゃんべやへもきてね、それがまあ、ちっとも家

へ帰ってもうたわないと思っていたら、まあ、とつぜん、いいだすのねえ。」

おかあさんはひどくうれしそうだった。なあんだ、そうだったのか……直樹はもうひとつ力がぬけ

たような気がする。

「へえ、ハンガリーと、日本のわらべ歌と、どうつながるのやろ。」

195

おばあさんが首をかしげた。

「それはつまりね、こういうことなのよ。わらべ歌というのは、子どもたちが代々、だれに教えられるともなく、うたいつづけてきたものでしょう？　そのなかにこそ、いろいろな民族の音楽の発生や、原始的なすがたがあるってことなの。つまり、かりものでない民族の音楽ね。」

「へええ、むずかしいもんやねえ。」

おばあさんが感心した。おかあさんは、そこからハンガリーと日本とのかんけいについて、一席のべたかったらしいが、ざんねんなことに、

「さあ、用意はいいか、車がきたようやぞ。」

おじいさんがそういって耳をすました。

「ほう、きたわきたわ。さ、のったり、のったり。」

おじいさんもいっしょにのりこみ、おばあさんひとりがとり残された。しきりに手をふっている。

ドアがバタンとしまった。

直樹は、ああ、これですべてがおわったと思った。しかし、そうではなかったのである。

196

20 りつ子からの手紙

直樹が東京へ帰って、一週間ほどしたとき、おかあさんはおばあさんの手紙を読みながら、直樹に声をかけた。

「りつ子さんておじょうさん、入院なさったんですってね。」

「えっ、ほんとう。なんで。なんの病気で。見せてよ手紙。」

直樹はおかあさんの手から、読みかけの手紙をひったくろうとして、手をたたかれた。

「人が読んでいるものを、取るんじゃありません。」

「だって、だって。」

「さあ、ここよ、読んでごらん。」

おばあさんの手紙は読みにくかった。ただ、りつ子さんもまた入院したようできのどくな、と書いてあり、直樹がおせわになったので、直樹からも手紙をするように、とあるだけだった。

「手紙をするようにっていったって、住所も書いてないじゃない。」

直樹は口をとんがらかし、あっ、といった。

「ねえ、おかあさん、また、って書いてあるね。」

「え、また、どこによ。」

「ほらさあ、また入院したって。りつ子ねえさん、前にも入院していたのかしら。」

「そうねえ、そういうことになるかしらねえ。」

おかあさんにも、わかりようがなかった。

しかし、りつ子からの手紙は、それから何日かしてとどいた。直樹はいそがしく手紙の封を切った。手紙のほかに、ボール紙をまるめたつつのようなものもとどいた。

　直樹ちゃん、このあいだはいろいろありがとう。直樹ちゃんにめぐりあえたことは、わたしの一生をかえるほど、たいへんなことでした。心からありがとうともうしあげます。

　直樹ちゃん、わたしはイーダなのです。あのいすがまちつづけていた、イーダこそ、わたしな

198

のです。けれど、このことは、直樹ちゃんとあっていたときにはわからなかったのです。

わたしは三さいになるかならないころ、原爆をうけ、たったひとりで、広島をさまよっていたのです。そして、いまの父と母にひろわれました。父と母は、じぶんたちの両親と、そこにたまたま、たった一晩あずけた三つの女の子をさがしに広島へ出て、そこでわたしを見つけたのです。

両親と、わが子は、朝ごはんでもたべていたのか、まるくならんだかたちに、骨になっていました。いっぺんに両親とわが子をうしなった父と母は、たったひとりでよちよち歩きまわっているわたしを見たとき、どうしてもこの子を育てたい、と思ったのだそうです。

わたしは、ぼろぼろのもんぺをはき、うわぎは半分やぶれてなく、かけていたはずの防空かばんや、防空ずきんも、なにひとつありませんでした。ただひとつ、赤いメリンスの、花もようのお手玉を、しっかりにぎっていたそうです。

わたしは、名まえはときかれたとき、イーダちゃん、とこたえました。年はというと、指を三本出しました。ぼろぼろのもんぺに書かれた名まえは半分取れていて、つ子というのだけ読めたそうです。

そこで新しい父と母は、わたしに、りつ子という名をつけ、育ててくれたのです。その後、父と母に子どもは生まれませんでした。ですから父と母は、わたしをひきとったことを、どれほど

199

しあわせに思ったかしれなかったといいます。

高校のとき、わたしはじぶんが、ほんとうの子でないことをしりました。ほんとうの父や母に、ひとめあいたいと、どのくらい思ったでしょう。原爆で一家じゅう死んだのか、それとも、どこかに生きているのか、わたしが考えるのは、いつもそのことばかりでした。そしてわたしは、父も母も生きているのだ、きっとどこかで、しあわせにくらしているのだ。ある日かならず、わたしはめぐりあえる、そうゆめ見るようになりました。

そのうちわたしは、からだがひどくだるくなり、首のところがはれて、いたみだしました。入院、原爆による白血病と診断されました。もちろん先生も、母も病名をかくしていました。死にいたる病気だからです。でもわたしは、じぶんの病名を、ふとしたことからしってしまったのです。原爆にあった人たちが、二十数年たったいまなお発病し、死んでいくおそろしい病気であることも……。

長いあいだ入院し、輸血をくりかえし、経過がよくて、わたしは元気になりました。そして退院し、ぶらぶらしているときにめぐりあったのが、直樹ちゃん、あなたです。

はじめわたしは、直樹ちゃんがなにを考えて、いすをつくった人をしりたいというのか、もちろん、ぜんぜんしりませんでしたし、それほど、ふかいこととは思わなかったのです。けれど、

200

あの古ぼけたカレンダーが、一九四五年八月六日、原爆投下の日をさいごに、めくられることが

なく、かけられていたことをしったとき、わたしはどうしても、直樹

ちゃんのひみつをしりたくなったのです。

直樹ちゃんの話をきいているうちに、いすがさがしている子がイーダちゃんとよばれていたと

いうことをしって、わたしはまたどきりとしました。さっきも書いたように、たったひとりぼっ

ちで焼けあとの広島をさまよっているとき、わたしはじぶんをイーダちゃんと名のったのですか

ら……。

わたしは直樹ちゃんに、あの家につれていってもらいましたね。あのとき、いちばんさいごに

わたしは、あとかたづけをするといって残ったでしょう？　わたしはゆう子ちゃんの出してきた

クレヨンをしまうために、おくの六畳にはいり、おしいれの中のおもちゃばこをひっぱり出しま

した。それはみかんばこに紙をはったものでしたが、その中から、小さな、赤い花もようのメリ

ンスでつくったお手玉を見つけたとき、わたしの心は期待で苦しくなりました。

「きっとわたし、なにもかも、はっきりさせてみせるわ。」

といったのは、そのときだったのです。

あの日、わたしたちはそれから、とうろう流しにいきましたね。そしてつぎの朝、ひどいめま

201

いでわたしはたおれ、そのまま広島の原爆病院に再入院しました。そして病院で直樹ちゃんが残

していった手紙を読んだのです。

わたしはどきどきして、先生の回診をまちました。先生が診察してくださってせなかの番に

なったとき、

「先生、わたしのせなかに、ほくろがありますか。」

って、さもなにげなさそうにききました。

「うんうん、あるよ。オリオン星座みたいに、三つならんだほくろがね、めずらしいねえ。」

先生のへんじがかえってきたとき、わたしはうれしくて、なみだがぽろぽろ出ました。

直樹ちゃんは、むなかたまきこ、が、イーダのおかあさんだとしらせてくれましたね。わたし

は、うれしかった。じつはあの絵本に、むなかたまきことという字を見つけたとき、わたしはがっか

りしてすわりこみたいくらいだったのです。わたしはそこに、むなかた〇つ子という名がほし

かったのです。みつ子でもいいし、えつ子でもいい、のつく名なら、わたしだと思ってい

たのです。けれど直樹ちゃんの手紙で、それがわたしのおかあさんの名まえだとわかって、わた

しはなみだを、そこでもぽろぽろ流しました。

あの本はきっと、おじいさんが外国から持って帰った本ではないかしら。それをおかあさんが

202

読み、そのつぎに、わたしの本になったのだと思います。そして、イーダとよばれるようになったのでしょう。

おじいさんのへやからひろった紙きれで、本籍らしいものがわかり、わたしは病院からその村へ問い合わせました。そして、おじいさんのことも、父や母のこともわかりました。母はひとりむすめで、父は養子にきたのです。父は戦死、母は、原爆のおちる一年前になくなっています。

そして、わたしの名は、いつ子だったとわかりました。その後わたしは祖父に育てられ、あの、どういうわけか、祖父とふたりで広島へ出かけ、原爆にあったのでしょう。おそらく祖父は原爆で死んだのでしょう。なぜわたしだけが無きずで生き残ったのか、いまとなってはしるすべもありません。

お手玉のことでは苦労しました。わたしを育ててくれた母が、そのことをはなしてくれたとき、いちど見せてくれたのですが、それっきり、どこかへしまいこんでしまったのです。なんといって、それを見せてもらったらよいのか、わからないのです。でもようやく、そのときはいていたぼろぼろのもんぺといっしょに、病院へ持ってきて、見せてもらいました。そのお手玉のもようと、あの家でひろったお手玉のもようは、ぴったりでした。もようもおなじなら、ぬい方も、糸も、なにもかもです。

203

このことは母にまだいってありません。もちろん、わたしを育ててくれた父や母は、わたしのほんとうの父母がわかったとしればよろこんでくれるでしょう。でも、もうすこし、ようすをみて、ゆっくりとはなそうと思っています。だってわたしにだって、なにもかも、まだゆめのようなのですもの……。

わたしは、からだのぐあいがすこしおちついたところで、ようやく一日だけ、家へ帰してもらいました。そして、あのふしぎな家……いいえ、わたしの生まれた家へいって、あの小さないすと、絵本を持ってきました。そのとき、たんすの中から、いつ子と書いたエプロンや、もんぺのはきかえも見つけました。そのもんぺは、わたしのはいていたもんぺと、おなじ布で、おなじ大きさにぬってありました……。

そうそう、そのとき、直樹ちゃんがわすれていったたいせつなものも見つけましたよ。別便で送ります。

わたしはあの家をきちんとしめ、それから、家へ帰っていすを組み立てました。父や母がへんな顔でいすを見ていましたっけ。いすは、ふしぎなほど、きちんともとどおりに組み立てられました。いま、わたしのベッドのそばにちょこんとおかれています。だれもいないとき、わたしはいすにはなしかけます。

204

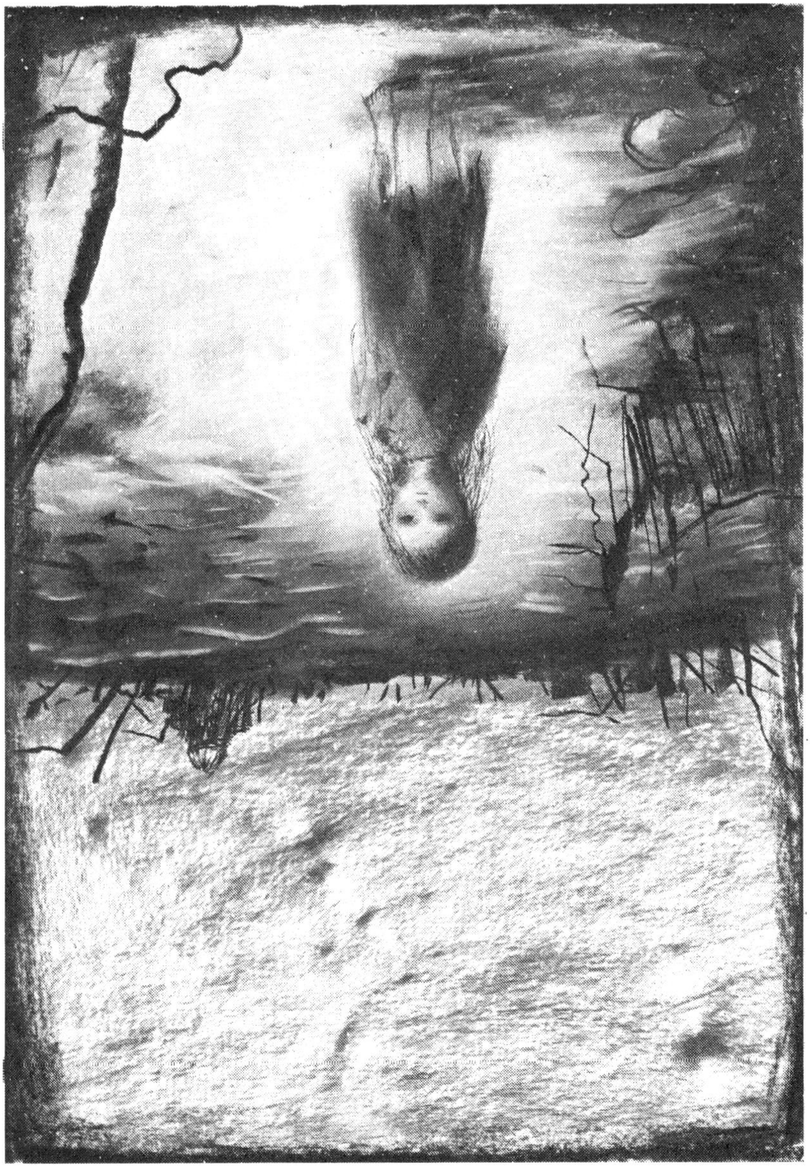

「わたしがイーダよ、わかる？　あなたに、小ちゃなおしりをのせていた、わたしがイーダよ。」

でもいすは、ふくれているのか、みとめたくないのか、へんじもしてくれません。小さなイーダが、こんなに大きくなってしまったということを、いすはどうしても、みとめたくないようです。

直樹ちゃん、長いあいださがしもとめていたわたしの父も、母も、祖父も、もうこの世にはなく、わたしは、たったひとりぼっちなのだと、これではっきりしました。それは、いいつくせぬほどのかなしみでした。でもわたしは、この小さないすが、コトコトと家の中を歩きまわりながら、この長い年月のあいだ、わたしをまちつづけていてくれたというだけでうれしいのです。

直樹ちゃん、わたしは、きっときっと元気になってみせますよ。ぜったい、死んだりしませんよ。

そして、あの家へ住もうと思うのです。かいづかの垣根は、きれいにかりこんでやりましょう。池にはきんぎょをおよがせましょう。しょうべん小僧には、噴水をいさましくとばしてもらいましょう。家もぬりかえてやりましょう。あじさいがむらさきのまるい重たい花をつけ、ばらはさきそろい、ふじだなからは、ふじの花がたれるでしょう。

わたしは女の赤ちゃんをうみましょう。そして、小さないすに、おすわりをさせましょう。そうしたらいすは、はじめてよろこんで、イーダだ、ほんとうのイーダが帰ってきたというでしょう……。

206

直樹ちゃん、そのときは、遊びにきてくれますね。

りつ子の手紙はそこでおわっていた。　直樹は長いあいだ、身うごきもせず、すわっていた。　それから、のろのろとボール紙のつつをひらいた。　出てきたのは直樹の絵だった。　あの日、絵をわすれてきたと思い出しても、直樹には取りにいく元気もなかったのだった。

じっと見ていると、あれはてた木々はみるみるかりこまれ、いきいきとばらが花ひらいてくるようだった。　ドアをあけて出てくるのはりつ子である。　白いうぶぎの赤ちゃんをだいている。

「いこうねえ。　おうちへいこうねえ。　おにいちゃんと、りつ子ねえちゃんと、ゆう子ちゃんと、みんなでいこうねえ。　いすちゃんのところへいこうねえ。」

いつのまにか、ゆう子がきていた。　うたうようにくりかえしている。　直樹の目になみだがあふれた。　おねえさんは死ぬもんか。　よくなるんだ。　ぜったいよくなるんだ。　そのときこそ、あの家も、いすも、よみがえるんだ。　しあわせな日が、もういちどくるんだ。

207

あとがき

いすとの出合いは、数年前であった。二、三さいほどの幼児がこしかける小さな木のい

すが、夜ふけて帰るわたしのあとを、コトリ、コトリ、コトリと、足をひきずってついてくる。

「ナイ……イナイ……ナイ、イナイ……。」

ひくくつぶやきながら、いすは、やがて、暗い横町へ消えていった。

そのあと、わたしはしばしばいすに出合った。人気のないへやの中を、いすはやっぱり、

足をひきずってコトリ、コトリと歩きまわっていた。

わたしにはときとして、物がこわいことがある。山深く、住民のことごとくが離村して

いった廃屋にころがる古ぐつとか、家族の歴史がいく変遷したのに、割れもせずぽつんと

残っているちゃわんとかが、いのちあるもののように思われる。いすはわたしのそういう

習癖をしっていたのかもしれない。

「だれをさがしているの。なぜ、歩きまわるの。」

この作品はいすとの対話からはじまった。相手がいすのことだから、たどたどしく、

二、三さいの女の子をさがしているとしかわからない。そのまま日がたった。そのあいだ、

わたしは二回ばかりこのいすを主人公にしたおさない子向けの作品を書き、やめてしまっ

た。書きつくせないなにかがいすの中にあるのを感じたからである。

もういちど、いすとの対話がはじまったのは去年の秋だった。そのあたりにいすのもと

208

めている場所があるように思われて、わたしは山口県岩国市へ旅立った。岩国には「びわの実学校」の同級生である沖井千代子さんがまっていてくれた。これから書く作品について、わたしはあまりはなさないほうだし、またはなすだけのまだなにもないわたしをむかえて、かの女は、ずいぶんこまったろうと思う。しかし、かの女は直観的にわたしのぞんでいる場所へつれていってくれた。

城山にひっそり身をよせている白い土べいのつづく町、山かげのあれはてた廃屋、おほり、すべていすの語るとおりの場所であった。また沖井さんはわたしの会いたいとねがっていた人たちに会わせてくれた。爆心地から〇・七キロメートルの地点で原爆をうけたかの女の友人たち、広島の周辺地区の人々、めぐりあう人々は奇跡的にいのちをまっとうし、からだに心に深いきずあとをひめた人々であった。

そうした話をきき資料をあさっていくうちに、わたしは無数の死者の群れが地の底から立ち上がってくるのを感じた。いすが愛し、さがしもとめている少女も、その中でおさない手をのばしているようにわたしには思われた。転生ということばがしきりに去来した。

その後、「原爆の図」をえがかれた丸木俊子さんにお会いする機会をえた。最近えがかれた、とうろう流しの図の前で、ま夜中、火の消えたとうろうが沖から潮にのって帰ってくる話をうかがった。「絵にもかけません。文にも書けません。」と、丸木さんはいわれた。

そのとき、わたしの中にコトリコトリと歩きつづけるいすの孤独なすがたと、潮にのっ

209

帰ってくるとうろうのすがたがダブってうかんだ。

「でも、書かなくてはいけませんね。」「そうです。二十一世紀の人たちになんらかの形で伝えることが、二十世紀に生まれたわたしたちの責任です。」みじかいやりとりであったけれど、ずしりと心に重かった。

少女の死ということにとらわれていたわたしだったが、りつ子の登場ですべてはおわった。りつ子は書いているうちに、ふいにあらわれた。わたしはとつぜんやってきたりつ子にとまどい、もういちどたしかめたくて広島へとんだ。原爆資料館で重文資料をとくにかしていただき、りつ子の存在が架空のものでないことをしってつらかった。非情な数字が死をしめしていた。

さいごの章を書きあげて、新広島ホテルのまどをあけると、慰霊碑の上にも、祈りのいずみの上にも、ちらちらと白く雪が舞っていた。

一九六九年二月七日。わたしはこの「あとがき」を書きました。そのときの心持ちを、いまでもまざまざと思い浮かべることができます。

それから七年の歳月をへたいま、司修さんの絵とともに、新しい版が世に出ていきますことを、どんなにうれしく思っているかしれません。ありがとうございます。

一九七六年六月

松谷みよ子

210

児童文学創作シリーズ

ふたりのイーダ（新装版）

2006年 7 月10日　第 1 刷発行
2014年 2 月 6 日　第 6 刷発行

著 者　松谷みよ子

画 家　司 修

発行者　鈴木 哲

発行所　株式会社　講談社
東京都文京区音羽 2-12-21（〒112-8001）
電話　出版部 03-5395-3535
　　　販売部 03-5395-3625
　　　業務部 03-5395-3615

印刷所　株式会社廣済堂
　　　　信毎書籍印刷株式会社

製本所　島田製本株式会社

この本は、子どもの文学傑作選シリーズで刊行されたものの改装新版です。
落丁本・乱丁本は、購入書店名を明記のうえ、小社業務部あてに
お送りください。送料小社負担にておとりかえいたします。
なお、この本についてのお問い合わせは児童図書第一出版部あてに
お願いします。定価はカバーに表示してあります。
本書のコピー、スキャン、デジタル化等の無断複製は
著作権法上での例外を除き禁じられています。
本書を代行業者等の第三者に依頼してスキャンやデジタル化することは
たとえ個人や家庭内の利用でも著作権法違反です。

©Miyoko Matsutani／Osamu Tsukasa 2006 Printed in Japan
N.D.C.913 210p 22cm　ISBN4-06-213533-7

松谷みよ子の本

全9巻 **オバケちゃんの本**
いとう ひろし／絵

森にすむおばけ一家のいたずらっこオバケちゃんが巻き起こす
ゆかいな事件の数々。ユーモアあふれる幼年童話シリーズ。

1．オバケちゃん
2．オバケちゃん ねこによろしく
3．オバケちゃんと むわむわむう
4．オバケちゃんと おこりんぼママ
5．オバケちゃんと いそがしおばさん
6．オバケちゃん アカオニにあう
7．オバケちゃん 学校へいく
8．学校おばけの おひっこし
9．オバケちゃんと はしるおばあさん

全6巻 **モモちゃんとアカネちゃんの本**
1～4巻：菊池貞雄／絵　5・6巻：伊勢英子／絵

モモちゃんが生まれてから、妹のアカネちゃんが小学校に入るまでの
ある家族のかたちをつづった大河童話。長く読みつがれる傑作シリーズ。

1．ちいさいモモちゃん
2．モモちゃんとプー
3．モモちゃんとアカネちゃん
4．ちいさいアカネちゃん
5．アカネちゃんとお客さんのパパ
6．アカネちゃんのなみだの海